The Horizons of Christopher Columbus

Using the Heavens to Map America

by Arne B Molander

The Horizons of Christopher Columbus: Using the Heavens to Map America

ISBN 978-1-105-86335-6

First Edition: June 2012

Copyright © 2012 by Arne B Molander

Author contact: amolander@verizon.net

Cover design: Mark Molander

Book assistance: Mark Molander

Printed on demand by Lulu Press

Order direct: www.lulu.com

To Anna: My late wife and "first mate," who for decades tolerated my devotion to Columbus and countless trips for research and presentations.

To Mark: An enormous thank you to my son Mark, who contributed countless hours preparing the manuscript. I could not have completed this book without his extensive assistance and continuous encouragement.

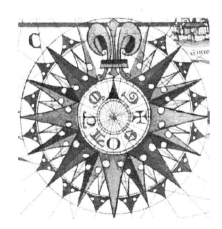

Contents

Preface

This book is the culmination of more than half a century of research into Christopher Columbus' 1492 voyage. I became interested in this historic voyage after a 1941 reading Richard Halliburton's *Seven League Boots* describing how he and Lowell Thomas moved a monument honoring Columbus' landfall from its Cat Island pedestal to the "correct" location on Watlings Island. They justified this shift by citing a mistranslated 16th century description of the landfall island as a "large bean." My teenage reaction to their map of Watlings Island was to scoff at its supposed resemblance to a bean; its coastline lacked the definitive curvatures needed to justify such a graphic metaphor.

A decade later, I was responsible for selecting some radar-tracking sites for the newly established missile test range at Cape Canaveral. Detailed charts for this task revealed that most of the Bahama island chain rested on two huge and very shallow banks. The smaller one, the Little Bahama Bank, had the distinctive shape of a 150-mile long kidney bean. I wondered if this might not be the "large bean" outlined in the sand by Indians unable to communicate orally with Columbus. If Columbus' landfall actually occurred anywhere on the Little Bahama Bank, it would mean that *all* of the many candidates then being considered for that honor were too far south by 100 miles or more. This insight made it important to re-open the vexing landfall question in time for the 1992 quincentennial celebration.

In 1967, after transferring to Washington, DC, I had the opportunity to evaluate the likelihood of a Little Bahama Bank landfall. I now had convenient access to the Library of Congress, where I pored through documents containing clues to the landfall's identity. Clues defining the second and third Bahama Islands discovered by Columbus had a compelling congruence with an island pair in the northern part of the archipelago. However, that pair couldn't be convincingly tied to *any* potential landfall island in the Little Bahama Bank. I shelved that "large bean" clue obtained from secondary sources and concentrated on evidence from Columbus' own description of his landfall island- evidence that established its latitude at northern Eleuthera, 90 miles north of the Watlings Island. Other clues from Columbus' *Journal* confirmed he had planted Spain's banner at a beach on Egg Island, a 200-acre islet on the northwest coast of Eleuthera.

Using all of the more than 100 clues contained in the *Journal*, I reconstructed Columbus' voyage from Egg Island to the three other islands he explored on his route to Cuba. In 1972 I summarized my findings in a 6-page paper and sent it to the nation's leading Columbus authority for review, Samuel Eliot Morison. He dodged my claim Columbus had navigated accurately by using latitude sailing rather than the universally-held view that error-prone dead reckoning had caused Columbus to drift 100 miles south of his measured latitude. I realized I'd have a difficult time promoting my landfall theory to entrenched historians.

After nearly a decade of inactivity, my son Mark persuaded me to resume my landfall studies, which led to a detailed 80-page study after a close inspection of Egg Island in 1980 with both he and my eldest son, Christopher. On that trip to the Bahamas, I flew over several of its islands and photographed features important to the landfall question. The photos supported my first published landfall article in the October 1981 issue of *Americas* Magazine. Around this time, I helped form the

Columbus Research Associates (CRA), an organization that would make four sailing trips to the Bahamas in search of landfall evidence. Members included: Dr. Peter Anderson, George Huson, Dr. Leonard Harris of NASA, Dr. Robert Roig of Mitre Corp, and Dr. Warren Tsuneishi of the Library of Congress.

The four CRA sailing trips in the Bahamas, all captained by Peter Andersen, contributed significantly to our understanding of Columbus' voyage a half millennium earlier. Other landfall enthusiasts joining one or more of our sailing expeditions included Bob Beach, Jack Colwell, Hans Frederikse, Tamas Gyorik de Salanky, Greg Huson, Col. Milton Kaufman, Chris Molander, Mark Molander, Col. Bill Naylor, Cdr. Peter Perkins, Glen Ruh, Robert Spedden and Paul Vassallo. A fifth and final cruise, dubbed our *Rendezvous with Columbus,* was an ambitious plan for celebrating the landfall quincentennial both at the *right place* (Egg Island, Eleuthera) and on the *right date* (October 21, 1992, after adjusting for the 9-day difference between the Julian and Gregorian Calendars). We enrolled 150 celebrants but our plans were wrecked by hurricane Andrew, which ironically swung due west upon reaching the exact latitude Columbus had followed 500 years earlier. The 22-foot tidal surge leveled northern Eleuthera and scattered most of the flotilla we had assembled at Miami. A score of diehards convened for a brief ceremony on Egg Island and Evelyn Guyton's installation of a time capsule on her Royal Island. Among those diehards were Peter Hanke, my wife Anna and her brother Pierre Bayard de Volo with his wife Louise, and my brother Lars.

Other contributors to my landfall knowledge include the membership of The Society for the History of Discoveries; especially those who, like Dr. Donald McGuirk and Jim Kelley, participated in the vigorous landfall debate we conducted for several years in our wide ranging round-robin letter. Special thanks are also due Robert Hightower, Charles Burroughs, and Thomas Sander, who provided me a valuable forum through meetings of The Washington Map Society and its respected journal, *The Portolan.* Finally, I owe immeasurable gratitude to William F. Buckley for allowing me to outline my theory at the US Naval Academy landfall debate in 1992.

As a teenager I had scoffed at the choice of Watlings as the landfall island because its coastline lacked the significant curvature of a "bean." Then, the accepted translation for the landfall's description was as a "haba." A half a century later, Spain's leading Columbian expert, Consuela Varela, showed me the true meaning of "haba" by her gesture of chopping a string bean. I immediately confirmed her translation in an old Spanish language dictionary defining "haba" as a bean pod "contiene cinco o seis semilias" (containing 5 or 6 seeds), as opposed to the single bean invented to bolster countless landfall theories. Her demonstration uniquely supported my choice of Eleuthera as the Columbus landfall because it's the only candidate shaped like a string bean.

While my original interest was limited to solving the landfall puzzle, its solution has been eclipsed by discoveries growing out of that effort. These include revelations that Columbus used the celestial sphere at both the northern and east/west horizons to navigate and map the New World, and compelling evidence his 1492 voyage was preceded by a voyage to the Bay of Fundy in 1477.

Introduction

This book follows Columbus's 1492 voyage sequentially, day by day, and log entry by log entry. The log entries are contextually interspersed with analyses and findings, with the log entries shown in *italics*.

In general, the leading authority on Columbus's 1492 voyage has been S. E. Morison. Therefore, many of the findings are compared and contrasted directly with Morison's theories, but with a fully refreshing new look at all the data.

Over the last 50 years I've uncovered a wide range of long-overlooked evidence concerning history's most important voyage, which I've woven throughout the chapters. My biggest findings and contributions are also highlighted directly below.

The 1477 Voyage

Chapter 1 reveals that Columbus braved the frigid North Atlantic in February 1477 in order to measure a rare solar eclipse just above his western horizon. His observations allowed Spain to accurately locate the longitude of a North American coastline long familiar to the Greenland settlements. We are fortunate the evidence of this expedition, in Columbus' son's biography, escaped deletion by Spanish authorities.

Latitude Sailing

Experienced sailors knew that undetectable currents made it impossible to cross the Atlantic on a constant latitude course solely by compass. Accurate sailing of latitudes required the guidance of a bright star culminating nightly, a few degrees above the route's northern horizon, for easy measurement. This celestial dependence dictated an August departure for Columbus, allowing Ursa Major's second magnitude star, Dubhe, to culminate in darkness a few degrees above his 28th latitude course. Columbus' mid-winter return by way of the Azores would be guided by Cassiopeia's nightly culmination above his 37th latitude.

League Length

Historians have speculated widely about the actual length of the leagues recorded by Columbus. Morison's assumption of 2.89 nautical miles would have forced Columbus to multiply his quadrant's degree readings by 20.76 to record his southerly progress in leagues. Surely, Columbus wanted to simplify his record keeping by using a league of three nautical miles, or exactly 20 leagues for each degree measured by his quadrant.

Lunar Planetary Conjunctions (LPC)

During his seven month voyage, Columbus had 26 potential opportunities (had weather permitted) to measure his longitude by using lunar conjunctions of the major planets. His August 3rd departure guaranteed that 18 of these measurements would occur over his eastern horizon, an orientation allowing simultaneous calibration by astronomers in Spain. The likelihood of 18 favorable orientations out of any given 26 LPCs is less than four percent. During his explorations of Cuba and Hispaniola, Columbus favored large harbors with lengthy, unobstructed water views in the direction of predicted LPCs.

The Landfall Latitude

Accurate latitude sailing would have carried Columbus to a landfall at the north end of Eleuthera, the island actually identified as his landfall on every 18th century Spanish map in the US Library of Congress.

San Salvador Maps

Chapter 3 demonstrates how the only surviving San Salvador map drawn by a voyage crew member matches the north coast of Eleuthera in impressive detail. Nearly two centuries later, a widely respected French cartographer confirmed the crew member's detailed landfall image of Eleuthera's Egg Island by adding a misoriented (but well-proportioned) image of nearby Little Egg Island.

Mastic Trees

In Chapter 4, Columbus marvels at the lush mastic trees still dominating Mastic Point, his anchorage at Andros Island. Morison believed this anchorage was at Long Island, a more arid island with no mastic trees when thoroughly surveyed by botanists in the early 20th century.

The Coast Curves Sharply to the Northeast ("*al nordeste haze una grande angla*")

Chapter 5 shows how the middle part of the Long Island coastline as described in the *Journal* and sailed by Columbus does indeed form a semi-circular cove oriented directly to the northeast. Morison's choice of Crooked-Aklins also forms a large cove, but is incorrectly oriented south of east.

The October 21st Solar Eclipse

Over the span of half a century, there were only three recorded attempts to measure New World longitudes using a solar eclipse. Columbus was well positioned for the first measurement on 13 February 1477 in Nova Scotia. The second potential opportunity occurred on 21 October 1492 when Columbus risked night-long exposure in uncharted waters to gain a sunrise view of the eastern horizon. Unfortunately, he had nothing to show for his efforts after this solar eclipse expired just below his horizon. Ferdinand Magellan viewed an almost total eclipse from Argentina's coastline on 17 April 1520.

Cuba's "Rio de Mares"

Chapter 6 lists nearly a dozen clues clearly identifying the "Rio de Mares" of Columbus as today's Puerto Padre. Morison inaccurately eliminated 25 nautical miles of Columbus' coastal explorations by proclaiming this westernmost Cuban harbor was "undoubtedly Puerto Gibara."

"Canoe-Days"

When Columbus first met the Taino, he approximated the distance their canoes could cover in one day as roughly 15 leagues. But after misreading the identity of a prominent Cuban cape he obligingly cut his "canoe-day" measure in half. Despite repeated evidence to the contrary, he stubbornly clung to this misinterpretation for the remainder of his voyage. Before Columbus had sailed one tenth of Hispaniola's perimeter he was able to accurately estimate its coastline as 200 leagues. If his Taino guides had given him their estimate in canoe-days, he would have misinterpreted it as 100 leagues. This appears to be another indication Columbus had access to accurate measurements made by the 1477 expedition.

Hispaniola's Peaks

Chapter 9 explains how Columbus made accurate distance estimates to several Hispaniola peaks barely breaking his horizon at distances ranging to 40 nautical miles. His astonishing accuracy suggests these "estimates" were actually read from an accurate chart–possibly drawn by fellow participants in the 1477 expedition who had viewed its eclipse at totality from the northern Bahama Islands.

Suspicious Loss of the Flagship

The half-knot westerly current sweeping the north coast of Hispaniola slowed progress as Columbus sailed its coastal shallows in search of an anchorage near a large Indian community. His frequent soundings must have alerted him when his flagship abruptly passed over the depths of a huge harbor crater (possibly the residue of a prehistoric meteor impact). This crater was too deep for anchorage. Rather than simply regaining the nearby shallows, for the first time on his voyage Columbus left his leaky flagship in the hands of a cabin boy and retired for the night. The westerly current soon carried the unanchored Santa Maria to its destruction on the harbor's reefs. It's possible Columbus deliberately sacrificed his flagship, perhaps to:

- Start a New World outpost with the men who couldn't fit in his then single remaining smaller ship, possibly at the behest of his Jewish sponsors in search of a safe haven for the Jews of Spain recently forced into exile or conversion.
- Eliminate the slowest ship in the fleet, which he was currently piloting – especially given Pinzón's current break-away on the faster Pinta. Columbus would not have wanted another break-away allowing another captain taking undue credit for the discoveries.
- Reduce the chance of a mutiny – one less boat to manage and the possibility to leave the least loyal crew members behind before the long voyage home.
- The natives were very nonthreatening and the exploration phase of the voyage was nearing completion – the focus was shifting to getting back home, so the need for a backup ship was diminishing.

Huge Longitude Error

On 14 January 1493 Columbus must have been stunned when the moon's unmapped orbital fluctuations introduced a 2400-mile error in his LPC-22 measurement of longitude. Columbus didn't immediately challenge this preposterous measurement that shifted his recorded location eastward by more than a tenth of the earth's circumference. Instead, for more than a month he dutifully followed a return route that would have carried him north of the British Isles.

Spanish Censorship

His January 6th 1493 *Journal* records the Indian's accurate estimate that the islands of Hispaniola and Jamaica are "distant from the mainland ten days journey in a canoe." This suggests that Spanish censors probably deleted an October 12th reference to a Florida coastline within four days of his landfall.

Gilded Fixation

Columbus occasionally expressed a desire to convert the natives to Christianity, but the primary objective of his voyage is suggested by his *Journal's* 153 surviving references to gold.

A Furtive Glance at Puerto Rico

When Columbus departed Hispaniola, his men were anxious for a prompt return to Spain in their leaky caravels. However, Columbus wanted to identify a suitable beacon for guidance on his return voyage to Puerto Rico, and claim its discovery. He got his way by covertly sailing the length of Puerto Rico in darkness while most of the crew was asleep.

The Lisbon Sidetrack

On February 26th 1493 Columbus changed his heading from Portugal's Cape Vincent to the equidistant port of Lisbon, which was out of the way. Some have blamed this change on heavy weather, but Columbus made this decision one day prior to the storm's onset.

Cantino Map

The Cantino map of 1502 includes the first mapping of America's southeast coast from the Mississippi Delta to the eastern tip of Long Island. More than half of its 22 place names can be associated with prominent features of that coast. Ponce de Leon has been improperly credited with the discovery of Florida a decade later. But, Ponce de Leon never got proper credit for using the heavens to accurately measure the latitude of the Columbus landfall.

Part I – To the New World (Once Again)

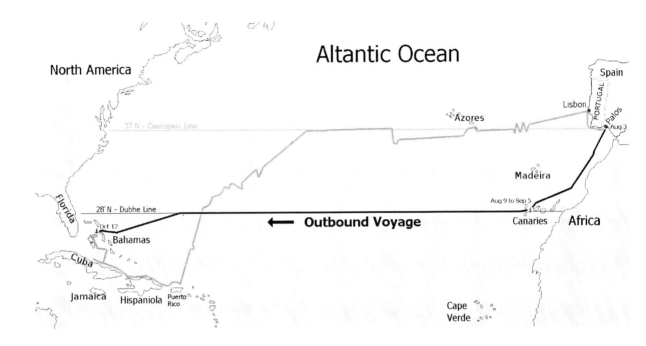

1 - The Voyage Plan

This is the First Voyage, and the courses and the way, that the Admiral Don Christopher Columbus pursued when he discovered the Indies, set forth in the form of a summary, save for the Prologue, which he addressed to the Sovereigns, and which is given in full, and which begins in this manner.

In this brief preface, Bishop Bartolemé de Las Casas introduces what has proven to be an indispensable abstract of the detailed *Journal* Christopher Columbus recorded during his historic 1492 voyage. In the mid 16th century Las Casas was granted access to a second-hand copy of the *Journal* then preserved in the Dominican Monastery of San Pablo as "The Barcelona Manuscript." From it this conscientious scholar abstracted 133 pages of background material for his *Historia de las Indies,* a comprehensive apology for Spain's brutal treatment of the New World's indigenous population. The Las Casas abstract eventually became the focus of much greater attention than his expiatory *Historia* after both the Barcelona Manuscript and its holographic original were lost, apparently forever. Even his abstract remained hidden for over 200 years until a Spanish naval historian, Martin Fernandez de Navarrete, rescued it from a dusty shelf in the Duke del Infantado's library. When eventually published in 1825, it was enthusiastically greeted as a surrogate for the long-missing *Journal* of the 1492 voyage. The abstract's re-emergence quickly stimulated interest in rediscovery of the 1492 landfall, then being mapped by cartographers as two different Bahamian islands — Eleuthera by the Spanish and Cat Island by the English. It soon became the primary source for defining most landfall attributes despite its many errors, omissions, and ambiguities, and especially its lack of cartography. These deficiencies opened the door to widely divergent interpretations of its frequently ambiguous and sometimes-conflicted landfall evidence, thereby fueling a contentious debate between hundreds of advocates.

What follows is the Las Casas abstract as translated into English in 1930 by Cecil Jane. His imperfect translation is herein defined as the *Journal* of Christopher Columbus, and printed in italics to distinguish it from my annotated commentary.

In the Name of our Lord Jesus Christ

Most Christian and most exalted and most excellent and most mighty princes, King and Queen of the Spains and of the islands of the sea, our Sovereigns: Forasmuch as, in this present year of 1492, after that Your Highnesses had made an end of the war with the Moors who reigned in Europe, and had brought that war to a conclusion in the very great city of Granada, where, in this same year, on the second day of the month of January, I saw the royal banners of Your Highnesses placed by force of arms on the towers of the Alhambra, which is the citadel of the city, and I saw the Moorish king come out of the gates of the city and kiss the royal hands of your Highnesses and of the Prince, My Lord, and afterwards in that same month, on the ground of information I had given to your Highnesses concerning the lands of India,...

As we shall soon see, a youthful Christopher may have obtained much of this *"information...concerning the lands of India"* on a 1477 voyage to Nova Scotia's Bay of Fundy. That earlier voyage would have shown him that the "Ocean Sea," previously thought to extend to the shores of Asia, was much narrower than had been assumed by cartographers who had known the earth's circumference accurately for two millennia. Regardless of whether Columbus really believed Nova Scotia was part of Asia in 1477, a decade later he was publicly proclaiming the golden temples of Cipangu (Japan) were only 2,400 miles west of the Canary Islands — less than a quarter of their actual distance. The conventional wisdom tells us he arrived at this absurd estimate by means of two totally unrealistic transformations. First, he shrunk the westerly sailing distance to Japan from its daunting 200 degrees of longitude to a manageable 60 by what can best be described as cartographic legerdemain. Secondly, he shortened each remaining degree of longitude 25 percent by replacing their actual 56 2/3 Arabic miles with a like number of shorter Roman *millas*. Small wonder it took Columbus seven years to overcome the reasoned objections of those royal cartographers who correctly understood the impossibility of provisioning a sea voyage to the far side of the earth.

However, this conventional wisdom conflicts with the Royal Capitulations (Articles of Agreement) for his 1492 Enterprise of the Indies, which suggest Columbus may have already convinced the Court he had discovered new lands in 1477 instead of simply reaching the shores of Asia. The preamble to these all-important Capitulations granted Columbus generous rights to both "what he hath discovered [que ha descubierto] in the ocean sea and for the voyage which with God's help he is now about to make thereon." The leading Columbian historian of the 20th Century, Samuel Eliot Morison, dismissed the intriguing implications of this passage with his observation, "The past tense has aroused no end of conjecture; but as it did not trouble contemporaries it need not trouble us." To Morison's credit he did observe, "The extraordinary thing about these documents is their failure to refer to a route to the Indies, indeed to mention the Indies in any manner whatsoever." Further examination of these issues might develop a fuller understanding of the events leading to history's most important voyage.

...and concerning a prince who is called Grand Khan, which is to say in our Romance tongue King of Kings, how many times he and his ancestors had sent to Rome to beg for men learned in our holy faith, in order that they might instruct him therein, and how the Holy Father had never made provision in this matter, and how so many nations had been lost, falling into idolatries and taking to themselves doctrines of perdition, and your Highnesses, as Catholic Christians and as princes devoted to the holy Christian faith and propagators thereof, and enemies of the sect of Mahomet and of all idolatries and heresies, took thought to send me, Christopher Columbus, to the said parts of India, to see those princes and peoples and lands and the character of them and of all else, and the manner which should be used to bring about their conversion to our holy faith, and ordained that I should not go by land to the eastward, by which way it was the custom to go, but by the way of the west, by which down to this day we do not know certainly that any one has passed;...

The uncertainty expressed here reminds us Columbus was aware of claims by others who may have anticipated his Enterprise of the Indies — that is, to reach those Oriental riches by sailing westward along the 28th parallel instead of retracing Marco Polo's grueling overland route. Fanciful tales still abound of Carthaginian and Phoenician sailors, Irish monks and Portuguese explorers crossing the Atlantic centuries ahead of Columbus, but his only certain precursors were the Vikings, who were known to have established settlements in northern Newfoundland and along Greenland's southwest coast half a millennium earlier. Ironically, after five centuries of battling harsh Arctic winters and hostile *Skrellings,* these weakened Viking colonies finally collapsed sometime between Columbus's 1451 birth and his 1492 voyage. Lack of contact with his North American colony had troubled Denmark's King Christian I, who is reported to have jointly arranged a Greenland expedition with Portugal's King Alfonso V in 1472-3. Denmark would have wanted to ascertain the status of their Greenland settlements, while Alfonso V's interest may have been a direct westward route to the wealth of the Indies as an alternative to Portugal's tedious progress down the west coast of Africa. Although any Portuguese records of this conjectured voyage failed to survive the great Lisbon earthquake of 1755, Danish archives suggest such an expedition, captained by the German Didrik Pinning and Denmark's Hans Potthorst, had been driven westward as far as the shores of Newfoundland or Labrador. Some claim they were accompanied by Norway's Johannes Scolp (or Scolus) and Portugal's Joao Vaz Corte-Reale, both of whose names appear on early 16th century maps of that region.

The Capitulation's reference to lands already *"discovered"* by Columbus suggests he may have signed on as a young shipmate for an exploratory voyage to the western Atlantic, perhaps even the Pinning-Potthorst expedition itself. Compelling evidence of Christopher's participation in an exploratory voyage to the North Atlantic is revealed in Fernando Columbus's biography quoting his father's claim that:

> "In the month of February, 1477, I sailed one hundred leagues [300 nautical miles] beyond the island of Tile [Thule], whose southern part is in latitude 73 degrees N, and not 63 degrees as some affirm; nor does it lie upon the meridian where Ptolemy says the West begins, but much farther west. And to this island, which is as big as England, the English come with their wares, especially from Bristol. When I was there, the sea was not frozen, but the tides were so great that in some places they rose twenty-six *braçias* [50 feet], and fell as much in depth."

It's generally acknowledged this extract reveals Columbus sailed the North Atlantic in 1477, but historians have limited his westward progress by assuming his "Thule" was Iceland. However, it will be shown here that a much stronger association of "Thule" can be made with Greenland. This transformation will lead us to the inevitable conclusion that Columbus was claiming to have reached the shores of North America 15 years before his historic 1492 voyage! It's easy to demonstrate that every facet of Fernando's quantitative extract supports this surprising conclusion.

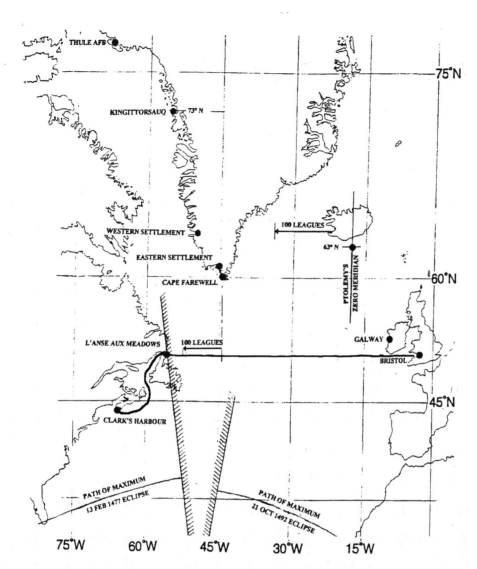

Figure 1-1. The 1477 Voyage of Columbus to the New World (to Clark's Harbour)

Thule - Morison proclaimed it "a certainty" that Columbus's "Thule" was Iceland. But "Thule" was not a permanent site — it was always identified with the most remote northern region known during any given historical epoch. "Thule" was Scandinavia when Ptolemy prepared his famous atlas early in the first millennium, but it had shifted to Iceland by the 9th century, and by 1477 even further westward to Greenland where that name survives today on the island's northernmost airfield. This toponymic migration gave Columbus sufficient reason to warn us that *new*-Thule was "much farther west" than the Ptolemaic zero meridian bisecting Iceland, the *old*-Thule. To make doubly certain we understood his *new*-Thule was Greenland rather than Iceland, he also asserted its "southern part" extended *a full 10 degrees north* of Iceland's 63-degree latitude. The intersection of *old*-Thule's latitude and longitude near the midpoint of Iceland's southern coast eliminate this island as a possible candidate for Columbus's *new*-Thule. This leaves Greenland as the only viable candidate for the actual island he "sailed 100 leagues beyond" in 1477.

Greenland - While Greenland fits Thule's longitude requirement for an island "much farther west" of Ptolemy's zero meridian, its southern terminus at Cape Farewell lies 13 degrees *south* of "Thule's" latitude. At first glance this apparent discrepancy is particularly troublesome because, unlike longitude, latitude measurements were generally accurate to within a fraction of a degree in the 15th century. Fortunately, this discrepancy can be fully resolved by two cartographic considerations. First, although Greenland lacks a true "southern part," its southwest coast, warmed by a branch of the Gulf Stream, became home to its only two Viking settlements. While the bearing line between this pair of settlements was closer to north-south than east-west, the Viking colonists always identified them as "Western" and "Eastern," designations consistent with viewing Greenland's sheltered southwest coastline as more "southern" than "western." Secondly, the northernmost cairn along this "southern" coastline had been erected at Kingittorsuaq, an island in the Upernavik Archipelago, at least a century earlier by Erling Sighvatsson, Bjarni Thordarson, and Enteritis Oddsson, three hardy Norsemen who chiseled its neat runes one bitter April day. Their cairn stood within *three* miles of the "73 degrees" Columbus attributed to Thule's "southern" coast, a truly remarkable congruence, especially when compared to that *600-mile* discrepancy with Iceland's southern coast. At least one of Greenland's several Catholic Bishops is likely to have conveyed this cairn's fundamental cartographic information to Rome, suggesting that Columbus, a Lisbon cartographer, was probably aware of "Thule's" Upernavik (Kingittorsuaq) latitude marker. If not, his "73 degrees" latitude reference is a truly astonishing coincidence.

Newfoundland - Columbus used a league of three nautical miles to measure his 1477 sailing limit as "100 leagues beyond the island of Thule," likely along the same fixed latitude sailing route from Bristol that John Cabot would follow 20 years later. If so, a constant-latitude voyage 300 miles beyond Greenland's settlements would have brought him to Cabot's subsequent Newfoundland landfall near the Viking's L'Anse aux Meadows. Columbus mildly inflated Newfoundland's 42,734 square miles to be "as big as" England's 50,000, but such proud exaggeration is mild compared with the sovereign-pleasing exaggerations of his 1492 discoveries, including the claim in his widely-distributed 1493 letter that Cuba's 44,218 square miles were "larger than England and Scotland together," a combination actually twice the size of Cuba.

Bay of Fundy - Columbus's most surprising observation was the 50-foot tidal range, assuming we accept the consensus belief his Genoese "braçia" had a length of 22.9 inches. Such an enormous tide can't be ignored as casual hyperbole, for in 1492 Columbus credited Tanamo Bay with Cuba's largest tidal range, which it has, by all of three inches! Only two North Atlantic locations, the Bay of Fundy and Ungava Bay, have tidal ranges approximating 50 feet, and both of these have spring tides very close to Columbus's observation. However, Ungava, at the mouth of Hudson's Bay, is ice-covered from November through May, leaving Fundy as the only realistic candidate for Columbus's huge tidal measurement where "the sea was not frozen" in February.

The specificity implied by *twenty-six* braçias also suggests the 1477 expedition actually measured Fundy's 50-foot tides firsthand rather than simply approximating Viking estimates as roughly 26 or so of their Genoese units. Historians have universally ignored this unique link with Fundy's tides by assuming Columbus interrupted his description of "this island" to recall the nearly 36-foot tides at the Avon River's mouth 25 miles east of Bristol, which he could have examined before sailing west had he both the time and inclination. But Fundy not only has a much closer congruence with Columbus's recorded tidal range, its protected haven was also his most accessible viewing site for measuring longitude by means of a February 13th solar eclipse.

The Solar Eclipse of February 1477 - Historians have never questioned why Columbus would forsake his sunny Mediterranean homeland to endure a frigid mid-winter cruise dodging the life-threatening icebergs of the North Atlantic. All have ignored a compelling motivation for his bitterly cold February voyage – a solar eclipse Johannes Mueller's *Ephemerides* predicted for the late afternoon of February 13th at the Bay of Fundy. Mueller's calculations informed European astronomers this eclipse would be ideally suited for accurately measuring the longitude of an extensive coastline the Vikings had discovered centuries earlier only 100 leagues west of their Greenland settlements. European geographers surely realized these Viking discoveries identified an unknown continent rather than China's east coast, known to lie more than 30 times that distance to the west. In February 1477 Columbus could have measured that coastline's longitude with surprising accuracy by observing the eclipse elevation angle while anchored in one of Nova Scotia's several harbors. But not just any harbor would do. He needed one with a southwesterly expanse of ocean in order to measure the eclipse elevation angle above a well-defined western horizon. That angle also needed to be high enough to minimize the effect of the horizon's known angular distortion, while low enough to maximize instrumental precision.

Clark's Harbour on the south edge of the Bay of Fundy was the nearest haven meeting both requirements of this critical and demanding longitude measurement. If anchored there at 5:09 PM Columbus could have observed a 60% solar eclipse elevated 8.9 degrees above his unobstructed WSW horizon, as shown in Figure 1-2. This was high enough to reduce the error introduced by horizon refraction to six miles of longitude. It may be just a coincidence that the best location for a sister ship to observe this eclipse *at totality* was in the northern Bahamas, precisely where Columbus first landed in 1492. But, it's surely significant that the Bay of Fundy was the nearest harbor offering an unobstructed view of the southwestern horizon directly below this late-afternoon eclipse.

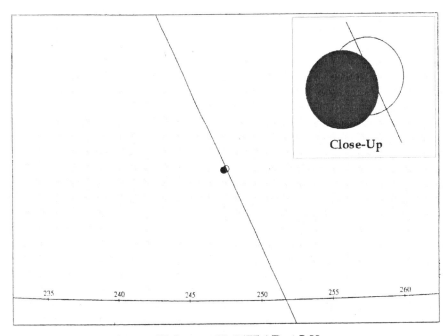

Close-Up

235   240   245   250   255   260

Eclipse of February 13, 1477 AD at 5:09 pm
Columbus (Clark's Harbour) - Elevation Above Horizon

Figure 1-2. Solar Eclipse of 1477 per Columbus's Vantage

Later we shall see how this compelling circumstantial evidence from his son's biography is partially validated in the *Journal's* December 21st entry, a critical portion of which has been deleted, probably by Spanish authorities. It's surprising his son revealed the Admiral's participation in the 1477 voyage given his family's continuing efforts to minimize the contributions of others to his father's singular 1492 accomplishment. And it's doubly fortunate this passage escaped the censor's knife because it also raises the possibility that Portugal's actual reason for rejecting his father's 1484 proposal was Corte-Reale's 1477 failure to find a westward passage to the Indies, rather than that route's extreme length. In any case, it's extremely unlikely Columbus believed the Orient was just a few thousand miles west of Spain. How could an experienced cartographer and remarkably precise navigator, who had already ranged over 50 degrees of the earth's latitude, have underestimated its circumference by more than 35 percent two millennia after Eratosthenes had measured it with less than one percent error?

...therefore, after having driven out all the Jews from your realm and lordships,...

Prior to Seville's 1391 pogrom, Spanish Jews had confidently practiced their religion countrywide, including several large cities where they actually outnumbered Catholics. But over the following century the Church's tolerance of other faiths continued to decline with the ebbing Moorish presence in Iberia. A few days after the fall of Grenada in January of 1492, Spanish Jews were given three choices: emigration with their religious beliefs intact, assimilation to Catholicism as *Conversos*, or outward conversion as *Marranos* ("swine") forced to conceal their continuing belief in Judaism from the prying eyes of informants. Many of those who chose emigration relocated to Morocco where *The National Geographic* photographed some descendants still hopefully cherishing the keys to Spanish homes confiscated from their ancestors 500 years earlier. Ironically, those Jews who chose to remain in Spain as Conversos contributed substantially to Columbus's Christian crusade. Luis de Santangel, the King's chief financial adviser and fundraiser for the voyage, along with his associates Juan Cabrero, Gabriel Sanchez and Alonso de la Caballeria, were four Conversos who promoted Columbus's Enterprise of the Indies to Ferdinand and Isabela. Henry of Trastámara, the illegitimate son of Alfonso XI's Jewish mistress, Leonora de Guzmán, had himself founded the Spanish royal house in the previous century. Even the family of our gentle transcriber, Bartolomé de Las Casas, had only recently converted from Judaism to the Catholic faith.

Jewish contributions to Columbus's 1492 voyage were more than just financial. Simon Wiesenthal, a Jewish historian and holocaust survivor, pointed out that Jewish cartographers, including the Cresques family of Majorca, had long been esteemed for their skill and knowledge. These "map Jews" were as respected as the "compass Jews" responsible for developing the instruments and astronomical knowledge Spain needed to support its growing sea power. Wiesenthal is convincing when he asserts "There can be no doubt that without the aid of these [Jews] who helped persuade the royal couple to sponsor the expedition, who gave financial aid, and who provided nautical documents, Columbus's voyage would never have taken place."

...In the same month of January, your Highnesses commanded me that, with a sufficient fleet, I should go to the said parts of India and for this accorded me great rewards and enabled me so that from that time henceforward might style myself don and be high admiral of the Ocean Sea, and that my eldest son should succeed to the same position, and so on from generation to generation...

Columbus took care here to remind his sovereigns of the generous Capitulations they had signed in April, which included 10 percent of *all* future net profits from his discoveries. Despite this reminder, 30 years of litigation by his heirs were to garner only token annuities as a hollow substitute for those immense promised rewards. The Columbus heirs eventually settled for honorary titles, which would later enable the 17th *"Admiral of the Ocean Sea"* to play a role in Spain's 1992 quincentennial celebration.

...And I departed from the city of Granada on the twelfth day of May in the same year of 1492, on a Saturday, and came to the town of Palos, which is a port of the sea, where I made ready three ships, very suited for such an undertaking,...

Columbus perhaps had a clockwise sailing plan — to the Indies with those easterly trade winds pounding the Canary Islands, and home with the west winds long observed at the Azores latitude. He would depart Spain's Palos de la Frontera with only the smallest of his three ships, the *Niña*, lateen-rigged for close-hauled sailing. Had he planned much upwind sailing he wouldn't have converted the *Niña's* lateen rig into the *"very suited"* square rigging of her sister ships upon reaching the Canary Islands.

...and I set out from that port, well furnished with very many supplies and with many seamen, on the third day of the month of August of the same year, on a Friday, half an hour before the rising of the sun,...

Some claim Columbus crossed the Rio Saltes bar on the same tide as the final boatload of Spain's 300,000 banished Jews. Queen Isabela had recently extended their expulsion deadline from 31 July to that very morning, so this final boatload may even have followed Columbus's wake along Africa's northwest coast as far as Casablanca in Spanish Morocco. What we do know is that several senior members of his crew were Jewish, including Luis de Torres of Murcia, the linguist who would serve as interpreter if Columbus should meet with the Great Khan. Some have even argued that Columbus himself was a Converso because his wife, Felipa Moniz Perestrello, was partially of Converso descent and converts tended to marry among themselves. Wiesenthal believed the very substantial Jewish support for Columbus's Enterprise derived from their expectations his discoveries might provide a haven from religious persecution.

...and I steered my course for the Canary Islands of your Highnesses, which are in the Ocean Sea, thence to set out on my way and to sail until I should arrive in the Indies,...

The *"Canary Islands"* were the logical launching site for his trans-Atlantic exploration because a decade earlier the Treaty of Alcáçovas had established their latitude as the northern boundary separating Portugal's southern hegemony from Spain's. Accurate sailing of that political boundary was critical if Columbus expected to claim those territories revealed by his 1477 voyage rather than simply *"arrive in the Indies."* Although latitude sailing (LS) would have been his simplest and most accurate method for following that boundary line, Morison assumed Columbus crossed the Atlantic using the dead reckoning (DR) navigation system favored by Mediterranean pilots. They had long relied on DR to measure their position from compass heading, speed, and elapsed time, adjusted for *estimated* drift caused by winds and ocean currents. While its unrestricted headings were an important advantage on short Mediterranean routes, DR was a poor choice for lengthy sea voyages restricted by an imprecise 15th century compass, crudely graduated in only 32 points instead of 360 degrees, and lacking the gimbals needed to reduce the wild oscillations of its undamped needles in oceanic swells. On a transatlantic crossing, just a quarter-point bias in reading a fluttering needle would be enough to throw a pilot 150 miles off course. Compass variation, unknown currents and leeway could easily double that error. Iberian political concerns aside, it would have been foolhardy for Columbus to cross the Atlantic without the accurate latitudes needed by any future rescue mission should his fleet become grounded on an uncharted reef. But Morison brushed aside such considerations because his postulated "90-mile error" in the landfall's latitude required Columbus to rely on inaccurate DR navigation.

Eva Taylor summarized DR deficiencies for trans-oceanic navigation in Volume III of "The Oxford History of Technology". She concluded "methods of navigation developed first for the enclosed Mediterranean Sea...were inadequate for the new ocean navigation of the early fifteenth century sponsored by the Portuguese Prince Henry the Navigator...In effect, the new method of navigation proposed was 'running down the latitude.'" So it was DR's deficiencies that led the prescient Prince Henry to school his navigators in the LS techniques Portugal would need to reach the Indies later that century. This celestial-based navigation system, developed during Greece's Golden Age, saw little use on short Mediterranean runs after the eighth century introduction of the compass, but it remained the preferred navigation method for seafaring Arabs and Vikings because of its simplicity and accuracy on their lengthy oceanic voyages.

LS allowed pilots to maintain an accurate east-west course by simply observing a suitable star's lower culmination angle when it was directly below the celestial pole and thus nearest the horizon. Any change in that elevation angle would immediately alert pilots to deviations from their east-west course. For maximum accuracy, pilots sought those combinations of sailing season and latitude that allowed bright stars to culminate slightly above their northern horizon. They also preferred constellations containing several bright stars that would create redundant non-culminating pairs in case atmospheric absorption dimmed a lower culminating star below the threshold of visibility. Northern hemisphere pilots probably ignored upper culminations at the southern horizon, as it was much easier to follow dimming stars to lower culminations than to detect them rising to brief visibility above the southern horizon.

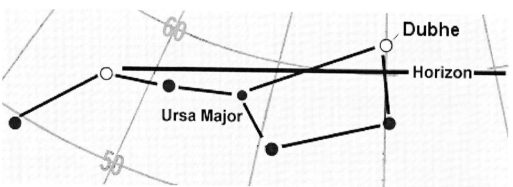

Figure 1-3. Lower Culmination of Ursa Major viewed from 28th Latitude, with Dubhe sweeping just above the horizon, ideal for easy measurement

Under favorable conditions, LS pilots learned to stay within a few miles of their course using only crude instruments to measure those small stellar elevation angles. One instrument widely used in the Indian Ocean was the kamal, a wood panel the size of a playing card with a multi-knotted string threaded through its center, shown in Figure 1-4. The pilot would extend the kamal towards the northern horizon with his teeth clenched on that knot defining his desired latitude, attained whenever the culminating star appeared at the card's upper edge while its lower edge rested on the horizon. Whenever stellar elevation angles were small enough, pilots could dispense with the *kamal* and simply measure elevation angles in finger widths by extending their open hands toward the horizon. In fact, the Arabic unit of angle measurement was the isba, defined as a finger width viewed at arms length — equivalent to about 90 miles of latitude. Ahmad b. Majid, an Arabian contemporary of Columbus, criticized those "careless pilots" who ignored angle differences of a quarter isba, by noting "This is a disgrace, especially when making landfalls on routes which are almost due east and west." (Imagine what Ahmad's reaction would have been to Morison's contention Christopher Columbus missed his latitude by four times this "disgraceful" error by ignoring the Big Dipper while crossing the Atlantic on his own "almost due east and west" course.)

Figure 1-4. Kamal – A Method Used for Latitude Sailing

Another defect of DR navigation was its unrecoverable loss of guidance during a tempest. LS pilots simply converged towards the latitude defined by their guide star's culmination angle after the storm had passed. DR navigation also required time measurements and estimates of speed, compass variation, leeway and currents, while LS needed only a single elevation angle — an angle easily measured as it slowly changed at lower culmination. According to Professor G. J. Marcus, "It cannot be too strongly emphasized that latitude sailing was the underlying principle of all ocean navigation down to the invention of the chronometer." Until accurate time pieces and sextants would finally make unrestricted oceanic navigation feasible, the whimsical, but nonetheless effective, British instructions for sailing constant latitudes to their North American colonies were to "head south until the butter melts, then due west."

...and deliver the embassy of Your Highnesses to those princes all that you commanded me to do. To this end, I thought to write all that I might do and see and experience, as will be hereafter seen. Moreover, Sovereign Princes, in addition to writing each night that which the day had brought forth and each day how I had sailed at night,...

Columbus's *"writing each night...and each day"* would become the earliest surviving example of systematic nautical record keeping, an innovation soon widely imitated. His detailed daily entries frequently describe a wide range of events in chronological sequence, suggesting he sometimes may have supplemented his twice-daily recordings with intervening observations. Following periods of intensive activity or heavy weather, his *Journal* occasionally reveals signs of deferred entries, and by his return voyage he had reduced their frequency to once a day.

...I design to make a new chart for navigation, in which I will set all the sea and lands of the Ocean Sea in their true places, under their bearings,...

To *"make a new chart for navigation"* it was essential for Columbus to record a *continuous* track connecting his landfall location to all his subsequent discoveries.

...and moreover to compile a book and to set down all, picturing everything by latitude from the equinoctial line...

Columbus couldn't picture *"everything by latitude from the equinoctial line"* without celestial assistance - even small DR errors would have accumulated to unacceptable latitude errors well before he had finished mapping his Caribbean discoveries. He could have measured latitude directly from the elevation of the north celestial pole if there had been a bright star marking its location. But the nearest bright star was Polaris, then orbiting the north celestial pole at a radius of 3°27'. This meant latitudes approximated by Polaris elevation angles could differ by as much as 414 miles! Despite this huge uncertainty, pilots still had two options for obtaining useful latitudes from Polaris elevation angles. A *direct* method used the Guard stars' rotation angle to establish when Polaris was approximately at the same height as the celestial pole.

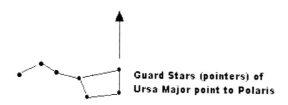

Polaris (North Star) •

Guard Stars (pointers) of Ursa Major point to Polaris

Ursa Major (Big Dipper)

Figure 1-5. Guard Stars of Ursa Major Point to Polaris

Although this method gave latitude directly, even a five-degree error in reading the Guard's rotation angle would throw a latitude measurement off by 18 miles. Thus, pilots often favored the simpler and more accurate indirect alternative of measuring Polaris elevation angles as they slowly changed near lower culmination. Since Polaris was almost 3 ½ degrees below the celestial pole, pilots had to differentiate their indirect measurements of the "height of the North Star" from the derived latitude. This distinction was made clear by Amerigo Vespucci in his 18 July 1500 letter to his sponsor, Lorenzo de Medici, when he characterized Cape May's latitude of 39 degrees as "far enough for the North Star to rise above our horizon 35 1/2 degrees." We'll soon see how Vespucci also may have made an accurate longitude measurement while presumably anchored at that New Jersey cape two months earlier.

Columbus could measure Polaris elevation angles using either of two instruments. His astrolabe was a circular disk, suspended vertically with its centrally pinned alidade rotated to the Polaris elevation angle. His quadrant was a suspended quarter-circle with a plumb bob defining the elevation angle when the instrument's edge was sighted to Polaris. Both instruments measured their angles relative to the local gravity vector, so it might be supposed their angle readings weren't very accurate when read from an unstable deck (an argument advanced by Morison and others to explain why Columbus supposedly had misread his 1492 latitudes by 90 miles). But John Gilchrist's comprehensive study of 80 latitude measurements from the 16th and 17th centuries concluded accuracies of readings taken at sea weren't notably different from those taken ashore. Gilchrist also noted that a score of latitude measurements attributed to Magellan, Verrazano and Cartier averaged only 15 miles error — the equivalent accuracy achieved a century later by Champlain. Such consistent performance over the span of a century suggests Columbus's proficiency with the quadrant a quarter century before Magellan was closer to 15 miles than the 90 miles needed to accommodate Morison's landfall theory.

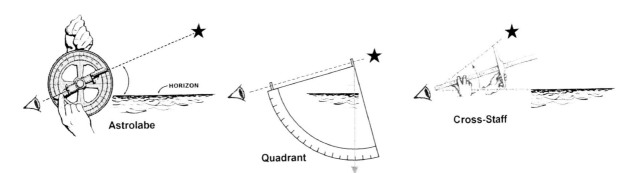

Figure 1-6. The Astrolabe, Quadrant, and Cross-staff

...and by longitude from the west...

Neither could Columbus measure *"longitude"* on his 225-day voyage by simply compiling his estimated progress while mid-ocean currents were shifting his location several undetectable miles every day. On a lengthy sea voyage there were only two useful means of measuring longitude, both based on the moon's retrograde rotation of about 12 degrees a day. The preferred method determined longitude directly from the moon's elevation angle during infrequent solar eclipses and planetary occultations. A less accurate but far more frequent opportunity to measure longitude was provided by the moon's lunar distance to nearby planets, a more demanding measurement requiring greater precision than available from either an astrolabe or quadrant.

The most precise instrument for measuring longitude by either method was the astronomer's cross-staff, a device conceived in 1342 by the Jewish scholar Levi ben Gersohn. Even a portable cross-staff only a few feet in length could measure elevation angles an order of magnitude more precisely than the astrolabe or quadrant. The German mathematician Martin Behaim claimed use of a cross-staff during his 1485 mapping of Africa's west coast for the Portuguese. Although Columbus never mentioned this instrument, Spain undoubtedly appreciated its importance for charting accurate longitudes of his discoveries, and could have supplied one for both his 1477 and 1492 voyages.

Despite its superior accuracy, the cross-staff wasn't suitable for overhead measurements because it required simultaneous reading of both ends of its crosspiece. In actual usage, the lower end of the crosspiece was always aimed at the horizon, so only its upper end required reading. When used in this manner its maximum precision was restricted to measurements of small elevation angles. But precision didn't automatically translate into accuracy when refraction at the horizon could bias celestial measurements of longitude by as much as a thousand miles. A reasonable compromise may have limited usages to elevation angles between 2 and 15 degrees, a range of usage supported by the fragmentary available evidence. If true, the half-century following February 1477 provided only two additional solar eclipses with potential for accurate measurement of New World coastlines. The first of these occurred on 21 October 1492, a rare opportunity apparently leading Columbus to risk standing off an entire moonless night in uncharted waters, presumably to observe this sunrise eclipse above an unobstructed eastern horizon. The second solar eclipse wouldn't occur until 17 April 1520 while Ferdinand Magellan was anchored off the east coast of present-day Argentina. His Puerto San Julien anchorage was ideally positioned for finding where the Pope's Line of Tordesillas divided the South American Continent between Spain and Portugal. At 7:06 AM Magellan could have observed a total eclipse just 4.4 degrees above the unobstructed eastern horizon needed for his longitude measurement.

These three rare solar eclipses, all of which would have been useful to early explorers, were likely augmented on 26 May 1500 by Vespucci's observation of Saturn's lunar occultation at his Cape May anchorage. At 4 AM Vespucci would have seen Saturn duck behind the Moon's slender crescent as they rose together 2 degrees above the eastern horizon. Within the hour (a time unit conveniently linking lunar motion to its diameter — 30 lunar diameters per hour) Saturn emerged from the Moon's dark upper edge, 18 degrees above the Sun now breaking the horizon. This lunar occultation may be responsible for his letter's remarkably precise claim of sailing "84 degrees from the meridian of the city and port of Cadiz," a longitude accurately establishing the Mississippi Delta as the western limit of Vespucci's New World explorations. (The 1502 Cantino Map of his discoveries appropriately named that delta "The Sea of Mud," a place name later trimmed from his map, but fortunately surviving on its several derivatives.)

The rare opportunities to obtain longitude from eclipses could be substantially augmented by also measuring the "lunar distance" between the moon and nearby planets. Though lunar distance opportunities were far more frequent, their findings were also much less accurate because they depended on the moon's variable angular rate rather than simply its elevation angle. That difference made lunar distance measurements 30 times as demanding as longitudes derived from eclipses. But even those stringent requirements weren't enough to discourage Gerard of Cremona from advocating a lunar distance method of finding longitude three centuries before the Columbus voyages. To avoid the horizon's obvious distortions, Gerard proposed measuring lunar distance when the moon and its nearby planet were overhead. While his proposed zenith measurements would circumvent the huge errors introduced by horizon refraction, no adequate zenith instruments were then available, a deficiency exacerbated by inclined lunar orbits that generated planetary separations averaging 10 lunar diameters at their closest approach. Under those conditions Columbus would have done well to estimate lunar distance within half a lunar diameter, or 450 miles of longitude. Except for infrequent lunar occultations, Gerard's zenith measurements of lunar distance would have to wait for development of a vastly improved navigational instrument — the 18th century's sextant.

However, a simple modification to Gerard's lunar distance method could have yielded useful longitudes even with 1492's crude instruments. Although unreported in navigation literature, Columbus could have followed the same procedure that made some solar eclipses accurate indicators of longitude. That is, he could have used a cross-staff to measure each lunar-planetary conjunction (LPC) while the moon and planet were both elevated a few degrees above the horizon reference; high enough to substantially reduce the obvious horizon distortions while low enough for accurate measurement by a cross-staff. To interpret the several-per-month LPCs during his voyage he would need an ephemeris predicting the daily celestial longitudes of the moon and planets. Morison informs us that Columbus did in fact carry a copy of Johannes Mueller's *Ephemerides* on his voyages. Mueller's 750-page tome tabulated those longitudes for a 30-year interval extending from 1477 through 1506, a span coincidentally and fully covering Columbus's Bay of Fundy voyage to the year of his death. Its tables provided two reciprocal usages for Columbus — first and foremost, finding his longitude from measurements of the celestial display and, secondarily, predicting the celestial display at a specified time and location. Columbus is known to have implemented this secondary usage when he frightened Jamaica's uncooperative natives into submission with his dramatic warning of a lunar eclipse rising "bloody and enflamed" early in the evening of 29 February 1504. His confident prediction of that rare celestial display at a known longitude suggests the reciprocal capability — measuring celestial displays to determine his longitude.

While Columbus couldn't have anticipated his Jamaican requirement, he surely realized the importance of longitude measurements on his 1492 voyage, and circumstantial evidence strongly suggests he frequently used his *Ephemerides* for this purpose. Solar interference would have obscured LPCs with the planet Mercury and several of those involving Venus, Mars, Jupiter and Saturn. As a result, during his 225-day voyage Columbus had access to no more than 26 potential LPC opportunities, an unknown number of which he would lose to cloud cover. Because of differential refraction with the moon and planet at differing elevations, he probably preferred to measure these 26 LPCs at higher angles than optimal for solar eclipses. By increasing this angle from 5 degrees to 15 he could have reduced the longitude errors caused by differential refraction from 100 miles to 18 for a typical lunar distance of 3 degrees. Determining the optimum elevation angles for a range of lunar distances would have been a suitable project for Prince Henry the Navigator, but any such use of his Sagres School is speculative. The *Journal* doesn't explicitly reveal how Columbus used LPCs, but we shouldn't expect such a revelation because he surely intended to conceal this innovative technique from Spain's competing naval powers.

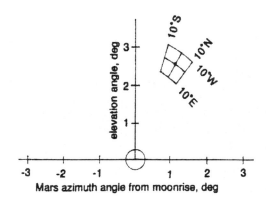

Figure 1-7. Vespucci's Lunar Distance Measurement

Two Columbus contemporaries, Ferdinand Magellan and Amerigo Vespucci, also appear to have used LPCs to measure longitude: Magellan made several LPC-correlated longitude measurements on his circumpolar quest 20 years after Amerigo Vespucci had used his *Ephemerides* to measure longitude using a lunar conjunction with Mars on 23 August 1499. In a letter to his patron, Vespucci wrote, "...when the Moon rose on our [unobstructed eastern] horizon...the Moon was one degree and several minutes to the east of Mars." Figure 1-7 shows the horizon geometry Vespucci would have observed from the Bay of Oyapac, a location reasonably inferred from his report. Historians have scoffed at Vespucci's claim, possibly because they didn't understand how he could have utilized a lunar-planetary conjunction that occurred well below his horizon. Vespucci's claim suggests both he and his friend Columbus knew how to obtain longitude from the lunar distance of LPCs occurring a few degrees *above* the horizon.

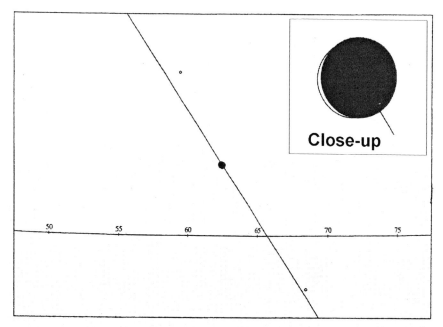

Eclipse of April 17, 1520 AD at 7:06 am
Magellan (Puerto San Julien) - Elevation Above Horizon
Figure 1-8. Solar Eclipse of 1520 per Magellan's Vantage

...and above all it is very fitting that I should forget sleep and give much attention to navigation, because it should be so. And these things will be a great labor.

Columbus has just recorded that he will measure his coordinates by the global coordinate system of *"latitude"* and *"longitude"* rather than the flat-earth Portolan chart then commonly used in the Mediterranean. Both global coordinates were best measured at night by celestial observation, so Columbus knew he would have to *"forget sleep and give much attention to navigation."* If he had intended to measure his coordinates by DR navigation he could have slept the night through, comfortable in the knowledge that his watch captains were keeping track of their course and distance.

At this point, Columbus is prepared to discover and map America. The rest of this book follows the *journal* entries day by day.

2 - The Atlantic Crossing

FRIDAY, AUGUST 3rd — *On Friday, the third of August, of the year 1492, at eight o'clock, we set out from the bar at Saltés. We went with a strong sea-breeze sixty millas to the southward, that is, fifteen leagues, before sunset;...*

This terse entry hardly seems an adequate introduction to a 225-day voyage that was to irrevocably alter the course of history. But it's brevity doesn't diminish its importance to the landfall question demonstrated when Morison expanded his undersized island candidate to the *Journal's* dimensions by assuming Columbus measured distances in Roman *"millas"* supposedly mistranscribed by Las Casas as *"leagues"* of four times that length. One of several arguments against Morison's landlubber-centric rationale is that all other verbatim *Journal* distances are recorded in *leagues*, while many summarized excerpts express distance in *millas* — an indication Las Casas frequently converted the sailor's *league* into the landlubber's *milla* in his summaries. Even this brief entry, with its unique use of both distance units, has the appearance of a summary carelessly misrendered into the first-person form Las Casas had just finished copying from the prologue. That prologue demonstrated Columbus wasn't shy about expressing his aims in passionate detail, so he probably recorded some of his innermost thoughts on this first day of his lifelong crusade. Thus it's surprising this "verbatim" entry has less than 10% the content of most of his first-person entries, and is even shorter than the average summarized entry. In fact, its compressed form — date, time, location, wind, course and distance — parallels many summarized *Journal* entries but none of those in the first person. From these arguments we can be fairly confident these *"sixty millas"* were a Las Casas conversion from *"15 leagues"* and that a seafaring Columbus always recorded distances in *leagues* rather than in *millas*.

...afterwards, to the southwest and south by west which was the course for the Canaries.

It will soon become clear that today's *"afterwards"* extends until tomorrow's sunrise, his normal break point between each day's *Journal* entry on his outbound voyage.

SATURDAY, AUGUST 4th — *They went to the southwest by south.*

SUNDAY, AUGUST 5th — *They went on their way, day and night together, more than forty leagues.*

MONDAY, AUGUST 6th — *The rudder of the caravel* Pinta, *in which was Martin Alonso Pinzón, jumped out of gear; this was believed or suspected to be due to the action of a certain Gomez Rascón and Cristóbal Quintero, to whom the caravel belonged, because that voyage was irksome to him. And the Admiral says that, before they set out, these men had been found to be inclined to oppose and pick holes, as they say. The Admiral was then much disturbed because he could not help the caravel without danger to himself, and he says that this anxiety was somewhat relieved because he knew that Martin Alonso Pinzón was a man of courage and good understanding. Eventually, day and night, they went twenty-nine leagues.*

Martin Alonso Pinzón's subsequent insubordination would soon anger Columbus, so this entry's favorable assessment of him as a *"man of courage"* supports the widely held belief Columbus seldom altered his *Journal* entries. With the exception of some transcription errors, one intriguing erasure, and several minor ellipses, the *Journal* abstracts recorded by Las Casas are probably an accurate representation of the Admiral's observations.

TUESDAY, AUGUST 7th — *The rudder of the* Pinta *again was unshipped and they repaired it, and they went on a course for the island of Lanzarote, which is one of the Canary Islands...*

Latitude Sailing (LS) was the preferred navigation system for constant-latitude ocean crossings, but useless on his southwesterly *"course for the island of Lanzarote."* On this first leg of his voyage Columbus had to rely on Dead Reckoning (DR) navigation over a distance of 600 miles, where even a quarter point of compass error could throw him off course by 30 miles. This threat had already established Lanzarote's 2200-foot volcanic peak as an important beacon visible at almost twice that distance. If overcast left a pilot empty handed at Lanzarote's latitude, he could always head southeast to sight another Canary Island or reestablish his bearings at Africa's nearby coastline.

...And they made twenty-five leagues, day and night together...

The evidence suggests Columbus would utilize fewer than half of his 26 LPC opportunities, possibly due to inclement weather, operational complications, or the limited utility of increasingly redundant measurements. But at 7:15 this evening he must have been eager to test his skill with LPC-1, when Saturn's bright beacon stood 15 degrees above his darkening eastern horizon and only 2 ½ degrees below the nearly full Moon. At this elevated viewing angle, the differential refraction error would have been reduced to less than 15 miles of longitude.

WEDNESDAY, AUGUST 8th — *Among the pilots of the three caravels there were different opinions concerning their position, and the Admiral proved to be nearest the truth...*

This morning, with position estimates in hand from the *Niña* and *Pinta*, Columbus could cautiously flaunt his superior measurements — understandably restrained given this was his first attempt. Some who doubt Columbus made use of LPCs have argued that today's *"position"* debate was stimulated by a Canary Island landfall, but Fernando's *Biography* reveals his father's fleet wouldn't sight the Canaries until tomorrow.

...He was anxious to go to Grand Canary, in order to leave the caravel Pinta *there, since she was steering badly and making water, and he wished to secure another there, if one were to be found. They were not able to arrive there on that day...*

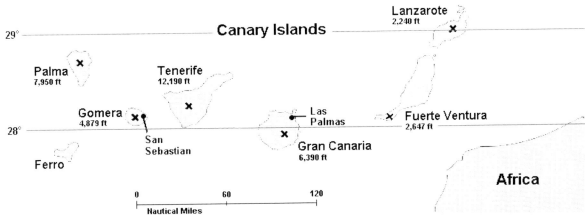

Figure 2-1. The Canary Islands

THURSDAY, AUGUST 9th — Until the night of Sunday, the Admiral could not make Gomera, and Martin Alonso, by order of the Admiral, remained off that coast of Grand Canary, because he could not steer...

From Fernando's biography we learn it was contrary winds and calms, rather than the *Pinta's* rudder problems that delayed the fleet's arrival at Grand Canary for three full days.

...Afterwards, the Admiral reached Canary or Tenerife,...

Fernando added some details about his father's Canary Island stopover. He reported the *Santa Maria* and *Niña* reached Gomera on August 12th and anchored there at the port of San Sebastián for almost two weeks while Pinzón was repairing the *Pinta's* rudder at Las Palmas. At San Sebastián Columbus could have observed lunar conjunctions of Jupiter (LPC-2) and Mars (LPC-3) from a known longitude in the early morning hours of August 20th. These observations may have helped Columbus correct for any slowly changing bias in his *Ephemerides* tabulations. At the least they gave him an opportunity to hone his celestial measurement skills.

...and with much labor and care on the part of the Admiral, of Martin Alonso, and of the others, they repaired the Pinta very well, and eventually they reached Gomera...

The *Pinta* wasn't *"repaired"* until three weeks after their first arrival at Gomera.

...They saw a great fire coming from the mountain of the island of Tenerife, which is remarkably lofty...

The Canary's highest peak soars 12,190 feet above sea level, 60 times the height of those Bahama Islands soon to welcome him to the New World. On the night of August 24th its fiery volcanic cone must have made an impressive display as the *Santa Maria* sailed within 20 miles on its way to rejoin the damaged *Pinta* at Las Palmas. Details from Fernando's biography reveal that his father's second anchorage in the Canary Islands extended from August 25th to September 1st, allowing Columbus to study LPC-4, the August 26th lunar conjunction with Venus, once again from a fixed location.

...They fitted the Niña *with square sails, for she had been lateen rigged. He returned to Gomera on Sunday, the second of September, with the* Pinta *repaired. The Admiral says that many honourable Spaniards, inhabitants of the island of Hierro, who were in Gomera with Doña Inéz Peraza, the mother of Guillem Peraza, who was afterwards first Condé de la Gomera, swore that every year they saw land to the westward of the Canaries, which is towards the setting sun; and others from Gomera affirmed exactly the same under oath. The Admiral says here that he remembers that, being in Portugal in the year 1484, one from the island of Madeira came to the king and asked of him a caravel, to go to this land which he saw, and that this man swore that he saw it every year and always in the same way. He also remembers that they said the same thing in the islands of the Azores, and that all these agreed concerning the direction and the manner of appearance and the size. Having taken in water and wood and meat, and the other things which the men, whom the Admiral had left in Gomera, when he went to the island of Canary to repair the caravel* Pinta, *had obtained, finally he set sail from the island of Gomera, with his three caravels, on Thursday, the sixth day of September.*

One might ask "Why did the expedition remain in the Canary Islands for a full lunar cycle instead of promptly embarking on its westward quest?" Surely consumables could have been replenished in a few days; repair of the *Pinta's* rudder wouldn't take much longer, nor would rigging the *Niña* with square sails. So why tarry a month in port while teredos and barnacles were reducing chances of a successful ocean crossing with each day's delay? In his *Admiral of the Ocean Sea*, Morison attributed Columbus's extended stay in this archipelago to a romantic interlude with the beautiful Doña Beatrix de Peraza. But Fernando's *Biography* dispels Morison's romantic speculation by revealing the two "lovers" remained islands apart during the Admiral's entire Canary Island layover.

Columbus's choice of this delayed sailing date can be explained by upcoming celestial events useful for his navigation and accurate mapping of discoveries. He planned for a voyage of only 2,400 miles, whether his anticipated landfall was actually Japan or the North American coastline *"he hath discovered"* on his 1477 voyage. According to Andrés Bernáldez, chronicler of his second voyage, Columbus's caravels should be expected to make those 2400 miles in less than three weeks when propelled by sustained easterly trade winds at the Canaries latitude. Departing Gomera on September 6th with the moon full he probably anticipated a landfall between 60° and 65° W longitude well before the next full moon on October 5th. That celestial event would present him with a rare opportunity for precisely measuring the longitude of his landfall with a penumbral *lunar eclipse*. And if foul weather should prevent that measurement, a much stronger opportunity might present itself on October 21st when a nearly total *solar eclipse* was predicted for the western Atlantic. Both eclipses would occur a few degrees above his *eastern* horizon, as required for longitude measurements of the North American coastline to his west.

His September 6th departure date would also allow Columbus to sharpen the navigation skills he needed for effective use of Ursa Major as his latitude-guiding constellation. For years he had observed this constellation as it culminated high above Spain's northern horizon. But while sailing the 28th parallel he knew Dubhe would be the constellation's only star culminating above the horizon, so close to the horizon its visibility would be diminished by atmospheric absorption. So Columbus needed to practice measuring selected pairs of Ursa Major's stars at the instant they shared the same elevation angle. His Canary Island observations over a full lunar cycle would enable him to identify which pairs of that constellation's stars were easiest to read under the variable viewing conditions he expected to encounter.

Longitude measurements could also be facilitated by practice with LPCs for all four major planets at his Canary Island anchorages. The last of these, LPC-5, was a lunar-Saturn conjunction on September 3rd during his final anchorage at Gomera, allowing Columbus to sharpen his skills while timing his New World landfall to accommodate both predicted eclipses.

THURSDAY, SEPTEMBER 6th — *He set out on that day in the morning from the harbor of Gomera and shaped his course to proceed upon his voyage; and the Admiral learned from a caravel, which came from the island of Hierro [Ferro,] that three caravels of Portugal were cruising there, in order to take him...*

While LS enabled pilots to maintain accurate courses, its limited choice of sailing dates and latitudes made their ships vulnerable to enemy interception. The 16th century probably saw more than one Spanish treasure fleet ambushed by privateers lurking along the return latitude to Cadiz. Forewarned of the *"three caravels,"* Columbus *"shaped his course"* in a southwesterly direction from San Sebastián to pick up his Ferro latitude well to the west of that island. That Portuguese fleet may have been stationed there not to intercept Columbus, but to serve as a reminder of Pope Sixtus IV´s 1481 confirmation of the Treaty of Alcáçovas establishing Portuguese dominion over any discoveries south of the Canary Islands. Next March, when their King Jao II learned of Columbus's New World discoveries he would immediately claim them for Portugal under the treaty's provisions. But by 1494 Spanish power and a Spanish Pope, Alexander VI, would rotate that line of demarcation from the Canary Island latitude into a *longitude* line giving Spain dominion over all of Columbus's discoveries to its west.

...This must have been due to the envy which the king felt because he had gone to Castile. And he went all that day and night in a calm, and in the morning he found himself between Gomera and Tenerife.

FRIDAY, SEPTEMBER 7th — *All Friday and Saturday, until three o'clock at night, he was becalmed.*

SATURDAY, SEPTEMBER 8th — *At three o'clock at night, on the Saturday, it began to blow from the northeast, and he shaped his route and course to the west. He shipped much sea over the bows, which made progress slow, and that day and night he went nine leagues.*

Columbus knew his lengthy *"course to the west"* could be severely distorted by undetectable changes in the ocean's current and/or earth's magnetic field. So it's well that Dubhe, a second-magnitude star in Ursa Major, would culminate just above his northern horizon as it took its nightly scoop from the North Atlantic. On clear moonless nights that angle was less than one finger width at arm's length above an artificial horizon defined by a sister ship's lantern a mile or so north of the *Santa Maria*. But this night the nearly full moon rose well ahead of Dubhe's culmination, so Columbus may have been guided by one of Ursa Major's several multi-star combinations. For example, in mid September, one pair, Megrez and Dubhe, could both be measured at four degrees shortly after 8 PM, well before the *waning* quarter moon rose near midnight. In late September, another pair, Megrez and Phad, would be visible seven degrees above the horizon in nautical darkness; well after the *waxing* quarter moon had set before midnight. Dubhe provided a rich variety of stellar pairs for maintaining the 28th latitude under a range of visibility conditions, so it's well

Columbus could study them over the full lunar cycle before his ocean crossing. But his preference would always be for solitary Dubhe's small culmination angle.

Fifteen centuries earlier, the three Magi had awkwardly expressed a similar preference for a solitary culminating star to guide them on their westward trek to Bethlehem. They could have maintained their latitude in the trackless desert with nightly guidance from Ursa Major's "stationary" star Alkaid as it culminated just two degrees above their cloudless northern horizon. The universal misconception about the Magi's "stationary" star is fixated on imagined celestial events above the *western* horizon that couldn't have provided the Magi useful guidance for more than a few hours each night. With no means for correcting course errors accumulated during their 20 or so unguided hours, any celestial guidance above the western horizon would have been essentially useless to the Magi.

Several navigation experts having no vested interest in the landfall question have lent their informed support to the circumstantial evidence Columbus navigated by LS instead of DR. In the National Geographic Society's *Men, Ships and the Sea*, Captain Allan Villiers wrote, "Masters achieved surprising accuracy by dead reckoning, but they avoided long voyages over open sea" in explaining why Prince Henry established his 15th century navigation school at Sagres. Tim Severin, a frequent author of maritime history for the NGS, reinforced this position when he wrote me that, "Columbus probably used LS because it is the only method that takes account of ocean currents, leeway and other variables which are inadequately covered by dead reckoning." It's difficult to square these informed opinions with those who apparently still believe Columbus avoided celestial distractions by crossing the Atlantic with a bucket over his head.

SUNDAY, SEPTEMBER 9th — *He made fifteen leagues that day, and he determined to reckon less than he made, in order that the crews might thus not become disheartened or alarmed if the voyage were lengthy. In the night he went a hundred and twenty millas, at ten millas an hour, which is thirty leagues. The sailors steered badly, letting her fall off to west by north and even to west-northwest; concerning this the Admiral many times rebuked them.*

While Columbus was a latitude sailor, this entry suggests his sailors were still relying on the non-celestial methods that had served them well on short Mediterranean runs. Fernando's *Biography* reveals the fleet had its last view of the Canaries this very night with Palma's 7730-foot peak off the stern's starboard quarter. If *"The sailors"* had foolishly kept Palma's peak at a constant bearing angle until it slipped below the eastern horizon, the fleet's heading that night would have slowly rotated clockwise towards *"west-northwest."* Upon arising, Columbus *"rebuked"* the men and re-established his due west course by compass, but he would have to wait for Dubhe's culmination that evening to correct for his sailor's 15-mile deviation from the 28th latitude. Regaining this lost latitude would have been guesswork for DR navigators, but Columbus merely needed a sighting of Ursa Major's culmination. The only contemporary description of Columbus's navigation methods appears in Antonio Galvano's *The Discoveries,* written in 1555 while serving as governor of the Maluccas. It is likely Galvano had been guided to his post by skilled Arabian pilots relying on LS navigation to cross the daunting expanse of the Indian Ocean. So it's of more than passing interest that his book's brief mention of Columbus's first voyage includes the declaration "Some affirme that they were the first that sailed by latitudes."

MONDAY, SEPTEMBER 10th — *In that day and night, he went sixty leagues, at ten millas, which is two and a half leagues, an hour. But he only reckoned forty-eight leagues in order that the crew might not be dismayed if the voyage were long.*

TUESDAY, SEPTEMBER 11th — *That day they sailed on their course, which was to the west, and they made twenty leagues and more. And they saw a large piece of the mast of a ship of a hundred and twenty tons, and they could not secure it. During the night, they went about twenty leagues, and he reckoned no more than sixteen, for the said reason.*

WEDNESDAY, SEPTEMBER 12th — *That day, proceeding on their course, they made in the night and day thirty-three leagues, counting less for the said reason.*

THURSDAY, SEPTEMBER 13th — *In that day and night, following their course which was west, they went thirty-three leagues, and he reckoned three or four less. The currents were against them...*

Beyond sight of land, Columbus could estimate ocean *"currents"* only by comparing his measured location with one calculated from frequent recordings of the *Santa Maria's* course and speed. Morison pointed out that water speed was accurately measured "by watching the bubbles or the gulfweed float by." But location measurements beyond sight of land required celestial assistance, and no LPC had occurred since departing his Canary Island anchorage. I suspect Spanish astronomers, anticipating tonight's LPC deficiency, provided Columbus with predicted longitudes for Rigel, the firmament's 7th brightest star in the constellation Orion. On a clear night Columbus would have seen this beacon rising at midnight just one degree above the waning quarter moon. If he measured this separation greater than predicted, he would have underestimated his actual progress, attributing the measured deficiency to imagined westerly *"currents."*

...On this day, at the beginning of the night, the needles turned northwest, and in the morning they declined northeast somewhat.

While awaiting Rigel's appearance, Columbus had time to observe the counter-clockwise orbit of Polaris about the north celestial pole. Las Casas, the landlubber, grossly distorted these observations by recording an outlandish compass swing of almost 90 degrees from *"northwest"* to *"northeast somewhat."* But Fernando, the sailor, recorded these compass deflections in his father's *Biography* as a more realistic "half a point to the northwest" in the evening and "a little more than half a point to the northeast" in the morning. This measured shift of a dozen degrees was nearly double the actual value, but a reasonable estimate for observations projected down to a fluctuating ship's compass. On this night Columbus still assumed Polaris marked the north celestial pole, making his compass appear to swing easterly as the pole star moved westerly through the night. The near symmetry of his evening and morning compass readings suggests there was minimal variation at tonight's location. This episode reinforces the fact that pilots simply couldn't rely on their compass for 3000 miles of oceanic navigation.

FRIDAY, SEPTEMBER 14th — *That day they navigated on their course westward, and during the night, and they went twenty leagues. He reckoned somewhat less. Here those in the caravel* Niña *said that they had seen a tern and a tropicbird; and these birds never go more than twenty-five leagues from land.*

SATURDAY, SEPTEMBER 15th — *He sailed that day with its night twenty-seven leagues and somewhat more on his westerly course. And on this night, at the beginning of it, they saw fall from the sky a marvelous branch of fire into the sea at a distance of four or five leagues from them.*

The Perseids meteor showers had peaked in mid-August and the Leonids weren't due until late November, so this unexpected display may have been all the more dazzling with the waning quarter moon still beneath the horizon early that evening.

SUNDAY, SEPTEMBER 16th — *He went on his westerly course that day and night. They must have made thirty-nine leagues, but he did not reckon more than thirty-six. That day there were some clouds, a little rain falling. Here the Admiral says that then and always after that time they met with very temperate breezes, so that it was a great delight to enjoy the mornings, and nothing was lacking except to hear the nightingales. He says "And the weather was like April in Andalusia." Here they began to see many tufts of very green seaweed, which, as it appeared, had not long been torn from the earth;...*

Four months later Columbus would validate Indian depictions of distant Caribbean islands by again noting the differences between benthic (bottom-growing) seaweed *"torn from the earth"* and the rootless pelagic seaweed floating in the Sargasso Sea. This week Columbus will make sporadic reference to seaweed, with peak readings of *"choked"* on 21 September and *"dense"* the following day.

... on this account, all judged that they were near some island, but not to the mainland, according to the Admiral, who says: For the mainland I take to be further on.

Barely a thousand miles beyond the Canary Islands, Columbus reveals knowledge of a *"mainland,"* unknown to most Europeans. Some of his crew may have also signed on to the earlier 1477 expedition, including some possibly anchored in the northern Bahamas to measure longitude with the solar eclipse at totality. Today's revelation of *"the mainland... further on"* may have been stimulated by this (Monday) morning's LPC-6 three hours before the end of today's *Journal* entry. At 2:52 AM Jupiter shone brightly 15 degrees above the darkened eastern horizon and only 4 degrees below the waxing Moon.

MONDAY, SEPTEMBER 17th — *He sailed on his westerly course, and they went in the day and night fifty leagues or more: he only counted forty-seven. The currents assisted them...*

Beginning today, all Columbus estimates of Atlantic Ocean *"currents"* will be correlated with an LPC. There's no record Columbus measured LPC-6 or LPC-7, but they were his only source for the longitudes needed to calculate ocean *"currents."*

...They saw much vegetation and it was very delicate and was weed from rocks; and the vegetation came from the westward. They concluded that they were near land. The pilots took the north, marking it, and they found that the needles declined northwest a full point; and the sailors were alarmed and depressed, and they did not say why. When the Admiral noticed this, he gave orders that they should mark the north again at dawn, and they found that the needles were true. The explanation was that the star appears to change its position and not the needles...

In their second description of an illusionary compass shift, Las Casas and Fernando both recorded the apparent nightly Polaris swing as one point *"northwest"* in the evening to *"true"* at dawn. This may be history's first recording of oceanic compass variation; roughly half a point westerly after factoring out the Polaris rotation about the north celestial pole. This rotation made his sailors *"alarmed and depressed,"* but Columbus had gained understanding since Thursday night and now realized *"that the star appears to change position and not the needles."* As then, tonight's Polaris observations were probably incidental to the reason Columbus was still on deck at 2:30 AM. His *Ephemerides* had alerted him to this morning's LPC-7 with Mars, at magnitude 1.8, only 1.0 degree above a waxing Moon perched 15 degrees over the eastern horizon.

...In the morning, on that Monday they saw much more weed, and it seemed to be grass from rivers, and in this they found a live crab, which the Admiral kept. And he says that these were certain signs of land, because they are not found eighty leagues from land. They found that the water of the sea was less salt, after they had left the Canaries, and the breezes constantly softer. They all went on their way greatly rejoicing, and as to the ships, she that could sail fastest went ahead, in order to be the first to sight land. They saw many dolphins, and the crew of the Niña *killed one. The Admiral says here that these indications came from the west: "Where I hope in that high God, in Whose hands are all victories, that very presently He will give us land." On that morning he says that he saw a white bird which is called a tropicbird, and which is not accustomed to sleep on the sea.*

TUESDAY, SEPTEMBER 18th — *He navigated that day and night and they made more than fifty-five leagues, but he did not reckon more than forty-eight. All these days, the sea was very smooth, like the river at Seville. On this day Martin Alonso in the* Pinta, *which was a fast sailer, did not wait; for he called to the Admiral from his caravel that he had seen a great crowd of birds go towards the west, and hoped to sight land that night, and for this reason he so went ahead. To the northward there appeared a great bank of dark clouds, which is a sign of being near land.*

With his fleet averaging more than 6 knots since Sunday's conjunction, Columbus was reluctant to sacrifice his fleet's steady progress to timely collection of position estimates from the *Niña* and *Pinta*. Transfer of their measurements to the *Santa Maria* would have to wait for Wednesday's calms.

WEDNESDAY, SEPTEMBER 19th — *He sailed on his course, and in the day and night went twenty-five leagues, since it was calm. He wrote down twenty-two. This day, at ten o'clock, there came to the ship a booby [alcatraz], and in the evening he saw another, and it is not their habit to go farther than twenty leagues from land. A few drops of rain fell without wind; this is a certain indication of land...*

Sailing ships were then an order of magnitude faster than land travel, giving the world's seamen the lead in developing a universal vocabulary for objects of mutual interest. Just as the Chinese distance unit, the "li," was phonetically similar to the nautical "league," the Iberian "alcatraz" bears an obvious phonetic relationship to the English "albatross." The *"alcatraz"* Columbus saw this day was probably an albatross, which, unlike the *"booby"* invented by Cecil Jane, does venture far out to sea.

...The Admiral did not wish to be delayed by beating to windward in order to make sure whether there was land in that direction, but he was certain that to the north and to the south there were some islands, as in truth there were, and he went thru the midst of them, because his wish was to press towards the Indies. "And there is time enough, for, God willing, on the return voyage, all will be seen." These are his words...

This entry confirms Columbus planned an Atlantic Ocean *"return"* to Spain rather than extending his westward route to a circumnavigation of the globe.

...Here the pilots gave their position. The pilot of the Niña *made it four hundred and forty leagues from the Canaries; the pilot of the* Pinta, *four hundred and twenty; the pilot of the vessel in which the Admiral was, four hundred exactly.*

The closely spaced pair, LPC-6 and LPC-7, gave Columbus his second opportunity for celestial longitude measurements at sea. They were followed today by his second oceanic position comparison, delayed three days to take full advantage of the favorable winds preceding today's *"calm."* The 20-league intervals separating these measurements define a single degree of equatorial longitude. This level of longitude accuracy is compatible with the 3 arc minutes of latitude error Morison attributed to Jacques Cartier's 1534 crossing of the Atlantic.

THURSDAY, SEPTEMBER 20th — *On this day he navigated west by north and west-northwest because, with the calm that prevailed, the winds were very variable. They must have made some seven or eight leagues. Two boobies [alcatraces] came to the ship, and afterwards another, which was a sign that they were near land, and they saw much vegetation, although on the previous day they had seen none. They caught by hand a bird which was like a tern; it was a river, not a sea bird; it had feet like a gull. There came to the ship, two or three land birds, singing, and afterwards, before sunset, they disappeared. Afterwards, a booby [alcatraz] came; it came from the west-northwest and went southeast, which was an indication that it left land to the west-northwest, for these birds sleep on land and in the morning go out to sea to look for food, and do not fly to a greater distance than twenty leagues.*

The albatross has long since disappeared from the North Atlantic, but a former nesting site has recently been discovered in Bermuda, then 400 leagues to the fleet's *"west-northwest."* Columbus had this direction right, but demonstrated surprising ignorance in limiting their ocean-spanning flights to *"twenty leagues."* Ornithological ignorance led Cecil Jane to consistently mislabel the soaring *"alcatraz"* as *"boobies"* of much shorter range.

FRIDAY, SEPTEMBER 21st — *Most of that day it was calm, and afterwards there was some wind. They must have gone, day and night together, including the distance which was on their course, and that which was not, some thirteen leagues. At dawn, they found so much weed that the sea appeared to be choked with it, and it came from the west. They saw a booby [alcatraz]; the sea was calm as river, and the breezes the best in the world. They saw a whale, which is a sign that they were near land, since they always remain near it.*

SATURDAY, SEPTEMBER 22nd — *He navigated west-northwest, more or less, inclining to one side or the other. They must have made thirty leagues; they saw hardly any vegetation. They saw some petrels and another bird. Here the Admiral says: "This head wind was very necessary to me, since my people were much excited, because they thought that in these seas no winds ever blew to carry them back to Spain. For some part of the day there was no seaweed, afterwards it was very dense."*

SUNDAY, SEPTEMBER 23rd — *He sailed northwestward and at times northwest by north and at other times keeping to his course, which was to the west. He made some twenty-two leagues. They saw a pigeon and a booby [alcatraz], and another river-bird, and other white birds; there was much vegetation and in it they found crabs. As the sea was calm and smooth, the people murmured, saying that, as there was no great sea, it would never blow so as to carry them back to Spain. But afterwards the sea, without wind, rose greatly, and this amazed them, for which reason the Admiral here says: "So that high sea was very necessary for me, because such a thing had not been seen save in the time of the Jews, when [those] of Egypt came out against Moses who was leading them out of captivity."*

MONDAY, SEPTEMBER 24th — *He navigated on his course to the west, day and night, and they went fourteen leagues and a half; he reckoned twelve. There came to the ship a booby [alcatraz], and they saw many petrels.*

Fernando's *Biography* describes the crew as becoming increasingly restive. Some of them even suggested they should heave Columbus overboard "and report back in Spain that he had fallen in accidentally while observing the stars," confirmation enough that Columbus wasn't crossing the Atlantic with a bucket over his head!

TUESDAY, SEPTEMBER 25th — *This day was very calm and afterwards it blew, and they went on their way to the west, until night. The Admiral talked with Martin Alonso Pinzón, captain of the other caravel, the* Pinta *concerning a chart which three days before he had sent to him to the caravel and in which, as it appears, the Admiral had certain islands depicted as being in that sea. And Martin Alonso said that they were in that neighborhood, and the Admiral replied that such was his opinion, but the fact that they had not reached them must be due to the currents which had carried the ships northeastward, and they had not gone as far as the pilots said. Having come to this conclusion, the Admiral asked him to send the chart to him, and, when it had been sent on a line, the Admiral began with his pilot and sailors to fix his position on it...*

For the third time on his voyage, Columbus evaluated oceanic *"currents"* and attempted to *"fix his position"* at sea. But this morning he didn't wait for inputs from the other pilots, suggesting his celestial opportunity to measure longitude may have occurred last night. This opportunity, LPC-8, came at sunset with Venus near maximum brightness as it glowed brightly 15 degrees above the western horizon and almost 5 degrees below the waxing crescent Moon.

...At sunset, Martin Alonso mounted the poop of his ship and in great delight called the Admiral, asking for a reward from him because he had sighted land. The Admiral says that, hearing this stated positively, he fell to his knees to give thanks to Our Lord, and Martin Alonso with his men said the Gloria in excelsis Deo. *The Admiral's people did the same, and those in the* Niña *all climbed the mast and into the rigging, and all affirmed that it was land...*

The sailors eagerly climbed the rigging to confirm Pinzón's imaginary *"land,"* possibly a low cloudbank backlit by the setting sun.

...The Admiral ordered the course, which was to the west, to be changed and they all made southwestward, where the land had appeared...

Cecil Jane's translation is misleading here because Columbus respected the political importance of Ferro's latitude, and had no intention of permanently changing his *"course...to the west"* in search of a phantom island. The Dunn/Kelley translation captures the sense of this entry with "The Admiral ordered the ships to leave their course, which was west, and for all of them to go southwest where the land had appeared." If their search proved futile, Columbus apparently intended to return to his baseline western course, as he did two days later.

...That day they sailed four and a half leagues to the west and in the night seventeen leagues to the southwest, a total of twenty-one. But he told the men that it was thirteen leagues, since he always pretended to his people that he had made a small distance, in order that the voyage might not appear lengthy to them. In this way he kept two reckonings on that voyage: the smaller which was false, and the greater which was true. The sea was very smooth, so that many sailors went swimming. They saw many dorados and other fish.

WEDNESDAY, SEPTEMBER 26th — *He sailed on his course to the west until after midday; then they went to the southwest, until it was found that what they had said was land was not land, but only a cloud. They made* *in the day and night thirty-one leagues, and he reckoned twenty-four to his men. The sea was like a river; the breezes sweet and very soft.*

THURSDAY, SEPTEMBER 27th — *He kept on his course to the west. He went in the day and night twenty-four leagues; he reckoned to his men twenty leagues. Many dorados came and they killed one; they saw a tropicbird.*

FRIDAY, SEPTEMBER 28th — *He kept on his course to the west. They made in the day and night, owing to calms, fourteen leagues; he reckoned thirteen. They found little vegetation; they took two dorados, and in the other ships they took more.*

SATURDAY, SEPTEMBER 29th — *He kept on his course to the west. They went twenty-four leagues; he reckoned twenty-one to his men. Owing to the calms which they experienced, they made little way in the day and night. They saw a bird which is called the frigate-bird, which makes the boobies [alcatraces] vomit what they have eaten in order to eat it itself and which maintains itself upon nothing else. It is a sea bird, but it does not settle on the sea, nor does it go more than twenty leagues from land; there are many of these birds in the Cape Verde Islands. They later saw two boobies. The breezes were very sweet and pleasant, so that he says that nothing was wanting save to hear the nightingale, and the sea was smooth as a river. There afterwards appeared, on three occasions, three boobies and a frigate bird. They saw much vegetation.*

SUNDAY, SEPTEMBER 30th — *He kept his course to the west. He went, owing to the calms, in the day and night fourteen leagues; he reckoned eleven. Four tropicbirds came to the ship, which is a great indication of land, since so many birds of one kind being together is a sign that they are not straying or lost. Four boobies [alcatraces] were also seen, on two occasions; there was much vegetation. Note that the stars which are called the guards, when night falls, are near the arm on the west side, and when dawn breaks, they are on the line below the arm to the northeast, so that it seems that in the whole night they move only three lines, which are nine hours; and this is the case every night. This the Admiral says here...*

The *"guards,"* Kolchab and Pherkab Major, form the far edge of Ursa Minor's cup, opposite Polaris. Since antiquity, Sailors have used this stellar pair as a heavenly clock read with the aid of a nocturnal (shown below in Figure 2-2) for measuring their 24-hour rotation about Polaris. A man's image superimposed on the North Pole, with "arms" extended east and west, facilitated the readings of this rotation. Tonight's measurement of *"nine hours"* for the length of *"the whole night"* is puzzling, especially when confirmed by Fernando For at the 28th parallel "nautical twilight" spans a full 10 hours and 25 minutes on this Columbian date. Even shrinking its duration to the interval defined as "astronomical twilight" (the sun an additional six degrees below the horizon) would leave it half an hour too long.

Figure 2-2. 16th century Italian nocturnal

...Moreover, at nightfall the needles decline a point northeast [norueste], and at daybreak they are right on the [north] star, from which it appears that the star moves as the other stars and that the needles always point truly.

On September 17th Columbus had measured compass variation as a half-point westerly. He reported the same variation today, a finding concealed by Cecil Jane's erroneous rendering of *"norueste."* From this one pair of measurements Willem Van Bemmelen conjectured a set of *hypothetical* isogonic contours that could have guided Columbus to Watlings Island had he actually been navigating by DR. Morison adopted Van Bemmelen's conjecture as *fact* to "prove" Columbus used DR navigation to reach landfall at Watlings! Not to be outdone, the *National Geographic Society* massaged those same conjectured isogonic contours to shift their own landfall guess further south to Samana Cay.

MONDAY, OCTOBER 1st — *He kept his course to the west. They made twenty-five leagues; he reckoned twenty leagues to his men. They had a heavy fall of rain. The Admiral's pilot on this day at dawn calculated that they had gone from the island of Hierro up to then five hundred and seventy-eight leagues westward. The smaller reckoning, which the Admiral showed to the men, made it five hundred and eighty-four leagues, but the true distance, which the Admiral calculated and kept secret, was seven hundred and seven.*

A few minutes before midnight, LPC-9 gave Columbus his fourth oceanic opportunity to measure longitude when a sparkling Saturn stood half a degree above the Moon on his western horizon. Once again he appears to have used the heavens to reckon his progress as *"seven hundred and seven"* leagues. And it is well he did because LPC-9 would prove one of the strongest measurement opportunities of his entire voyage with only 3 miles of differential refraction error at the assumed elevation angle of 15 degrees.

TUESDAY, OCTOBER 2nd — *He kept on his course, night and day, for thirty-nine leagues, to the west; he reckoned to the men, a matter of thirty leagues. The sea was always smooth and calm. "To God many thanks be given," the Admiral says here. Weed was floating from east to west, contrary to that which was generally the case. Many fish appeared; one was killed. They saw a white bird which seemed to be a gull.*

Columbus has reached the location where the Atlantic's circular North Equatorial Current (NEC) flows in an *"east to west"* direction. Yesterday morning's LPC-9 had given him the accurate longitude measurement needed for estimating ocean currents when beyond sight of land.

WEDNESDAY, OCTOBER 3rd — *He followed his ordinary course; they went forty-seven leagues; he reckoned forty leagues to the men. Petrels appeared; there was much vegetation, some very faded and others very fresh and bearing something like fruit. They did not see any birds, and the Admiral believed that they had left behind the islands which he had depicted on his chart. The Admiral says here that it had not been his wish to keep beating about during the past week and on the days when he saw so many indications of land, although he had information of certain islands in that region, in order not to delay, since his aim was to pass to the Indies and, if he were to have delayed, he says that it would not have been good judgment.*

Today's estimate *"they had left behind the islands"* was recorded more than 24 hours after Monday's LPC-9, so it might be considered uncorrelated to that event. However, Las Casas omitted an important phrase from today's *Journal*, which was transcribed by Fernando as, "in the afternoon of Wednesday following, the *Niña's* pilot claimed they had sailed 540 leagues, while the *Pinta's* set the figure at 634." So these belated position estimates do satisfy the 72-hour multi-ship correlation window. Both fall far short of the *"seven hundred and seven"* leagues recorded by Columbus because only he knew how to measure his location celestially.

Fernando added "The Admiral's people wished to turn off in one direction or another to look for those lands, but he refused because he feared to lose the fair wind that was carrying him due west along what he believed to be the best and most certain route to the Indies. Besides, he reflected that he would lose respect and credit for his voyage if he beat aimlessly about from place to place looking for lands whose position he had claimed to know accurately." And the mention of *"information of certain islands in that region"* may refer to a possible undocumented mapping of the northern Bahamas in 1477, which was at an optimum viewing site for the eclipse — at totality a few degrees above the western horizon.

THURSDAY, OCTOBER 4th — *He kept on his course to the west; they went, day and night together, sixty-three leagues; he reckoned forty-six to his men. There came to the ship more than forty petrels in a body, and two boobies [alcatraçes], and a boy in the caravel hit one with a stone. A frigate bird came to the ship and a white bird like a gull.*

FRIDAY, OCTOBER 5th — *He kept on his course; they made eleven millas an hour and in the night and day they went fifty-seven leagues, since during the night the wind freshened somewhat. He reckoned forty-five to his men. The sea was calm and smooth. "To God," he says, "many thanks be given." The air was sweet and temperate; there was no vegetation; birds, many petrels. Many flying fish flew into the ship.*

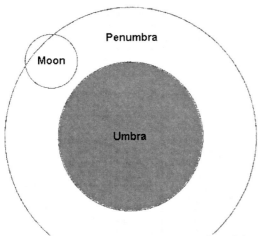

Figure 2-3. Partial Lunar Eclipse October 5th

Figure 2-3 above shows the full moon at 6:00 PM. The penumbra defines the region where the moon is partially shadowed by the earth, and the smaller umbra where it lies totally within the earth's shadow. At his longitude of 65 W tonight's penumbral eclipse occurred just 45 minutes after moonrise, reducing the impact of timing errors.

If the 1477 expedition informed Columbus the Bahamas were less than 1100 leagues west of the Canary Islands, he would have expected landfall in late September at the average 50 leagues a day that Bernáldez claimed for caravels. Then he could have utilized tonight's penumbral lunar eclipse, one whose fullness, horizon proximity, and date of occurrence were well suited for measuring the longitude of his anticipated landfall. But the trade winds had frequently failed Columbus, leaving him 200 leagues short of his objective. Neither Las Casas nor Fernando mentions this evening's eclipse, possibly because cloud cover thwarted an observation, or Columbus considered any additional mid-ocean measurements pointless.

SATURDAY, OCTOBER 6th — *He kept on his course westwards; they went forty leagues in the day and night; he reckoned thirty-three to his men. On this night Martin Alonso said that it would be well to steer southwest by west, and the Admiral thought that Martin Alonso did not say this on account of the island of Cipangu; and the Admiral saw that, if they missed it, they would not be able to reach land so soon, and that it was better to go at once to the mainland and afterwards to the islands.*

Martin Alonso Pinzón was a day early anticipating Columbus's decision to change the fleet's course from due west to southwesterly.   Perhaps Pinzón sensed the huge flocks of migratory land birds flying southwesterly from Bermuda were a more reliable indication of land than his rival's *"information of certain islands in that region."* If Columbus had followed Martin Alonso's suggestion to reduce their due west course by three compass points, rather than the two he would order tomorrow, the fleet may have actually made landfall at Watling's Island instead of Eleuthera, thereby averting decades of future controversy. But Columbus was reluctant to order a course change until he could claim the idea as his own.

SUNDAY, OCTOBER 7th — *He kept on his course to the west; they made twelve millas an hour for two hours, and afterwards eight millas an hour; and up to an hour after sunrise he went twenty-three leagues. He reckoned eighteen to his men...*

Las Casas converted Columbus's recording of the fleet's gale-driven speed from the mariner's three leagues an hour into the landlubber's vernacular of *"twelve millas an hour."* The Bernáldez assertion that caravels could make 72 leagues on a "good" day may have been based on this one *Journal* entry.

...On this day, at sunrise, the caravel Niña, *which went ahead as she was a fast sailer, and they all went as quickly as they could in order to be the first to sight land and secure the reward which the Sovereigns had promised to whomsoever should first sight it, hoisted a standard at the mast-head and fired a lombard, as a sign that they saw land; for so the Admiral had ordered. He had also ordered that, at sunrise and sunset, all the ships should join him, since these are the two periods when it is most possible to see for a distance, the mists clearing. In the evening the land, which those in the* Niña *thought they had seen, was not sighted, and a great flock of birds passed from the direction of the north to the southwest, which led him to believe that they were going to sleep on land or were, perhaps, flying from the winter which was about to come to the lands whence they came. As the Admiral knew that most of the islands which the Portuguese held had been discovered through birds, the Admiral decided to abandon the westward course and to steer west-southwest, with the resolve to proceed in that direction for two days...*

Columbus belatedly accepts Martin Alonso's suggestion to change course, but not until he can put his own stamp on it by reducing the change from three compass points to two. He also limits its scheduled duration to *"two days,"* soon doubled to compensate for the weakening winds. By chance, their Atlantic crossing coincided with the autumnal migration of immense flocks of blackpoll warblers returning from eastern Canada to the West Indies by way of Bermuda. At any other time of the year Columbus might have held his due west course, passing just north of the Bahama Islands to a landfall near Daytona Beach after a powerful northward boost from the Gulf Stream. Constrained physically by this northerly stream and legally by the Treaty of Alcáçovas, he might have coasted northward in search of a harbor, planting his standard at St. Augustine eight years before Amerigo Vespucci mapped its future coquina quarry as "the red headland" and twenty-one years before the well-connected Juan Ponce de Leon received undue credit for its "discovery." Thousands of those warblers responsible for deflecting Columbus's course would soon be greeted near the end of their exhausting flight by swarms of laughing gulls feasting on their vulnerable victims. Surely these determined little songbirds have earned a footnote in history for possibly diverting Spain's New World focus from the North American continent to the Caribbean.

...He began to do so one hour before sunset. They made in the whole night a matter of five leagues, and twenty-three in the day; in the night and day together, they went in all twenty-eight leagues.

In 1942 Morison's *Admiral of the Ocean Sea* identified Watlings as the landfall island by assuming unreliable DR navigation had pulled Columbus 90 miles south of his due west course. But in 1971 his *The European Discovery of America, The Northern Voyages,* praised another Genoese, Giovanni Cabotto (John Cabot) for using LS to cross the Atlantic in 1497 with only four miles of latitude error. When I pointed out that accurate LS navigation by Cabot was inconsistent with unreliable DR navigation by Columbus, Morison privately admitted "Of course Columbus was attempting LS..." Three years after this admission, Morison's companion text, *The Southern Voyages,* finally acknowledged (page 54) that Columbus "proposed to reach the Indies by the same traditional 'latitude sailing' practiced by northern seaman." But by the following page he had regressed to his 1942 claim that "Columbus relied almost completely on dead reckoning."

MONDAY, OCTOBER 8th — *He navigated west-southwest, and day and night together they went about eleven and a half or twelve leagues, and it seems that at times in the night they made fifteen millas an hour, if the text not be corrupt. They had a sea like the river of Seville. "Thanks be to God," says the Admiral, "the breezes were softer than in April in Seville, so that it is a pleasure to be in them: they are so laden with scent." The vegetation seemed to be very fresh; there were many land birds, and they took one, and they were flying to the southwest, terns and ducks and a booby [alcatraz].*

      The Barcelona Manuscript, the source of this *Journal*, was indeed *"corrupt"* in claiming *"fifteen millas [3.75 leagues] an hour,"* a speed 25 percent greater than the fleet's maximum. With the sea as calm as *"the river of Seville,"* the *"softer"* breezes, heralding tomorrow's strong northerly wind, actually limited today's progress to *"twelve leagues,"* or only 0.5 leagues an hour. A stickler for details, Columbus recorded tonight's top speed as *"0.75 leagues an hour,"* inflated to 3.75 by some careless scribe. Frequent transcription errors warn us no item of *Journal* evidence can be taken for granted when evaluating landfall clues. Each clue must be probed for reasonable alternative readings to find the strongest possible synoptic interpretation of the total available evidence.

TUESDAY, OCTOBER 9th — *He sailed southwestward; he made five leagues. The wind changed and he ran to the west by north, and went four leagues. Afterwards, in all, he made eleven leagues in the day and in the night twenty and a half leagues; he reckoned seventeen leagues to the men. All night they heard birds passing.*

      Today's course changes confirm Columbus was contending with a norther's disruption of the Atlantic's easterly trade winds. The typical norther's clockwise cycle begins with its easterly winds diminishing (yesterday) as it veers southerly. When the front arrives it blows strongly from the northwest before subsiding as it rotates back to northeasterly. Morison points out that Columbus couldn't sail within five compass points of the wind. So this morning's initial *"southwestward"* course tells us the norther was probably blowing strongly from the W by N at daybreak. After the norther worked its way clockwise to the NNW, Columbus could compensate for his starboard tack with a port tack of *"four leagues"* to the W by N, a textbook maneuver returning him to his baseline WSW course.

WEDNESDAY, OCTOBER 10th — *He navigated west-southwest; they made ten millas an hour and at times twelve and sometimes seven, and in the day and night together they went fifty-nine leagues; he reckoned to the men forty-four leagues, no more...*

      The norther having blown itself out, strong easterly trade winds now rapidly drove his fleet toward its Eleuthera landfall, *"at times"* reaching hull speeds of *"twelve millas,"* or nine knots.

...Here the men could now bear no more; they complained of the long voyage. But the Admiral heartened them as best he could, holding out to them bright hopes of the gains which they could make, and he added that it was in vain for them to complain, since he was going to the Indies and must pursue his course until, with the help of Our Lord, he found them.

THURSDAY, OCTOBER 11th — *He navigated to the west-southwest; they had a rougher sea than they had experienced during the whole voyage. They saw petrels and a green reed near the ship. Those in the caravel* Pinta *saw* *a cane and a stick, and they secured another small stick, carved, it appeared, with iron, and a piece of cane, and other vegetation which grows on land, and a small board. Those in the caravel Niña also saw other indications of land and a stick loaded with barnacles. At these signs, all breathed again and rejoiced. On this day, to sunset, they went twenty-seven leagues. After sunset he steered his former course to the west;...*

Wilson's Petrels, small dark birds seen skimming the wakes behind today's luxury liners, still return to their Bahamian rookeries every evening. Once again, Columbus's avian timing was fortuitous because these landfall harbingers would soon be migrating back to their Antarctic nesting grounds. But on this day their sunset flight towards Eleuthera signaled Columbus to return to his baseline western course just hours before history's most important landfall. His 400 miles of DR navigation to the WSW these past four days probably added more uncertainty to his landfall latitude than he had accumulated over almost 3000 miles of celestial navigation. Summation of his recorded transatlantic components tells us his landfall latitude was very close to 26° N., although deviations of up to a quarter degree (15 miles) are within reason.

...they made twelve millas an hour, and up to two hours after midnight they had made ninety millas, which are 22 leagues and a half. And since the caravel Pinta was swifter and went ahead of the Admiral, she found land and made the signals which the Admiral had commanded. The land was first sighted by a sailor called Rodrigo de Triana...

The waning quarter moon rose at 9:30 PM and now stood behind Rodrigo's left shoulder, high enough to brightly illuminate the alabaster coral beaches and low-lying white limestone cliffs defining the eastern edge of the Bahama Islands. There were at least two "Rodrigos" among the *Pinta's* company, so we can't be sure who deserves the honor for first sighting the New World, though most historians give that credit to Juan Rodriguez Bermejo of Molinos, a small town near Seville.

...although the Admiral, at ten o'clock in the night, being on the sterncastle, saw a light. It was, however, so obscured that he would not affirm that it was land, but called Pero Gutierrez, butler of the Kings dias, and told him that there seemed to be a light, and that he should watch for it. He did so, and saw it...

This eyewitness wasn't able to confirm the Admiral's suspect claim after he became one of the 39 men Columbus would later maroon to perish on Española.

...He said the same to Rodrigo Sanchez de Segovia, whom the King and Queen had sent as veedor, and he saw nothing since he was not in a position from which it could be seen. After the Admiral had so spoken, it was seen once or twice, and it was like a small wax candle, which was raised and lowered. Few thought that this was an indication of land, but the Admiral was certain that they were near land. Accordingly, when they had said the Salve, which all sailors are accustomed to say and chant in their manner, and when they had all been gathered together, the Admiral asked and urged them to keep a good look out from the forecastle and to watch carefully for land, and to him who should say first that he saw land, he would give at once a silk doublet apart from the other rewards which the Sovereigns had promised, which were ten thousand maravedis annually to him who first sighted it...

No feasible landfall candidate offers a plausible explanation for this *"light"* four hours before the actual sighting by Rodrigo de Triana. The trade winds drove the fleet 36 miles westward during that four-hour interval, while Bahama's highest elevation, 206 feet on Cat Island, was only visible to 20 miles. If the Admiral's "sighting" had been abeam rather than ahead, prudent seamanship would have compelled him to investigate it before plunging ahead in the darkness under gale force winds. And if his "sighting" had been real, Columbus wouldn't have left its substantial reward in place, even boosting it with his offer of a *"silk doublet."* Columbus's *"small wax candle"* is more suggestive of nearby oceanic phosphorescence than the glow of Indian campfires well below a distant horizon. Its likely Columbus contrived his "sighting" to keep the prize money and the honor for himself, and, in fact, he acquired both rewards upon his return to Spain. According to a possibly apocryphal story, Rodrigo de Triana was so distraught at being unfairly deprived of an annuity equivalent to a sailor's annual wage that he gave up his Spanish citizenship and converted to the Muslim faith.

...Two hours after midnight land appeared, at a distance of about two leagues from them...

By the light of a waning quarter moon, a jubilant Rodrigo's first view of the New World was the gale-driven surf pounding the rocky coast of barren Man Island lying just six miles ahead of the *Pinta* off the NE corner of Eleuthera. The caravel's cannon proudly thundered the successful conclusion to a voyage school children would commemorate each October for centuries to come. After an intrepid 38-day sail across a trackless ocean, Columbus and his elated crew weren't about to distract themselves from their joyful celebration by computing the landfall longitude for posterity. But it has since been pieced together from *Journal* entries as roughly 1100 leagues west of the Canary Islands; only a marginally useful longitude measurement, whatever its derivation.

Latitude, on the other hand, could easily be measured with enough accuracy to unambiguously identify the landfall island, so Las Casas could have saved us all a lot of trouble by transcribing it from the *Journal.* Unfortunately all we now have from Columbus is a somewhat ambiguous latitude description in the letter written to his sovereigns during his return voyage. This condensed account of his discoveries includes only this one latitude reference, "it is distant from the equinoctial line twenty-six degrees." In the inaugural issue of *The American Neptune* Samuel Eliot Morison assured his readers this latitude referred to the landfall, noting Watlings Island "only" missed it by almost 120 miles while ignoring its proximity to Eleuthera. Most historians now claim the "26 degrees" refers to Cuba or Española, in what would be an incredibly large latitude error, an order of magnitude worse than a minimum acceptable threshold specified by the historian Andres Bernáldez. This is yet another example of how Columbus's reputation has been sacrificed to sustain unfounded landfall theories.

An Eleuthera landfall is supported by three contemporary accounts. In his brief record of Columbus second voyage, Bernáldez wrote "No one is regarded as a good pilot and master who, although he has to pass from one land to another far distant without seeing any sign of other land, makes an error of 10 leagues, even if the crossing be one of 1000 leagues." Bernáldez would not have written this passage, so closely matching the conditions of Columbus's first voyage, had his friend misread latitude by the 30 leagues claimed by Morison. The "even if" in this passage is an added inference Columbus navigated by LS, where latitude errors are independent of distance, instead of DR, where they increase with the distance traveled.

Juan Ponce de Leon also identified Eleuthera as the Columbus landfall in the surviving accounts of his 1513 "discovery" of Florida. This well-placed nobleman had sailed on Columbus's second voyage prior to his installation as *Puerto Rico's* first colonial governor; so few men then living were better qualified to correctly identify the landfall. Juan wrote how he had anchored at the Columbus landfall for nearly a fortnight before crossing *"The Windward Gulf of the Bahamas."* The only gulf shown on 16th century charts of the Bahama Islands is easily identified as the Northeast Providence Channel separating Eleuthera from The Little Bahama Bank. More significantly, Juan also recorded the landfall's only contemporary latitude measurement as 25° 40'; just 6 miles north of Eleuthera, while 93 miles from Watlings Island. This latitude measurement should carry some weight because Juan soon demonstrated his proficiency with the quadrant by measuring Cape Canaveral's latitude within 12 miles of true.

The historian Gonzalo Fernandez de Oviedo gave us the third contemporary landfall fix in 1535. He specified its location as "40 leagues from Bimini," an island the Chaves *Rutter* correctly positioned near the western end of Providence Channel. To establish the length of this important waterway, Oviedo tied its eastern opening to the well-known Columbus landfall. This fortuitous landfall identification provides longitudinal confirmation of Eleuthera, which lays 43 leagues east of Bimini, impressively close to Oviedo's specification. In contrast, Watlings Island and the other southern landfalls lie far across the archipelago at *twice* this specified distance from Bimini. It would have made about as much sense for Oviedo to reference the location of Watlings to Bimini as it would to reference Madagascar's location to the Canary Islands.

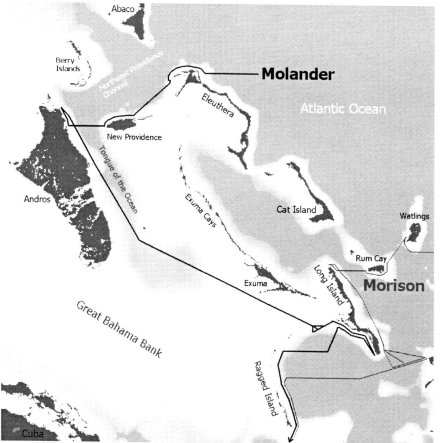

Figure 2-4. Morison and Molander route theories converging before Cuba

Figure 2-4 shows overall map of Bahamas highlighting above features of Morison (grey line) and Molander (black line) routes from first landfall to where they converge at Cuba.

Part II – The Bahamas

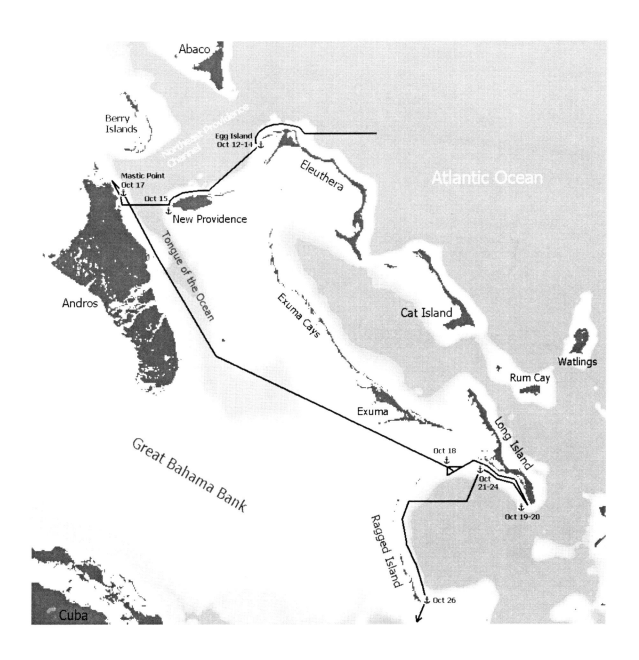

3 - San Salvador: Gateway to a New World

...They took in all sail, remaining with the mainsail, which is the great sail without bonnets, and kept jogging, waiting for day, a Friday, on which they reached [llegaron] a small island [una isleta] of the Lucayos, which is called in the language of the Indians "Guanahani."

With gale-driven surf pounding Eleuthera's rocky coast, Columbus ordered all sails furled except for the mains - enough canvas that stormy night to carry his fleet to the mouth of Northeast Providence Channel, the northeast gateway to the Bahama Islands. A jubilant Columbus surely recorded significant features of Eleuthera's coast while jogging outside its fringing reef, clearly revealed by the ominous breakers reflecting the light from the rising quarter moon. But Las Casas, focused on the needs of his planned *Historia*, ignited today's contentious landfall debate by omitting tonight's landfall descriptions from his *Journal* excerpts. Despite his omissions we can still imagine the astonished Taino Indians clustering along the coast at dawn. They must have gazed in wonder as huge sails of colorful canvas, billowing in the brisk trade winds, magically drove this magnificent fleet WSW towards the reef's first opening at Egg Island. This 250-acre islet, marking the first entrance to Eleuthera's shallows, remains the evening destination of modern yachtsmen following those same trade winds along the very reef that had guided Columbus to Egg Island, his first anchorage in the New World.

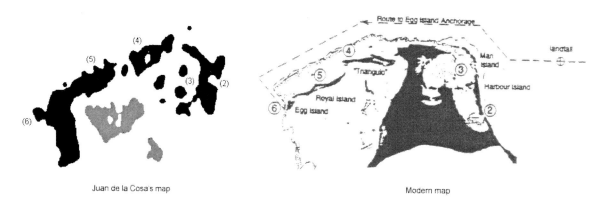

Figure 3-1. "Guanahani" as traced by Harrisse from Juan de la Cosa's map (left) and a modern map of north Eleuthera (right), comparing only the coastline seen by Columbus

Given the dearth of surviving landfall descriptions, it's fortunate Columbus chartered the *Santa Maria* as his flagship because her owner-master, Juan de la Cosa, left us the only eyewitness mapping of *"Guanahani"* in his New World Map of 1500. Even this vital evidence might have been lost to the landfall debate had not Henry Harrisse, the tenacious 19th century historian, traced a copy from Cosa's fading cartographic masterpiece. While some have questioned the accuracy of his copy, the original's curator at Madrid's Museo Naval gave me his blessing of Harrisse's "exactamente" cluster of islets depicting *"Guanahani."* His blessing should have aroused the attention of today's landfall advocates, who have ignored this clustered image of *"Guanahani"* because of their fixation on solitary islands. They miss the many unique Eleuthera features depicted in the enlargement of Cosa's ¼-inch-wide rendering of *"Guanahani,"* drawn eight years after that dramatic night of discovery. Consider that:

1. Northern Eleuthera is the only landfall candidate having the multiple islets and coastline seen by Juan de la Cosa as he coasted from Harbour Island to Egg Island.

2. With the moon up four hours, Juan could see Harbour Island's brightly illuminated limestone entrance centered on Eleuthera's slightly concave coastline. Persistent trade winds could lock his fleet inside this narrow entrance for weeks on end, so Columbus patiently waited for a less confining anchorage on Eleuthera's west coast.

3. Moonlight also illuminated Harbour Island's tranquil shallows, depicted on Cosa's map by three small dots, then a cartographic symbol for shoal water.

4. Seeking an opening in the reef, the fleet sailed past the closely clustered triangle of St. Georges, Russell and Charles Islands, which merged into a single islet ("Triangulo") in the dawn's early light. Cosa's map rotates their merged coastline 30 degrees to the same ENE-WSW course he had sailed eight years earlier.

5. The strongest feature of Juan de la Cosa's ¼-inch mapping of *"Guanahani"* is his pattern of three equally spaced cusps along the WSW-ENE coastline of an island drawn immediately west of Triangulo. In a truly remarkable congruence, these cusps mirror both the spacing and orientation of three cusps uniquely defining Royal Island's north coast.

6. It was daylight when Columbus anchored inside the first accessible break in Eleuthera's fringing reef, so darkness can't be blamed for three discrepancies in Cosa's mapping of Egg Island. These three mapping errors and possible explanations are:

   • Cosa merged Egg and Royal into a single island, possibly because their separation would be mapped at only .05 millimeters.

   • Guanahani's west coast is shown paralleling Eleuthera's shoal rather than Egg Island's coastline, an unsurprising error in a map drawn eight years after the landfall, and,

   • The small blob at the west end of *"Guanahani"* doesn't match Egg Island's coast. Possibly it was added to mark Columbus's first anchorage in the New World.

7. This tiny triangular mass (shown below in Figure 3-2) is clearly incongruent with northern Eleuthera, but it does match the island's southern region, which Cosa may have mapped during his 1499 homeward voyage from Española. If Cosa had intended to revisit the 1492 landfall on that voyage, Eleuthera's interior shallows would have diverted him to the island's east coast, bringing within view of Little San Salvador's gaping West Bay, which were well depicted and positioned on his miniature mapping. Unlike its adjacent namesake, Little San Salvador managed to avoid the 19th century's misguided relocation.

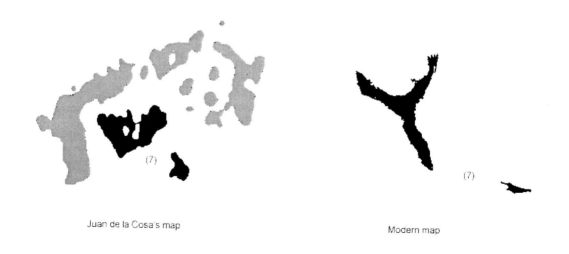

Juan de la Cosa's map

Modern map

Figure 3-2. Triangulo (7) of southern Eleuthera with gaping Little San Salvador

This list of congruencies assures us Juan de la Cosa was identifying Eleuthera as the landfall island, an association always depicted on 18th century Spanish maps as "San Salvador," the name Columbus gave to the Indian's *"Guanahani."* Eleuthera's cartographic claim to the landfall should have been validated by the wealth of evidence uncovered when the Las Casas *Journal* extracts were recovered in 1791. Ironically, superficial analysis of this comprehensive new evidence led to the opposite result after geographers fixated on a single mistranscribed clue while ignoring more than 100 others in this third-hand copy. This narrow approach uprooted San Salvador from its well-established Eleuthera location and shifted it 90 miles south to Watlings Island. This shift spawned scores of divergent landfall theories because none could demonstrate a convincing congruence with most of the *Journal's* 100 other clues.

Cecil Jane's first step in reinforcing Watlings Island's tenuous landfall claim was to enlarge the *Journal's* definitive *"isleta"* from an "islet" to a "small island." He made this shift to accommodate a Watlings Island that sprawled over 20,000 acres, a hundred times larger than scores of isletas described both by Columbus and in the *Chaves Rutter.* Most Watlings advocates now accept the correct translation while arguing that an *"isleta"* from a summarized third-hand excerpt can't be given much weight. But Las Casas was compiling his transcript as background for his *Historia,* not as a resource for the landfall debate. So surely he didn't intend to mislead himself when he repeated *"isleta"* in his marginal note, one of the few postils he appended to Columbus's description of *"Guanahani."* Cecil Jane might have translated *"isleta"* correctly had he been aware of the contemporary Spanish practice of grouping a shoal's islets under the name of its main island. Then he would have realized Columbus used *"llegaron"* precisely to describe his *arrival* at one of Eleuthera's islets far removed from his landfall sighting rather than to a continually visible Watlings Island less than an hour ahead. That realization might have helped him understand why Las Casas' *Historia* gave *"Guanahani"* a length 15 of leagues, four times that of Watlings while closely matching the extent of Eleuthera's coastline seen by Columbus in 1492. The lines are clearly drawn on this important issue because 250-acre Egg Island fits comfortably with the contemporary definition of *"isleta,"* while Watlings Island is far too large.

Figure 3-3. Likely landfall beach of Columbus on southern end of Egg Island

*...Immediately they saw naked people, and the Admiral went ashore in the armed boat, and Martin Alonzo Pinzón and Vincente Yañez, his brother, who was captain of the Niña. The Admiral brought out the royal standard, and the captains went with two banners of the Green Cross, which the Admiral flew on all the ships as a flag, with an **F** and a **Y**, and over each letter their crown, one being one side of the + and the other on the other. When they had landed, they saw very green trees and much water and fruit of various kinds...*

History's most important landing was recreated in Alain Manesson Mallet's 1685 Guanahani map (shown on left side of Figure 3-4, and on book's cover in color) from his widely read five-volume atlas. Although his depiction of *five* ships and *eight* boats reveals Mallet was no historian, this engineer-cartographer reportedly gathered first-hand information for many of his maps. Even if derived from secondary sources, this 17th century map of Guanahani deserves careful scrutiny for its stunningly accurate portrayal of some unique Egg Island topography. Congruent features include a semicircular southern beach, correctly sized, shaped and oriented, and appropriately bracketed by a rounded pedestal of land to its west and a more rectangular one to its east. An even stronger feature gives adjacent Little Egg Island the proper length, distance and direction from that beach, as well as its slender aspect. The foreground's major mismatch is its incorrect orientation of Little Egg Island, a discrepancy possibly resulting from a written description of how it lay "athwart" the fleet's approach to its anchorage. Taken at face value, Mallet suggests Columbus planted Spain's Royal Standard on Egg Island's shallow southern beach rather than its exposed western one, a view supported by his need to "take the soundings" reported by Oviedo.

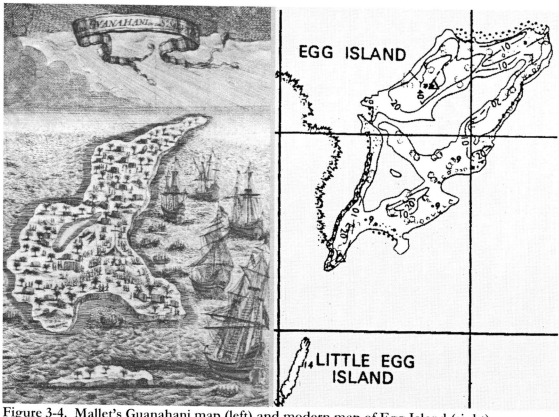

Figure 3-4. Mallet's Guanahani map (left) and modern map of Egg Island (right)

...The Admiral called the two captains and the others who had landed, and Rodrigo de Escobedo, secretary of the whole fleet, and Rodrigo Sanchez de Segovia, and said that they should bear witness and testimony how he, before them all, took possession of the island, as in fact he did, for the King and Queen, his sovereigns, making the declarations which are required, as is contained more at length in the testimonies which were there made in writing. Soon many people of the island gathered there. What follows are the actual words of the Admiral, in his book of the first voyage and discovery of these Indies. "I," he says, "in order that they might feel great amity towards us, because I knew that they were a people to be delivered and converted to our holy faith rather by love than by force, gave to some among them some red caps and some glass beads, which they hung around their necks, and many other things of little value. At this they were greatly pleased and became so entirely our friends that it was a wonder to see. Afterwards they came swimming to the ships' boats, where we were, and brought us parrots and cotton thread in balls, and spears and many other things, and we exchanged for them other things, such as small glass beads and hawks bells, which we gave to them. In fact, they took all and gave all, such as they had, with good will, but it seemed to me that they were a people deficient in everything. They all go naked as their mothers bore them,...

These *"naked"* natives must have been impressed by their strange visitors, carried to their island in huge vessels driven faster by the wind than their dugout canoes could be paddled. The Taino may have been *"deficient in everything,"* but they still could have offered their visitors two useful gifts had Watlings Island actually been the landfall. One would have been the potable water. A second would have been the giant iguana, a vulnerable delicacy still surviving on Watlings Island. Egg Island lacks both of these features, so the Taino resorted to attractive substitutes, such as the *"parrots"* still thriving in Abaco Island's nature preserve directly across Northeast Providence Channel.

...and the women also, although I saw only one very young girl. And all those whom I did see were youths, so that I did not see one who was over thirty years of age; they were very well built, with very handsome bodies and very good faces. Their hair is coarse almost like the hairs of a horse's tail and short; they wear their hair down over their eyebrows, except for a few strands behind, which they wear long and never cut. Some of them are painted black, and they are the colour of the people of the Canaries, neither black nor white, and some of them are painted white and some red and some in any colour that they find. Some of them paint their faces, some their whole bodies, some only the eyes, and some only the nose. They do not bear arms or know them, for I showed to them swords and they took them by the blade and cut themselves through ignorance. They have no iron. Their spears are certain reeds, without iron, and some of these have a fish hook at the end, while others are pointed in various ways. They are generally fairly tall, good looking and well proportioned. I saw some who bore marks of wounds on their bodies, and I made signs to them to ask how this came about, and they indicated to me that people came from other islands, which are near, and wished to capture them, and they defended themselves. And I believed, and still believe that they come from the mainland [tierra firme] to take them for slaves...

The question here is whether *"tierra firme"* should be interpreted in a narrow sense as the Florida *"mainland,"* or in a broader sense as the larger island of Eleuthera adjacent to their *"isleta"* landfall. Watlings Island is larger than its closest neighbors, forcing Cecil Jane to overlook several problems with the *"mainland"* interpretation dictated by his landfall selection. First, Watlings Island is more than 300 miles from Florida's east coast over shoal-water routes that offered the mainland's powerful tribes more convenient opportunities to acquire their *"slaves"* at several intervening populated islands. Second, it would have been illogical for Columbus to assume these raiders came from a mainland 10 times as far as *"other islands, which are near."* Finally, Las Casas would introduce *"Florida"* twice in lieu of *"mainland"* in his November 21st abstract, so it seems likely he would have been equally specific here, if appropriate. Instead, Columbus was probably employing *"tierra firme"* in its broader sense as the main island of Eleuthera viewed from adjacent Egg Island. This broader interpretation provides a logical basis for Columbus assuming the slavers came to Egg Island directly from neighboring Eleuthera rather than 30 miles from Abaco or New Providence islands, *"which are near."* Solitary Watlings Island can't accommodate this broader interpretation of *"tierra firme,"* perhaps leaving Morison to wonder why Columbus assumed the slavers rowed 100 leagues from Florida rather than the 10 indicated by Indians.

...They should be good servants and of quick intelligence, since I see that they very soon say all that is said to them, and I believe that they would easily be made Christians, for it appeared to me that they had no creed. Our Lord willing, at the time of my departure I will bring back six of them to your Highnesses, that they may learn to talk...

These docile Caribbean natives were not merely potential *"good servants."* Three years later Columbus would anger Isabela by sending her 500 in chains as compensation for the financial failure of his second voyage.

...I saw no beast of any kind in this island, except parrots." All these are the words of the Admiral.

The Smithsonian Institution's 20th century survey of Bahamian reptiles lists *none* for Egg Island compared with *eight* distinct species on Watlings, including the giant iguana. While the iguana possibly survived on Egg Island until 1492, its vulnerability to the nearby Taino makes that unlikely.

But there's no doubt it was thriving on Watlings Island the morning Columbus rowed ashore to claim *Guanahani* for Spain. This dichotomy makes *"no beast of any kind"* a strong point of evidence favoring Egg Island. But David Henige, in his *"In Search of Columbus,"* downplayed this evidence by falsely suggesting Columbus *"confined his observing to the vantage point of shipboard."* Henige closed his 282-page diatribe by asserting that my approach was *"an argument from silence at its most vulnerable."* He was clearly mistaken on both counts because the *Journal* informs us Columbus *"went ashore"* to take possession of the landfall island, and *"saw no beast of any kind."* This is no "argument from silence" - it's an emphatic negative observation almost certainly appropriate for tiny Egg Island but assuredly not for Watlings.

SATURDAY, OCTOBER 13th — *As soon as day broke, there came to the shore many of these men, all youths, as I have said, and all of good height, very handsome people. Their hair is not curly, but loose and course as the hair of a horse; all have very broad foreheads and heads, more so than has any people that I have seen up to now. Their eyes are very lovely and not small. They are not at all black, but the colour of Canarians, and nothing else could be expected, since this is in one line from east to west with the island of Hierro in the Canaries...*

Columbus apparently forgot Guanahani was actually 2½ degrees south of Ferro's latitude after his four-day southwesterly jog to follow the birds. He may have over-looked this course change because it had been suggested by his rival Pinzón. No one has yet offered an explanation for the disquieting fact Watlings Island is another 1½ degrees south of Ferro, a latitude discrepancy almost an order of magnitude greater than Columbus's measurement capabilities.

...Their legs are very straight, all alike; they have no bellies but very good figures. They came to the ship in boats [almadias], which are made of a tree trunk like a long boat and all of one piece. They are wonderfully carved, considering the country, and large, so that in some forty or forty-five men came. Others are smaller, so that in some only a solitary man came. They row them with a paddle, like a bakers peel, and they travel wonderfully fast. If one capsizes, all at once begin to swim and upright it, baling it out with gourds which they carry with them...

Lacking appropriate terminology for the Taino dugouts, Columbus stretched the meaning of the Spanish word *"almadias"* for "rafts." Within a fortnight he began identifying them by their Indian name "canoas," a term that had gained universal usage by the time Las Casas recorded his abstract. This terminology shift prompted Las Casas to add a postil clarifying the use of *"almadias"* in this excerpt.

...They brought balls of spun cotton and parrots and spears and other trifles, which it would be tedious to write down, and they gave all for anything that was given to them. And I was attentive and laboured to know if they had gold, and I saw that some of them wore a small piece hanging from a hole which they have in the nose, and from signs I was able to understand that, going to the south or going around the island to the south [bolviendo la isla por el sur], there was a king who had large vessels of it and possessed much gold...

Everette Larson, Chief of the Library of Congress Hispanic Division, has interpreted the alternative route of *"bolviendo la isla por el sur"* as a rounding of the landfall island itself rather than a pointless pirouette around some intervening island en route to Cuba. It would have served no purpose to round Watlings before heading south, leaving its advocates stuck with the pointless pirouette as their only alternative. Larson's interpretation makes sense at Egg Island where the more cautious Taino may have doubted whether the shallows south of The Tongue of The Ocean

(TOTO) could accommodate the huge ships of Columbus. Those doubters may have suggested the longer but more reliable alternative of a deep-water clockwise circuit of Eleuthera.

...I endeavoured to make them go there, and afterwards saw that they were not inclined for the journey. I resolved to wait until the afternoon of the following day, and after that to leave for the southwest,...

His decision to risk the direct *"southwest"* route to Cuba gave Columbus an extra day to perform two important tasks at *"Guanahani."* One, the exploration of Eleuthera's expansive harbor would require most of the following day. The second, measurement of its longitude by observing LPC-10, apparently wasn't executed, even though Jupiter was less than a degree higher than the Moon when they rose together shortly after midnight. The failure to take advantage of this exceptional celestial opportunity could have resulted from any number of factors, including his October 17th observation that it rained *"every day"* in the Indies. Another possibility is that intensive landfall activities had sapped the energy demanded by a dozen miles of midnight rowing to reach Russell Island's unobstructed view of the eastern horizon.

Celestial measurement of Guanahani's longitude had to wait until 1513 when Juan Ponce de Leon's company reached Eleuthera on March 14th where they "made ready one ship to cross the Windward gulf of the islands of the Lucayos" on their way to Florida. Their 10-day Eleuthera anchorage had nothing to do with the simple crossing of Northeast Providence Channel: it was dictated by a pair of celestial opportunities for measuring the longitude of the Columbus landfall island. The first of these was a lunar eclipse on March 21st. While this celestial event lacked the crisp definition of a solar eclipse, it facilitated measurement by peaking near the horizon. A stronger opportunity would occur two days later when the Moon rose at 9 PM with Saturn barely one degree above it. While Antonio de Herrera's fragmentary account of the voyage doesn't tell us when Ponce departed Eleuthera, we do know he sailed 120 miles northwest from there to reach the west end of Grand Bahama Island on the 27th of March. This arrival date is consistent with an Eleuthera departure on the 24th of March, the morning after Saturn's LPC. While waiting for this pair of celestial events his men may have dug the water wells giving the community of Spanish Wells the name it carries to this day. These clever wells were created by simply stacking several open-ended water barrels deep into the sand to facilitate collection of rainwater pooling above the limestone backbone of St. George's Cay.

...for, as many of them indicated to me, they said that there was land to the south and to the southwest and to the northwest, and that those to the northwest often came to attack them...

Exploration literature abounds with examples of indigenous peoples providing remarkably accurate maps to European explorers. And we know Columbus was vitally interested in Caribbean cartography, both to expedite his quest for gold and *"to set all the sea and lands of the Ocean Sea in their true places"* for his sovereigns. So we can be almost certain the Taino sketched maps for Columbus. Those aggressive Indians *"to the northwest"* are suggestive of Abaco's Cherokee Sound, 30 miles northwest of Egg Island. Ponce de Leon would find its Indians unusually hostile when he scoured the northern Bahamas 21 years later in his fruitless search for the Fountain of Youth.

....So I resolved to go to the southwest, to seek the gold and precious stones...

His restated resolve to chance the shorter, less certain, *"southwest"* route through the shallows hasn't deterred several landfall advocates from force-fitting their track reconstructions to some *unrecorded* course change supposedly made the following day. While these imagined course changes may have bolstered many a sagging landfall theory, they certainly would have played havoc with Columbus's pledge to *"to set all the sea and lands of the Ocean Sea in their true places."*

...This island is fairly large [bien grande isla]...

To validate the Watlings Island landfall claim, Cecil Jane enlarged yesterday's *"isleta"* into a *"small island."* Today's entry forced him to make the opposite adjustment by shrinking *"very large"* into a *"fairly large"* more appropriate to that same island. If accurately translated, these supposed descriptions of Watlings Island would be even more conflicted because yesterday's *"isleta"* had to be much smaller than today's *"bien grande isla."* At Eleuthera this seeming contradiction is readily resolved if Columbus was following the same toponymic rules as the *Chaves Rutter* published 40 years after his landfall. This closely held nautical guide to New World discoveries seldom gave independent names to islets sharing the same shoal with a larger nearby island. For example, the *Rutter* included both the Grenadines and their much larger neighbor, Granada, under a single place name, Caribiara. If Columbus had made landfall at one of the Grenadines he could have written he *"arrived at an islet which is called in the language of the natives* Caribiara," and the following day observed without contradiction that nearby Grenada is *"bien grande isla."* In the same way Egg Island can be viewed as an unnamed islet of the much larger Eleuthera, the *"Guanahani"* honored by Spanish cartography until the end of the 18th century. Other landfall advocates, fixated on solitary islands instead of the islet cluster on Eleuthera's shoal, have overlooked this simple explanation reinforced by the 16th century naturalist, Oviedo, who used the plural "islas blancas" to describe Guanahani.

...and very flat; the trees are very green and there is much water...

The first two components of this clue don't have much evidentiary value because every landfall candidate is *"flat"* compared to the soaring Canary Island peaks Columbus had departed a month earlier, and most are *"green"* enough to fit that description. But the only *"water"* of interest was the potable kind, then, as now, a scarce commodity on many of these islands. Although there are no wells on Egg Island, the fresh water ponds on adjacent Royal Island and its nearby islets were surely made known to Columbus in time for this evening's *Journal* recording. Watlings Island has numerous brackish ponds, but today most of its potable water comes from man-made wells carved into the island's limestone base with metal tools lacked by the Taino.

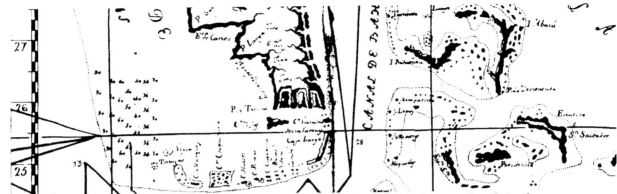

Figure 3-5. 1782 Spanish (Bernard de la Orta) map identifying Eleuthera as San Salvador, with key latitude marked slightly below 25.5° N – matching Egg Island's actual 25.48° N

Figure 3-6. 18th Century Spanish Map (unattributed, from Library of Congress collection) identifying Eleuthera as San Salvador (between Abaco and "del Gato" – Cat Island)

...In the center of it, there is a very large lake [laguna en medio muy grande];...

Cecil Jane followed most other translators in misrendering *"laguna"* to conceal Watlings' lack of a large central lagoon. Even its central "lake" is actually a composite of several meandering for miles through terrain so rugged that even two weeks, let alone two days, would have been inadequate for exploring their perimeters. Columbus's *"laguna en medio muy grande"* was Eleuthera's 40 square-mile lagoon clearly visible from the *Santa Maria's* deck as he recorded its appropriate description in the evening twilight.

...there is no mountain, and all so green that it is a pleasure to gaze upon it. The people also are very gentle and, since they long to possess something of ours and fear that nothing will be given to them unless they give something, when they have nothing, they take what they can and immediately throw themselves into the water and swim. But all that they do

51

possess, they give for anything that is given to them, so that they exchange things even for pieces of broken dishes and bits of broken glass cups. I even saw one give sixteen balls of cotton for three ceotis *of Portugal, which are a* Castillian blanca, *and in these balls there was more than an* arroba *of spun cotton. I should forbid this and should not allow anything to be taken, unless it be that I command all, if there be a quantity, to be taken for Your Highnesses...*

This passage demonstrates Columbus's wish to treat the Indians fairly by prohibiting his men from trading a few copper coins for 25 pounds of spun cotton. He also may have been reminding his sovereigns that today's fair treatment would facilitate their later conversion to the Faith.

...It grows here in this island, but owing to lack of time, I can give no definite account;...

Cotton became the leading money crop for English colonists on several of these islands, making its modern distribution of little evidentiary value.

...and here is also produced that gold which they wear hanging from the nose...

The nearest sources of *"gold"* were Haitian riverbeds more than 400 miles from these Bahamian limestone pedestals that rise a mile from their Caribbean seabed. Columbus sometimes misread Indian signs in ways he knew would impress his Sovereigns.

...But in order not to lose time, I wish to go and see if I can make the island of Cipangu. Now, as it was night, they all went to land in their boats.

As transcribed by Las Casas, Columbus was anxious to reach *"Cipangu"* (Japan) which he supposedly took to be Cuba, the large island to the *"southwest"* mapped for him by his Taino guides. But this cartographer surely knew Marco Polo's Oriental journey had traversed less than a quarter of the Earth's circumference, so accurately measured more than a millennium earlier. With each LPC his *Ephemerides* reminded Columbus that 10,000 miles separated his discoveries from Japan.

SUNDAY, OCTOBER 14th — *At dawn, I ordered the ship's boat and the boats of the caravels to be made ready...*

At dawn's first light Columbus ordered the flotilla's three boats provisioned and lowered from their deck brackets for today's exploration of the landfall island.

...and went along the island [al luengo de la isla] in a north-north-easterly direction...

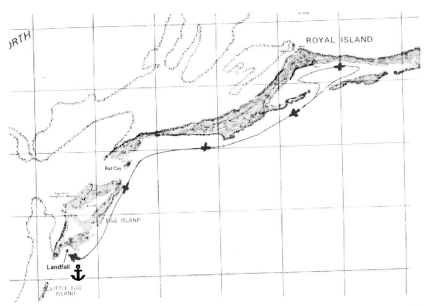

Figure 3-7. Egg-Royal map showing one-mile markers enroute to Royal's sheltered harbor

The precise translation of *"al luengo de la isla"* is "the length of the island," a phrase informing us they rowed the full length of Egg Island *"in a north-north-easterly direction."* The length and direction of his rowing route both create problems for Watlings advocates. First, they must assume Columbus delayed his eagerly anticipated first anchorage in the New World by sailing past sheltered French Bay to find an exposed anchorage at Long Bay on the island's west coast. Secondly, an exploration originating at Long Bay could have rowed only half "the length of the island." Finally, the first three miles from a Long Bay anchorage would have been more *westerly* than *easterly*.

...to see the other part, which lay to the east, and its character [que habia],...

Here Columbus actually wrote *"la parte del este que habia,"* adding the last two words to emphasize this *"isleta"* had a separate eastern *"part,"* like Royal Island, not merely the eastern part common to all islands. Cecil Jane and his followers have consistently mistranslated this simple phrase in wondrous ways to conceal yet another fundamental deficiency of Watlings Island.

...and also to see the villages. And I soon saw two or three, and the people all came to shore, calling us and giving thanks to God. Some brought us water, others various eatables:...

This first mention of *"villages"* confirms Royal Island had the potable water Egg Island lacked, and why the Indians delayed their offer of water until Columbus had reached this eastern part, *"que habia."* There would have been no reason to withhold the offer of fresh water for two full days on Watlings Island as its brackish ponds were no sweeter along Columbus's conjectured rowing route than near his supposed anchorage.

...others, when they saw that I was not inclined to land, threw themselves into the sea and came, swimming, and we understood that they asked us if we had come from heaven. One old man got into the boat, and all the rest, men and women, cried in loud voices: 'Come and see the men who have come from heaven; bring them food and drink.' Many came and many women, each with something, giving thanks to God, throwing themselves on the ground and raising

their hands to the sky, and then shouting to us that we should land. But I feared to do so, seeing a great reef of rocks [una grande restinga de piedras] which encircled the whole of that island,...

According to the Spanish linguist, Everette Larson, *"una grande restinga de piedras"* could describe either the "ledge of exposed rock" lining Royal Island, or a "submerged coral reef" if that reef were very close to shore. Royal Island's jagged ledge of aeolian limestone rising several feet above the heaving surf was the menacing *"grande restinga de piedras"* that led Columbus to decline the Taino invitations. Ironically, this dark ledge, extending the *"whole"* length of Royal's south coast, echoed his last view of the Old World where Ferro's *"Cabo de Restinga"* derives its name from the volcanic ledge ringing its southern cape.

Figure 3-8. Forbidding jagged ledge of rock rimming most of Egg and Royal Islands

Figure 3-9. Closer view of collapsed section of jagged ledge on Egg and Royal Islands

The west coast of Watlings lacks a ledge, forcing Morison to assume today's rowing route was outside the island's girding reef. That reef is more than a mile from shore, too far for Taino *"shouting"* to be heard above the breaking surf. And why would Columbus ignore a short and protected route within that reef to contend with a longer and more difficult rowing route? If he had taken that outer route, several reef openings would have allowed his rowboats to slip through to the Taino beckoning from the beach.

...while within [entremedias] there is deep water,...

Columbus's *"entremedias"* could be translated as *"within"* when it has a pair of antecedents, but with only one antecedent here it must be read as *"halfway."*   Cecil Jane misrendered it as a synonym for "dentro de" to accommodate Watlings's lack of dual antecedents. Its correct translation accurately positions Royal Island's harbor entrance at the midpoint of its rocky shelf, a topographic detail Columbus deemed worth noting in his *Journal*.

...and a harbour large enough for all the ships [naos] in Christendom,...

After finding *"deep water"* in Royal Island's small enclosed harbor, Columbus could now promote yesterday's 40 square-mile *"laguna"* into an outer roadstead *"large enough for all the [naos] in Christendom"* to anchor while awaiting harbor access. Today's capacity estimate is identical with his December 20th entry sizing the 40 square-mile roadstead adjoining Haiti's small inner harbor at Acul Bay. But Columbus knew the importance of realistically sizing the harbors he discovered; e.g., his November 20th entry characterizes the 10 square-mile *"laguna"* forming Cuba's Puerto Cayo Moa as only *"large enough for all the ships of Spain."* These carefully considered harbor comparisons should have made Morison wonder why Columbus would have described Watlings' miniature harbor as larger than Puerto Cayo Moa when it's less than half its size. And while it may seem odd to measure harbor capacity by its roadstead, Columbus clearly did just that today and again on December 20th when he sized Haiti's tiny Acul Bay by its large outer roadstead.

...the entrance to which is very narrow. It is true that inside the reef there are some shoals, but the sea is no more disturbed than the water in a well...

Columbus described Royal Island's *"very narrow"* opening through that rock shelf to its inner harbor with *"some shoals"* within its 200 acres of remarkably placid surface, sheltered from the trade winds by large trees and rocky crags. He had happened upon one of the finest natural harbors in the Bahama Islands where modern yachtsmen can still ride out fierce hurricanes.

Morison's choice of Grahams Harbour has many problems, starting with an entrance that's a mile wide rather than *"very narrow."* And its exposure to wind and swells has led the authoritative *Yachtsman's Guide to The Bahamas* to describe how it "always seems to carry a surge though it," as opposed to *"no more disturbed than the water in a well."*

...And in order to see all this, I went this morning, that I might be able to give an account of all to Your Highnesses and also say where a fort could be built. I saw a piece of land, which is shaped like an island although it is not one [pedaço de tierra que se haze como Isla aunque que no lo es], on which there were six houses; it could be converted into an island in two days,...

Rowing back to the Egg Island anchorage, the boats passed through the narrow channel separating Royal Island's west end from Rat Cay. This three-acre islet, appropriately sized for *"six houses,"* was convenient to Royal's abundant fresh water while still well situated for escape from raiding slavers by land or by sea. Although *"shaped like an island,"* it's still *"not one* [suitable for a fort]*"* because the marl bottom connecting it with Royal Island remains today — as judged by Columbus 500 years ago — too shallow to offer protection from potentially hostile Indians. His reasonable estimate of *"two days"* for removing a few hundred cubic yards of this marl suggests they probed the soft bottom with their oars as they rowed directly over it.

The case for Watlings Island rests on Las Casas' marginal note, "peninsula," a common term Columbus himself surely would have used, if appropriate, in place of his awkward 13-word phrase. Even if the Las Casas speculation were applicable to Watlings, its windswept limestone peninsula is covered with scrubby xerophytic vegetation and several miles removed from potable water — hardly a favorable site for *"six houses."* And, lacking dynamite and bulldozers, neither would it have been possible in two *thousand* days to excavate the thousands of cubic yards of limestone needed to convert this huge peninsula into an island.

...although I do not see that it is necessary to do so, for these people are very unskilled in arms, as Your Highnesses will see from the seven whom I caused to be taken in order to carry them off that they may learn our language and return. However, when Your Highnesses so command, they can all be carried off to Castile or held captive in the island itself, since with fifty men they would be all kept in subjection and forced to do whatever may be wished...

His proposed method for assimilating the Taino is overshadowed by ominous hints of his future slaving activities.

...Near the said islet, moreover, there are the loveliest group of trees that I have ever seen, all green and with leaves like those of Castile in the month of April and May, and much water...

While the cocoanut palms behind Royal's western beach aren't indigenous to the Bahamas, the limestone ridge to their windward has always provided enough rainwater run-off and trade-wind shelter to create one of the more favorable arboreal sites in the eastern Bahamas. Whatever trees thrived there in 1492 were only a stone's throw from Rat Cay, the nearby *"said islet"* Columbus considered for a possible *"fort."*

Finding that *"loveliest group of trees"* near Watlings' windswept peninsula has always been problematic. In addition, Columbus continues to identify his potential fortress site as *"the said islet"* rather than the *peninsula* concocted by Las Casas.

...I examined the whole of that harbour, and afterwards returned to the ship...

Today's inspection trip to Royal Island was a leisurely seven-mile tour. The conjectured Watlings Island route of triple that distance would have required sustained speeds of almost two knots from sailors who had done little rowing for more than a month.

...and set sail...

Friday morning's sail the length of Eleuthera's threatening reef must have convinced Columbus to avoid night sailing in these dangerous shallows until he had gained confidence in his Taino guides. Yesterday he had planned to weigh anchor *"in the afternoon,"* but his Royal Island inspection seems to have taken longer than anticipated. The resulting delay made it risky to set sail in the late afternoon for the gain of a few hours. Tomorrow's *Journal* entry will make it clear Columbus prudently *"stood off"* Egg Island until dawn.

...I saw [vide] so many islands that I could not decide to which I would go first. Those men, whom I had taken, made signs to me [dezian por señas] that there were very many, so many that they could not be counted, and they mentioned by name more than a hundred...

The many small islets visible from Egg Island would have been of little interest to Columbus, and no other landfall candidate has *"many"* islands in view. It seems *"vide"* should be interpreted here as he *"saw"* these islands on maps sketched by his Taino guides.

...Finally, I sought for the largest and resolved to steer for it, which I am doing...

Having twice declared he would sail the shortest route to Cuba, the Taino maps tell Columbus his *"southwest"* course will take him by way of New Providence, the *"largest"* neighboring island along this route. Many landfall advocates argue Columbus quietly changed his *"southwest"* course to whatever heading supports their theories, so it bears repeating Columbus could not *"set all the sea and lands of the Ocean Sea in their true places"* unless he faithfully recorded his every course change for Spanish cartographers.

...It is five leagues away from this island [de esta isla] of San Salvador,...

Columbus may have used *"de esta isla"* rather than *"del isla"* to inform Spanish cartographers he was measuring this distance from his Egg Island anchorage instead of the main island of Eleuthera. New Providence Island can't be seen from Egg Island, nor is Rum Cay visible from Watlings Island, so this conservative distance estimate must have come from Taino who as yet had only an approximate sense of the league length Columbus was using.

...and of the others, some are more and some less distant...

While all landfall theories offer candidates for the *"largest"* island, few of the others have *"some less distant"* such as the several visible between Egg Island and New Providence.

....All are very flat, without mountains, and very fertile; all are inhabited and they make war upon one another, although these people are very simple and very well formed men.

4 - The Islands of Santa Maria and Fernandina

MONDAY, OCTOBER 15th — *I stood off that night, fearing to come to anchor before daylight, as I did not know whether the coast was free from shoals. At daybreak I hoisted sail...*

If the fleet had been anchored at Watlings Island there would have been little reason to stand off all night wallowing in the ocean's swells. But this would be a wise precaution at Egg Island where Eleuthera's huge shoal exposed the fleet to more than a million acre-feet of tidal flow. Its one-knot pull on the *Santa Maria's* anchor chain had already warned Columbus this opposing flow would peak near daybreak. Realizing it could pin him to his anchorage if the morning winds turned contrary, Columbus wisely *"stood off that night,"* beyond reach of Eleuthera's strong tidal current.

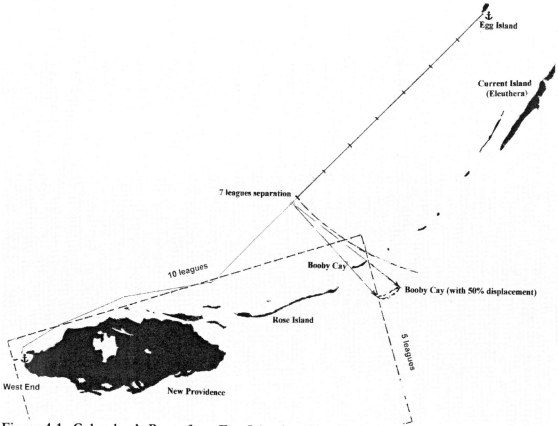

Figure 4-1. Columbus's Route from Egg Island to West End of New Providence

...And as the island was more than five leagues distant, rather being about seven...

His *"southwest"* course from Egg Island would bring Columbus to New Providence Island, but the distance proved to be 11.5 leagues instead of *"about seven."* This discrepancy may have resulted from differences in how the Taino and Spanish mapped New Providence Island. The Taino saw Columbus was focused on the larger islands, so they may have simply sketched New Providence without including any of its adjacent islets, an assumption supported by the 2-to-1 aspect ratio Columbus read from their map. But the Spanish, in the manner of Chaves, would have included its adjacent islets, such as Rose Island, in their elongated mapping of New Providence. On the *Santa Maria's* southwest course from Egg Island, the first New Providence islet visible from its forecastle would have been Booby Cay, a barren rookery *"seven"* leagues from Egg Island.

...and the tide [marea] was against me,...

His *"southwest"* course to New Providence carried Columbus to a ringside view of the turbulent whitecaps marking where that island's strong tidal flows twice daily challenge the currents of Northeast Providence Channel. This dramatic tidal clash underscores the importance of this landfall clue because there's no measurable *"tide"* at Rum Cay or, for that matter, along any other suggested sailing route. For this reason, advocates of other landfall theories have either ignored this important clue, or claimed Columbus was describing oceanic rather than tidal currents. But there's little doubt today's *"marea"* was a tidal current, because Columbus always used *"corrientes"* when describing ocean currents.

...it was about midday when I arrived at the island. I found that the side which lies toward the island of San Salvador runs north and south for a distance of five leagues, and the other side which I followed, runs east and west for more than ten leagues...

Columbus's uncanny ability to estimate the distances to several Haitian peaks will become evident in his December 6th *Journal* entry. But the lack of elevated Bahama landmarks made today's distance estimates dependent on his ability to measure speed through the water. While impressively accurate, they exposed his distance estimates to the variability of ocean currents, which could be significant in the Bahamas where the Atlantic Ocean's NEC generally exceeds half a knot. During his half day sail along this coast (presumably from Booby Cay's east cape to the west end of New Providence) a deflected NEC may have inflated its length of 9.9 leagues to *"more than ten leagues."*

While Morison's choice of Rum Cay provides an excellent match to both the direction and distance of this morning's sail, this small island suffers from two major deficiencies. First, it must ignore the *"side which I followed"* by having Columbus sail <u>two</u> sides of Rum Cay to avoid a dangerous reef on its north coast. A more troublesome deficiency is its length of barely 3 leagues, which Morison finessed by assuming Columbus used a short "land league" when "estimating the length of a coastline." But Columbus didn't resort to a "land league" for coastal measurements of other islands on December 6th and March 4th. Colonel Don Antonio de Alcedo had already made Morison's invention pointless in 1780 when his *West Indies Word Atlas* observed, "after [Columbus] discovered land he touched at New Providence and Andros Island."

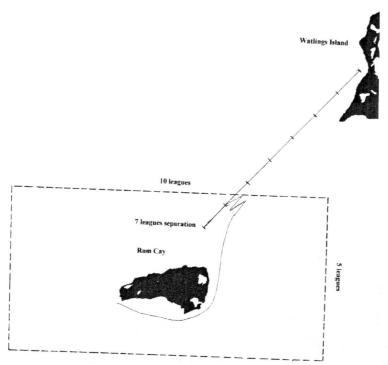

Figure 4-2. Morison's Route from Watlings Island to West end of Rum Cay

...And as from this island I saw [vide] another and larger [otra mayor] to the west,...

Colonel Alcedo identified Andros as the obvious candidate for this *"larger island to the west,"* while Morison's best choice was Long Island. Either would have been well below Columbus's horizon, so *"vide"* must describe a map reading rather than an actual sighting.

...I set sail to go all that day until night, since otherwise I should not have been able to reach the westerly point [cabo]...

By noon a *"southwest"* heading at five knots had carried the fleet to the beautiful beaches of Paradise Island, the popular tourist mecca off the north coast of New Providence. Strong tidal currents in Nassau's narrow entry channel prevented Columbus from taking advantage of its magnificent harbor, and anchorage anywhere along Providence's exposed coast would have been risky. Improving communication with the Taino had identified New Providence's western *"cabo"* as a suitable anchorage, so Columbus unfurled all his sails in a race to complete this 10-league run before sunset.

...To this island I gave the name Santa María de la Concepción,*...*

Unlike the name he had given to his landfall island, this unwieldy choice for his second discovery doesn't appear on any surviving map, apparently because its unwieldy name was shortened; almost immediately to Santa Maria, and finally to Samana. These suggested changes are tacitly confirmed in the *Chaves Rutter* when it positions the island of Samana 24 miles WSW of the Columbus landfall. This association is supported by three Samana features listed in the *Rutter*: namely, *size* (24 miles E-W by 12 miles N-S), *a harbor at its northeast corner* (New Providence has

Nassau while Rum Cay lacks even an exposed anchorage,) and *a latitude of 25 degrees* (within 4 miles of New Providence while 77 miles from Rum Cay.)

...and about sunset, I anchored off the said point [cabo]...

Columbus's immediate objective was West Bay at the west end of New Providence Island, the closest anchorage for caravels unable to cope with Nassau's strong tidal currents. Racing against the clock with all sails set for the afternoon's 30-mile run, he reached this tranquil haven as the sun was setting across The Tongue of the Ocean (TOTO.) The afternoon's exhausting run gave Columbus sufficient reason to defer today's *Journal* entry until tomorrow morning.

...to learn if there were gold there, because those whom I had caused to be taken in the island of San Salvador told me that they wore very large golden bracelets on their legs and arms. I can well believe that all that they said was a ruse in order to get away...

A modern-day Columbus wouldn't have much difficulty finding *"golden bracelets"* at West Bay, a yacht haven for some of the world's wealthiest families.

...It was nevertheless my wish not to pass any island without taking possession of it, although when one has been annexed, all might be said to have been. And I anchored...

Until late Tuesday morning the fleet remained anchored in West Bay, a well-protected harbor embraced by Simms Point to its north and Clifton Point to its south. Morison's Rum Cay doesn't have a harbor, and its only anchorage, Port Nelson, is actually much closer to the island's east coast than its west "cape." Constrained by the *Journal's* evidence, Morison has Columbus sail all afternoon to barely make the 9 miles to Rum Cay's west "cape." This exposed "cape" had been credited with a "temporary anchorage" by older editions of *The Yachtsman's Guide*. However, the Guide's editor wrote me this exposed anchorage had been deleted from newer editions because its "seven fathoms with poor holding ground was extremely dangerous." It seems Rum Cay's "temporary anchorage" was an artifice created to accommodate Morison's theory, an accommodation making Columbus look foolish while exposing modern yachtsmen to needless risk.

...and was there until today, Tuesday, when at dawn I went ashore in the armed boat and landed...

This excerpt confirms Columbus didn't always honor his promise of *"writing each night that which the day had brought forth and each day how I sailed at night."* He can be excused for his negligence here because it was well into Monday evening before the *Santa Maria* was securely anchored after a half day of coasting New Providence Island's unfamiliar shallows. Columbus also neglected to measure LPC-11 when the Moon rose at 2 AM Tuesday morning with Mars just four degrees above it. Exhaustion may explain his apparent reluctance to row half the night to gain an unobstructed view of this LPC on the eastern horizon. It's worth noting that both of his first two New World LPC opportunities occurred during the second half of the lunar cycle, as they would for Cabot in 1497, Vespucci in 1499 and Cabral in 1500. This lunar phasing was expected to allow comparison of LPC readings taken by New World explorers with those by astronomers at known longitudes in Europe. Columbus must have been disappointed to find that eastern oceanic horizons weren't readily accessible at either of his first two New World anchorages.

...The people, who were many, were naked and of the same type as those of the other island of San Salvador; they allowed us to go through the island and gave us what we asked of them...

New Providence was densely populated 500 years ago for many of the same reasons 150,000 Bahamians call it their home today — adequate rainfall, abundant flora, and sheltered harbors. The Taino must also have valued its placid shoal water routes for their dugout canoes, so vulnerable to frequent swamping in the open ocean. Rum Cay lacks all of these attributes, explaining why it still has fewer than 100 residents, many of them descendants of the hardscrabble salt harvesters who depended on its frequent droughts to dry their salt pans. Small wonder Rum Cay has yielded so little archeological bounty compared with the extensive finds on New Providence.

....And as the wind blew more strongly across from the southeast, I was unwilling to wait and went back to the ship...

The nighttime cooling of sub-tropical landmasses can create substantial onshore morning breezes. Those at his West Bay anchorage apparently disrupted the easterly trade winds until mid-morning, leaving Columbus roughly eight hours to make the 23 miles to Andros Island by sunset.

...A large canoe was alongside the caravel Niña, *and one of the men of the island of San Salvador, who was in her, threw himself in to the sea and went off in it, and in the evening before midnight the other threw himself overboard* [lacuna], *and went after the canoe, which fled so that there was not a boat that could have overtaken it, since we were a long way behind it. In the end it reached land and they left the canoe, and some of my company went ashore after them, and they all ran off like chickens. The boat which they had abandoned we brought on board the caravel* Niña. *To her, there now came from another direction* [de otro cabo] *another small canoe with a man who wished to barter a ball of cotton,...*

Cecil Jane concealed Rum Cay's lack of a second cape embracing Columbus's anchorage by mistranslating *"de otro cabo"* as *"from another direction"* instead of *"from the other cape."* The *Journal's* 13 other usages of *"derrota"* were all correctly rendered by Jane. The correct translation is accommodated at New Providence Island where his anchorage in West Bay was embraced by nearby Simms Point to his north and Clifton Point less than a mile to his south.

...and some sailors jumped into the sea and took him, because he would not come on board the caravel. I was on the poop of the ship and saw everything, and I sent for him and gave him a red cap and some small beads of green glass, which I put on his arm, and two hawks bells, which I put in his ears, and ordered his canoe, which was also in the ship's boat, to be given back to him and sent him ashore. After that I set sail to go to the other large island [otra grande isla], *which I saw to the west...*

Columbus must have been viewing Andros Island on Taino sketches, because this *"other large island"* directly across TOTO (Tongue of the Ocean) from his West Bay anchorage, was well below his western horizon.

...I commanded that the other canoe, which the Niña *was towing astern, should be set adrift also. Afterwards, on land, when the other, to whom I had given the things mentioned and from whom I had refused to take the ball of cotton, although he wished to give it to me, reached it, I saw that all the rest clustered around him, and that he was dazzled and quite sure that we were good people and that the one who had run away had somehow wronged us and that accordingly we had carried him off. It was to create this impression that I had so acted with him, ordering him to be set free and giving him the presents, in order that we may be held in his esteem so that when Your Highnesses again*

send here, they may not be unfriendly. All that I gave to him was not worth four maravedis. So I departed at about ten o'clock, with a southeast wind that veered southerly,...

Today's clockwise rotation of a dying wind was a harbinger of tomorrow afternoon's norther that would prevent him from circling Andros to the north.

...in order to pass over to the other island. It is very large and there all these men, whom I carry with me from the island of San Salvador, make signs that there is much gold and that they wear it as bracelets on their arms and on their legs, and in their ears and noses and around their necks. From this island [desta isla] of Santa Maria to the other was some nine leagues, from east to west,...

Use of the contraction *"desta"* rather than *"del"* confirms New Providence had the multiple islets lacking at Rum Cay, a usage consistent with the contemporary practice of letting a single name serve multiple islands on the same shoal. Columbus couldn't see Andros Island from his anchorage, so *"nine leagues, from east to west"* was estimated from a Taino sketch of still uncertain scale.

...and all this side of the island runs from northwest to southeast...

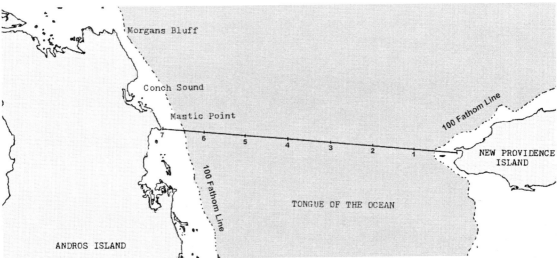

Figure 4-3. The seven leagues from West end of New Providence to Mastic Point on Andros

This approximate coastline orientation was read from Taino sketches drawn without benefit of a magnetic compass. After reaching Andros Island, Columbus would correct this Taino mapping by rotating its coastline clockwise a full two compass points.

...It seems to me that on this side the coast may extend for twentyeight leagues or more;...

The east coast of Andros Island extends for nearly 96 miles (32 leagues), demonstrating the Taino had already gained a better understanding of Spanish metrics with their estimate of *"twentyeight leagues or more."* Morison's candidate, Long Island, falls far short with a length of 19 leagues.

...the island is very flat, without any mountains, as are San Salvador and Santa Maria,...

This usage of *"very flat"* is appropriate because Andros Island is the flattest island in the entire archipelago. Long Island is a misfit to this clue because its east coast is the most dramatic in the Bahamas with steep cliffs looming nearly a hundred feet above his supposed anchorage

Figure 4-4. Prominent high white cliffs on Long Island's east coast

...and all the coasts are free from rocks [todas playas sin roquedos],...

This egregious mistranslation was designed to accommodate Long Island's few scattered beaches. Correctly translated, this excerpt accurately describes the east coast of Andros Island as *"all beaches without rocks."* If Columbus had been characterizing Long Island's east coast, he surely would have emphasized its dominating cliffs instead of the occasional short stretches of beach at their base. And had he somehow overlooked that coast's dominant feature, this conscientious chronicler surely would have included the missing article and verb concocted by Cecil Jane.

...except that they all have some reefs [peñas] near the land under water, on which account it is necessary to keep a sharp lookout when it is proposed to anchor, and not to anchor very near the shore, although the waters are always very clear and the depth can be seen...

When exploring his *Guanahani* landfall Columbus had used *"restinga de piedras"* to describe Royal Island's exposed rock shelf, while today he used *"peñas"* for the <u>underwater</u> reefs fronting

Andros Island. Cecil Jane's translation offers no hint why Columbus would have used different names for similar submerged reefs at Watlings and Long Island.

....At a distance of two lombard shots from land, the water off all these islands is so deep that it cannot be sounded...

The lombard was a carriage-mounted cannon, somewhat larger than the swivel gun carried by many 15th century caravels. To establish congruency with Long Island, Morison put its range between 500 and 1000 yards; a conservative estimate given that the hand-drawn Turkish war bow could reach 500 yards. Morison must have based his estimate on *effective* range, a measure that begs the question of target vulnerability, a factor differing widely for targets ranging from fortress walls to unarmored men. For universal understanding Columbus surely was defining the lombard's *maximum* range, an easily measured attribute independent of target vulnerability. Based on contemporary artillery performance, the lombard's maximum range was probably between 1000 and 1500 yards. But Columbus would measure several distances of a "quarter league" on this journey, so he had no need for a redundant length unit of 1500 yards. So, my estimate for his usage ranges from 1000 yards (1/6 of a league) to about 1200 yards (1/5 of a league.)

Columbus recorded this entry while standing off Mastic Point where breakers clearly marking the Andros reef parallel the coast at almost 2500 yards (*"two Lombard shots"*) as far as one can see in either direction. He also correctly observed that the world's third-longest barrier reef is so steep the bottom *"cannot be sounded"* beyond these breakers. While Andros Island has a satisfying congruence with this clue, Morison acknowledged Long Island's east coast is incongruously steep-to within just a few yards of shore. Long Island does have a shelf at sounding depth, but it wanders erratically and would have been invisible to Columbus, lacking the breakers that mark the Andros reef.

...These islands are very green and fertile and the breezes are very soft, and it is possible that in them are many things, of which I do not know, because I did not wish to delay in finding gold, by discovering and going about many islands. And since these men gave these signs that they wear it on their arms and legs, and it is gold because I showed them some pieces of gold which I have, I cannot fail, with the aid of Our Lord, to find the place whence it comes...

Columbus's fixation on Taino gold seems to have taken precedence over his Prologue's call for their *"conversion to our holy faith."*

...Being in the middle of the channel [golpho] between these two islands, that of Santa Maria and this large island, to which I gave the name Fernandina,...

Columbus was precise in using *"gulf"* rather than *"channel"* to describe TOTO; so identified on early Bahama maps. Cecil Jane's use of *"channel"* attempts to rescue its weak congruence with the body of water between Rum Cay and Long Island, which is in no sense a *"gulf"* and only marginally qualifies as a *"channel."*

...I found a man alone in a canoe on his way from the Island of Santa Maria to that of Fernandina. He was carrying with him a piece of their bread, about as large as the fist, and a gourd of water and a piece of brown earth, powdered and then kneaded, and some dried leaves, which must be a thing highly prized among them, since already at San Salvador they presented me with some of them...

These *"dried leaves"* were the first tobacco ever seen by Europeans. Columbus had stumbled upon the New World's richest treasure whose future market would far exceed the value of the gold he was avidly seeking.

...He also carried with him a basket of their make, in which he had a string of glass beads and two blancas, through which I knew that he came from the Island of San Salvador and had crossed to that of Santa Maria and was on his way to Fernandina...

The arrival of *"men who have come from heaven"* at Egg Island had been as big an event for the Taino as it was for Columbus. This momentous news had to be relayed promptly to Andros, an especially fertile island, centrally situated for a regional authority. The 20 leagues from Egg Island to mid TOTO probably required at least two days for one man canoeing from sunrise to sunset. If so, he would have departed Egg Island no later than Sunday morning, possibly during Columbus's harbor inspection. He then could have followed the shallow to Simms Point before tackling TOTO, fortuitously tranquil as diminishing winds heralded the arrival of tomorrow's norther.

...He came alongside the ship. I made him come on board, as he asked to do so, and caused him to bring his canoe on board also and all that he had with him to be kept safe. I commanded that bread and honey should be given to him to eat, and something to drink, and thus I will carry him to Fernandina and will give him back all his belongings, in order to give him a good opinion of us, so that when, please God, Your Highnesses send here, those who come may receive honour and the Indians will give to us all that they have.

Cecil Jane exercised poetic license here by substituting *"Indians"* for the non-committal *"they"* Columbus recorded one day before his initial claim of reaching the *"Indies."* Today's excerpt wasn't recorded until Tuesday afternoon while Columbus was anchored off Andros Island. He redeemed his delinquency with a midday Wednesday recording of the following entry, repeating some of his Tuesday observations before describing Wednesday morning events.

TUESDAY AND WEDNESDAY, OCTOBER 16th — *I departed from the islands [las isla] of Santa Maria de Concepción...*

Cecil Jane interpreted this ambiguous *Journal* entry as plural, reinforcing the concept Columbus applied one name to multiple islands on the same shoal. Dunn/Kelley interpreted it as singular, but when the article and noun disagree in number, errors of omission seem more likely than those of commission.

...when it was already about midday...

In Tuesday's entry Columbus had informed us they departed at *"about ten oclock,"* a fresh recollection likely closer to the truth.

...for that of Fernandina, which loomed [a muestra ser] very large to the westward,...

Both Cecil Jane ("loomed") and Dunn/Kelley ("showed up") took liberties with a phrase that might better be read as "shown to be" on his Taino sketches.

...and I navigated all that day in a calm. I could not arrive in time to be able to see the bottom in order to anchor in a clear place, for it is necessary to exercise great care in this matter so as not to lose the anchors, and accordingly I stood off and on all that night until day when I came to a village, where I anchored...

Columbus *"stood off and on all that night"* until Wednesday morning when he was *"able to see the bottom"* behind Andros Reef and *"anchor in a clear place"* near Mastic Point. Morison knew anchorage was unlikely anywhere in the pounding surf and poor holding ground fronting Long Island, his candidate for *Fernandina*. So he pretended this anchorage was never attempted when he wrote "Since the previous evening the fleet had been standing off-and-on, as the lee shore was so steep-to as to make anchoring unsafe. At noon October 17 the fleet got underway..."

...and from which had come the man whom I found the day before in that canoe in the middle of the channel [golfo]. He had given so good a report of us that all night there was no lack of canoes alongside the ship; they brought us water and what they had. I ordered something to be given to each of them, that is to say, some small beads, ten or a dozen of glass on a string, and some brass timbrels, of the kind which are worth a maravedi each in Castile, and some leather thongs; all these things they regarded as most excellent. When they came on board the ship, I also commanded molasses to be given to them to eat And afterwards, at the hour of tierce, I sent the ship's boat ashore for water, and they with good will showed my people where the water was and themselves carried the full casks to the boat, and they were delighted to give us pleasure...

Columbus hadn't refilled his water casks at New Providence, possibly because none of its several wells were convenient to his West Bay anchorage. But this morning he was anchored near the largest fresh water reservoir in the Bahamas. Heavy rainfall over the flat terrain of Andros Island creates an immense freshwater lens supplying most of the potable water for Nassau's tourist trade. Each day during the busy winter months, huge freshwater containers are towed from northern Andros loading docks to Nassau. Not only had Columbus anchored near this abundant source of fresh water, but its lading would be facilitated by a gently sloping terrain to a calm anchorage, no small consideration given that he and his 90 companions had consumed several tons of drinking water during their ocean crossing.

This *Journal* excerpt makes no sense at Long Island. The only sources of water near his conjectured Burnt Ground "anchorage" were limestone potholes holding a few gallons of poor quality hardly worth the collecting. Even if those potholes had been freshened by recent rainfall, those *"full casks"* of water, each weighing several hundred pounds, would have to be lowered by rope to the base of the cliff, loaded onto rowboats in a pounding surf, rowed through ocean swells to the "anchorage" and finally hoisted aboard heaving and rolling ships from the bobbing boats.

...This island is very large, and I am resolved to round it, because, as far as I can understand, there is in it or near it a gold mine. This island is distant from that of Santa Maria about eight leagues, almost from east to west [8 leguas quasi leste gueste]...

Those *"8 leguas quasi leste queste"* should be read as *"almost 8 leagues east to west,"* more precisely matching today's 23-mile *"east to west"* route from Simms Point to Mastic Point. Morison's proposed route from Rum Cay to Long Island is only 18 miles in length, 25 percent short of today's TOTO crossing. The Taino errors of roughly 10 percent in both the length of Andros Island and its separation from New Providence demonstrate their proficient cartography and improving ability to communicate this information to Columbus.

...and this point [cabo], where I came, and all this coast runs north-northwest and south-southeast;...

From his anchorage Columbus noted the Andros coastline actually ran NNW - SSE, two points clockwise from the NW - SE bearing approximated on his Taino sketches. Las Casas recorded the coastline bearing here as NNW - SSW, but the weight of evidence tells us this awkward configuration was just another one of his many transcription errors. For if this SSW direction were correct, then the Taino estimate of SE, the two subsequent Columbus SSE observations, and his informed decision to follow that coast to the SE would all have to be grossly in error.

That evening the dimly lit shallows of Conch Sound gave Mastic Point the appearance of a "cabo" protruding from Andros along the same NNW-SSE coastline as the island itself. There isn't a hint of a cape near Burnt Ground, let alone one with a NNW-SSE orientation, a deficiency compelling Cecil Jane to mistranslate "cabo" as a much less prominent "point."

...I saw quite twenty leagues of it, but it did not end there...

This entry is a puzzle for all track reconstructions because Columbus, who had yet to coast Fernandina, could see barely half this span when anchored off any of these low-lying islands. My resolution of this conundrum is that *"twenty leagues"* measures tomorrow night's difficult coasting of Andros. When Columbus belatedly realized he had omitted this important measure from his *Journal,* I believe he recorded it as a clarifying afterthought incorrectly inserted here. For Long Island advocates this *partial* length has necessarily taken on a life of its own as a substitute for *"twentyeight leagues,"* the only measure of Fernandina's *full* length. But Long Island even fails this watered-down test because it's only 19 leagues long and clearly does *"end there."*

...Now, as this is being written, I have set sail with a south wind in order to try to round the whole island and go on until I find Samoet, which is the island or city where there is gold, for so say all those from the island of San Salvador and from that of Santa Maria have told us. These people are like those of the said islands and have the same speech and manners, except that these here seem to me to be somewhat more domesticated and tractable, and more intelligent, because I see that they have brought here cotton to the ship and other trifles for which they know better how to bargain than the others did. And in this land also I saw cotton cloths made like mantillas, and the people are better disposed and the women wear in front of their bodies a small piece of cotton, which scarcely hides their secret parts...

Not surprisingly, these *"more domesticated and tractable, and more intelligent"* of the Taino had laid claim to the abundant fresh water and substantial bio-diversity of Andros Island. This same verdant landscape would encourage Sir Neville Chamberlain's family to develop a sisal plantation there in the 1890's. Great Britain's ill-fated future prime minister was charged with managing this non-productive venture, which soon failed at the same time a similar effort was enjoying success several hundred miles to the southeast in the semi-arid Caicos Islands.

...This island is very green,...

The University of North Carolina has a large botanical garden dedicated to William C. Coker, the pioneering head of its botany department. A century ago Johns Hopkins University Press published Dr. Coker's comprehensive study of Bahamian flora, which has yet to be equaled in scope or detail. At one north Andros site Coker observed, "Here for the first time we met with a forest in the Bahama Islands," listing several tall species with trunk diameters exceeding 2 feet. In stark contrast, he repeatedly described Long Island as "extremely xerophytic" with only scrubby trees of "15 to 20 feet" in height, obviously inadequate candidates for the many Taino dugouts reported by Columbus.

...and flat...

Except for a few low hills, most of Andros consists of "vast areas of shallow water and swamp," according to the *Yachtsmans Guide*. It contrasts waterlogged Andros with Long Island's "bold headlands" and "towering cliffs" that offer "an unusual treat for visitors." If Columbus had somehow managed to anchor beneath Long Island's dominating cliffs, how could he have described the island as "*flat*"?

...and very fertile,...

Northern Andros was far better suited for Taino vegetable gardens, with twice the rainfall and much slower drainage than the xerophytic hills of Long Island.

...and I have no doubt that all year they sow and reap Indian corn [panizo], and equally other things...

Columbus lacked a word for the New World's most valuable food gift to the Old, the *"Indian corn"* thriving in the fertile soil of Andros. He selected *"panizo"*, the millet of European bakeries, a choice left uncorrected by Las Casas a half century later.

...I saw many trees very unlike ours, and many of them had many branches of different kinds, and all coming from one root; one branch is of one kind and one of another, and they are so unlike each other that it is the greatest wonder in the world. How great is the difference between one and another! For example: one branch has leaves like those of a cane and another like those of a mastic tree, and thus, on a single tree, there are five or six different kinds all so diverse from each other. They are not grafted, for it might be said that it is the result of grafting; on the contrary, they are wild and these people do not cultivate them...

If Columbus were given a list of modern place-names for locations described in his *Journal*, the one he would surely recognize is Mastic Point, the Andros Island *"cabo"* still home to large groves of the *"mastic tree."* A century ago, Dr. Coker's exhaustive survey described those groves on Andros Island, but not a single specimen on Long Island. Columbus was obviously confused by Mastic Point's tangle of mastic trees, still intertwined with tall grasses, decorated with colorful bromeliads and festooned with the Bahamian Love Vine. Locals, who brew "stiff cock tea" from the milky fluid filling those hollow vines, have long esteemed it as an aphrodisiac. Woodrow Wilson believed Taino servants brewing a "brown tea" in Puerto Rico may have inspired Ponce de Leon's search for The Fountain of Youth. Perhaps this adventurous conquistador mistook the natives' "vid" for "vida" in transforming their "fountain vine" into an imagined "fountain of life." What's certain is that Ponce de Leon spent several months exploring the northern Bahamas after the Gulf Stream's strong current prevented his slow fleet from rounding Cape Canaveral. That certainty is confirmed by his accurate latitude measurements for Guanahani, St. Augustine and Cape Canaveral. After detouring to Abaco Island in the Bahamas he recorded three additional latitude measurements over the remaining months of his voyage. Two of them slice though Abaco Island, while none come within 150 miles of the Key West he supposedly discovered.

Figure 4-5. Large mastic trees in Mastic Point, Andros Island

Celestial evidence suggests the official purpose of Ponce de Leon's voyage was to determine the longitudes of Florida's east coast mapped by Amerigo Vespucci more than a decade earlier. Ponce spent 37 days coasting the 100 miles from St Augustine's Inlet to Cape Canaveral. His painfully slow progress along that coast could be due to several excellent celestial opportunities for measuring longitude; no less than seven compact LPCs, with four of them having lunar-planetary separations of less than two degrees. This rare opportunity for multiple longitude measurements of Florida's coast occurred in 1513, which should put to rest widespread uncertainty about the year of Ponce de Leon's voyage.

Ponce de Leon's secondary objective may have been an entrepreneurial venture – to locate and exploit "The Fountain of Youth." In addition to those two latitude measurements, there's ample evidence his search led him back to the Bahamas rather than into the Gulf of Mexico. First, Ponce de Leon surely knew these tea-drinking Indians came from the Bahama Islands, and not from as yet unexplored southern Florida. Second, Ponce described the Gulf Stream's intense northerly flow at Cape Canaveral as having "more force than the wind, and would not let the ships go forward," giving him no reasonable alternative but to sail southeasterly towards Abaco Island and anchor "close to a village called Abaioa," a likely misreading of Abacoa. Third, the Love Vine he sought grows in the northern Bahamas, but not near the Florida Keys. Fourth, Ponce gave the name "Los Martires" to a "line of islets and rocky islets" which "as they rose to view appeared like men who were suffering." This graphic metaphor is inappropriate for the Florida Keys, but has an intriguing congruence with *"The Yachtsman's Guide"* description of Basin Harbour Cay as "undoubtedly the most spectacular cay in the whole Bight (of Abaco)...[it has] limestone cliffs which rise in places to a height of 50 feet...Many of the prominent headlands around the coast have been sculpted by wind and weather into forms closely resembling "gargoyles or the heads of grotesque animals." Fifth, a contemporary comment on the naming of "Los Martires" was "the name has remained fitting, because of the many that have been lost there since." This comment is apt for Abaco Island, which lay astride the heavily trafficked trade route from the Caribbean to Spain. Despite this wealth of compelling contrary evidence, Key West and Tampa Bay will probably play a misleading role in a 2013 quincentennial celebration of Ponce de Leon!

Figure 4-6. Three examples of the "suffering men" Ponce de Leon found in Abaco Sound

...No creed is known to them and I believe that they would be speedily converted to Christianity, for they have a very good understanding...

This *"more domesticated and tractable"* Andros community seems to have revived Columbus's interest in religious conversion of the Taino.

...Here there are fish, so unlike ours that it is a marvel; there are some shaped like dories, of the finest colors in the world, blue yellow, red and of all colors, and others painted in a thousand ways, and the colors are so fine that no man would not wonder at them or be anything but delighted to see them...

The diversity at Andros reef biota has established it as one of the world's favorite scuba diving sites. While Columbus didn't have access to scuba gear, he did enjoy a bird's eye view of this shallow reef while being rowed across its crystal-clear waters to Mastic Point. From his perch he could see schools of brilliantly colored reef fish a few feet beneath his boat as they fed on tender filamentous algae thriving in the reef's sheltered waters.

Reef fish are scarce near Long Island's Burnt Ground because the filamentous algae they prefer can't survive its pounding surf. And those few fish tolerating its leathery algae must feed far below its turbulent surface. While fish are visible to depths of 100 feet throughout the Bahamas, those *"finest... red"* colors observed by Columbus begin fading at depths of 10 feet and shift to a blue-green tint by 30 feet. It is unlikely Columbus could have written this passage at Burnt Ground where reef fish would have been reluctant to leave their safe depths to examine a threatening boat bobbing far above them in the ocean's swells. Small wonder scuba divers at the Stella Maris Resort near Long Island's Burnt Ground are now ferried to the sheltered west coast of Conception Island to gain their viewing of reef fish.

...There are also whales...

This clue became difficult to evaluate after 19th century whalers decimated the Atlantic's whale population, completely eradicating some species, including the Gray whale. We do know that the shoal waters near Andros offered a calving environment for Atlantic Gray whales similar to the Gulf of California lagoons still used by their surviving Pacific cousins. Whale Cay, in the nearby Berry Islands, lends some support to this conjecture.

...I saw no land animals of any kind, except parrots and lizards. A boy told me that he saw a large snake. I did not see any sheep or goats or other animals, but I have been here a very short while, as it is now midday. None the less, if there had been any I could not have failed to see one...

Substantial populations of *"parrots and lizards"* and *"snakes"* make Andros Island a likely candidate for these sightings. The assertion *"if there had been any...sheep or goats or other animals...I could not have failed to see one...in a very short while"* is added reason to doubt Columbus could have overlooked Watling's iguanas five days earlier, as posited by Henige.

...I will describe the circuit of this island when I have rounded it.

As the norther's winds rotate to southerly, Columbus temporarily modifies his sailing plan to add a counterclockwise rounding of Andros Island. If actually implemented, this deep-water *"circuit"* of Andros probably would have shifted his Cuban landfall westward 150 miles.

WEDNESDAY, OCTOBER 17th — *I set out from the village at midday from my anchorage and from where I had taken water in order to round this island of Fernandina, and the wind was southwest and south. It was my wish to follow the coast of this island, from where I was to the southeast, because it all trended north-northwest and south-southeast, and I desired to take the route to the south-southeast, because in that direction, as all the Indians whom I have with me say and as another indicated, towards the south lies the island which they call Samoet, where there is gold...*

For the first time Columbus refers to his Taino guides as *"Indians"* rather than *"natives,"* a perplexing shift in terminology considering his *Ephemerides* revealed India remained half a world further on. Taken at face value, this shift suggests growing confidence the Taino's *"Samoet"* was Japan and that he was now sailing in the East Indies.

...And Martín Pinzón, captain of the caravel Pinta, *in which I sent three of these Indians, came to me and told me that one of them had very definitely given him to understand that the island could be rounded more quickly in a north-northwesterly direction...*

Columbus still prefers the direct southern route to Cuba from Andros, but one of the Taino remains doubtful whether these large ships *"from heaven"* can make it through the extensive shallows south of TOTO. So this guide recommends a deep-water alternative, a lengthy counter-clockwise rounding of Andros through Northwest Providence Channel. Such a recommendation would have been ludicrous at Burnt Ground where the direct southern route is the only sensible one for, as Morison himself acknowledged, "Nothing larger than a boat can pass around the leeward side of Long Island."

...I saw that the wind would not help me for the course which I wished to steer and that it was favorable for the other course, and I sailed north-northwest...

The continuing rotation of the wind forces Columbus to accept the guide's recommendation for a lengthy northern detour circumnavigating Andros.

...And when I was about two leagues from the head of the island, I found a very wonderful harbor...

Proceeding slowly northward in light winds, Columbus soon came upon the opening to Conch Sound with its several square miles of shallows lying exactly *"two leagues"* south of Morgan's Bluff, the dominating *"head of the island."* These 60-foot heights earned their notorious identity in the 17th century when the English pirate, Henry Morgan, reportedly used it as his lookout for intercepting Spanish galleons homeward bound with their New World treasures.

...with a mouth, or rather it may be said with two mouths, since there is an islet [isleo] in the middle, and both mouths are very narrow, and within it is more than wide enough for a hundred ships, if it be deep and clear and there be depth at the entrance...

While the English language doesn't distinguish *"isleta"* from *"isleo,"* the Spanish usually restricted use of the latter term to those islets lying very close to larger islands or to the mainland. Although no *"isleo"* now bisects the sandbars embracing its narrow entrance, five centuries of hurricanes have occasionally reshaped its shallows. Such reshaping is suggested by British Admiralty Charts depicting multiple *"isleos"* at the entrance to Conch Sound two centuries ago. The one constant at Conch Sound is its expanse *"more than wide enough for a hundred ships,"* although its light color warned Columbus it might not *"be deep"* enough to serve as a harbor.

...I thought it well to examine it closely and to take soundings, and so I anchored outside it, and went into it with all the ships boats, and we saw that it was shallow...

Hopes for a large harbor at Conch Sound were dashed after Columbus anchored inside the Andros reef to launch the *"boats"* confirming his doubts.

...And as I thought, when I saw it, that it was the mouth of a river,...

Taino sketches revealed Andros was a very large island, but they probably couldn't convey its swampy interior to Columbus. So it was natural for him to assume Conch Sound was *"the mouth of a river"* flowing from the island's interior. Morison's candidate for this harbor, Newton's Cay, fails congruence here in several respects. It looks more like the mouth of a small creek than a *"river,"* it's much closer than *two leagues"* from Long Island's head, it's far too small for *"100 ships,"* and much of it's actually *"deep"* enough to serve as a harbor.

...I had ordered casks to be brought to take water, and on land I found some eight or ten men, who immediately came to us and showed us a village near there, where I sent people for water, some of them with arms and some with casks, and so they took it. And as it was some distance away, I was kept there for the space of two hours...

Nichol's Town, two miles north of Conch Sound, is a likely site for the *"village near there"* with its still flowing water wells convenient to the ship's boats.

...During this time I walked among the trees, and they were the loveliest sight that I have yet seen; they seemed to be as green as those of Andalusia in the month of May, and all the trees are as different from ours as day is from night, and so is the fruit and the grasses and the stones and everything else. It is true that some trees were of the kind that are found in Castile, but yet there is a great difference, and there are many other kinds of trees which no one could say are like or could be compared with those of Castile...

Columbus had no trouble finding lovely trees to stroll under near Nichol's Town where 19th century British Admiralty Charts show extensive stands of 100-foot pines within a few miles. Professor Coker's survey lists five large trees indigenous to the Bahamas — Horseflesh, Wild Tamarind, Mahogany, Pine, and Mastic — all of which "attain their greatest size on Andros." The only one of these five species that could survive Long Island's droughts was the Wild Tamarind ("of reduced size"). It's unlikely Columbus tasted any *"fruit"* during his Andros Island stroll. Coker found all ten indigenous varieties as "hardly equal to our persimmon" and "not worthy of cultivation."

....All these people are like those already mentioned. They are of the same type and as naked and of the same height, and they give what they have for whatever is given to them. And here I saw that some boys from the ships exchanged some little pieces of broken dishes and glass for their spears. The others, who went for the water, told me how they had been in their houses and that inside they were thoroughly swept and clean, and that their beds and coverings are like nets of cotton...

These cabin boys were the first Europeans to discover Indian "hamacas" formed of *"nets of cotton."* Clean, comfortable and convenient, these hammocks soon became universal replacements for the wooden platforms the boys had to sleep on that night.

...They, that is the houses, are all like tents and very high and with good chimneys, but among the many villages which I have seen, I have not seen one of more than from twelve to fifteen houses...

These *"chimneys"* created light breezes by drawing heat out through a roof opening, a passive cooling system widely utilized throughout our southern states before the introduction of electric fans and air conditioning.

...Here they found that married women wore cotton drawers, but girls did not, except some who were already eighteen years old. There are here mastiffs and small dogs, and here they found a man who had in his nose a piece of gold, which might have been half the size of a castellano, on which they saw letters. I was angry with them because they had not bargained for it and given whatever might be asked, in order that it might be examined and seen what money it was, and they replied that they had not dared to bargain for it...

Columbus rebuked his men for not obtaining a coin that might have confirmed contact with a more advanced *"mainland"* civilization.

...After the water had been taken, I returned to the ship and set sail, navigating so far to the northwest that I discovered all that part of the island until the coast runs east and west...

Columbus differentiated the prominent cape at Morgan's Bluff from the island's *"east and west"* coast two miles to its *"northwest."* Sailing 10 miles from his *"midday"* anchorage in the light afternoon winds might have taken about three hours. If so, a *"two hour"* stopover at Nichol's Town would put Columbus off the Andros *"east and west"* coast about 5 PM. (If much later he might have referenced his arrival time to sunset.) Morison's Long Island lacks an east-west coastline, forcing him to interpret the phrase *"the coast runs east and west"* as an awkward surrogate for that island's slender north cape.

...And afterwards all these Indians repeated that this island was smaller than the island of Samoet and that it would be well to turn back in order to arrive at it sooner...

One cautious Taino had recommended a lengthy deep-water detour around Andros, but most still favored a direct route to Española through the shallows south of TOTO. By now they may have seen Columbus's huge ships *"from heaven"* drew less than nine feet of water, allowing easy passage through those shallows. In an illuminating marginal note, Las Casas added the mid-sixteenth century identity of *"Samoet"* as *"Española."*

...There the wind presently fell and began to blow from the west-northwest, which was contrary for the course which we had been following. I therefore turned back...

So the wind change, not his Indian guides, was responsible for turning Columbus *"back"* to the direct route to *"Samoet"* gold. If this norther had arrived but a few hours later Columbus would have continued his circuit of Andros Island before scudding southward with these same winds, perhaps with a boost from the Gulf Stream's powerful eddies along Florida's east coast. We can only speculate how a 1492 Florida landfall might have reordered Spain's New World priorities, but this wind shift could rank with history's most important.

...and navigated all that night in an east-southeasterly direction, sometimes due east and sometimes southeast; this was done in order to keep clear from the land, because there were very thick clouds and the weather was very heavy...

By now his Taino guides had scaled the language barrier to convince Columbus that TOTO was clear of nautical hazards, so he confidently sailed *"all that night"* through *"thick clouds."* None of his recorded sailing directions make much sense off the coasts of either Andros or Long Island, possibly because Columbus was ignoring his gyrating compass that dark and stormy night. It would have been easier for him to simply parallel the coast of Andros on a SSE course, while maintaining a safe enough distance to *"keep clear from the land."* Then he could have monitored tonight's progress against coastal features shown on his Taino map rotating this coastline to *"northwest to southeast."* If so, tonight's actual track would have been *"sometimes"* ESE to clear Andros, and then *"sometimes"* SSE along that island's coast.

There remains the mystery of why Columbus claimed to have *"navigated all that night in an east-southeasterly direction."* The answer may lie in one of the *Journal's* many lineouts of compass headings mistranscribed by Las Casas. In this instance Las Casas superimposed *"southeasterly"* above his original lined out heading transcription, while leaving intact its introductory *"east."* If Las Casas had intended to line out the complete original heading, his *"southeasterly"* correction would have paralleled the Andros coastline as mapped by the Taino.

...There was little wind [el era poco] and this kept me from coming to shore to anchor...

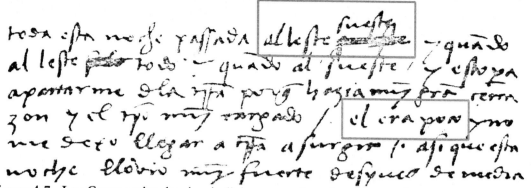

Figure 4-7. Las Casas script, boxing in "el era poco" to demonstrate how easy it would be to misread

Cecil Jane's creative translation, *"there was little wind,"* assumes one of the *Journal's* copyists had dropped *"viento"* from the original's *"el era poco."* This assumption may support Morison's belief Columbus made little overnight progress, but detailed U.S. meteorological data for Palm Beach, Florida show October northers almost always retain full strength until their winds have rotated back to northeasterly. In addition, rather than preventing him from anchoring on this reef bound coast, *"little wind"* probably would have facilitated that delicate operation. Finally, *"el"* rather than *"hay"* would be unusual usage as the "el" is usually *implied* like in "llovia" for "it was raining." What probably kept Columbus from anchoring that night were the norther's low clouds which sailors in every vernacular need to see "rise" from the surface before anchoring in unfamiliar waters. I believe *"el era poco"* was a misreading of Columbus's explanation he couldn't anchor because "eleva poco," that is, because the clouds "rose little." A transcriber ignorant of nautical terminology could easily have misread a scrawled "v" as an "r" and partitioned this original phrase into three familiar words found in every landlubber's lexicon.

...Then this night it rained very heavily from after midnight until near daybreak, and it is still cloudy with a threat of rain. We are at the end of the island to the southeast [nos al cabo de la Isla de la parte de el sueste],...

Cecil Jane distorted his translation of this passage to make it fit a Long Island lacking a distinct *"parte de el sueste."* No distortion is necessary for Andros Island, which is segmented by three separate "Bights" allowing Indian canoes convenient access to the island's west coast. South Bight is a narrow channel separating northern Andros from *"the island's southeastern part,"* a slightly rotated orientation revealing the Admiral's continued reliance on his skewed Taino map. The eastern entrance to this channel is marked by Driggs Hill, a singular elevation at the *"cape of the island's southeastern part."* It would give the Admiral his last view of Andros Island as he turned southeasterly towards TOTO's exit channels. Despite tonight's gale he managed to measure the distance from Morgan's Bluff to Driggs Hill to within one league when he later recalled *"I saw quite twenty leagues of* [Andros], *but it did not end there."* But he created confusion by inserting his recollection in his "Tuesday and Wednesday" entry instead of today's "Wednesday" entry.

Columbus should have reached Driggs Hill by 2 A.M., assuming a hull speed of 9 knots during the gale and allowing two hours for course changes. This performance would put into question Cecil Jane's self-serving assumption of a present tense for the missing verb.

...where I hope [espero] to anchor until the weather clears, so that I can see the other islands to which I propose to go...

The *Journal* actually used the preterit form *"hoped,"* but Cecil Jane misrendered it as the present tense to support his guess for the missing verb timing the arrival at Driggs Hill. Jane needed this consistency to prevent The Admiral of The Ocean Sea from over-running those few remaining miles of Long Island's coastline. But Columbus had little reason to jog in place for several hours during a norther that could expedite his quest for Samoet's gold. Although Columbus earlier had *"hoped to anchor until the weather clears,"* clearing skies allowed him to take advantage of the norther's express delivery to Española's gold.

...So it has rained, more or less, every day since I have been in these Indies. Your Highnesses may believe that this is the best and most fertile and level and good land that there is in the world.

These *"every day"* rainstorms may have contributed to his failure to measure longitude celestially while anchored at Egg and New Providence Islands. His *Ephemerides* warned him he wouldn't have another opportunity until the evening of October 27th, so a timely excuse to his sovereigns was in order, an excuse sugar-coated with a glowing description of his discoveries.

THURSDAY, OCTOBER 18th — *When the weather had cleared, I sailed before the wind, and continued the circuit of the island when I could do so [quanto pude],...*

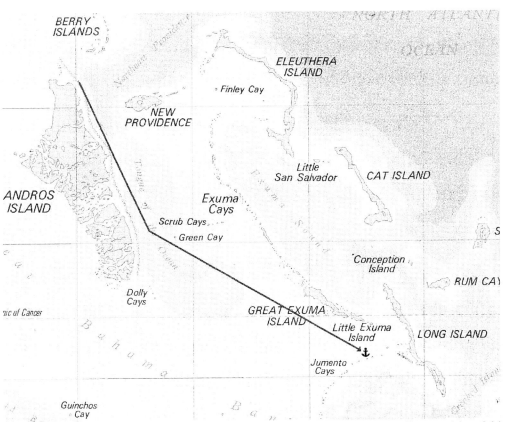

Figure 4-8. The 60 league route from northern Andros to Jumento Cays, taking 26 hours with the favorable wind

Morison thought *"When the weather had cleared"* brought an end to Columbus's jogging, but it could be improving visibility that allowed him to venture a crossing of TOTO. Dunn/Kelley corrected the last phrase to read *"as much as I could,"* an accurate translation signaling Columbus's intention to *"circuit"* those impassable shoals he viewed as a southeastern extension of Andros Island. They are bordered on their northeast by a 60-mile wide shelf of the Bahama Bank whose 20-foot depth bridges TOTO's sailing basin to the Atlantic Ocean. Over countless millennia the tides across this bank have scoured its sandy surface into several closely spaced channels giving the appearance of a hand print left by some colossal Neptune pulling himself from the depths. The permanence of these channels is implied by names such as Queens, Lark, Blossom and Thunder, the latter being the likely choice of his Indian guides. Although today's yachtsmen usually shun this beautiful sailing basin, it has long been recognized as a shipping lane, even identified as "The Route to New Providence" on at least one 18th century French chart. Several of these channels were more than deep enough for Columbus to slip through before scudding ESE across the bank in a following wind. Today the *U.S. Sailing Directions for The West Indies* acknowledge their utility with "Vessels of not more than an 18-foot draft may cross the southern part of Great Bahama Bank with local knowledge or the assistance of a pilot." With ships of only half that draft, the fleet confidently crossed the Bank behind the *Niña,* guided by Taino pilots familiar with its sand bars.

...and anchored when [al tiempo] it was not well to navigate. But I did not land, and at dawn I set sail.

Columbus feared it would not be *"well to navigate"* after 6 P.M. as they neared the end of nautical twilight. He realized it would be after midnight before the rising crescent moon could illuminate a safe passage though breakers defining the lengthy arc of the Jumentos Cays. That string of reefs and islets separating Great Bahama Bank's shallows from the Atlantic's depths offered a wide choice of safe anchorages. One likely choice was No Bush Cay, a few sandy acres explaining why Columbus *"did not land."* Their twilight anchorage had given them 16 hours to sail the 130 miles from Driggs Hill at an average speed of about 8 knots, well within the fleet's capabilities in a strong norther. They did have to remain on watch for coral heads during their entire 8-hour crossing of the bank, a demanding routine explaining why a drained Columbus delayed recording this, the *Journal's* briefest entry, until *"dawn."*

5 - The Island of Isabela

FRIDAY, OCTOBER 19th — *At dawn I weighed anchor and sent the caravel* Pinta *to the east-southeast, and the caravel* Niña *to the south-southeast, while I in the ship went to the southeast. I gave orders that they should follow their courses until midday, and that both should then change their course and rejoin me...*

At dawn's first light the fleet glided from the bank's translucent shallows onto dark oceanic swells extending to the horizon's southeastern arc, the direction to Long Island mapped on his Taino charts. Columbus fanned out his three ships in search of that island; a risky tactic if the weather were to suddenly turn, for reassembling a scattered fleet could be problematic before the advent of telegraphy. So he maintained the integrity of his flotilla by limiting this maneuver to six hours. His generous time allowance and today's reduced sailing distances tell us the norther had spent its fury.

Figure 5-1. Columbus's route along western side of Long Island

...And presently, before we had sailed for three hours, we saw an island to the east, towards which we steered, and all three vessels reached it before midday, at its northern point...

Three hours at six knots in the diminishing winds carried the *Pinta* within 3 leagues of Long Island, giving its captain, Martin Alonso Pinzón, the first sighting of its low-lying west coast. The roar of the *Pinta's* cannon signaled his sighting to the *Santa Maria*, sailing halfway between its sister ships. The *Pinta* and the *Santa Maria* were standing off New Found Harbour at the western tip of mid section of Long Island when the *Niña* closed its seven-league gap *"before midday."*

...where there is an islet [un isleo] and a reef of rocks [restinga de piedra] on its seaward side to the north and another [otro] between it and the main island...

The shallows near New Found Harbour have been reshaped by five centuries of hurricanes and by the decades of salt raking operations facilitated by Long Island's protracted droughts. Despite substantial landscape alterations, Dollar's Cay is still recognized as *"un isleo"* and Conch Cay as *"another between it and the main island."* An elevated rock shelf running the *"seaward side"* of Dollar's Cay, also confirms the appropriate description of a *"restinga de piedra."* Morison's candidate for *"un isleo"* is Bird Rock at the northwest corner of Crooked Island. To support this identification Cecil Jane must convert Columbus's exposed rock shelf into a *"reef,"* repeating the error he made at Royal

Island. But Crooked Island's most evident discrepancy has *The Yachtsman's Guide* wondering why Columbus found Bird Rock's anchorage "greatly to his liking. Why, we'll never know, as there is always an unforgivable surge running through it."

...These men from San Salvador, whom I have with me, called this island "Samoet,"...

Eagerly anticipating its golden treasures, Columbus accepts his guides' premature identification of Long Island as *"Samoet,"* but after sailing its length he will realize *"it is an island separated from that of Samoet."*

...and I named it Isabela...

The *"Isabela"* of Columbus is identified as the Taino's "Yuma" in 16th century cartography. Although neither place name survives, today's Exuma Island is an evident contraction of "ex Yuma." The relative locations implied by its name identify Long Island as the Taino's "Yuma" and the *"Isabela"* of Columbus.

...There was a north wind,...

Although the norther had slackened, today's *"north wind"* would prove adequate for exploration of Long Island's west coast.

...and the said islet lay on the course from the island of Fernandina, from which I had navigated from east to west [el dicho isleo en derrota de la Isla Fernandina de adonde yo avia partido]...

Cecil Jane's twisted translation had been a stumbling block for every credible landfall theory. Dunn/Kelley rendered this excerpt correctly as *"the said isleo lay on an east-west course from the island of Fernandina, from which I had departed."* Their translation reminds us Dollar's Cay rests directly upon the east-west line from Andros Island.

...Afterwards the coast ran from the islet to the west [Isleo al gueste] and extends for twelve leagues to a cape,...

To guide cartographers, Columbus anchored his measurement of Long Island's west coast to Dollar's Cay, the western *"isleo"* of the pair extending three miles beyond the island's west cape. He measured those 32 miles from this *"islet to the west"* to Long Island's southern *"cape"* as *"twelve leagues."* His 8 or 9 miles of sailing under the influence of the half-knot westerly NEC may account for those extra four miles. Dunn/Kelley not only deny existence of a second *"isleo,"* but also arbitrarily reject *"gueste"* as "Almost certainly a copying error for sueste." Their evidence alterations seem hardly worth the trouble given that Morison's conjecture accounts for barely half the *"twelve leagues"* measured by Columbus.

...which I also named Cabo Hermoso. It is on the west coast and it is indeed lovely, round and in deep water, with no shoals off it...

Columbus reached Long Island's southern cape in the late afternoon in time to see its towering alabaster cliffs still bathed in brilliant sunlight. He went on to accurately describe this *"Beautiful Cape"* as *"in deep water, with no shoals off it,"* contrasting it with this morning's shallows at

New Found Harbour. Even Morison wondered how Columbus could have given this name to his candidate cape at Fortune Island whose "dark, weathered Aeolian limestone is far from a beautiful rock." While beauty may lie in the eye of the beholder, there's no escaping the fact that the entire eastern half of Morison's cape is embedded in *"shoals."*

...At first the shore is stony and low, and further on there is a sandy beach which is characteristic of most of that coast,...

Directly north of his *"Beautiful Cape"* Columbus could see its rocky precipice drop abruptly to a low shelf and *"further on...a sandy beach"* extending northward beyond the horizon.

...and there I anchored this night, Friday, until morning...

Columbus's timing was fortunate because he would have found no anchorage near this exposed cape had he arrived a few hours earlier while the wind was still northerly. But the wind's clockwise rotation through the afternoon had brought him a wide choice of anchorages echoed 500 years later in the *U.S. Sailing Directions for The West Indies*. This guide informs today's yachtsmen that "...Good anchorage during the prevailing easterly winds can be taken anywhere along the southwestern side of Long Island." Columbus may have anchored behind a projection near the lagoon's north end.

...All this coast, and the part of the island which I saw, is mainly a beach; the island is the loveliest thing that I have ever seen, for, if the others are very lovely, this is more so. It has many trees, very green and tall,...

Safely anchored for the night, Columbus recorded Long Island's most impressive west coast features. Neither its west coast nor that of Morison's Fortune Island has many *"green and tall"* trees, but from his anchorage Columbus could admire Long Island's most verdant region, sheltered from trade winds by its eastern ridge of hills that still divert rainwater to the lagoons near his anchorage.

...and this land is higher than the other islands which have been discovered...

Columbus could hardly have ignored Long Island's backbone rising far *"higher"* than the swamps of Andros Island. Morison's choice of Crooked Acklins fails this height comparison.

...There is in it one elevation [alguno altillo], which cannot be called a mountain, but which serves to beautify the rest of the island,...

Any yachtsmen retracing the Columbus route across TOTO's shallows will be rewarded by a view of the same miniature Mount Fujiyama that had so enthralled the Admiral. This symmetric 110-foot rise behind Clarence Town still slopes gently to forested sea level lagoons. Twenty years ago it remained without visible human alteration to the green canopy so pleasing to Columbus. No unique and beautifying elevation exists along Morison's route, possibly explaining why the Dunn/Kelley translation misread its singular form as *"some small heights"* which somehow manage *"to beautify the rest of the island."*

LONG ISLAND DISTRICT

Pinders
Bowers
Duncanson Point
Grays
Upper Channel Cay
Andersons
New Found Harbour
Old Grays
Lower Deadmans Cay
Sandy Cay
DEADMANS CAY
Junker's Landing
Buckleys
Cartwright
McKenzie
Buckley's Point
Mangrove Bush
CLARENCE TOWN
Scrub Hill
Stevens
Victoria Village
Turnbull
Dunmore
Hard Bargain
McKenzie
Taits
Roses
Berrys
Cabbage Point
Ford
Mortimers
Gordon's
South End
Cape Verde

Figure 5-2. The "Angla" of Long Island

...and it seems to me there is much water in the center of the island. On this northeastern side, the coast curves sharply, [de esta parte al nordeste haze una grande angla]...

     Cecil Jane took liberties here with the *Journal's* punctuation and translation. Dunn/Kelley corrected both by pointing out *"the center of the island"* wasn't the location of *"much water"* but of an *"angla,"* universally accepted as a corruption of the Portuguese "angra" for cove. So far so good, but they went on to claim Columbus had used *"angla"* in two *opposite* meanings, four times for *"cape"* and a like number for *"bay."* Such topographic nonsense would be equivalent to using the same word to describe a "peninsula" and a "gulf." The Dunn/Kelley rationalization is unnecessary, because all four of their imaginary *"capes"* adjoin the *"coves"* Columbus was actually describing. In this case it was a large cove, centered on the island and oriented to the northeast. His apt description can be appreciated by visualizing the *"grande angla"* at the foot of "Mount Fuji" as an 8-mile bow drawn on a target directly to its northeast. While the curving coastline on Morison's route also forms a large cove, it fails congruency in two significant ways; it extends the full length of the coast, rather than just its *"center,"* and it's aimed easterly instead of northeast.

...and it is very thickly wooded with very large trees. I wished to go to anchor there, in order to land and to see such beauty, but the water was of little depth and I could only anchor at a distance from the shore, and the wind was very favorable for reaching this point where I am now lying at anchor, and which I have named Cabo Hermoso, because such it is. So I did not anchor within that curve [angla] and also because I saw this cape, so green and lovely, at a distance...

The slight concavity of this *"angla"* offered little protection from the day's northerly winds, forcing Columbus to sail a dozen more miles to Cabo Hermoso. This *"green and lovely cape"* was at hand when he recorded tonight's entry, but *"at a distance"* he had first seen it as a purple sliver resting on the southern horizon.

...All the other things and lands of these islands are so lovely that I do not know where to go first, and my eyes never weary of looking at such lovely verdure so different from that of our own land. I believe, moreover, that here there are many herbs and many trees which will be of great value in Spain for dyes and as medicinal spices, but I do not recognize them and this causes me much sorrow. When I arrived here at this cape, there came from the land the scent of flowers or trees, so delicious and sweet, that it was the most delightful thing in the world. In the morning, before I go from here, I will land to see what is here at this point. There is no village, except further inland, where these men, whom I have with me, say there is a king and that he wears much gold. Tomorrow I wish to go far inland to find the village and to see or have speech with this king,...

The Taino village needed convenient access to canoe routes and the freshwater drainage from the island's western slopes. Likely *"further inland"* sites meeting both requirements could have been anywhere north of Duncanson Point along the base of the island's backbone.

...who, according to the signs these which men make, rules all these neighboring islands and is clothed and wears on his person much gold, although I do not put much trust in what they say, both because I don't understand them well and because they are so poor in gold that any small amount which this king may wear would seem to be much to them. This point here I call Cabo Hermoso. I believe that it is an island separated from that of Samoet, and even that there is another small island between them...

By now Columbus had seen enough of Long Island to convince himself it wasn't a likely candidate for *"Samoet."* His Taino charts apparently mapped Crooked-Acklins as *"another small island"* on his route to Española, the true Samoet.

...I make no attempt to examine so much in detail, since I could not do that in fifty years, because I wish to see and discover as much as I can,...

His *Ephemerides* revealed he had a week before his next celestial opportunity to measure longitude, giving him ample time to *"discover as much as I can"* before reaching Cuba.

...in order to return to Your Highnesses in April, if it please Our Lord...

Columbus now reveals the date of his planned return, thoughtfully scheduled for celestial measurement of both his longitude and latitude. His *"April"* return will accommodate a mid-January *longitude* measurement of his discoveries using an extremely rare lunar occultation of Venus. And the constellation Cassiopeia will be phased to guide him home along Cape Vincent's latitude, just as Ursa Major had guided his outbound voyage along Hierro's latitude.

...It is true that, if I arrive anywhere where there is gold or spices in quantity, I shall wait until I have collected as much as I am able. Accordingly, I do nothing but go forward in the hope of finding these.

SATURDAY, OCTOBER 20TH — *Today at sunrise, I weighed anchor from the place where I was with the ship, anchored off the southwest point [cabo del sudueste] of this island of Samoet,...*

Confusion in keeping track of Indian and Spanish island names may account for this erroneous identification of *"Samoet"* by Las Casas. The mix up might also be blamed on Columbus, but his growing doubts about judgments by his Taino guides *"so poor in gold"* make it unlikely he would so quickly forget yesterday's disappointment in his quest for Samoet's gold.

...to which point [cabo] I gave the name Cabo de la Laguna and to the island that of Isabela,...

This first mention of *"Cabo de la Laguna"* has led several landfall analysts to speculate Columbus secretly (and foolishly) relocated his anchorage during the dark of a moonless night. A less bizarre explanation is that he simply remained anchored all night behind the lagoon's northern projection one mile from the island's southern cape (*Cabo Hermosa.*).

...in order to steer to the northeast and east [navigar al nordeste y al leste] from the southeast and south [de parte del sueste y sur]. For there, as I understood from these men whom I have with me, was the village with its king...

Cecil Jane interpreted both of these compass points as sailing directions in his attempt to fit this entry to Crooked-Acklins Island. Dunn/Kelley treated the first as sailing directions and the second as island configuration, similar to the "sur y sudoeste" that Chaves would later apply to the dogleg shape of Abaco Island's east coast. If true, Columbus may have been describing how Long Island's west coast extends *"southeast"* from New Found Harbour to the *angla* where it doglegs *"south"* to Cabo Hermoso. To reach *"the village with its king"* near Duncanson Point he now needed to *"steer to the northeast and east."*

...I found the water everywhere so shallow that I could not enter or navigate to that point...

The *Yachtsman's Guide* maps the shoals still blocking all inland routes from New Found Harbour.

...and I saw that, following the route to the southwest [el camino del sudueste], it would be a very great detour [muy grande rodeo]...

Dunn/Kelley point out Columbus will use *"camino del"* on October 29th to clearly mean the *"route from"* rather than the *"route to"* assumed here by Cecil Jane. The *"route from"* is also more appropriate for connecting his known location with the uncertain location of the *"village."* Based on the Dunn/Kelley interpretation, a counterclockwise *"very great detour"* of Long Island *"from the southwest"* would have tripled the length of a direct route through New Found Harbour.

...Therefore I determined to return by the way which I had come, to the north-northeast [del nornordeste] from the west [de la parte del gueste], and to round this island in that direction,...

Columbus seems to be restating his decision to try the shorter route by way of New Found Harbour. This redundancy suggests his recording might have been interrupted by an important distraction, possibly the solar eclipse his *Ephemerides* predicted for tomorrow's sunrise. Once again Cecil Jane obscured the distinction between sailing directions *("del nornordeste")* and island configuration *("de la parte del gueste.")*

...and the wind was so light that I was unable to proceed along the coast except in the night, and as it is dangerous to anchor off these islands except in daytime, when it is possible to see with the eye where to let go the anchor, since the bottom varies everywhere, some parts being clean and some not, I proceeded to stand off under sail all this Sunday night. The caravels anchored, because they found themselves near land earlier, and they thought that from the signals which they were in the habit of making, I should come to anchor, but I did not wish to do so.

Columbus ignored his *"caravels"* call to *"anchor"* by standing off this moonless night in hazardous waters where *"the bottom varies everywhere."* He took this risk to gain an unobstructed sunrise view of the North Atlantic's first potentially useful solar eclipse since 1477. His *Ephemerides* told him he was 20 degrees too far west to observe this event, but he hoped this prediction had a large easterly error. Unfortunately, the error proved to be of opposite polarity, so Columbus gained nothing by standing off all night, and Spain would have to wait another 21 years for Ponce de Leon's celestial measurements.

SUNDAY, OCTOBER 21st — *At ten oclock I arrived here at this Cabo del Isleo and anchored, as did the caravels...*

Columbus would have stationed his *Santa Maria* about five miles seaward of New Found Harbour if he hoped to observe this morning's solar eclipse above an unobstructed eastern horizon. The failure of this effort would have been apparent as soon as the sun rose free of the moon shortly after 6 A.M. The four hours needed to reach the anchorage indicate the norther had fully run its course, as foretold by yesterday's observation that *"the wind was so light."* The *Santa Maria* may have been towed to its anchorage by boats, with little help from its sails or a tide peaking at 8 A.M.

...After having eaten, I went ashore, and there was there no village but only a single house, in which I found no one, so that I believe that they fled in terror, because in their house were all their household goods. I allowed nothing to be touched, but only went with these captains and people to examine the island. If the others, which have already been seen, are very lovely and green and fertile, this is much more so, and has large and very green trees. There are here very extensive lagoons [unas grandes lagunas],...

Columbus might have oversold Long Island's west coast to his sovereigns, but he wasn't exaggerating about the *"grandes lagunas"* within view of this morning's anchorage. Crooked-Acklins lacks the *multiple* lagoons described by Columbus, a deficiency concealed when Dunn/Kelley mistranslated this phrase as *"some big lakes."*

...and by them and around them there are wonderful woods, and here and in the whole island all is as green and the vegetation is that of Andalusia in April. The singing of little birds...

The singing birds possibly including survivors from the same flock of warblers that had lured him from the 28th parallel on October 7th.

...is such that it seems that a man could never wish to leave this place; the flocks of parrots darken the sun, and there are large and small birds of so many different kinds and so unlike ours, that it is a marvel. There are, moreover, trees of a thousand types, all with their various fruits and all scented, so that it is a wonder. I am the saddest man in the world because I do not recognize them, for I am very sure that all are of some value, and I am bringing specimens of them and also of the herbs. As I was going round one of these lagoons, I saw a snake [sierpe] which we killed, and I am bringing its skin to Your Highnesses. When it saw us, it threw itself into the lagoon and we went in after it, for the water was not very deep, until we killed it with our spears. It is seven palms [palmos] in length; I believe that there are many similar snakes here in these lagoons...

Although Columbus described the New World's first kill as a *"snake,"* its length of almost 5 feet and its vulnerability to *"spears"* assures us Fernando's biography correctly identified this creature as an iguana.

...Here I recognized the aloe, and tomorrow I am resolved to have ten quintals brought to the ship, since they tell me it is very valuable...

Columbus's limited botanical knowledge may have made him *"the saddest man in the world,"* but it left him room for the gathering of half a ton of worthless palmetto leaves.

...Further, going in search of very good water, we arrived at a village near here, half a league from where I am anchored...

The British Admiralty Office conducted the first thorough mapping of the Bahama Islands early in the 19th century. One of their priorities was identification of potable water sources, most of which they found in the northern Bahamas. This morning Columbus had anchored near one of the two wells the Admiralty would later identify on Long Island. Both are more than 30 miles from Burnt Ground where Morison supposed the Admiral filled his empty water casks five days earlier.

...The inhabitants, when they saw us, all fled and left their houses and hid their clothing and whatever they had in the undergrowth. I did not allow anything to be taken, even the value of a pin. Afterwards, some of the men among them came towards us and one came quite close. I gave him some hawks bells and some little glass beads, and he was well content and very joyful. And that this friendly feeling might grow stronger and to make some request of them, I asked him for water; and, after I had returned to the ship, they came presently to the beach with their gourds full,...

Although pottery could be obtained through occasional mainland trade, the limestone base of the Bahama Islands meant drinking water was usually stored in gourds. These small containers made proximity to reliable wells a primary factor in selecting village sites such as Royal Island instead of Egg Island.

...and were delighted to give it to us, and I commanded that another string of small glass beads should be given to them, and they said that they would come here tomorrow. I was anxious to fill all the ships casks with water here;

accordingly, if the weather [el tiempo] permit, I shall presently set out to go round the island, until I have had speech with this king and have seen whether I can obtain from him the gold which I hear that he wears...

Columbus hadn't given up his effort to reach the "gold-bedecked king," but saw that the shallows behind New Found Harbour blocked a direct route. So he revived his alternative plan of a lengthy circuit *"round the island"* if *"el tiempo"* permits. Heavy *"weather"* wasn't his present worry, and it would have been more precise to use "viento" if adequate winds were his concern. He was probably using "el tiempo" in a temporal sense to warn that a lengthy circuit of Long Island might prevent him from reaching Cuba before the next LPC six days from now.

...After that I wish to leave for another very large island, which I believe must be Cipangu, according to the signs which these Indians whom I have with me make; they call it 'Colba'...

While Columbus was obviously mistaken (or misleading) in identifying *"Colba"* as Japan, it's certain this *"very large island"* was Cuba, one of the few Carib place names to survive the conquest. In his 1493 letter Columbus reveals he had named this island "Juana" in honor of Spain's crown prince. But that name was replaced by "Cuba" shortly after the death of the frail young prince. For clarity, Las Casas substituted "Cuba" for "Juana" in all 27 subsequent *Journal* references to this island. Though not an important alteration in itself, it does show the Las Casas transcript was not always completely faithful to the *Journal.*

...They say there are ships and many very good sailors there. Beyond this island, there is another which they call Bohio, which they say is also very large...

Columbus still believed *"Bohio"* was the Taino's name for the *"very large"* island of Española. He didn't realize that his Taino guides were identifying locations of Indian villages on Española, the island they called *"Samoet."* A half century later Las Casas was aware the Taino's name for Española was *"Samoet,"* but a stubborn Columbus would always call it *"Bohio,"* a name surviving today as Cuba's word for "hut."

...The others, which lie between [entremedio] them, we shall see in passing,...

Cecil Jane added an extraneous *"them"* to imply these *"others"* lay between Cuba and Española. As correctly translated by Dunn/Kelley, Columbus might see these smaller islands before reaching Cuba.

...and according to whether I shall find a quantity of gold or spices, I shall decide what is to be done. But I am still determined to proceed to the mainland [tierra firme] and the city of Quinsay and to give the letters of Your Highnesses to the Grand Khan, and to request a reply and return with it.

Columbus used *"tierra firme"* to define the Asian mainland Marco Polo had visited two centuries earlier on his journey to the Grand Khan's court in *"Quinsay,"* the modern city of Hangchow.

MONDAY, OCTOBER 22nd — *All this night and today I have been here, waiting to see if the king of this place or other personages would bring gold or anything else of importance. There did come many of these people, who were like the others in the other islands, just as naked and just as painted, some white, some red, some black, and so* *in various ways. They brought spears and some skeins of cotton to exchange, and they bartered these with some sailors for bits of glass from broken cups and for bits of earthenware. Some of them wore some pieces of gold, hanging from the nose, and they gladly gave these for a hawks bell, of the kind made for the foot of a sparrow-hawk, and for the glass beads, but the amount is so small that it is nothing. It is true that whatever little thing might be given to them, they still regarded our coming as a great wonder, and they believed that we had come from heaven. We took water for the ships in a lagoon which is here near Cabo del Isleo, for so I named it...*

Long Island's mid-section's northwest cape is only a few hundred yards from Conch Cay, the *"Isleo"* Columbus had discovered on Friday. Today this cape is called Wells Point, possibly as a result of the British Admiralty's discovery of nearby potable water. Three hundred years before their mapping, Columbus *"took water for his ships"* from a large lagoon behind Wells Point.

....And in the lagoon, Martin Alonso Pinzón, captain of the Pinta, *killed another snake, like that of yesterday, seven palms long; and here I caused to be collected as much aloe as was found.*

TUESDAY, OCTOBER 23rd — *I wished today to set out for the island of Cuba, which I believe must be Cipangu, according to the indications which these people give me concerning its size and riches. I did not delay longer here or [lacuna] round this island to go to the village, as I had determined, to have speech with this king or lord, in order not to delay too long, since I see that there is no gold mine, and since to round these islands there is need of various winds, and it does not blow just as men may wish, and since it is well to go where there is much business. I say that it is not right to delay, but to go on our way and to discover much land, until a very profitable land is reached. My impression, however, is that this is very rich in spices, but I have no knowledge of these matters, which causes me the greatest sorrow in the world, for I see a thousand kind of trees, each of which bears fruit after its kind and is as green now as in Spain in the months of May and June, and a thousand kind of herbs, also in bloom. And in all this I recognize only the aloe, of which I have ordered much to be brought to the ship to carry to Your Highnesses. I have not set nor am I setting sail for Cuba, because there is no wind, but a dead calm, and it is raining heavily and it rained heavily yesterday, without being at all cold. On the contrary, the day is hot and the nights mild as in May in Spain in Andalusia.*

WEDNESDAY, OCTOBER 24th — *This night, at midnight, I weighed anchor from the island of Isabela, from Cabo de Isleo, which is on the north side where I had stayed, for the island of Cuba, which I hear from these people is very large and has much trade, and has in it gold and spices and great ships and merchants, and they indicated I should steer west-southwest to go there. This I am doing, for I believe that, if it be as all the Indians of these islands and those whom I carry with me in the ships give me to understand by signs, for I do not know their language, it is the island of Cipangu, of which marvellous things are recounted; and in the spheres which I have seen and in the drawings of mappemondes, it is in this region. And I navigated until day to the west-southwest,...*

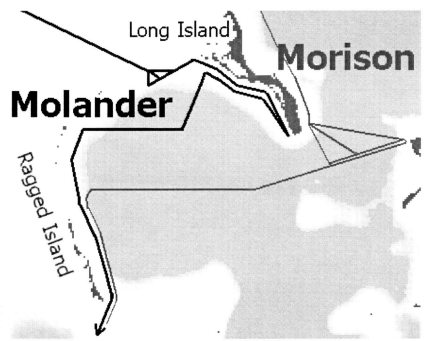

Figure 5-3. Routes from Long Island to Cuba comparing Molander and Morison theories

Las Casas frequently demonstrated carelessness in transcribing compass headings. Up to this point his holographic *Journal* transcript already reveals eight canceled incorrect headings in addition to the uncorrected NNW-SSW error for Fernandina's east coast. These recording mistakes should alert us to consider alternative headings whenever the transcribed ones don't make sense. Such is the case here; for Columbus surely realized the shortest route to Cuba's gold was SSW, perpendicular to the island's coastline depicted on his Taino map. Given Las Casas' demonstrated trouble with sailing directions, I have assumed Columbus actually followed a sensible direct SSW course from Wells Point to Cuba rather than the transcribed detour to the *"west-southwest."*

...and at dawn the wind fell and it rained, and so it was almost all night. I was thus with little wind until after midday, and then it began to blow very gently, and I set all my sails on the ship, the mainsail and two bonnets, and the foresail and spritsail, the mizen, main topsail and the boats sail on the poop. So I went on my course until nightfall, when Cape Verde [el cabo verde], in the island of Fernandina, which is on the south side in the western part [de la parte de sur a la parte de gueste], lay to my northwest, and was seven leagues [a el siete leguas] distant from me...

COLUMBUS'S "SANTA MARIA"

Figure 5-4. Santa Maria

These *"seven leagues"* must have shocked Spanish cartographers when Martin Fernández de Navarrete recovered the Las Casas abstract of the *Journal*. For three centuries they had relied on evidence from Juan de la Cosa, Juan Ponce de Leon, Alonso Chaves, Alain Manesson Mallet, Don Antonio de Alcedo, and others, all identifying Eleuthera as the San Salvador of Christopher Columbus. But now they were confronted with contrary evidence from the great explorer himself, and these recorded *"seven leagues"* restricted San Salvador's location to the central Bahamas! Lacking detailed topographic and meteorological data, flora and fauna distributions, and tidal flows, anchorages and harbors to compare with his *Journal* descriptions; they had little choice but to shift San Salvador southward to the central Bahamas. Watlings Island soon became the favorite candidate for a "correct" identification of San Salvador, despite its many incongruities.

At the same time these "seven league boots" were kicking the northern Bahamas out of the landfall hunt; they were battering the door open to dozens of southern landfall theories. These disparate speculations proliferated rapidly because none were congruent with the other hundred or so clues in the *Journal*. Every new landfall theory quickly came under critical review by judges who couldn't resist the temptation to advocate their own "better" southern solution. For more than a century the Columbus landfall debate expanded in scope and intensity until the Bahamas Parliament officially honored Watlings Island in 1926 and Samuel Eliot Morison gave it his imprimatur in 1942.

But should this single datum be allowed to override more than a hundred other items of evidence, especially when *"seven leagues"* could easily have been just one more recording error in this third-hand copy of the *Journal?* Obviously *"el cabo verde"* implies this cape was not only verdant, but already known to Columbus. Both of these attributes hold true for Mastic Point on Andros Island, while neither fits the limestone cliffs dominating Long Island's southern cape. And from *"seven leagues"* south of this cape he would have seen its limestone cliffs only as a thin blue line on his horizon with no hint of its green mantle. And surely this distance wasn't just idle speculation about barely visible limestone cliffs new to Columbus. What probably triggered this entry was realization the track connectivity he had promised Spain's cartographers had been disrupted by the distraction of last week's storm. Columbus knew this connectivity was essential *"to set all the sea and lands of the Ocean Sea in their true places,"* so he belatedly recorded his estimate of the distance and bearing to Mastic Point, the Andros site he had tied to Guanahani. On Morison's route *"seven leagues"* fails to establish the required connectivity to Long Island's Burnt Ground, its last mapped location. This oversight would have left Spain's cartographers to grapple with the unmeasured gap to the island's southern cape.

Columbus was once again accurate in estimating the bearing to Mastic Point within 8 degrees. But his distance estimate is a complete mismatch to the actual 62 leagues, a difference explained only by a transcription error in *"a el siete leguas."* One possible culprit is the introductory *"el,"* an extraneous word appearing in only 3 of the *Journal's* 240 other league distances. Collins Dictionary supports this possibility with their example "está a siete km de aquí" meaning "it is 7 km (away) from here." Their coincidentally apt example reveals *"el"* is an unnecessary appendage to the *"siete leguas"* transcription and suggests how a transcriber might have misread an accurate Columbus distance estimate of "60 leagues." If he had actually recorded the number of leagues as "sesenta," his penmanship could easily have been misread as "el siete," especially when "60 leagues" was at odds with the 21 much smaller distance measurements Las Casas had just transcribed from the Bahamas. We don't have access to Columbus's original script, but examples of Las Casas' handwriting show that transcription of handwriting was an uncertain process.

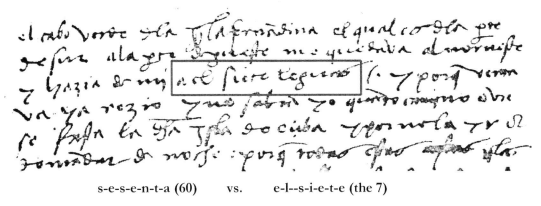

s-e-s-e-n-t-a (60)   vs.   e-l--s-i-e-t-e (the 7)

Figure 5-5. Snippet of 3 lines of text from Las Casas script including "el siete leguas"

There remains one additional barrier to accepting Mastic Point as *"the green cape"* of Columbus — his definition of this Andros location as *"de la parte de sur a la parte de gueste."* Normally one would think of Mastic Point as lying in the northern part of Andros Island, but the *"western part"* is a reasonable alternative if Columbus was still being influenced by that two-point rotation of his Taino map. If so, the *"south side"* of that western part might indicate Columbus was carefully accounting for the one league separating the north and south ends of Mastic Point.

...And as it now blew hard, and I did not know what distance it was to the island of Cuba, and in order not to go in search of it at night, because all these islands lie in very deep water, so that no bottom can be found beyond two lombard shots distance, and then it is all patchy, one part being rocky and another sandy, and hence it is impossible to anchor safely, except when it is possible to see, I decided to take in all sail, except the foresail, and to proceed under it. After a short while, the wind became much stronger and I made a considerable distance,...

This *"considerable distance"* has to be a major portion of the *"less than two leagues"* Columbus soon claims for his entire 12 hours of night sailing. As such, it suggests he had made very little distance before the winds finally picked up while still within sight of New Found Harbour.

...at which I felt misgivings, and as there were thick clouds and it was raining, I ordered the foresail to be furled, and that night we went less than two leagues, etc.

This entry marks the end of the verbatim *Journal* passages Las Casas began transcribing on the October 12th. It reveals Columbus chose to drift slowly under reduced sail. What Columbus couldn't detect was an ocean current pushing his fleet northwest at roughly the same speed.

THURSDAY, OCTOBER 25th — *After sunrise, until nine o'clock, he navigated to the west-southwest. They made five leagues...*

The more sensible course for Columbus was still *south*-southwest, the shortest route to Cuba. He followed this course for three hours, making *"five leagues"* at an average speed of five knots.

... Afterwards he changed the course to the west...

After last night's scant progress, the Admiral realized he couldn't reach a Columbus Bank anchorage before the waxing crescent moon set at about 9 PM, putting him at risk of a moonless arrival at the southernmost Ragged Islands if he continued his SSW course. So *"he changed the course to the west"* to reach that islet chain in daylight and follow it southward at a safe distance. The transcribed WSW course doesn't provide a rationale for Columbus turning west. In fact, if Columbus had simply continued on a WSW course he would have arrived sooner, both at the Ragged Islands and his Columbus Bank anchorage.

...He went eight millas an hour until an hour after midday, and from then until three o'clock, and they went forty-four millas [11 leagues]...

Having reverted from a verbatim transcription to an abstract of this *Journal* entry, Las Casas was again free to convert Columbus's two leagues an hour into *"eight millas an hour,"* a velocity measure familiar to his fellow landlubbers. The fleet maintained this speed for four hours before slowing to six millas an hour for the next two hours, bringing his westerly travel to *"forty-four millas,"* as converted from the 11 leagues recorded by Columbus.

...Then they sighted land and it was seven or eight islands in a row, all lying north and south. They were five leagues from them, etc.

Fifteen miles to his west Columbus could see the Jumentos Cays, a chain of barren islets stretching 100 miles towards his southern horizon. Their delineation of Fernandina's eastern shallows defined a safe deep-water route to the Columbus Bank anchorage recommended by his Taino guides. Those *"seven or eight islands"* in view probably included Water, Lanzadera, Torzon, Flamingo, Man of War, Jamaica, and Seal Cays.

FRIDAY, OCTOBER 26th — *He was to the south of the said islands. It was everywhere shallow water for five or six leagues. He anchored there;...*

Columbus confidently sailed on through the night, keeping the line of limestone cays a safe distance to starboard as he converged back towards his base course extending SSW from New Found Harbour to Cuba. He probably anchored in the early afternoon *"to the south of the said islands"* near the north edge of the Columbus Bank.

...the Indians whom he carried with him said that from these islands to Cuba it was a journey of a day and a half for their boats, which are small vessels of a single piece of wood carrying no sail. These are canoes....

Columbus would measure 21 leagues for tomorrow's *"journey of a day and a half"* from *"these islands to Cuba."* This measurement would allow him to scale his Taino maps by translating their canoe-day into a distance of about 14 leagues.

...He set out there for Cuba, because from the signs which the Indians made to him concerning its greatness and its gold and pearls, he thought that it was that land, that is to say, Cipangu.

These Taino *"signs"* included maps revealing *"Cuba"* as much larger than Andros Island; large enough to be the Japan Columbus claims to be seeking.

SATURDAY, OCTOBER 27th — *They weighed anchor at sunrise from those islands, which he called Las Islas de Arena, on account of the little depth of water which there was to the south of them for a distance of six leagues...*

The *"little depth of water...for a distance of six leagues"* along his baseline SSW course suggests last night's anchorage was near the north edge of these shallows.

...He made eight millas an hour to the south-southwest until one o'clock...

Thursday night's southerly coasting along the Jumentos Cays had returned Columbus to his baseline SSW course extending from Long Island's New Found Harbour to Cuba's Bahia Bariay, a course Las Casas was now transcribing correctly.

...and they went about 40 millas [10 leagues],...

Instead of only *"40 millas"* Columbus should have made 56 in seven hours at *"eight millas an hour."* This discrepancy suggests Las Casas sometimes interpreted recordings of maximum speed as an average.

...by nightfall they had gone twenty-eight millas [7 leagues] more on the same course, and before night they saw land...

Today's scant progress of 17 leagues was enough to bring them within four leagues of Cuba's coastline late that afternoon. From there they could see the bold white ridge of Cerro Yaguajay as it rose 870 feet into the darkening sky nearly 15 miles to their SSE.

...They spent the night on watch [al reparo] while it rained heavily...

Columbus elected to stand 12 miles off Cuba's coast and spend *"the night on watch"* instead of seeking safe harbor in these unfamiliar waters. His justification for putting his fleet at risk this rainy night was LPC-12, a pre-dawn lunar conjunction of Saturn, his third opportunity to measure longitude in the New World. On both previous occasions he had been stymied by inconvenient anchorages, so tonight he would remain at sea to gain an unobstructed WSW horizon beneath the setting moon. His perseverance appears to have been fruitless because *"it rained heavily"* while he was *"on watch,"* making it unlikely he could even see Saturn. A successful measurement could have given him one of the most accurate longitude measurements of his voyage because his *Ephemerides* was in error by only three arc minutes for this date.

...On Saturday, up to sunset, they went seventeen leagues to the south-south-west.

In his wrap-up of today's transcription, Las Casas reverted to the nautical units recorded in the *Journal*, confirming he had correctly converted those *"seventeen leagues"* into the 68 (*"40"* plus *"twenty-eight"*) millas familiar to his readers.

Part III – Cuba

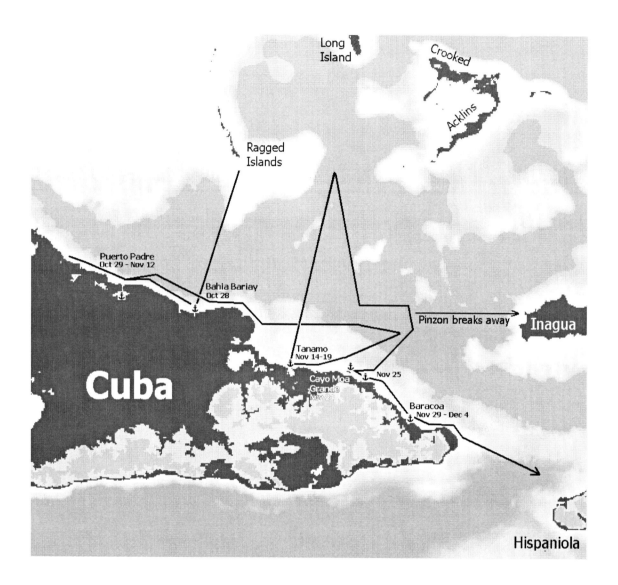

6 - Cuba's Rio de Mares

SUNDAY, OCTOBER 28th — *He went from there in search of the nearest point in the island of Cuba to the south-south-west,...*

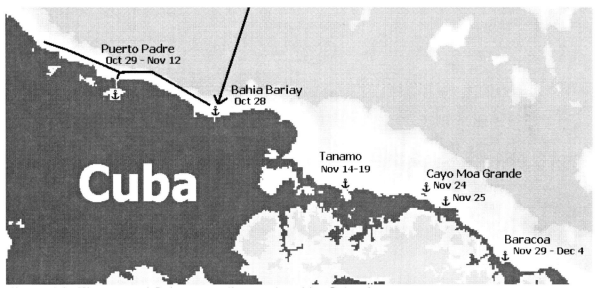

Figure 6-1. First part of Cuban coastline explored by Columbus

Columbus held his SSW course towards Cuba's *"nearest point"* instead of turning to heights now piercing the SE horizon in the dawn's first light. His confidence the *"nearest point"* lay directly ahead suggests his Taino guides had mapped his direct SSW route to Cuba while the fleet was still anchored at Long Island's New Found Harbour. If true, both of the *Journal's* "WSW" transcriptions should be read as "SSW," and except for his jog to acquire the Jumentos Cays, Columbus had followed the Taino's SSW direct course from Long Island to Cuba's *"nearest point."* His DR navigation error of less than three degrees along this SSW course was an impressive display of seamanship. But even this small error demonstrates why he relied on LS for crossing the Atlantic's daunting unknown.

...and he entered a very lovely river, very free from the danger of shoals or of other obstacles,...

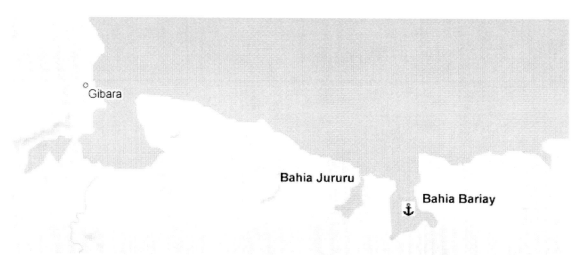

Figure 6-2. Bahia Bariay, Bahia Jururu, and Puerto de Gibara

His SSW course brought him to one of Cuba's many excellent harbors, Bahia Bariay, correctly identified by most historians. This sheltered haven was *"very free from the danger of shoals or of other obstacles"* that had menaced his fleet when they sailed the "Baja mar" (shallow sea} giving the Bahamas its name.

... and the water all along the coast, where he went, was very deep and clear up to the shore. The mouth of the river was twelve brazas deep,...

Historians give the "braza" a length of 5.6 feet, a scaling that brings Columbus's depth reading into close agreement with the 66-foot maximum near the center of Bahia Bariay's opening.

...and it is fully wide enough to beat about. He anchored, as he says, a lombard shot within it...

Shortly after sunrise Columbus took his first Cuban anchorage, possibly in 20 feet of sheltered water 1200 yards inside the harbor's wide mouth.

...The Admiral says that he had never seen anything so beautiful. All the neighborhood of the river was full of trees, lovely and green, and different from ours, each one with flowers and fruit after its kind; there were many birds and small birds, which sang very sweetly. There were a great number of palms, different from those of Guinea and from ours, of moderate height, and their trunk had no bark, and the leaves were very large; they cover their houses with them...

Columbus provided an apt description of the Royal Palm, one of Cuba's few indigenous varieties. Instead of *"bark"* this handsome palm is sheathed in a column of leaf bases supporting its magnificent sunburst of fronds, a source of roofing thatch impervious to Cuba's tropical rainstorms.

...The land is very flat...

Bahia Bariay is surrounded by waterlogged swashes sustaining dense thickets of low growing mangroves.

...The Admiral jumped into the boat and went to shore, and he came to two houses, which he believed to be those of fishermen, who fled in terror...

The mouth of a river 800 yards within Rio Bariay gave these fleeing *"fishermen"* convenient access to both fresh and saltwater fishing.

...In one of them he found a dog that never barked...

Las Casas was surprised to learn these dogs "just growl in their gullets, and are like Spanish dogs, and only differ in that they do not bark." Domesticated by the Indians as a source of protein, rather than as pets or watchdogs, this abandoned canine may have been left tethered near the kitchen pot while its owners fled in terror at the sight of the Spaniards. According to Morison, those "peros mudos" that did manage to escape the cooking pot would become a feral nuisance to Spanish farmers. A more severe canine revenge would soon be wrought upon the Indians by conquistadors terrorizing them for sport with packs of wolfhounds trained to brutally kill their victims.

...and in both houses he found nets of palm fiber and lines and horn fishhooks, and bone harpoons, and other fishing tackle, and many fires in the houses. He believed that in each of the houses many persons lived together. He commanded that none of these things be touched, and so it was done. The vegetation was as abundant as in Andalusia in April and May. He found much purslane and amaranth. He returned to the boat and went a good distance up the river, and it was, as he says, so great a joy to see the verdure and the trees and to hear the singing of the birds that he could not leave it to return. He says the island is the most lovely that eyes have ever seen; it is full of good harbors and deep rivers, and it seems that the sea can never be stormy, for the vegetation on the shore runs down almost to the water, which it does not generally do where the sea is rough...

The Rio Bariay meandered into the harbor a mile from his anchorage. This placid estuary is lined on both banks by mangrove trees anchoring their exposed roots in brackish waters still teeming with a rich diversity of fish and crustaceans.

...Up to that time he had not experienced a high sea among all those islands...

This observation helps account for the excellent progress Columbus made while that north wind was driving him south from Andros to Long Island.

...He says that the island is full of very beautiful mountains, although there are no very long ranges, but they are lofty, and all the rest of the island is high like Sicily. It is full of many waters, as he was able to gather from the Indians whom he carried with him and whom he had taken in the island of Guanahani; they told him by signs that there are ten large rivers,...

These *"signs that there are ten large rivers"* would have been challenging to convey in the game of charades seemingly advocated by naysayers who would deny the Taino even the most basic of cartographic skills. Today's sequence of events suggests these *"Indians"* quickly learned how to depict Cuba's *"ten large rivers"* in the European manner by observing Columbus map his first river cruise in the New World.

...and they cannot go around it in their canoes in twenty days...

Two days earlier, while anchored on the Columbus Bank, Columbus had learned that Indian canoes could make the remaining 63 miles to Cuba in *"a day and a half,"* suggesting a "canoe-day" was roughly 14 leagues. Today's estimate of more than *"twenty days"* for the island's circuit limits their canoe-day to less than 20 leagues. The compatibility of these estimates suggests that the Tainos ranged widely throughout the Caribbean and had a good sense of its dimensions.

...When he went near the shore with the ships, two boats or canoes came out, and as they saw that the sailors entered the boat and rowed about in order to see the depth of the river, to know where they should anchor, the canoes fled. The Indians said that in that island there are gold mines and pearls; the Admiral saw that the place was suited for them, and that there were mussels, which are an indication of them. And the Admiral understood that the ships of the Grand Khan come there, and that they are large; and that from there to the mainland [tierra firme] it is ten days journey...

It's likely the Taino associated inquiries about the fabled palaces of the *"Grand Kahn"* with those magnificent Mayan temples in Yucatan, the nearest *"mainland."* One of its largest cities, Tulum, stood on Yucatan's east coast, directly behind Cozumel. It was still surviving in 1517 when a chaplain with Juan de Grijalvo's party marveled that it was "so large that the city of Seville could not be better or larger." The Taino estimate of *"ten"* canoe-days for the 660-mile route from Bahia Bariay to Tulum is remarkably consistent with more than *"twenty days"* for Cuba's circuit, another indication of their cartographic competence. In 1519 Hernando Cortes would test Cozumel's anchorages before sailing on to Vera Cruz to launch his remarkable conquest of Montezuma's Aztec empire. Neither of these two future adversaries were yet teenagers when Columbus mapped this milepost pointing the way to their impending confrontation.

...The Admiral called the river and harbour San Salvador.

Columbus gave his first Cuban landfall the same reverential name he had assigned to Guanahani, his first landfall in the New World.

MONDAY, OCTOBER 29th — *He weighed anchor from that harbor and navigated to the west in order, as he says, to go to the city where he thought that the Indians told him that the king resided...*

Morison speculated that this royal residence was near Holguin, only 35 miles from his anchorage. It will be shown that Cardenas, 300 miles west of Holguin, is a stronger candidate for *"the city where...the king resided."*

...One point of the island ran out six leagues to the northwest; from there another point ran out to the east ten leagues...

Intervening heights blocked his view of all coastal features *"east ten leagues"* from his Bahia Bariay anchorage. And it's unlikely his Taino guides could provide this level of unseen detail 200 miles from their Egg Island home. This suggests Columbus mapped both of these distances later than implied by this Las Casas extract. If true, the obvious candidates for these two points become Puerto Padre, exactly *"ten leagues"* west of Bahia Bariay, and Bahia de Manati, an additional *"six leagues"* beyond Puerto Padre. Both of these distances were correctly transcribed by Las Casas, so he can be excused for not referencing them to Puerto Padre. NOAA viewed this coast through the eyes of Columbus when it mapped this harbor pair as the only two features identified on this coast in their "Straits of Florida and Approaches."

...He went another league and saw a river with a smaller mouth, to which he gave the name Rio de la Luna...

Bahia Jururu is the "Rio de la Luna," the *"river with a smaller mouth"* less than one *"league"* west of Bahia Bariay. Its entrance channel, a narrow crescent accentuated by its rock cliffs, inspired the Admiral's lunar comparison. His generous distance estimate may have been measured from his anchorage inside Bahia Bariay

...He went on until the hour of vespers. He saw another river, much larger than the former, and so the Indians told him by signs, and near it he saw fair villages of houses...

The conventional view identifies this *"river"* as Puerto Gibara, a small harbor barely two leagues west of this morning's anchorage. But Columbus had coasted with the trade winds until mid-afternoon and normally would have mentioned the extremely light winds had he averaged less than a knot for the better part of a day. A stronger candidate for his *"river"* is Puerto Padre, both *"much larger"* and exactly *"ten leagues"* from Bahia Bariay, a distance consistent with a ship speed of several knots. Puerto Padre would become the Admiral's base of operations for a fortnight, making its identification key to tracking his coastal explorations. Almost a dozen *Journal* clues bear on this issue, and every one favors Puerto Padre over Puerto Gibara as this *"river"* of Columbus.

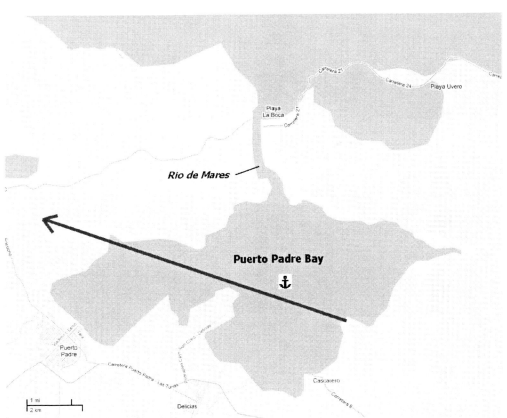

Figure 6-3. Puerto Padre - indicates site for observing potential lunar eclipse and bearing line to the setting moon

...He called the river the Rio de Mares...

The plural name Columbus gave this important harbor suggests multiple *"Mares"* of considerable extent, such as the pair forming Puerto Padre's bifurcated 10,000-acre harbor. His grandiose appellation fails both tests at Puerto Gibara, the conventional wisdom's *solitary* and *undersized* basin.

...He sent two boats to a village to have speech, and in one of them an Indian of those whom he carried with him, because by now they understood something and showed themselves to be well pleased with the Christians. All, men, women and children, fled from these houses, abandoning them with all that they had, and the Admiral commanded that nothing should be touched. The houses, so he says, were quite the most lovely that they had seen, and he believed that the nearer they came to the mainland [tierra firme,] the better they would be...

Ignoring the accumulating evidence of a subsistence society, Columbus pretends to have reached Japan, known to lie east of the Asian *"mainland."* He will soon replace this pretense with the claim that Cuba is an extension of the mainland, despite compelling contrary evidence from his Taino guides.

...They were made in the manner of tents, very large, and they looked like tents in a camp, with no regular streets, but one here and another there. Inside they were well swept and clean, and their furnishing very well arranged: all were made of very beautiful palm branches. They found many images made like women and many heads like masks, very well worked. He did not know if they had them for their beauty or whether they worship them. There were dogs that never bark; there were wild birds, tamed, in their houses; there were wonderful outfits of nets and hooks and fishing tackle. They did not touch any of these things. He believed that all those on the coast must be fisherman who carry the fish inland, for that island is very large and so lovely, that he was never weary of speaking well of it. He says that he found trees and fruit with a very wonderful taste, and he says that there should be in it cows and other herds, since he saw skulls which seemed to be those of cows...

From his service as its first military chaplain, Las Casas knew Cuba didn't have any *"cows"* until their introduction by Spanish colonists, so he added a marginal note identifying these manatee *"skulls."*

...There are birds, large and small, and the chirping of the crickets went on all night, at which all were delighted; the air all night was scented and sweet, and neither hot nor cold. And further, on the voyage from the other islands to that island, he says there was great heat, and that in this island there was not, but it was as temperate as May. He attributes the heat of the other islands to the fact that they are very flat and that the wind there blows from the south and is thus warm. The water of those rivers was salt at the mouth; they did not know where the Indians found drinking water, although they had fresh water in their houses. In this river the ships could turn to go in and go out, and they have very good signs or landmarks. The water was seven or eight brazas [44 feet] deep at the mouth...

Columbus seems to have passed directly over Puerto Padre's maximum depth of 45 feet at the center of the harbor's entrance.

...and five [28 feet] within...

Puerto Padre's large anchorage in its *"eastern sea"* has depths appropriately ranging from 20 to 30 feet. Puerto Gibara has a maximum depth of only 15 feet tapering to a beach girding most of its undersized harbor.

...All that sea, as he says, seems to Him to be always as calm as the river of Seville,...

Puerto Padre is *"as calm as the river of Seville,"* thanks to a long and narrow entry channel isolating it from the Caribbean. In contrast, the *Sailing Directions for the West Indies* warn of wide-open Puerto Gibara's "swell when the prevailing wind is blowing," as likely during today's westerly exploration.

...and the water suited for the cultivation of pearls. He found large periwinkles, tasteless and not like those of Spain. He described the character of the river and the harbor, which he mentioned above and which he named San Salvador, as having lovely mountains near and lofty as la Peña de los Enamorados. One of them has on its summit another peak, like a beautiful mosque...

This entry harks back to his Cuban landfall in recalling a *"peak, like a beautiful mosque"* near Bahia Bariay. This mountain had seemed unique when first viewed by the Admiral, but its form is commonplace among the limestone terraces of eastern Cuba. Cecil Jane informed his readers "La Peña de los Enamorados (Lover's Leap) is a rock halfway between Antequera and Archidona, in Andalusia. According to a fifteenth century legend, a Christian warrior and his Moorish beloved leaped to their death from the rock to escape their pursuers." In a pair of postils Las Casas incorrectly identified this harbor as the site of Cuba's first Spanish settlement at Baracoa, a displacement of 200 miles. His mistake is surprising considering his lengthy service there as chaplain under Diego Velásquez, who founded the settlement in 1513.

...This river and harbor, in which he then was, has on the southeast side two quite round mountains...

Las Lomas Cupeycillo, a pair of *"quite round mountains,"* rise 800 feet above lush sea level terrain seven leagues *"southeast"* of Columbus's Puerto Padre anchorage. A half millennium later, this conspicuous pair still serves as an important nautical landmark in the *Sailing Directions for the West Indies.*

...And on the west-northwest side a lovely cape which projects outwards.

Punta Cobarrubia is the *"lovely cape which projects outwards"* three leagues to the *"west-northwest"* of Puerto Padre's entrance.

TUESDAY, OCTOBER 30th — *He went from the Rio de Mares to the northwest and saw a cape full of palms, and he named it* Cabo de Palmas. *After having gone fifteen leagues,...*

Dunn/Kelley clarified Cecil Jane's ambiguous rendering by affirming this *"cape full of palms"* is *"fifteen leagues"* beyond the *"Rio de Mares"* harbor. Their translation identifies Punta Maternillos is the "Cabo de Palmas" of Columbus. This cape is only 14 leagues northwest of Puerto Padre's entrance, but to reach it this morning he had *"gone fifteen leagues"* from his sheltered anchorage deep within that harbor.

...the Indians who were in the caravel Pinta *said that behind the cape there was a river, and that from the river to Cuba it was four days' journey. The captain of the* Pinta *said he understood that this Cuba was a city, and that land was a very extensive mainland which stretched far to the north,...*

Bahía la Gloria is the closest of several connected narrow bays forming a 240-mile coastal waterway behind a compact string of cays fronting Cuba's north coast. It was only a *"river"* in the sense of Florida's Banana River, and was surely a major artery for Taino canoes coasting the island in its sheltered waters. Cardenas, the western terminal of that artery, may be the *"Cuba was a city"* identified by the *"captain of the* Pinta." Its strategic location, at the west end of that sheltered route; would have been a *"four days' journey"* for canoes capable of 20 leagues a day.

... and that the king of that land was at war with the Grand Khan, whom they called "cami," and this land or city they called "Saba" and by many other names...

The modern name for the string of cays shielding the route to Cardenas is "The Archipiélago de Sabana," apparently one of the Caribbean's few surviving Taino place names.

...The Admiral resolved to go to that river and send a present to the king of the land, and send him the letter of the Sovereigns. For this purpose he had a sailor who had gone to Guinea in the same way,...

Columbus "resolved" to sail 20 leagues northwest from Puerto Padre to the waterway's eastern entrance between Cayo Sabinal and Cayo Guajaba,. From that entrance a round trip to Cardenas by canoe would require about eight days, putting its likely return date squarely in the middle of his *Journal's* upcoming five-day recording gap. Columbus makes no further reference to this emissary, neither here nor in next year's letter summarizing his first voyage to the New World.

...and certain Indians from Guanahani who were ready to go with him, on condition that afterwards they might return to their own land...

Apparently Columbus had no intention of honoring this commitment: he would deliver his Taino "trophies" to his sovereigns upon his triumphant return to Spain.

...In the opinion of the Admiral, he was distant from the equinoctal line fortytwo degrees to the north,...

Columbus hadn't needed a quadrant to maintain his constant-latitude crossing of the Atlantic – he simply monitored Dubhe's small elevation angle at lower culmination. But he lost the use of that simple guide well before he reached Cuba's latitude where all of Ursa Major was culminating below his northern horizon. To measure latitudes along Cuba's north coast Columbus used Polaris, the nominal "pole star" then orbiting the North Pole at a radius of $3° 27.'$ That small orbit meant Polaris culminated a full 18 degrees above his northern horizon, a large angle best measured with a quadrant. Columbus demonstrated a surprising lack of experience with this simple instrument by misreading his latitude by more than 20 degrees.

...if the text from which I have copied this is not corrupt;...

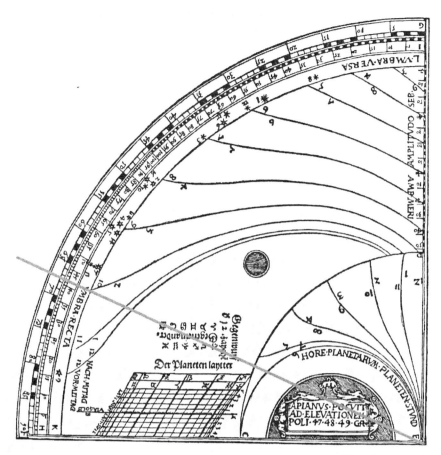

Figure 6-4. Apian Quadrant showing two scales (p.73 of Jane) - radial line added at 0.42

But this *"text"* was apparently not *"corrupt"* because Columbus would repeat this wild reading three days hence. Jim Kelley has proposed a convincing explanation for this reading error by noting that many 15th century quadrants carried dual scales; one calibrated in degrees for reading celestial angles, the other in tangents for estimating the distance to known elevations. With such an instrument, a tangent reading of 0.42 would correspond to an elevation angle of 22° 47', much closer to the truth, but still nearly a degree higher than Columbus should have read at the entrance to Bahía Jigüey.

...and he says that he must attempt to go to the Grand Khan, for he thought that he was in that neighborhood, or to the city of Catay, which belongs to the Grand Khan, which, as he says, is very large, as he was told before he set out from Spain. He says that all this land is low-lying and lovely, and the sea deep.

WEDNESDAY, NOVEMBER 31st *[sic]* — *All night, Tuesday, he was beating about,...*

The incorrect heading to the *Journal's* first 36-hour recording interval suggests Columbus delayed recording this October 31st passage until Thursday morning (November 1st). This delay could account for his careless *"November"* heading, the *Journal's* only dating error. Perhaps he had risen late in the day after *"beating about"* most of the night while trying to make sense of his quadrant readings.

...and he saw a river where he could not enter because the mouth was shallow, and the Indians thought that the ships could enter as their canoes entered it. And navigating farther on, he found a cape which jutted out very far and was surrounded by shallows, and he saw an inlet or bay, where small vessels might enter,...

Punta Maternillos is the prominent *"cape"* jutting several miles seaward immediately northwest of Nuevitas. It's *"surrounded by shallows"* sheltering a small *"inlet or bay"* accessible only to *"small vessels."*

...and he could not make it, because the wind had shifted due north and all the coast ran north-northwest and southeast. Another cape which he saw jutted still farther out...

No significant portion of this coastline comes within 15 degrees of the *"north-northwest"* transcribed by Las Casas. A transcription error seems likely because Punta Maternillos is where the coastline breaks <u>*west-north west and southeast.*</u> Columbus followed this coast to a longitude of about 77° 40' W where he could see a 233-foot rise on a *"cape which...jutted still further out."*

...For this reason and because the sky showed that it would blow hard, he had to return to the Rio de Mares.

Today the Enterprise of the Indies had reached its western limit at a longitude whose measurement would support Spanish territorial negotiations with Portugal. Columbus surely was disappointed in Saturday's failure to measure LPC-12, but he knew Sunday's lunar eclipse would give him another chance. This prospect motivated Columbus *"to return to the Rio de Mares,"* his harbor with the unobstructed western horizon essential for accurate measurement of this eclipse.

THURSDAY, NOVEMBER 1ˢᵗ — *At sunrise, the Admiral sent the boats to land, to the houses which were there, and found that all the people had fled, and after some time a man appeared, and the Admiral ordered that he should be allowed to become reassured, and the boats returned to the ships. After eating, he proceeded to send ashore one of the Indians whom he carried with him, and who, from a distance, called out to them, saying that they should not be afraid, because these were good people and did harm to no one, and were not from the Grand Khan, but in many islands to which they had been, had given of what they had possessed. And the Indian threw himself into the water and swam ashore, and two of those who were there took him by the arms and brought him to a house, where they questioned him. And when they were certain that no harm would be done to them, they were reassured, and presently there came to the ships more than sixteen boats or canoes, with spun cotton and their other trifles, of which the Admiral commanded that nothing should be taken, in order that they might know that the Admiral sought nothing except gold, which they call "nucay." So all day they were going and coming from the land to the ships, and they went to and fro from the Christians to the shore with great confidence. The Admiral did not see any gold among them. But the Admiral says that he saw on one of them a piece of worked silver, hanging from the nose, which he took to be an indication that there was silver in that land. They said by signs that within three days many merchants would come from the interior to buy the things which the Christians brought here, and that they would give news to the king of that land, who, as far as he could understand from the signs which they made, was four days journey from there,...*

This may be the same four-day journey to Cardenas mentioned two days earlier.

...because they had sent many men through the whole land to tell of the Admiral. "These people," says the Admiral," are of the same character and have the same customs as the others who have been found, having no creed that I know, since up to this moment I have not seen those whom I carry with me offer any prayer, but they say the Salve and the Ave Maria with their hands raised to heaven, as they are shown, and they make signs of the cross. There is,

moreover, one language for them all, and they are all friends, and I believe that all these islands are so and that they are at war with the Grand Khan, whom they call 'cavila,' and his province, 'Basan'; and they all go naked like the others." This the Admiral says. He says that the river is very deep and at its mouth they could bring ships alongside the land. The fresh water does not come within a league of the mouth and it is very fresh,...

Puerto Padre's *"river is very deep"* near its eastern bank where strong tidal surges have scoured its depth to 40 feet. Morison's choice of Puerto Gibara fails this simple test because both of its shallow rivers meander to the harbor through tidal flats.

...and "It is certain," says the Admiral, "that this is the mainland, and that I am," he says, "before Zayto and Quisay, a hundred leagues, a little more or less, distant from one and the other, and this appears clearly from the sea, which is of a different character from what it has been to the present, and yesterday, going to the northwest, I found that it was becoming cold."

Columbus had initially accepted the Taino's correct mapping of Cuba as a large island requiring more than *"twenty days"* to circuit in their canoes. Three days later Martin Alonzo Pinzón considered it the *"mainland,"* a view Columbus now accepts despite the lack of any supporting evidence. Perhaps he was recalling the geographic concepts depicted on Martin Behaim's 1492 globe. Behaim incorrectly mapped China's *"Zayto and Quisay"* (Quanzhou and Hangchou) along an *east-west* coastline near the Tropic of Cancer. While Behaim's latitude and orientation of the mainland's coast correspond with Cuba's, he reversed the positions of ocean and land, perhaps the basis for Las Casas' trenchant marginal commentary, "I don't understand this gibberish."

FRIDAY, NOVEMBER 2ⁿᵈ — *The Admiral decided to send two men, Spaniards: one was called Rodrigo de Jerez, who lived in Ayamonte, and the other was a certain Luis de Torres, who had lived with the adelantado of Murcia and had been a Jew, and who, as he says, understood Hebrew and Chaldee and even some Arabic. With these, he sent two Indians: one from among those whom he brought with him from Guanahani, and the other from those houses which were situated on the river. He gave them strings of beads with which to buy food, if they were in need of it, and appointed six days as the time within which they must return. He gave them specimens of spices to see if they found any, and instructed them how they were to ask for the king of that land, and what they were to say on behalf of the Sovereigns of Castile, how they had sent the Admiral to present letters on their behalf and a gift. They were also to learn of his estate, establish friendship with him, and favor him in whatever he might need from them, etc...*

Those *"six days"* didn't allow enough time for this multi-ethnic quartet to visit the king's palace in Cardenas, four canoe-days to the west, nor would their *"strings of beads"* have impressed his royal household. It appears this expedition was soon scaled back to an inland search for local chieftains.

...and they should gain knowledge of certain provinces and harbors and rivers, of which the Admiral had information, and learn how far they were from this place, etc...

From his longitude measurements Columbus knew the Orient lay more than 10,000 miles to the west. So his *"knowledge of certain provinces and harbors and rivers"* must refer to New World features mapped by the Taino or the 1477 expedition.

...Here the Admiral took the altitude on this night with a quadrant, and found that he was fortytwo degrees from the equinoctial line,...

Three days earlier Columbus had obtained the same quadrant reading while he was 36 miles further north, a latitude difference more than twice the resolution capability of his quadrant. This suggests Columbus took this pair of readings at differing times of the night, unaware that Polaris was orbiting the North Celestial Pole.

...and he says that according to his estimate, he found that he had gone from the island of Hierro one thousand one hundred and fortytwo leagues,...

His *"estimate"* of 1142 leagues was only 70 leagues greater than the total he had recorded crossing the Atlantic. Columbus had since sailed at least 140 leagues in the New World, whatever his landfall. In reviewing his *Journal,* Columbus seems to have overlooked some of his entries.

...and he still affirms that this is the mainland.

His first mission proclaimed in the *Journal's* prologue was to bring *"our holy faith"* to a *"Grand Khan"* ruling over *"the lands of India."* Yesterday his guides repeated their identification of Cardenas as Cuba's ruling city. To link its imagined palaces with the *"Grand Khan,"* Columbus must identify Cuba as the *"mainland,"* despite Taino cartography mapping it as an island of more than *"twenty days"* circuit.

SATURDAY, NOVEMBER 3rd — *In the morning, the Admiral entered the boat, and as the river at its mouth forms a great lake, which makes a very remarkable harbor, very deep and free from rocks, with an excellent beach on which to careen ships and with much wood, he went up the river until he came to fresh water, which was a distance of some two leagues. And he ascended an eminence, in order to see something of the land, and he could see nothing, owing to the large groves, luxuriant and odorous, on which account he did not doubt that there were aromatic plants...*

This solitary *"eminence"* was Loma Jibara, barely cresting the luxuriant forest canopy *"two leagues"* upstream from Puerto Padre. After Columbus *"ascended"* this height he realized its *"luxuriant"* growth would block his view of tomorrow morning's potential lunar eclipse on the western horizon.

...He says everything he saw was so lovely that his eyes could not weary of beholding such beauty, nor could he weary of the songs of birds, large and small. That day there came many boats or canoes to the ships, to barter articles of spun cotton and the nets in which they sleep, which are hammocks.

The ships' boys had seen these *"hammocks"* in native huts on Andros Island, and tonight some might actually get to use them. The popularity of this bedding spread rapidly after these fortunate few were rocked to sleep in Puerto Padre.

SUNDAY, NOVEMBER 4th — *Immediately at dawn, the Admiral entered the boat and went ashore to hunt some of the birds which he had seen on the previous day. After his return,...*

Expedition activities normally didn't start until *"morning,"* but today Columbus went ashore *"Immediately at dawn,"* supposedly *"to hunt some of the birds which he had seen on the previous day."* But the real reason for his early start was a potential lunar eclipse shortly before sunrise. That meant the event would occur within a few degrees of the horizon, allowing measurement with his lengthy cross-staff instead of his tiny quadrant. So Columbus *"went ashore"* to measure it from a stable site at the water's edge, possibly a half mile east of Punta Betancourt. This viewing site would give him an unobstructed horizon five miles across Puerto Padre on the moon's predicted bearing angle of 288 degrees. He knew his *Ephemerides* wasn't accurate enough to determine if the full moon would actually be eclipsed as it passed by the earth's shadow. As it turned out, Columbus returned empty-handed to the *Santa Maria* after the moon skirted the earth's penumbra, just a few arc minutes beyond reach. Today's failed attempt paralleled his failure to covertly measure the solar eclipse just beyond his reach on October 21ˢᵗ.

...Martin Alonso Pinzón came to him with two pieces of cinnamon, and said that a Portuguese, whom he had in his ship, had seen an Indian who was carrying two large handfuls of it, but that he did not dare to barter for it, owing to the penalty which the Admiral had imposed upon anyone who should barter. He said further that this Indian was carrying some bright red things like nuts. The boatswain of the Pinta *said that he had found cinnamon trees. The Admiral immediately went there and found that they were not cinnamon. The Admiral showed to some Indians of that place cinnamon and pepper — I suppose some of that which he had brought from Castile as a specimen — and they recognized it, as he says, and indicated by signs that there was much of it near there, towards the southeast. He showed them gold and pearls, and certain old men replied that in a place which they called "Bohío" there was a vast amount,...*

"*Bohío*" was the Taino word for their huts, but Columbus stubbornly continued to interpret it as the island of Española, a confusion clarified fifty years later in a Las Casas marginal note.

...and that they wore it round the neck and on the ears and legs, and also pearls. He further understood that they said that there were large ships and merchandise, and that all this was to the southeast. He also understood that far from there were men with one eye, and others with dogs noses who ate men, and that when they took a man, they cut off his head and drank his blood and castrated him. The Admiral determined to return to the ship to await the two men whom he had sent, intending himself to go in search of those lands if they did not bring some good news of the things they sought. The Admiral says further: "These people are very mild and very timorous, naked, as I have said, without arms and without law; these lands are very fertile; they are full of mames, which are like carrots and which have the taste of chestnuts; and they beans and kidney beans very different from ours, and much cotton, which they do not sow, and it grows wild in great trees; and I believe that the season for gathering it is all the year round, since I saw bolls open and others about to open and flowers, all on one tree; and there are a thousand other kinds of fruit, which it is impossible for me to write down; and all must be of value." All this says the Admiral.

MONDAY, NOVEMBER 5th *— At dawn, he ordered the ship beached for careening, and the other vessels, but not all at the same time, so that two should always be at the place where they were for safety, although he says that those people were very confiding and that they might have beached all the vessels at one time without fear...*

It had been three months since Columbus had sailed from Spain, and would be another four until his return. If there was to be a single hull cleaning during his voyage, today's *"careening"* at Puerto Padre was appropriate in both date and location.

...While this was going on, the boatswain of the Niña *came to ask a reward from the Admiral, because he had found mastic; but he did not bring a specimen, because he had dropped it. The Admiral promised him a reward, and sent Rodrigo Sanchez and master Diego to the trees, and they brought a little of it. He kept it to take back to the Sovereigns, and also a piece of the tree, and says that he recognized that it was mastic, although it should be gathered at the due season, and in that district there was enough to collect a thousand quintals every year. He found, so he says, a good deal of that wood there which seemed to him to be aloe. He says further that the harbor of Mares is one of the*

best in the world and has a better climate and milder inhabitants, and since it has a point which is a rocky hillock, it would be possible to establish a fort there, so that, if that place proved to be rich and important, merchants could be there in safety from any other nations...

Once again Columbus demonstrated a good eye for promising defensive sites. Punta Carenero is a rocky prominence dominating the narrow entrance channel to Puerto Padre's magnificent harbor, truly *"one of the best in the world."*

...And he says: "May Our Lord, in Whose hands are all victories, order all that is for His service." He says that an Indian told him by signs that the mastic was good for those suffering stomach pains.

TUESDAY, NOVEMBER 6th — *Yesterday, in the night, says the Admiral, the two men whom he had sent into the interior came back, and they told him that they had gone twelve leagues, as far as a village of fifty houses, where, he says, there would be a thousand inhabitants, since many live in one house...*

Rodrigo de Xerez and Luís de Torres returned from their scaled-down trip ahead of schedule, returning from those *"twelve leagues"* in less than four full days.

...These houses are like very large tents. They said that they had been received with great solemnity, according to their custom, and that all, men and women alike, came to see them, and that they were lodged in the best houses. These people touched them and kissed their hands and feet, wondering at them and believing that they came from Heaven, and so they gave them to understand. They gave them to eat of what they had. They said that when they arrived, the most honorable persons of the village led them by the arms to the chief house, and gave them two chairs on which they seated themselves, and they all sat on the ground around them...

Fernando's *Biography* added that these chairs "were made of one piece and in a strange shape, for it resembled some short-legged animal with the tail as broad as the seat of the chair and lifted up for convenience to lean against; this chair had a head in front with eyes and ears of gold. They call these seats *dujos* or *duchos.*"

...The Indian, who went with them, told them how the Christians lived and how they were good people. Afterwards the men went out and the women entered, and sat in the same way round them, kissing their hands and feet, fondling them, trying to find if they were of flesh and bone like themselves; they asked them to stay there with them for at least five days. They exhibited the cinnamon and pepper and other spices which the Admiral had given to them, and the others told them by signs that there was much of it near there, to the southeast, but they did not know if there was any in that place. Having found that there was no indication of any city, they returned, and it was so that if they had been willing to admit those who wished to come, more than five hundred men and women would have come with them, because they thought that they were going back to heaven. There came with them, however, a chief man of the village and his son, and a servant. The Admiral spoke with them, doing them much honor. The Indian indicated to him many lands and islands which there were in that neighborhood. The Admiral thought of bringing him to the Sovereigns, and he says that he does not know what the chief imagined — I suppose that he was afraid — and in the darkness of the night he was anxious to go ashore. And the Admiral says that since he had the ship on dry land, not wishing to offend him, he let him go; the Indian said that he would return at dawn, but he never came back. On the way the two Christians found many people, who were on their way to their villages, men and women, with a brand in their hands, the herbs for smoking which they are in the habit of using...

Fernando's *Biography* mentions the dual usage of these firebrands for lighting cigars, "the smoke of which they inhale," and "for roasting those roots of which they had given the Christians to eat and which are their principal food."

...They found no village of more than five houses on the way, and all gave them the same reception. They saw many kinds of trees and plants and scented flowers; they saw birds of various kinds, different from those of Spain, with the exception of partridges and nightingales which sang, and geese, of which there were many. They saw no four-footed beasts, save dogs, which do not bark. The land is very fertile and very cultivated with "mames" and beans and kidney beans very unlike ours; they saw the same Indian corn and a great quantity of cotton gathered and spun and worked, and in one single house they had seen more than five hundred arrobas, and they considered that it would be possible to get four thousand quintals every year. The Admiral says that it seems to him that they do not sow it, and that it gives fruit all the year; it is very fine and has a large boll. He says that those people give everything they have for a very low price, and that a great bundle of cotton is given for a lace end, or anything else which is given for it. "They are," says the Admiral, "a people very free from wickedness and unwarlike; they are all naked, men and women, as their mother bore them. It is true that the women wear only a piece of cotton, large enough to cover their privy parts and no more, and they are of very good appearance, and are not very black, less so than those of the Canaries. I hold, most Serene Princes," the Admiral says here, "that having devout religious persons, knowing their language, they would all at once become Christians, and so I hope in Our Lord that Your Highnesses will take action in this matter with great diligence, in order to turn to the Church such great people and to convert them, as you have destroyed those who would not confess the Father and the Son and the Holy Ghost, and after your days, for we all are mortal, you will leave your realms in a most tranquil state and free from heresy and wickedness, and you will be well received before the eternal Creator, whom may it please to give you long life and great increase of many kingdoms and lordships, and the will and inclination to spread the holy Christian religion, as you have done up to this time. Amen. Today I refloated the ship and I am preparing to set out on Thursday in the name of God, and to go to the southeast to seek for gold and spices and to discover land." All these are the words of the Admiral,...

Thursday's planned departure date implies the sequential careening process was expected to span Monday, Tuesday and Wednesday – one full day for each of his ships. The *Santa Maria* would be *"refloated"* early enough Tuesday to complete the careening of both caravels by Wednesday evening.

...who thought to set out on the Thursday, but, as he had a contrary wind, he was not able to set out until the twelfth day of November.

While Puerto Padre's narrow two-mile channel had provided Columbus with a well-sheltered anchorage, its strong tidal currents restricted his departure times. According to the *Sailing Directions for the West Indies,* "tidal currents in the entrance attain a rate of 2 knots and sometimes cause strong eddies that make full speed and a lot of rudder angle necessary." His planned *"Thursday"* departure, just four days after the full moon, would have shackled Columbus with a rising tide from dawn until nearly noon, a constraint exacerbated by the *"contrary wind."* He could have waited until daybreak Saturday for a two-hour window allowing him to exit the harbor on a slack tide. But he delayed his departure until Monday, November 12th, for reasons possibly concealed by the *Journal's* only multi-day recording gap. One reason for his delay could have been LPC-13, his first lunar-planetary opportunity to measure the western limit of his voyage. Sunday morning Jupiter would rise five degrees ahead of the Moon a few minutes after midnight. Puerto Padre offered an ideal viewing site along an unobstructed bearing of 78 degrees to its eastern mangrove swashes six miles across the harbor. As it turned out, biases in his *Ephemerides* would have overstated his westward travel by 1800 miles, an obvious error whose correction would have to wait until they returned to Spain. It doesn't take much imagination to envisage the pilots struggling with their biased longitude measurements that Sunday morning. And surely Las Casas would have considered their technical discussion of little use to his planned history of the Indies. Whatever his motivation, he omitted the next five daily *Journal* entries, before resuming his transcription on November 12th.

MONDAY, NOVEMBER 12th — *He left the harbor and river of Mares at the end of the quarter of dawn,...*

Columbus delayed departing from *"the harbor and river of Mares"* until early morning, giving him a full day's rest after yesterday's possible celestial observations. By *"the end of the quarter of dawn"* he had cleared the bar at the mouth of Puerto Padre's narrow entrance channel.

...in order to go to an island which the Indians, whom he carried with him, vigorously affirmed was called "Babeque,"...

The Dunn/Kelley concordance lists 21 *Journal* occurrences of this island name in six different versions ranging from *"baneque" to "veneque."* These variations suggest there are frequent errors in the two-stage transcription of the original *Journal.*

...where they said, according to the signs which they made, that the people of the place gather gold on the shore at night with candles, and afterwards, as he says, with a mallet they make bars of it...

His obsession with *"gold"* leads Columbus to misinterpret the Indian's simple demonstration of crabbing techniques as the gathering of nuggets *"at night with candles"* before hammering them into bullion. *The National Geographic's* 1986 landfall article pictures modern Caribbeans still crabbing by torchlight, but leaves the use of their crab feast *"mallets"* to the reader's imagination.

...To go there, it was necessary to steer east by south...

Columbus follows an *"east by south"* course towards Great Inagua Island, where they supposedly *"gather gold on the shore"* by candlelight. This course would eventually carry him the full length of Cuba's Oriente Province.

....After having gone eight leagues farther along the coast, he found a river,...

In retracing Columbus's eastward route, Las Casas focused his transcription on major coastal features he had ignored during last month's westerly exploration. Puerto Gibara, the first *"river"* discovered today, is exactly *"eight leagues"* east of Puerto Padre.

...and, having gone on from there another four leagues, he found another river, which seemed to be of great volume and larger than any of the others which he had found...

As abstracted by Las Casas, Columbus ignored Bahía Jururu and Bahía Bariay, the harbor pair already recorded at his Cuban landfall. His *Journal* also overlooks his passage by the narrow serpentine opening to Bahía Vita. But it does record the Admiral's sighting of Bahía Naranjo, the conspicuous harbor *"four leagues"* beyond Puerto Gibara on his *"east by south"* course from Puerto Padre.

...He did not wish to wait or enter any of them for two reasons: the first and principal was because the weather and wind were favorable for going in search of the island of Babeque; the other, because, if in it there were some populous or important city near the sea, it would be seen, and to ascend the river small vessels were needed, and those which he had were not, and so much time would be lost, and such rivers are a thing to be explored separately. All this coast was inhabited, especially near the river to which he gave the name Rio del Sol...

Columbus's first view of Bahia Naranjo was Punta Barlovento, a red cliff dominating the harbor's entrance. Its fiery reflection of the afternoon sun may have inspired his graphic name, "Rio del Sol," which evolved into today's more subdued "Orange Bay."

...He said that on the previous Sunday, the eleventh of November,...

Evidence Columbus had maintained his daily *Journal* during that five-day gap in the Las Casas transcription.

...it had appeared to him that it would be well to take some persons from that river, in order to carry them to the Sovereigns, that they might learn our language, in order to discover what there is in the land, and that, on their return, they might be tongues for the Christians and adopt our customs and the things of our faith: "Because I saw, as I recognize," says the Admiral, "that these people have no creed and they are not idolaters, but they are very gentle and do not know what it is to be wicked, or to kill others, or to steal, and are unwarlike and so timorous that a hundred of them would run from one of our people, although they jest with them, and they believe and know that there is a God in Heaven, and they are sure that we come from Heaven, and they are ready to repeat any prayer that we say to them and they make the sign of the cross. So your Highnesses should resolve to make them Christians, for I believe that, if you begin, in a little while you will achieve the conversion of a great number of peoples to our holy faith, with the acquisition of great lordships and riches and all their inhabitants for Spain. For without doubt there is a great amount of gold in these lands, so that it is not without reason that these Indians, whom I carry with me, say that there are places in these islands where they dig gold and wear it around their necks, in the ears, and on the arms and legs, and that there are very large bracelets, pearls of great value and an infinite amount of spices. And by this river of Mares, from which I departed this night, there is without doubt a very great quantity of mastic, and more can be had if more is desired, for the same trees, being planted, readily take root, and they are many and very large and they have a leaf like the mastic and fruit, except that it is larger, as are both the trees and the leaf, as Pliny says, than I have seen in the island of Chios in the archipelago. And I ordered many of these trees to be tapped, in order to see if they would give resin to bring back, and as it rained continuously during the time that I was in the said river,...

These rains may have thwarted attempts to measure LPC-13 on November 11th.

...I was unable to get any of it, save a very small amount, which I am bringing to Your Highnesses, and it may also be that it is not the season for tapping them, for I believe that the suitable time is when the trees begin to recover from the winter and are about to flower, and here they had fruit which was almost ripe...

Columbus frequently reveals a limited knowledge of flora and fauna, but he did understand the need to tap resin during its spring flow.

....And there is also a great amount of cotton here, and I believe that it would be marketed very well here, without bringing it to Spain, taking it only to the cities of the Grand Khan, which will doubtless be discovered, and to the many other cities of other lords who will delight to serve Your Highnesses, and where other things can be supplied from Spain and from lands of the east, since these lands are to the west of us. And here there is an infinite amount of aloe,

although that is not a thing to produce great gain, but from the mastic much may be expected, since there is none save in the island of Chios, and I believe that they derive quite fifty thousand ducats, if my memory does not play me false...

His youthful experience marketing *"mastic"* from *"the island of Chios"* stimulates his anticipation of eventually harvesting this money crop on Andros Island.

...And there is here at the mouth of this river the best harbor that I have seen so far, clear and wide and deep, and a good situation for making a town and fort, and such that any ships whatever could lie alongside the walls,...

The harbor of Bahía de Naranjo is *"clear and wide and deep,"* its entrance dominated by Punta Barlovento's red cliffs, which Columbus saw as a *"good situation for...a fort."* The conventional candidate for this harbor, Bahía Sama, lacks these distinctive features.

...and the land very temperate and high, and very good waters. It was so that yesterday there came to the side of the ship a boat with six youths, and five came on board the ship; I ordered them to be kept and I will bring them with me. And afterwards I sent to a house which is near the river to the west, and they brought seven head of women, small and large, and three children. I did this, in order that the men might conduct themselves better in Spain, having women of their own land, than if they had not, because already it has many times occurred that men were brought from Guinea, that they might learn the language in Portugal, and afterwards when they had returned it was thought that use might be made of them in their own land, on account of the good company which they had had and the gifts which had been given to them; but when they reached their own land this result never appeared. Others did not so act. So that, having their women, they will be willing to do what is laid upon them, and also these women will do much to teach our people their language, which is one and the same throughout these islands of India, and they all understand one another, and they go all about them in their canoes, which is not the case in Guinea, where there are a thousand differing languages, so that one does not understand the other. This night there came to the side in a canoe the husband of one of these women and father of three children, one male and two female, and asked if I would allow him to come with them and implored me greatly, and they are now all consoled, so that they must all be related. And he is a man of already forty-five years." All these are the exact words of the Admiral. He also says above that it was somewhat cold, and for this reason it would not be wise in winter to navigate northwards to discover. On this Monday he sailed before sunset *eighteen leagues to the east by south* as far as a cape, which he named Cape Cuba.

Today Columbus had sailed *"eighteen leagues to the east by south"* from Puerto Padre to reach Cabo Lucretia. This prominent cape bulges eastward midway between Punta Maternillos and Punta Maisi, the island's eastern cape. Columbus can be excused for wrongly identifying Cabo Lucretia as Punta Maisi because of a striking similarity in size and shape, apparently well depicted in his Taino sketch of Cuba's coastline. Based on their October 26th estimate of canoe performance, the Taino would have measured those 73 leagues from Punta Maternillos to Punta Maisi as about five of their "canoe-days." Although Columbus had sailed just 37 leagues of Cuba's coast, he thought he had reached Punta Maisi, so he obligingly halved his October estimate of their "canoe-day" to seven leagues. He will soon exhibit doubts about his identification of Cabo Lucretia, but he will never restore his truncated "canoe-day" to a realistic measure.

7 - The Quest for Baneque's Golden Nuggets

TUESDAY, NOVEMBER 13th — *The whole of this night he stood "a la corda", which is to beat to and fro and to make no progress,...*

For only the second time, a *Journal* entry doesn't open until *"night."* Perhaps Columbus slept late this morning after beating *"beat to and fro...the whole of this night"* to observe LPC-14 shortly after 2 AM as the Moon rose 4.2 degrees beneath Mars.

...because he had seen a pass, which is an opening in the mountains, as between one range and another, which began to show at sunset, where two very lofty mountains appeared. It seemed that this was the parting between the land of Cuba and that of Bohio, and this the Indians, whom he carried with him, said by signs...

Ten leagues south of Cabo Lucretia the Rio Mayari slices Oriente Province's dominating backbone between *"two very lofty mountains,"* Sierra del Nipe and Sierra del Cristal. This gap's enduring significance to coastal pilots is demonstrated in the *Sailing Directions for the West Indies* by "These ranges are separated by a valley, which is a good mark from Punta del Mulas." But Columbus stubbornly clung to his belief he had reached Cuba's eastern cape at Punta Maisi, and in the fading glow of *"sunset"* misread Taino *"signs"* as indicating a *"parting between the land of Cuba and that of Bohio."*

...The dawn having come, he made sail for land and passed a point, which at night seemed to him to be some two leagues away, and entered a great gulf [golpho] five leagues to the south-southwest,...

In the October 15th *Journal* entry Cecil Jane had mistranslated *"golpho"* as *"channel"* to conceal the lack of a *"gulf"* between Rum Cay and Long Island. Today he was free to render it correctly as the *"gulf"* spanning the *"five leagues"* between Punta del Mulas and the entrance to Bahia Levisa.

...and there remained another five before reaching the cape, where midway between two large mountains there was a cutting,...

It's *"another five"* leagues inland from Bahia Levisa's entrance to the prominent saddle point separating Sierra de Nipe from Sierra del Cristal.

...and he could not decide whether or not it was an entrance to the sea...

Bahia Levisa does have an *"entrance to the sea,"* but Columbus couldn't confirm it from a distance of six leagues. His fixation with Great Inagua Island's tantalizing "gold nuggets" left him no time for resolution of this question.

...He wished to go to the island which they called "Beneque," where he understood from information he had received, that there was much gold; and that island lay to the east...

Yesterday Columbus would have assumed *"Beneque"* (Great Inagua Island) was a short distance northeast of the Cabo Lucretia he had misinterpreted as Cuba's eastern cape. But this morning's coastal discoveries may have modified his initial reading of the Taino map, for he now accepts the possibility that the island of *"much gold...lay to the east"* of Cabo Lucretia, not the north-northeast.

...And since he saw no great center of population, where he could find shelter against the violence of the wind which rose higher than ever before, he decided to run out to sea and go to the east before the wind which was north; and he went eight millas an hour, and from ten o'clock when he took that course until sunset, he went fifty-six millas, which are fourteen leagues, to the east, from Cape Cuba...

Despite *"the violence of the wind"* rising *"higher than ever before,"* Columbus averaged less than 6 knots in sailing *"fourteen leagues"* east *"from ten o'clock...until sunset."* Under similar conditions on October 17th he had placed his fate in the hands of his Taino guides by racing through the darkness at nearly hull speed. Not only was today's sail to the island of *"much gold"* conducted at a slower pace, it was also terminated at *"sunset,"* possibly because Columbus was reluctant to approach an unfamiliar island in darkness. A Taino sketch would have scaled today's 30-league sail to *"Beneque"* as two of their "canoe-days," misinterpreted by a stubborn Columbus as the *"fourteen leagues"* he had already sailed today. So prudence dictated he wait for dawn instead of challenging what he thought were the nearby island's uncharted reefs on a moonless night.

...And of the other land of Bohio, which he left to the leeward,...

With the wind *"north,"* the *"land of Bohio"* (Española) would have seemed *"to the leeward"* because Columbus still believed his *"fourteen leagues"* beyond Cuba's eastern cape had carried him close to Great Inagua Island's longitude.

...beginning from the cape of the above-mentioned gulf, he discovered, in his opinion, eighty millas, which are twenty leagues. And all that coast runs east-southeast and west-northwest...

From a short distance northeast of Cabo Lucretia at dawn, Columbus easily *"discovered"* the six leagues of coastline to Bahia Levisa's entrance. The remainder of today's *"twenty leagues"* came into view during today's sail *"fourteen leagues to the east"* along the coast running *"east-southeast and west-northwest"* between Punta Guarico and Bahia Levisa. This sail exposed Columbus to the full force of the Atlantic Gyre. With Cuba's coast continually in view, it would be surprising if this greater than half-knot current had still escaped his notice.

WEDNESDAY, NOVEMBER 14th — *All the night of yesterday he went cautiously [al reparo] and beating about...*

For the second (and final) time in his transcript Las Casas recorded *"al reparo"* to describe Columbus *"cautiously"* awaiting an event of presumable importance. His first usage had occurred with LPC-12 on the night of October 27th, and this one on *"the night of yesterday"* coincided with Tuesday morning's LPC-14. The probability of randomly associating both usages of *"al reparo"* with LPC events is less than one in sixty.

... because he said that it was not wise to navigate among those islands by night, until they have been examined. For the Indians, whom he had with him, told him yesterday, Tuesday, that it was three days journey from the Rio de Mares to the island of Baneque, by which must be understood days journey for their canoes, which are able to go seven leagues...

The 53 leagues from Puerto Padre (*Rio de Mares*) to Great Inagua Island (*Baneque*) was a *"three days journey"* for Taino canoes capable of 15 to 20 leagues a day. But Columbus stubbornly sticks with the *"seven leagues"* he had calculated Monday when he confused Cabo Lucretia with the actual "Cabo de Cuba."

...The wind also failed him, and having to go eastward, he could only go east by south, and owing to other obstacles, which he mentions there, he had to wait until morning. At sunrise, he resolved to go in search of a harbor, since the wind had changed from north to northeast,..

November winds in eastern Cuba blow from the *"northeast"* quadrant nearly half the time. Columbus could only sail within five points of today's *"northeast"* wind, so *"he could only go east by south,"* instead of continuing due east to those imagined golden nuggets awaiting harvest on Great Inagua Island.

...and if he did not find a harbor, it would be necessary for him to go back to the harbors which he had left in the island of Cuba. He reached land, having gone that night twenty-four millas [6 leagues] to the east by south; he went south...millas to the shore, where he saw many inlets and many islets and harbors. And as the wind was strong, and the sea very rough, he did not dare to attempt the entrance, but ran along the coast to the northwest by west, looking for a harbor, and he saw that there were many, but not very clear. After he had thus gone sixty-four millas [16 leagues], he found a very deep inlet, a quarter of a milla [1125 feet] wide, and a good harbor and river,...

While the *Journal's* first ellipsis conceals today's recording of headings and distances, several *"harbor"* descriptions over the next few days make it clear Columbus ended today's sail in the outstanding harbor of Bahía de Tánamo. Its *"very deep inlet"* exceeds 70 feet, and its width of nearly 1000 feet matches the Admiral's *"quarter of a milla"* approximation. Finding his route to Tánamo is problematic because of the ellipsis and variable coastal currents. One way to bring him there is to assume *"16 leagues"* measures today's total sailing distance – six leagues *"east by south"* to Punta Guarico," followed by 10 leagues *"northwest by west"* along the coast to Tánamo. It will soon be evident Punta Guarico was his second premature attempt to identify Cuba's eastern cape.

...where he entered, and steered to the south southwest and afterwards south until he reached the southeast, all very wide and very deep...

This description of Tánamo's narrow twisting entrance channel seems to have lost a comma between *"south"* and *"southwest."* Columbus must have feared he might be locked in this harbor for a week or more by Cuba's prevailing northeasterly trade winds. But he willingly assumed this risk because his Taino maps indicated the harbor was ideally configured for a Saturday night measurement of LPC-15 to the ESE.

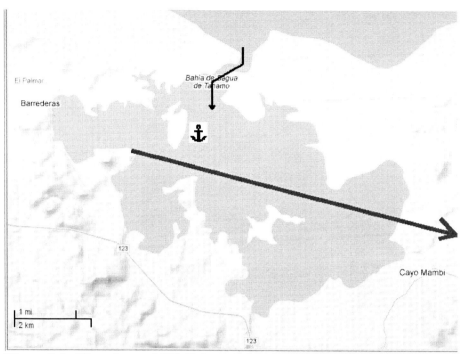

Figure 7-1. Direction to LPC-15 from Columbus's viewpoint in the harbor of Tánamo

...There he saw so many islands that he could not count them, all of good size and very high lands, full of various trees of a thousand kinds and an infinity of palms. He marvelled greatly to see so many islands and so lofty,...

Tánamo's most distinctive feature is its *"lofty"* islets, several exceeding elevations of 100 feet, with one, Cayo Alto, soaring 250 feet above the harbor.

...and he assured the Sovereigns that the mountains which he has seen since the day before yesterday, and those of these islands, are in his opinion higher than any in the world, and more lovely and clear, with no cloud or snow,...

Oriente Province's tallest peak is less than one third the height of the Canary Island volcano, Pico de Tiede, whose dramatic eruptions had enthralled Columbus on August 9th. His outrageously hyperbolic claim of *"higher than any in the world"* reveals his unbridled enthusiasm for today's discoveries.

...and very great depth of water at their foot...

Columbus seems to have anchored in 50-foot depths at the very "foot" of those steep cliffs lining Cayo Alto's east edge, as shown in Figure 7-1.

...And he says that he believes that these islands are those without number which in the mappemondes are placed at the end of the east. And he said that he believed that in them there were very great riches and stones and spices, and that they extend very far to the south, and spread out in every direction. He gave the sea the name Mar de Nuestra Señora,...

Tánamo's *"sea"* covers almost 10 square miles, second in area only to Puerto Padre's 15 square miles.

...and to the harbour which is near the mouth of the entrance to the islands he gave the name Puerto del Principe. *He did not enter it more than to see it from without, until another visit which he made on the Saturday of the following week, as will appear there...*

Dunn/Kelley notes Las Casas wrote his observation "in the left margin of the manuscript with a plus sign in the text marking where the insertion should be made."

...He says so many things and so much concerning the fertility and beauty and loftiness of these islands which he found in this harbor, that he tells the Sovereigns that they must not wonder that he praises all so much, because he assures them that he believes he has not said the hundredth part. Some of them seemed to touch the sky, and they were fashioned like diamond points; others, over their highest point, have, as it were, a table on top,...

In the late 19th century, Harvard's Professor Louis Agassiz likened these limestone terraces to "a series of gigantic ant-heaps and disconnected saddle-like ridges."

...and at their foot is very great depth of water, so that a very large carrack could reach them; they are full of trees and are not rocky.

THURSDAY, NOVEMBER 15th — *He decided to go among these islands with the ships' boats, and he says marvellous things of them, and that he found mastic and great quantity of aloe. Some of them were cultivated with the roots from which the Indians make their bread, and he found that fire had been lighted in some places. He did not see fresh water. There were some people and they fled. Everywhere he went, he found a depth of fifteen and sixteen brazas [82 to 88 feet], and all "basa," which means that the bottom is sand and not rocks, a thing which sailors greatly desire, because the rocks cut the cables of the ships anchors.*

Columbus seems to have limited today's harbor survey to its northern section where the water depths generally exceed 88 feet. *"He did not see fresh water"* there because the harbor's three major streams all discharge into the shallows along its remote southern coast.

FRIDAY, NOVEMBER 16th — *Because in all the places, islands and lands, where he entered, he always left a cross set up, he went into the boat and proceeded to the mouth of these harbors, and on a point of the land he found two very large pieces of timber. One was larger than the other, and the one on top of the other made a cross, so that he says a carpenter could not have made them better proportioned. And, having adored that cross, he commanded a very great and lofty cross to be made of the same logs. He found canes on that shore, and he did not know where they had grown and believed that some river had carried them down and cast them on the beach; and here he was right. He went to a creek within the entrance to the harbor, to the southeast. A creek is a narrow entrance by which the water of the sea enters into the land...*

Esteron Pescarito is a likely candidate for the *"creek"* to the harbor's *"southeast."*

...There was rocky height and peak like a cape, and at its foot the water was very deep, so that the largest carrack in the world could lie alongside the land,...

His boating explorations carried him to Punta Gorda where *"the water was very deep, so that the largest carrack in the world could lie alongside the land."*

...and there was a place or corner, where six ships might lie without anchors as in a hall. It seemed to him that a fort could be made there at small cost, if any considerable trade should develop at any time in that sea of islands...

Although *"without anchors"* is a hyperbolic claim, the semicircular hill embracing a quarter-mile cove on the northwest side of Cayo Largo provides a likely candidate for this sheltered anchorage.

...Having returned to the ship, he found the Indians, whom he carried with him, fishing for very large periwinkles which there are in those waters. He made the people dive there and search for nacaras, *which are the oysters in which pearls are produced. They found many, but no pearls, and he attributed this to the fact that it was not the season for them, which he believed to be May and June...*

Once again Columbus demonstrates a quaint understanding of natural history by claiming pearls are in *"season"* only when the oysters aren't.

...The sailors found an animal which seemed to be a taso *or* taxo...

Fernando's biography adds that when these *"sailors"* found the badger's tropical relative, they quickly dispatched it with their swords.

...They also fished with nets and found a fish, among many others, which seemed to be a very pig, not like a dolphin, which, he says, was all shell, very hard, and it had no soft place except the tail and eyes, and it had an opening under it to void its superfluities. He ordered it to be salted, in order to take it for the Sovereigns to see.

Trunk fish are widely distributed in the Caribbean's shallow grasses and coral reefs. These slow moving bottom-feeders are encased in a *"shell, very hard"* affording them protection from most predators.

SATURDAY, NOVEMBER 17th — *He entered the boat in the morning and went to examine the islands, which he had not visited, on the southwestern side. He saw many others and very fertile and very lovely, and between them there was very great depth of water...*

This morning's boat trip mirrors his efforts to observe a potential lunar eclipse on November 4th when he was rowed to Puerto Padre's east side for an unobstructed view of the setting moon. Today he needed to observe LPC-15 at moonrise, so he was rowed in the opposite direction, supposedly *"to examine the islands...on the southwestern side"* of Tánamo harbor. There aren't any islands there, but that vantage point would give him a 5-mile unobstructed path for viewing Venus and the Moon in near occultation as they rose together shortly after 5 AM.

During his 40 days in Cuba his *Ephemerides* would alert Columbus to five longitude measurement opportunities: four LPC's and the potential lunar eclipse of November 4th. LPC-12 and LPC-14 coincided with the *Journal's* only two transcriptions of the verb "to observe." More significantly, today's LPC-15 and the potential lunar eclipse both occurred after Columbus had been rowed to harbor locations offering optimal viewing sites. Nothing is known of his plans for LPC-13 because Las Casas failed to transcribe *Journal* entries during that time frame.

....Streams of fresh water divided some of them, and he believed that water and those streams originated from some springs which spouted forth in the heights of the mountains of the islands. Going farther on from there, he found a stream very lovely and fresh, and it flowed very cold in its narrow bed...

Possible candidates for this *"stream"* are the Rio Tánamo to the south and Rio Gamboa to the southwest.

...There was a very fair meadow and many very lofty palms, taller than those he had already seen. I believe that he says that he found large nuts like those of India and also large rats like those of India,...

These "large rats" were Caribbean hutia, rabbit-sized rodents nearing extinction in the 21st century.

...and very large crayfish. He saw many birds and there was a strong smell of musk, and he believed that there must be some there. On this day, of the six youths he took in the Rio de Mares, and whom he ordered to be kept on the caravel Niña, *the two oldest escaped.*

SUNDAY, NOVEMBER 18th — *He went out again in the boats with many people from the ships, and went to set up the great cross which he had ordered made from the two logs mentioned, at the mouth of the entrance of the Puerto del Principe, in a prominent position and one free from trees; it is very lofty and a very lovely thing to see. He says that the sea rises and falls there much more than in any other harbor which he has visited in that land, and that it is not surprising considering the many islands,...*

Columbus's tidal estimate coincided with the new moon's tidal peak. His observation that Tánamo had Cuba's widest tidal range is true, but overstated. Its tide exceeds the others by a mere two inches according to the *Sailing Directions for the West Indies.*

...and that the tide is in the reverse of ours, because there when the moon is the southwest by south, it is low tide in that harbor...

A Dunn/Kelley footnote points out *"the moon in the southwest by south"* was the seaman's way of defining time on a compass card viewed as a 24-hour clock with north representing midnight. So Columbus was estimating this harbor's low tide to occur at 2:15 PM with tonight's new moon.

...He did not set out from here, because it was Sunday.

MONDAY, NOVEMBER 19th — *He departed before sunrise and with a calm,...*

With the winds now *"calm,"* Columbus took advantage of an ebb tide helping his rowboats tow his fleet out of Tánamo harbor through its twisting entrance channel.

...and afterwards, at midday, it blew somewhat from the east, and he navigated north-northeast...

Still intent on reaching the "island of gold nuggets," Columbus may have cursed the Gods for conspiring against him as the shifting wind still *"blew somewhat"* from the direction of Great

Inagua Island. But he resolutely held his *"north-northeast"* course; hoping the wind would soon accommodate a southeasterly tack to *"Baneque."*

....At sunset, Puerto del Principe lay to the south-southwest, and was seven leagues distant. He saw the island of Baneque due east, from which he was distant sixty millas [15 leagues]...

The Taino seem to have accurately mapped *"the island of Baneque due east"* at a distance of 28 leagues, but Columbus stubbornly halved their canoe-day estimate to *"15 leagues."*

...He navigated all this night to the northeast; he made rather less than sixty millas [15 leagues], and up to ten oclock on the next day, Tuesday, another twelve [3 leagues], which in all amounts to eighteen leagues, and that to the northeast by north.

Columbus realizes today's sailing route would have bisected the island of Baneque had Cabo Lucrecia actually been Cuba's eastern cape. So he shifts that identity eastward to the Punta Guarico discovered a week earlier, while ignoring the implied lengthening of the Taino's canoe-day.

TUESDAY, NOVEMBER 20th — *Baneque, or the islands of Baneque, lay to the east- south-east,...*

This morning's *"east-south-east"* direction to Great Inagua Island suggests Columbus was now correctly scaling his Taino charts. Had he continued to cut the Taino's distance measurements in half he would have assumed this island lay to his south.

...from which direction the wind blew so that it was contrary. Seeing that it did not change and that the sea was rising,...

Possibly the Admiral cursed the wind for playing games as its relentless clockwise rotation continued to deny him access to "the island of gold nuggets."

...he resolved to return to Puerto del Principe, whence he had set out, which was twentyfive leagues away...

Yesterday's daylight sail of *"seven leagues"* and his nighttime sail of *"eighteen leagues"* differed in course by a single compass point, allowing Columbus to sum them as *"twentyfive leagues"* with negligible error.

...He did not wish to go to the islet which he called Isabela, *which was twelve leagues from him where he might have reached anchorage that day,...*

Columbus read the mapped distance from his dawn position to the *"islet which he called* Isabela," as *"twelve leagues,"* a reasonable but somewhat optimistic estimate to the actual distance of about 17 leagues.

...for two reasons: the one, because he saw two islands to the south, which he wished to examine;...

Great Inagua and Española were probably those *"two islands to the south."*

...the other, because the Indians whom he carried with him, whom he had taken in Guanahani, which he called San Salvador and which was eight leagues from that Isabela, might get away,...

Figure 7-2. String of islets (Exuma Cays) running to within "8 leagues" of the southwestern cape of Eleuthera

No credible landfall theory offers a *"San Salvador"* only *"eight leagues from...Isabela."* In Morison's reconstruction, Watlings Island is more than 22 leagues north of Crooked Aklins Island. At first glance the congruence is even weaker in my reconstruction because Eleuthera's southern cape is fully 24 leagues from Long Island. However, this discrepancy may have resulted from hurried Taino mapping of the several hundred islets bordering Exuma Sound, a sailing basin stretching from Long Island to southern Eleuthera. Individual mapping of this islet chain would have been tedious, so the Taino may have represented them by a narrow band stretching to their extreme northern limit at Ship Channel Cay, exactly *"eight leagues"* west of Eleuthera's nearest cape.

...and he says that he needed them and wanted to take them to Castile, etc. They had understood, so he says, that, gold being found, the Admiral would allow them to return to their native land...

Columbus secretly hopes the Taino will lead him to Great Inagua's *"gold"* before he carries them off to Spain.

...He reached the neighborhood of Puerto del Principe, but he was unable to make it, as it was night and the currents carried him away to the northwest...

The Atlantic Ocean's NEC runs at least half a knot *"to the northwest"* along Cuba's north coast.

...He went about and steered to the northeast, with a high wind. The wind lessened and changed at the third quarter of the night; he steered to the east by north. The wind was south southeast, and at dawn it changed to due south, and veered towards southeast. At sunrise he was off Puerto del Principe, and it lay to the southwest and almost southwest by west and he was distant fortyeight millas from it, which are twelve leagues.

WEDNESDAY, NOVEMBER 21st — *At sunrise, he steered to the east with a south wind; he made little progress, because the sea was against him. Up to the hour of vespers, he had gone twentyfour millas [6 leagues]...*

Columbus was well positioned for a final attempt at Great Inagua with the wind now finally abeam, but the *"south wind"* was so weak that he made only six leagues in nine hours against the Atlantic's unrelenting NEC.

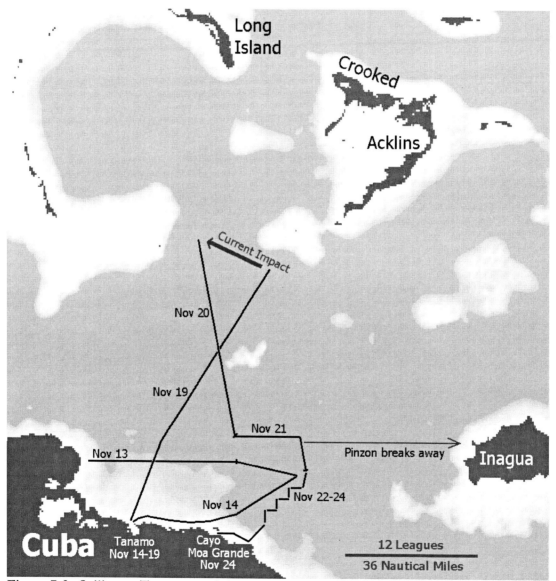

Figure 7-3. Sailing to Tanamo, and then exploring before reaching Cayo Moa Grande

...Afterwards, the wind changed to the east, and he went to the south by east, and at sunset he had gone twelve millas [3 leagues]...

Once again the capricious winds frustrated him by blowing directly from Great Inagua, so he altered his course back towards Cuba's shore, making only three leagues before sunset.

...Here the Admiral found that he was fortytwo degrees from the equinoctial line, to the north, as he had been in the harbor of Mares. But here he says that he has abandoned use of the quadrant until he reaches land, in order that he could repair it [que lo adobe]...

Columbus measures the Pole Star's elevation angle a third time, and again comes up with a value of *"fortytwo degrees."* He recognizes today's *"quadrant"* reading as a fruitless effort, declaring he will abandon further usage*" until he reaches land."* *"Adobe"* is the present subjunctive tense of "adobar," whose modern meaning suggests Columbus intended to "calibrate" his quadrant when *"he reaches land"* rather than *"repair"* this simple instrument.

...It was accordingly his opinion that he was not so far distant, and he was right, since it was impossible, these islands being only ... degrees. He was led to believe that the quadrant was correct, as he says, because the north star was as high as in Castile,...

This second ellipsis in the *Journal* (between *"only"* and *"degrees"*) conceals reference to a latitude lying between today's 21 degrees and Eleuthera's 26, the only latitude recorded in his 1493 letter. His measurement of a *"north star as high as in Castile"* confirms Columbus was reading his quadrant's tangent scale instead of its elevation angle because the 42nd latitude slices though *"Castile."*

...and if this be true, he had come very near and was as high as Florida. But then where are these islands now which he had close at hand? To this he added that it was, as he said, very hot. But it is clear that if he were off the coast of Florida, he would not have had heat but cold, and it is also manifest that at forty-two degrees it is not to be believed that there is heat in any part of the earth, unless it be for some accidental reason, and this I do not believe has been known up to the present...

Las Casas was introducing his own ideas here because Ponce de Leon didn't coin the name *"Florida"* until 1513.

...From this heat, which the Admiral says that he experienced there, he argued that in these Indies and there where he was, there must be much gold. This day Martin Alonzo Pinzón, with the caravel Pinta, went away, without the permission and against the wish of the Admiral, through greed, as he says, thinking that an Indian, whom the Admiral had ordered to be placed in that caravel, would give him much gold; and he went away without waiting, without the excuse of bad weather, merely because he wished to do so; and the Admiral says here: He had done and said many other things to me.

Pinzón wasn't about to wait for his Admiral's *"permission"* to harvest Great Inagua's imaginary gold nuggets. He could have rejoined the fleet after realizing his disappointment, but chose to stay out of contact for 46 days. This delay would give him first crack at real gold deposits on the island of Española.

THURSDAY, NOVEMBER 22nd — *On Wednesday, in the night, he steered to the south by east, with an east wind, and it was almost calm; at the third quarter, it blew from the north northeast. He was still going southward, in order to examine the land which lay in that direction from him, and when the sun rose, he found himself as far from it as on the previous day, owing to the contrary currents, and the land lay forty millas [10 leagues] away from him...*

By now Columbus was clearly aware of the *"contrary currents"* flowing parallel to Cuba's coast, currents that would play a major role in the tumultuous events of Christmas night.

...On this night, Martin Alonso followed an easterly course, in order to go to the island of Baneque, where the Indians say there is much gold; he was within sight of the Admiral and might have been some sixteen millas [4 leagues] away. The Admiral sailed within sight of land all night, and he caused some sail to be taken in and kept a lantern alight all night, because it seemed that Martin Alonso was coming towards him and the night was very clear and the wind light and good for him to come to him, if he wished.

FRIDAY, NOVEMBER 23rd — *The Admiral steered all day towards the land to the south, always with a light wind, and the current never permitted him to reach land, but he was today as far from it at sunset as he had been in the morning. The wind was east northeast and satisfactory for going to the south, except that it was light; and beyond this cape there stretched out another land or cape, which also trended to the east, which those Indians whom he had with him called "Bohio"...*

This day Columbus had seen *"beyond"* Punta Guarico to *"another land or cape, which also trended to the east."* These were the heights of Yunque de Baracoa, the "anvil" of a mountain dominating Cuba's coast southeast of Punta Guarico. Columbus wasn't about to acknowledge his second premature "discovery" of Cuba's eastern cape, so he shifted this mountain range east to the neighboring island of *"Bohio."*

...They said that this land was very extensive and in it were people who had one eye in the forehead, and others whom they called Cannibals...

This imaginative claim was to become one of Spain's rationales for their brutal treatment of the Indians.

...Of these last, they showed great fear, and when they saw that this course was being taken, they were speechless, he says, because those people ate them and are very warlike. The Admiral says that he well believes that there is something in this, but that since they are armed, they must be an intelligent people, and he believed that they may have captured some men and that, because they did not return to their own land, they would say that they were eaten. They believed the same of the Christians and of the Admiral, when some first saw them.

SATURDAY, NOVEMBER 24th — *He navigated all that night and at nine in the morning he made land at the level island, the same place to which he had come the previous week, when he was going to the island of Baneque...*

The *"level island"* of Cayo Moa Grande is an important Columbus landmark on Cuba's coast. Dense mangrove thickets blanket a 500-acre sandbar shielding its large anchorage from the Caribbean's fury. The colonists responsible for its "Grande" name would have been unlikely to view the 20,000 acres of Watling's Island as an "isleta."

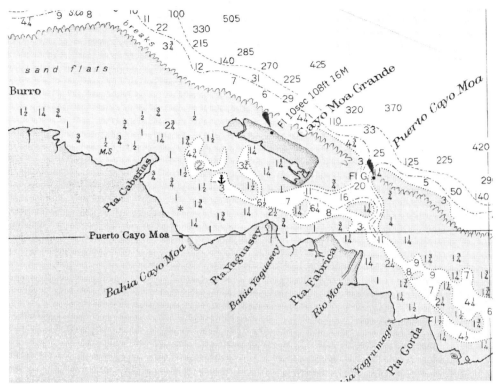

Figure 7-4. The Anchorage at Cayo Moa Grande

....At first he did not dare to approach the land, because he thought that the sea broke heavily at the opening in the mountains...

An exposed reef, extending twenty miles or more along the coast, has a convenient *"opening"* providing access to a well-protected anchorage behind Cayo Moa Grande. Columbus had not tried to land there when he *"first"* saw it on November 14th because then *"the sea broke heavily at the opening in the mountains."*

...Finally he reached the Sea of Nuestra Señora, where there were many islands, and entered the harbor which is near the mouth of the entrance among the islands. And he says that if he had known of that harbor before and had not spent his time in examining the islands of the Sea of Nuestra Señora, it would not have been necessary for him to go back, although he says that he felt that the time was well spent, since he had visited the said islands...

Searching for a positive spin, Columbus attributes discovery of Tánamo Bay's magnificent harbor to his November 14th decision to forgo anchorage at Cayo Moa Grande.

....So, having come to land, he sent the boat and sounded the harbor, and found a very good bottom, at six brazas [33 feet] depth and sometimes as much as twenty [110 feet], and clean, sandy everywhere. He entered it, steering to the southwest, and afterwards going to the west, the flat island lying to the north...

An entrance channel more than 100 feet deep extends one mile to the *"southwest."* After reaching it Columbus followed a second channel *"west"* to anchor in the shallows off Punta Pajaros, the south cape of Cayo Moa Grande, *"the flat island lying to the north."*

...This island, with another near it,...

A narrow channel lined with mangroves separates Cayo Moa Grande from its smaller neighbor, Cayo Chico. Their separation would have been visible only after Columbus *"sent the boats and sounded the harbor."*

...forms a bay [laguna] in which all the ships [naos] of Spain could lie...

Today's lagoon is less than one fifth the size of Eleuthera's, leading Columbus to trim his capacity estimate from *"all the ships of Christendom"* to *"all the ships of Spain."* In a marginal note Las Casas added its name, Puerto Sancta Cathalina, after realizing he had dropped it from his abstract.

...and could be safe from all winds without anchors [amarras]...

Cecil Jane was a nautical expert who surely realized the impossibility of his careless translation. Columbus was referring to the mooring cables installed in many sandy harbors to snag dragging anchors. Some Caribbean harbors still have their *"amarras"* from 500 years ago.

....And this entrance on the southeast side, which is made steering south southwest, has a way out to the west, very deep and very wide, so that it is possible to pass between the islands if one knows them, as it is the direct course along their shores for any one who comes from the open sea to the north...

From the west end of Cayo Moa Grande the boating party could observe *"a way out to the west, very deep and very wide."* They had the width right, but they would soon discover that impassable shallows blocked this potential exit.

...The islands lie at the foot of a big mountain, which stretches away from east to west and which is of great length and loftier and longer than any other on this coast, where there are innumerable mountains. Seaward, a reef extends the whole length of [al luengo de] the said mountain, like a bar, which reaches as far as the entrance; all this is on the southeastern side...

A lofty mountain range parallels Cuba's coast for more than 15 miles towards the southeast. Columbus could see a reef extending the *"whole length"* of that mountain range, and this time Cecil Jane chose to translate the phrase correctly. Had he done the same for the *"al luengo de"* of October 14th he would have made it clear Columbus had rowed Egg Island's *"whole length,"* not just part of Watlings.

...On the side of the flat island there is also a reef, although it is small, and so between the two there is a wide space and much depth of water, as has been said. Immediately at the entrance, on the southeastern side, within the same harbor, they saw a large and very lovely river, and of greater volume than those which they had hitherto seen, and the water was fresh as far as the sea. At the entrance, it has a bar, but afterwards, within, it is very deep, eight and nine brazas [50 feet]. It is all surrounded by palms and many trees, like the others.

Directly southeast of the harbor entrance, the *"large and very lovely"* Rio Moa disgorges its huge volume of fresh water onto a sand bar a mile inside the reef's opening to the sea. Eons of silt deposits have formed a large bar at its mouth, but the *Sailing Directions for the West Indies* confirms this river still deepens *"within."*

SUNDAY, NOVEMBER 25th — *Before sunrise, he entered the boat and went to examine a cape or point of land to the southeast of the flat island, a matter of a league and a half, because it seemed to him that there should be a good river there...*

Punta Gorda is a prominent coastal feature almost *"a league and a half"* to the *"southeast"* of the *"flat island."*

...Directly at the beginning of the cape, on the south eastern side, having gone two crossbow shots, he saw a large stream of very fine water flowing; it came down from the mountain and made a great noise...

The first river he came to was the Rio Fabrica, a mile southeast of his anchorage.

...He went to the river and saw some stones shining in it, on which were some veins the color of gold, and he remembered that in the river Tagus, at the mouth of it, near the sea, gold is found, and it seemed to him to be certain that there must be gold here, and he ordered some of those stones to be collected to take them to the Sovereigns. While they were there, the ships boys shouted that they saw pines. He looked towards the mountain and saw them, so tall and wonderful that he could not overstate their height and straightness, like spindles, thick and slender. From these he realized that ships could be built, and a vast quantity of planks secured and masts for the largest ships in Spain,...

Modern Cuba's Cuchillas de Pinal (Crests of Pine), 13 miles to his west, suggests favorable conditions for *"pines"* along the north slopes of Oriente Province.

...He saw oaks and strawberry trees, and a good river, and means for constructing sawmills. The land and the breezes were more temperate than any so far, owing to the height and beauty of the mountain ranges. He saw on the beach many other stones, the color of iron, and others which some said came from silver mines. All these were brought down by the river. There he secured a yard and a mast for the mizzen of the caravel Niña. *He reached the mouth of the river and entered a creek, at the foot of that cape, on the southeast, very deep and large, in which a hundred ships could lie, with no cables or anchors. The harbor was such that eyes never saw another like it; the mountains were very lofty and from them descend many very fine streams; all the high ground was full of pines, and everywhere were very diverse and lovely groves of trees. Two or three other rivers lay behind...*

The largest of these *"rivers"* is the Rio Yagrumague, one league southeast of his anchorage.

...He praises all this very highly to the Sovereigns, and declares that he felt inestimable pleasure and delight at seeing it, and especially the pines, because here could be built as many ships as might be wished, bringing out the materials, except timber and pitch, of which there would be an abundance there. And he affirms that he has not praised it to the hundredth part of that which might be said, and that it pleased Our Lord always to show him something better, and that continually in his discoveries up to then he had gone from good to better, as well in the matter of the lands and trees, herbs, fruit and flowers, as in that of the people, and always in a different manner, and as this was the case in one place, so it was in the next. The same was true of the ports and waters, and finally he says that if he who has seen it feels so great wonder, how much more wonderful will it be to one who hears of it, and that no one will be able to believe it if he has not seen it.

8 - Cuba's "very remarkable" Harbor of Baracoa

MONDAY, NOVEMBER 26th — *At sunrise, they weighed anchor from the harbor of Santa Catalina, where he was within the flat island,...*

While transcribing today's entry Las Casas realized he had failed to record that Columbus had dedicated *"the harbor of Santa Catalina"* to Alexandria's martyred Saint Katherine. So he added a marginal note to his November 24th abstract pointing out Columbus had entered this harbor on the eve of Saint Katherine's feast day.

...and he steered along the coast...

Here Columbus used *"de luengo de la costa"* to describe his partial coasting of Cuba east of Cayo Moa Grande. This contrasts with his October 14th usage of *"al luengo de la isla"* for coasting the full length of Egg Island, rather than part of Watlings.

...with little wind from the southwest, in the direction of Cape el Pico, which was to the southeast....

Ten miles further *"along the coast"* at Punta Guarico, Columbus could see the coastline curving smoothly towards its southern end in an arc tracing the parrot's beak suggested by *"Pico."*

...He reached the cape in the evening, because the wind dropped, and when he had arrived there, he saw to the southeast by east, another cape, which was sixty millas [15 leagues] from him;...

When Columbus *"reached"* Punta Guarico, *"he saw to the southeast and east, another cape"* at a distance of *"15 leagues."* From that vantage point every peak near Punta Maisí was hundreds of feet below his horizon. Columbus must have seen Cuba's eastern cape on an accurate chart; one mapping its location to within a fraction of a league and a few degrees.

...and near there [de alli] he saw another cape, which was southeast by south of the ship, and it seemed to him that it was twenty millas [5 leagues] away, and to it he gave the name Cape Campana [bell]...

Cecil Jane's misleading translation of *"de alli"* obscures the meaning of this passage. When the *Santa Maria* reached Punta Guarico's "beak" Columbus *"saw [from] there"* the bell-shaped 1000-foot elevation of El Viento that defined *"another cape...5 leagues"* to the *"southeast by south of the ship."*

...He was unable to reach it that day, because the wind again sank entirely. He may have made in the whole of that day thirtytwo millas, which are eight leagues,...

Punta Guarico stands at the head of a southeasterly coastline that diverts the Atlantic's NEC into an even stronger northwesterly coastal current. After Columbus passed Punta Guarico his progress against this current slowed dramatically as sometimes *"the wind again sank entirely"* and he made only *"eight leagues...in the whole of that day."* Those *"eight leagues"* were enough to carry Columbus from his Cayo Moa Grande anchorage to El Viento's "Cape Campana."

...in the course of which he noticed and marked nine well outlined harbors, which all the sailors marvelled at, and five large rivers, because he continually went near the shore, in order to see everything well...

There are a number of *"well outlined harbors"* along the coast from Punta Guarico to El Viento. Five shown on DMA charts are identified as Bahia Cañete, Bahia Yamaniguey, Bahia de Taco, Puerto Cayaguaneque and Puerto Navas.

...All that land has very high mountains, very lovely, and not dry or rocky, but all accessible, and very beautiful valleys. The valleys, as well as the mountains, were full of lofty and leafy trees, so that it was bliss to see them, and it seemed that there were many pines. And also behind Cape el Pico, to the southeast, there are two islets, each one of which is about two leagues in circumference, and within them three marvellous harbors and two large rivers...

Directly below Punta Guarico are *"two islets,"* Cayo Medio and Cayo Chico, neither with a circumference exceeding one mile. Las Casas appears to have garbled his transcription because *"two leagues in circumference"* accurately sizes the bay *"behind Cape el Pico"* containing those *"two islets...three marvellous harbors and two large rivers."*

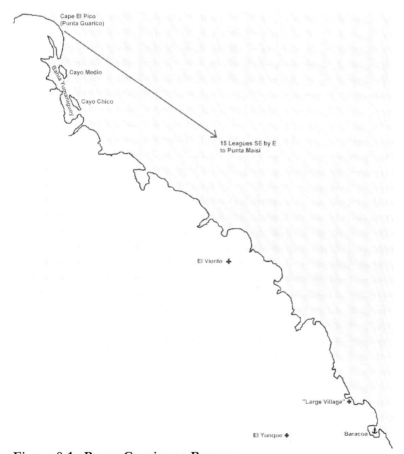

Figure 8-1. Punta Guarico to Baracoa

...On all this coast he saw no inhabited place from the sea; there may have been some, and there were indications that this was so, because wherever they landed they found signs that there had been people and many fires. He considered that the land which he saw today to the southeast of Cape Campana was the island that the Indians called Bohio; this seems so because the cape is apart from that land...

While rounding Punta Guarico in the late afternoon Columbus may have relied on Taino charts pinpointing Cabo Maisí, *"15 leagues"* to his *"southeast by east."* After working his way down the coast to El Viento's small cape, that bearing angle would rotate one compass point *"to the southeast."* Despite his Taino charts, Columbus was still burdened with the misconception that Cuba's Cabo Maisí lay at the west end of Española, *"the island which the Indians called Bohio."* Possibly his judgment was influenced by open ocean to his *"southeast"* that made it appear *"the cape is apart from that land."*

....All the people who have been found up to this time have, he says, the very greatest fear of those Caniba or Canima,...

"Caniba" would soon become a universal term for savages reputed to dine on human flesh.

...and they say that they live in this island of Bohio, which must be very large, as it appears, and he believes that those of Caniba take these people, since they are very cowardly and know nothing of arms, from their lands and houses. It seems to him that for this reason those Indians, whom he has with him, are not accustomed to settle on the coast of the sea, because their land is near Caniba...

His astute observation will be validated tomorrow when Columbus finds a large coastal village at an effective defensive location.

...He says when that they saw that he was going in the direction of that land, they were speechless, fearing that they would be eaten, and he could not calm their terror; and they said that the people there had only one eye and the face of a dog. The Admiral believed that they were lying, and he thought that they must be under the dominion of the Grand Khan who captured them.

TUESDAY, NOVEMBER 27th — *Yesterday, at sunset, he arrived near a cape which he called Campana, and as the sky was clear and the wind slight, he did not wish to go to land to anchor, although to the leeward he had five or six marvellous harbors...*

"Yesterday, at sunset" informs us today's *Journal* entry covers a 36-hour interval beginning with a redundant description of his Monday arrival near El Viento *"in the evening."* With *"the wind slight"* Columbus drifted down the coast Monday night, possibly reaching Puerto Navas, one of those *"nine well marked harbors"* mapped by his Indian guides.

...Because he had delayed more than he had intended, owing to the desire which he had and the pleasure which he derived from seeing and wondering at the beauty and freshness of those lands, wherever he approached them, and in order not to delay the execution of his projects, for these reasons he remained that night beating about and standing off until day. As the drifts and currents had carried him that night more than five or six leagues to the southeast, beyond the point where he had been when night fell, and where the land of Campana had come in sight,...

Although this entry introduces some uncertainty, it does establish his Tuesday morning position as *"more than five or six leagues to the southeast...[of] where the land of Campana had come into sight."* To reach El Viento's cape with *"the wind slight,"* Columbus may have sailed close enough to the coast to take advantage of *"the drifts and currents"* created by eddies of the Atlantic Ocean's NEC. Some have suggested *"southeast"* is an erroneous recording for the *northwest* flow of the NEC. But mistakes in both bearings seems unlikely when the *Journal's* error rate was less than 10 percent in transcribing "este" or "oeste," and apparently zero for "norte" and "sur." Even with the wind sometimes *"slight"* Columbus could have averaged slightly more than a knot to reach El Viento that evening after rounding Punta Guarico against the current.

...and as beyond that cape a big opening appeared, which seemed to part one land from another and make as it were an island in the midst, he decided to go back with the wind southwest, and he came to the place where the opening had appeared. And he found that it was only a large bay,...

The phrase *"go back with the wind southwest,"* informs us Columbus took advantage of a strengthening wind abeam to turn back for a closer look at Bahia Yumaniguey, the *"large bay"* directly south of Punta Guarico to see whether it separated Cuba from *"Bohio."* He soon realized *"it was only a large bay"* that didn't *"part one land from another and make as it were an island in the midst."*

...and at the end of it, to the southeast side, there was a cape, on which there was a mountain, lofty and square, which seemed to be an island...

Morison assumed this *"mountain"* was El Yunque, the highest peak *"southeast"* of Bahia Yumaniguey. But this peak still lay hidden far behind several mountains much closer to Columbus. The closest was Loma San Juan, *"lofty and square, which seemed to be an island"* dominating a full 15 degrees of his *"southeast"* horizon. Its lengthy elevated crest may be the one that would impress Professor Agassiz four centuries later.

...The wind veered to the north, and he again turned to a southeasterly course, in order to run along the coast and to discover all that was there...

As the *"wind veered to the north"* Columbus *"again turned to a southeasterly course"* within view of eastern Cuba's verdant landscape. The *Journal's* description of today's coasting may have been abridged by Las Casas, but it remains the longest surviving daily entry. And it's detailed enough for us to follow the fleet's progress from Puerto Cayaguaneque to a large Indian settlement at a cove one mile northwest of Baracoa.

...Presently he saw at the foot of that Cape Campana [El Viento] a marvellous harbor and a large river; and a quarter league from there another river; and a half league from there another river; and a further half league on another river; and a league from there another river; and another league from there another river; and another quarter of a league from there another river; and another league from there another large river, from which to Cape Campana was some twenty millas [five leagues], and they were to the southeast of him...

This entry introduces a minor uncertainty by summing its seven distance components to 4½ leagues instead of the five recorded by Las Casas. A slightly better cartographic fit suggests Columbus doubled counted one of his *"half league"* measurements instead of Las Casas dropping one in his transcript. In either case, today's sail carried Columbus to a well-protected cove nearly 10 miles southeast of Puerto Cayaguaneque, just one mile short of Baracoa's far superior harbor. This distance of only 3.2 leagues suggests Columbus may have overestimated his progress by ignoring the NEC's enhanced flow rate along this northeasterly coastline.

...Most of these rivers had large entrances, wide and clear, with wonderful harbors for the very largest ships, without bars of sand or rocks, or reefs. Coming so along the coast, on the southeast, from the last-named river, he found a large village, the largest that he had found up to this time,...

Elevated coastal lookouts would have enhanced communal survival in an age when hostile canoes could outrace fleeing villagers. Lookouts posted on the adjacent 340-foot hill could have given this *"large village"* several minutes more warning time than available in Baracoa's otherwise superior harbor.

...and he saw an infinite number of people come to the seashore, shouting loudly, all naked, with their spears in their hands. He wished to have speech with them, and lowered the sails, and anchored,...

This cove lacked overnight protection for the caravels, but offered adequate day anchorage.

...and sent the boats of the ship and of the caravel, in an ordered manner, that they should do no damage to the Indians and should receive none, commanding them to give them some trifles from their articles of barter. The Indians made a show of not allowing them to come ashore and of resisting them, and then seeing that the boats came nearer to the shore and that they were not afraid, they drew off from near the sea. And believing that, if two or three men landed from the boats, they would not be frightened, three Christians went on shore, telling them in their own language that they should not fear, for they knew something of it from intercourse with those whom they had with them. Eventually the Indians took to flight, neither large nor small remaining. The three Christians went to the houses, which are of straw and of the form of the others which they had seen, and they did not find anyone or anything in any one of them. They returned to the ships and they hoisted sail at midday to go to a beautiful cape which lay to the east, at a distance of some eight leagues,...

Cuba's Cabo Masaí *"lay to the east at a distance of some eight leagues."* This precise distance to a cape still well below his horizon informs us Columbus was probably basing his estimate on a very accurate map.

...Having gone half a league through the same bay, the Admiral saw toward the south a very remarkable harbor,...

"Having gone half a league through the same bay," put Columbus within view of the entrance to Baracoa's *"very remarkable"* bowl-shaped harbor.

...and on the southeast some marvellously beautiful lands, as it were a hilly tract of land in the midst of these mountains, and much smoke and large villages appeared among them, and the lands seemed to be very cultivated. Accordingly, he determined to run into this harbor and to make an attempt to have speech or dealings with them. The harbor was such that if he had praised the other harbors, he says that he praised this the most, with its lands and temperate climate and its surroundings and populousness. He says wonders of the beauty of the land and of the woods, where there are pines and palms, and of the great plain, which, although it is not entirely flat and stretches away to the south southeast, but is undulated with smooth and low elevations, is the most lovely thing in the world, and through it flow many streams of water, which come down from these mountains...

The view from Baracoa was breath taking. Four miles to the west, El Yunque's dominating "anvil" rose 2000 feet above the jungle canopy, while between Loma Majavara to the east and Loma California to the south, the undulating plain was irrigated by *"many streams"* flowing from the rain-drenched coastal mountains of Oriente Province.

...After the ship had been brought to anchor, the Admiral jumped into the boat to take soundings in the harbor, which is like a bowl. When he was opposite the entrance to the south, he found the mouth of a river, which was wide enough for a galley to enter it, and of such a nature that it was invisible until it was reached. Entering it a boat's length, he found five [27 ½ feet] and eight brazas [44 feet] depth of water...

The Rio Macaguanigua follows Baracoa's circular perimeter to a sandy mouth *"wide enough for a galley to enter"* from this beautiful harbor. It's not surprising this placid coastal *"river"* remained *"invisible until it was reached."* Las Casas seems to have garbled *"depth of water"* measurements more appropriate to the river's width.

...Proceeding by it, it was a marvellous thing to see the trees and the verdure and the very clear water and the birds, and its attractiveness, so that, as he says, he felt that he did not wish to leave it. He went on, telling the men whom he had in his company that, in order to give an account to the Sovereigns of the things which they had seen, a thousand tongues would not suffice for the telling nor his hand to write it, for it seemed to him that he was enchanted. He wished that many other persons, prudent and creditable, could see it, he says, being certain that they would not praise it less than he does. Here the Admiral continues in these words: "How great will be the benefit which can be derived from this land, I do not write. It is certain, Sovereign Princes, that were there are such lands, there must be innumerable things of value, but I do not delay in any harbor, because I wish to see as many lands as I can, in order to give an account of them to Your Highnesses, and moreover I do not know the language, and the people of these lands do not understand me, nor do I or anyone I have with me understand them. These Indians also, whom I carry with me, I often misunderstand, taking one thing for the contrary, and I have no great confidence in them, because many times they have attempted to escape. But now, please Our Lord, I will see as much as I can, and little by little I shall come to understand and know, and I will cause persons of my household to learn this language, for I see that all, so far, have one language. And afterwards the benefits will be known, and an effort will be made to make all these peoples Christian," for that will be easily achieved, since they have no creed and are not idolaters. And Your Highnesses will command that in these parts a city and fortress be established, and these lands will be converted. And I certify to Your Highnesses that nowhere under the sun do I think that there can be found lands superior in fertility, in moderation of heat and cold, in abundance of good and healthy water, and the rivers are not like those of Guinea, which are all pestilential. For, praise to be Our Lord, up to the present among all my people I have not found one who has had a headache or who has been in bed from illness, except one old man through pain from gravel, from which he has suffered all his life, and he was speedily well at the end of two days. This I say is the case in all three vessels...

Maybe there was *"not one who has had a headache,"* but many of Columbus's crew were surely infected by *Treponema pallidum*, the spirochete responsible for syphilis, a disease still unknown in Europe while endemic in the Western Hemisphere. Deluded by its lengthy incubation period, Columbus was unaware his men would ignite an explosive European epidemic shortly after his return to Spain.

....So it may please God that Your Highnesses send here or that there come here learned men, and they will see the truth of all. And since above I have spoken of the situation for a town and fortress on the river Mares, on account of the good harbor and of the surrounding district, it is certain that what I said is true, but it has no comparison with this place, nor has the Sea of Nuestra Señora...

Columbus's enthusiastic *"comparison"* of Baracoa's harbor with the far larger *"Mares"* (Puerto Padre) and *"Sea of Nuestra Señora"* (Tánamo) overlooked its "exposure to northers and the prevailing northeast trades" reported in the *Sailing Directions for the West Indies*. His glowing assessment and its strategic location near native population centers would lead Diego Velásquez to select it as Cuba's first Spanish settlement. Velásquez knew its *"large villages"* would have to be pacified before his settlement could be secured, so he summoned Father Las Casas from Española to serve as the region's chaplain. At Baracoa, Las Casas would observe firsthand his countrymen's mistreatment of Cuba's indigenous population, which, through disease and abuse, would plummet from three million to barely three thousand by the time he transcribed this description of Baracoa a half century later.

...For here inland there must be great centers of population and innumerable people and things of great value, so that I declare that here and in all else that I have discovered and which I have hopes of discovering before I go to Castile, all Christendom will find trade, and more especially Spain, to which all must be subject. And I say that Your Highnesses must not allow any stranger, except Catholic Christians, to trade here or set foot here, for this was the alpha and omega of the enterprise, that it should be for the increase and glory of the Christian religion and that no one should come to these parts who was not a good Christian. All these are his own words...

This rousing proclamation of faith imbedded within the *Journal's* longest transcribed entry may have been stimulated by anticipation of Baracoa's prospective enrichment of Christendom.

...There he went up the river and found some branches of the river,...

The Rio Macaguanigua *"branches"* 500 yards upstream from the river's mouth, within easy reach of an afternoon exploration.

...and going around the harbor he found that at the mouth of the river were some very lovely groves, like a very delectable orchard, and there he found a boat or canoe made of a single piece of wood, as large as a fusta of twelve seats,...

The *"fusta"* was a medieval galley, a long narrow sailing vessel propelled principally by oars.

...very lovely; it was beached under a boat-house or shed made of timber and covered with large palm leaves, in such a way that neither the sun nor the rain could injure it. And he says that there was a suitable place for building a town or city and fortress, on account of the good harbor, good water, good land, good surroundings and abundance of wood.

This laudatory coda may have helped influence Baracoa's selection as Spain's first expansion beyond its Española colony.

WEDNESDAY, NOVEMBER 28th — *He remained in that harbor that day, because it rained and was very cloudy, although he could have run all along the coast before the wind, which was southwest and would have been astern. But because he would not have been able to see the land well and because, not knowing it, it is dangerous for ships, he did not set out. The people from the ships landed to wash their clothes. Some of them went a certain distance inland; they found large villages and the houses empty, because all had fled. They returned down another river, larger than that in which they were harbored.*

This *"larger"* river may be the Rio Miel, which meandered into a wide bay about two miles southeast of their Baracoa anchorage.

THURSDAY, NOVEMBER 29th — *As it rained and the sky was accordingly overcast, he did not set out yesterday. Some of the Christians went to another village, near the northwestern side, and in the houses they found no* *one and nothing. On the way they came up with an old man who was unable to run away from them. They took him and told him that they did not wish to hurt him, and gave him some trifling articles of barter, and let him go. The Admiral would have liked to have seen him, in order to clothe him and have speech with him, because the felicity of that land and its suitability for the formation of a settlement greatly contented him; and he judged that there must be large centers of population. In one house they found a lump of wax which he brought to the Sovereigns, and he says that where there is wax, there must also be a thousand other good things. The sailors also found in one house a man's head [cabeza] in a small basket, covered with another basket, and hanging to a post of the house. They found another of the same kind in another village. The Admiral believed that they must be the heads of some principal ancestors, because those houses were of a kind so that many persons find shelter in one house, and they could only be relations, descendants of one common ancestor.*

This *Journal* isn't the only exploration record still being misread by historians and cartographers. Another prime example is the Cantino World Map of 1502 that features an obvious mapping of North America's southeast coastline from the Mississippi Delta to New York's Montauk Point. Cantino's map reinforces this identity with several place names linking unique coastal features to their locations. These include "pûta Roixa" (a once prominent red coral outcropping at St. Augustine), "Rio de las almadias" (the unique vegetation *rafts* in the St. Johns River), "Rio de los largartos" (Savannah River alligators), "las cabras" (the hazards at Frying Pan Shoals), "Costa alta" (Jockey's Ridge, the coast's highest elevation), "Cabo de bōa ventura" (the winds of Cape Hatteras), and "Costa del mar uçiano (coast of the Oceanic Sea - where the US coastline opens up on the homeward voyages, which is off the eastern tip of Long Island). The westernmost Cantino place name was cropped by one of its owners, but shows up on its several derivatives as "lago de lodo." an apparent reference to the largest "muddy lake" of the Mississippi Delta. Additionally, several of its South American place names match those in Amerigo Vespucci's 18 July 1500 report to Lorenzo di Pierfrancesco. His New World voyage of 14 months allowed ample time for a North American coastal exploration that gave him its naming rights.

Despite the Cantino's obvious depiction of North America's east coast, several historians have variously claimed its "mystery" coastline represents Florida, the Yucatan, or even a *duplicate* mapping of Cuba. One historian was even honored by the American Geographical Society for his 1924 study claiming many of the Cantino's place names originated with *Journal* descriptions of Cuba; three of which were supposedly recorded while Columbus was anchored in Baracoa. One of these was today's gruesome discovery of two "cabeças" that the historian claimed evolved to "cabezas," and then "cabzas," before it resurfaced as "las cabras" a decade later on the Cantino Map. But why would this important map have given Baracoa a place name so tenuously linked to a brief mention in the *Journal*? A stronger linkage can be established with Frying Pan Shoals; an ongoing threat to coastal shipping, which the Cantino appropriately mapped 1000 miles *north* of Baracoa. Those dangerous shoals still evoke appropriate images, such as "meterle a uno las cabras en el corral," an idiomatic expression for "filled with fear."

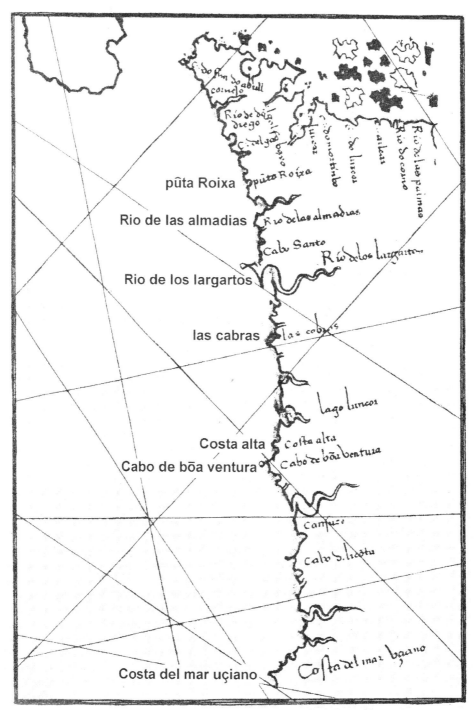

Figure 8-2. Southeast Coast of United States on Cantino Map (1502) – oriented to easily read the place names (south is pointing up)

FRIDAY, NOVEMBER 30th — *He was not able to set out because the wind was east, very contrary to his course...*

Exiting Baracoa through its narrow entrance would have been awkward in the prevailing easterly trade winds. Columbus would remain locked in this harbor until Tuesday by an opposing wind and the morning's tidal pull of a nearly full moon.

...He sent eight well-armed men, and two Indians with them, from among those whom he carried with him, to visit some villages inland and have speech. They reached many houses, and found no person or thing, for they had all fled. They saw four youths who were digging in their fields. When they saw the Christians, they turned at once in flight, and the Christians could not overtake them. They went, he says, a considerable distance; they saw many villages and very fertile land and all cultivated, and large streams of water. Near one they saw a boat or canoe, ninetyfive palms long, made of a single piece of wood, very beautiful, and in which a hundred and fifty persons could be contained and navigate.

The implied precision of *"ninetyfive palms"* suggests Columbus had its 66-foot length stepped off to provide his sovereigns with an accurate description of this *"very beautiful...boat or canoe."*

SATURDAY, DECEMBER 1st — *He again did not set out because of the contrary wind and because it rained heavily. He set up a great cross on some bare rocks at the entrance of that harbor, which, I believe, he called* Puerto Santo. *The point is that which is on the southeastern side at the entrance of the harbor,...*

Columbus *"set up a great cross on some bare rocks...on the southeastern side at the entrance"* of Baracoa, the harbor he had named "Puerto Santo." When Diego Velásquez established Cuba's first capital at Baracoa, he crowned this rocky prominence with the colony's first fortification.

...and whoever wishes to enter this harbor must go rather to the point which is on the northwestern side than to that on the southeast, because, although at the foot of both points, near the rock, there is a depth of twelve brazas [66 feet,] and very clear water, yet at the entrance of the harbor, near the southeastern point, there is shoal above the surface of the water. This is far enough from the point for it to be possible to pass between if there is need, for between the end of the shoal and the cape there is everywhere a depth of twelve and fifteen brazas [~75 feet.] At the entrance, the course is to the southwest.

Baracoa's entrance is bracketed by water depths of 60 feet, with 70 to 80 feet *"everywhere"* between. A threatening *"shoal"* still rises *"above the surface"* 30 yards from *"the southeastern point"* of Punta Barlovento, a gap barely wide enough *"to pass between if there be need."*

SUNDAY, DECEMBER 2nd — *The wind was still contrary and he could not leave. He says that every night there is a land breeze, and that however many ships might be there, they need have no fear of any storm whatsoever since it could not reach the ships inside, on account of a shoal which is at the entrance of the harbor, etc. He says that at the mouth of that river a ships boy found some stones which seemed to bear gold. He brought them to show to the Sovereigns. He says that there are large rivers at a lombard shot from there.*

Those *Journal* omissions indicated by *"etc"* might have clarified this jumbled extract. For starters, there's no *"shoal...at the entrance of"* Baracoa. Instead, *"at the foot of both points, near the rock, there is depth of twelve brazas."* There is a shoal at the entrance to Rio Miel, but this complex river delta is several lombard shots from Baracoa.. Possibly the single *"lombard shot from there"* was intended to measure Rio Miel's distance from Punta Estevé, a commanding elevation at the south end of Baracoa's rock cliff.

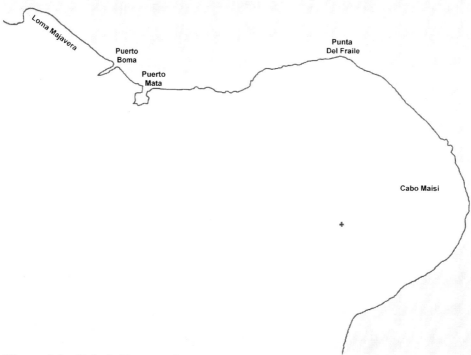

Figure 8-3. Cuba's Eastern Cape - Cabo Maisi (Punta Maisi)

MONDAY, DECEMBER 3rd — *Owing to the fact that the weather was always unsuitable, he did not leave that harbor, and decided to go to see a very lovely cape, a quarter of a league from the harbor, to the southeast. He went with the boats and some armed men...*

Two months earlier Columbus had capped his Egg Island anchorage with an exploration of Royal Island's beautiful harbor. On this, his last full day at Baracoa, he planned to inspect the two remaining Cuban harbors identified by his Indian guides. Heading *"southeast,"* his men rowed past Punta Estevé, the *"very lovely cape"* slightly more than *"a quarter league from the harbor."* This strategic height at the south end of Baracoa's rock cliff was destined to support a Spanish fortress.

...At the foot of the cape there was the mouth of a good river; he steered southeast to enter it, and it was a hundred paces [passos] wide; it was a fathom [braza] deep at the entrance or mouth, but within it was twelve fathoms, five, four and two,...

The boats continued *"southeast"* the length of Loma Majavara to reach Puerto Boma, the harbor fed by a *"good river"* at *"the foot of the cape."* Columbus again demonstrated his keen eye by precisely estimating the entrance channel's width as *"a hundred passos"* (150 yards) where the Rio Boma's depth tapers to one *"braza"* (5.6 feet.) However, the maximum depth *"within"* that entrance channel is barely half the recorded *"twelve fathoms,"* a discrepancy possibly resulting from a copyist misreading a scrawled *"seis"* as *"doce."*

...and as many ships [navios] as there are in Spain could lie there...

In his November 24th entry Columbus had characterized Cayo Moa Grande as large enough for all the *"naos"* in Spain. In today's entry he appropriately limits Puerto Boma's much smaller capacity to all the *"navios"* in Spain. The Cecil Jane and Dunn/Kelley translations both ignored his attempt at differentiation by translating their capacities as "ships." A distinction can be found in the 19th century dictionary of Casares, where *"navios"* is defined as the warships Spain had in far fewer numbers than its fleet of mercantile *"naos."* A century later the Spanish Armada set sail with 22 *"navios"* of the Spanish Royal Navy in a fleet augmented by 108 converted merchant vessels. Spain surely had fewer than 22 *"navios"* in 1492, possibly few enough to *"lie"* in Puerto Boma's tiny basin, 150 yards wide and a quarter mile in length.

...And leaving a branch of that river, he went to the southeast and found a creek, in which he saw five very large boats, which the Indians call "canoes," like fustas, very beautiful and carved, so that he says that it was a delight to see them...

This mention of ubiquitous Indian *"canoes"* stimulated that 1924 historian to link a second Cantino place name, "River of Rafts," to Baracoa's harbor. He ignored the obvious fact that *"canoes"* lacked both the uniqueness and permanence for meaningful identification of coastal features. And he forgot that the Cantino had mapped this place name hundreds of miles south of the same "las cabras" he had already assigned to Baracoa. In my view the Cantino Map was identifying the unique rafts of vegetation tethered by lengthy roots to the floor of Florida's St. Johns River. Three centuries later William Bartram observed how these same "floating islands present a very entertaining prospect." It's likely Amerigo Vespucci had also been entertained by this unique spectacle of floating islands when he recorded their distinctive place name at the appropriate Cantino latitude.

...At the foot of the mountain, he saw that it was everywhere cultivated. They went under very thick trees, and going along the way which led to them, they came upon a houseboat, very well arranged and roofed, so that neither sun nor water could do damage, and in it there was another canoe, made of a single piece of timber like the others, of the size of a fusta of seventeen benches, and it was a pleasure to see its workmanship and beauty. He ascended a mountain and found its top all level and sown with pumpkins and other products of the land, so that it was glorious to behold, and in the middle of it there was a large village...

Loma Majavara is a *"lofty and square"* coastal ridge rising 500 feet above sea level along the coast southeast of Baracoa.

...He came suddenly upon the people of the village, and as soon as they saw them, men and women took to flight. The Indian, one of those whom he carried with him, who accompanied him, reassured them, saying that they need not fear, for they were good people. The Admiral caused them to be given hawks bells and brass rings, and small green and yellow glass beads, with which they were well content,...

His endless supply of cheap trading goods, while appealing to simple natives, would have been inappropriate in the elegant court of China's Grand Khan.

...having seen that they had no gold and nothing else of value, and that he might well leave them in peace, and that all the neighborhood was inhabited, the others having fled from fear. And the Admiral assures the Sovereigns that ten men would make ten thousand take to flight; so cowardly and fearful are they, that they do not bear arms, except some spears, at the end of which there is a sharp stick, hardened in the fire. He decided to return. He says that with some

cleverness he took the spears from them, bartering for them so that they gave them all up. Returning to the place where they had left the boats, he sent some Christians to the place to which they had ascended, because it had seemed to him that he had seen a large apiary. Before those whom he had sent came back, many Indians gathered and came to the boats where the Admiral had now collected all his men again. One of them went forward into the river near the stern of the boat and made a great oration, which the Admiral did not understand, except that the other Indians from time to time raised their hands to heaven and shouted loudly. The Admiral thought that they were reassuring him and that they were pleased with his coming, but he saw the Indian, whom he carried with him, change his expression and become as yellow as wax and tremble greatly, saying by signs that the Admiral should leave the river because they wished to kill him. And he went up to a Christian who had a loaded crossbow and pointed this out to the Indians, and the Admiral gathered that he was telling them all because that crossbow carried far and slew. He also took a sword and drew it from its sheath, exhibiting it and saying the same. When they heard this, they all took to flight, the above-mentioned Indian still trembling from cowardice and faint-heartedness; and he was a man of good stature and strong. The Admiral would not leave the river until he had himself rowed to the shore where they were; they were many, all stained red and naked as their mothers bore them, and some of them had feathers on their heads and other plumes, and all had handfuls of darts. I went towards them and gave them some mouthfuls of bread and asked them for the darts; and I gave to some a hawks bell, to others a small brass ring, to others some small beads, with the result that they were all pacified and they all came to the boats, and they gave whatever they had for what was given to them, whatever it might be. The sailors had killed a tortoise and the shell was in pieces in the boat, and the ships boys gave a piece of it as large as a fingernail, and the Indians gave them a handful of darts. They are people like the others whom I have found, says the Admiral, and they have the same belief and think that we have come from heaven. Whatever they have they give at once for anything that may be given to them, without saying that it is little, and I believe that they would do so with spices and gold, if they had any. I saw a beautiful house, not very large, and with two entrances, for so have they all, and I entered it, and I saw a wonderful arrangement like rooms, made in a certain manner that I know not how to describe, and hanging from the ceiling of it were shells and other things. I thought that it was a temple and called them, and I asked them by signs if they offered prayer in it; they said, no. One of them went up above and gave me everything that was there, and I took some of it.

Today's examination of Puerto Boma left the rowing party insufficient time to study Puerto Mata, the last remaining unexplored harbor on Cuba's north coast.

TUESDAY, DECEMBER 4th — *He set sail with a light wind and left that harbor,...*

With this morning's *"light wind"* Columbus took advantage of an ebbing tide to ease his fleet out of Baracoa's harbor.

...which he named Puerto Santo...

Before leaving Baracoa we should consider the third Cantino place name the 1924 historian attributed to this single harbor. He argued that Baracoa's *"Puerto Santo"* was initially transformed to "Punta Santo" before eventually appearing as "Cabo Santo" on the Cantino Map. But he failed to explain why the Cantino Map would have put this third place name several hundred miles from the pair he had already attributed to Baracoa.

...At two leagues distance he saw a good river, of which he spoke yesterday...

The Rio Boma's mouth, *"two leagues"* southeast of his Baracoa anchorage, identifies it as the same *"good river, of which he spoke yesterday."*

...He went along the coast and all the land ran past the said cape, to the east southeast, and west northwest, as far as Cape Lindo, which is to the east by south of Cape del Monte, and it is five leagues from one to the other...

Punta del Fraile is the modern name for *"Cape Lindo...five leagues...to the east by south of Cape del Monte"* at the north end of Loma Majavara. Columbus was obviously impressed by the beauty of Punta del Fraile's "steep white cliffs" described in the "Sailing Directions for the West Indies."

....A league and a half from Cape del Monte there is a large river, somewhat narrow. It seemed to have a good entrance and to be very deep,...

This measurement confirms Puerto Boma is a *"league and a half"* beyond Punta Rama, a distance consistent with his earlier recording of *"two leagues"* from Baracoa.

...and from there at a distance of three-quarters of a league he saw another very large river, which must have come from a very great distance...

This *"very large river"* flows into Puerto Mata, the final harbor on Cuba's north coast, lying just beyond reach of yesterday's truncated rowing expedition. It is 1¾ miles southeast of Puerto Boma, a distance Columbus inflated to *"three-quarters of a league."*

....At the mouth it is a good hundred paces wide and there is no bar at it, and at the mouth there are eight brazas [44 feet] of water and the entrance is good, because he sent to see and to take soundings from the boat. The fresh water comes down to the sea, and the river is one of the most considerable he has found, and there must be large villages on it...

Puerto Mata's entrance is more than 200 paces in width, but only a "good hundred paces" have adequate depth for shipping. In all other respects its characteristics match those given by Columbus.

...After Cape Lindo there is a great bay, which might be a good passage to the east northeast and southeast and south southwest.

Las Casas abstracted these ENE, SE and SSW bearings from untranscribed text that may have explained their significance. They may represent directions to the three nearest large islands on his Taino maps: *"east northeast"* to Great Inagua, *"southeast"* to Española, and *"south southwest"* to Jamaica.

Part IV – Hispaniola

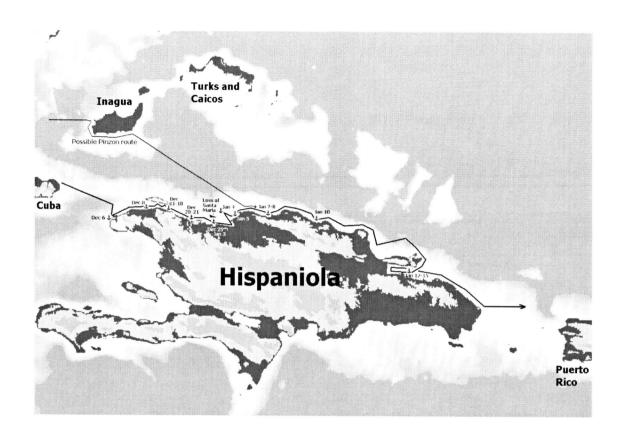

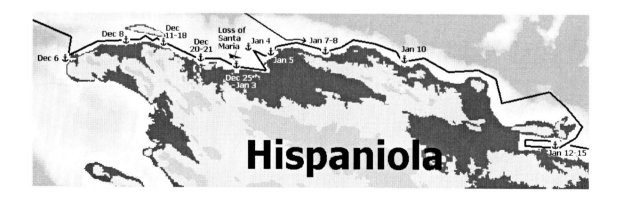

9 - The Island of Hispaniola

WEDNESDAY, DECEMBER 5th — *All this night he beat about off Cape Lindo, where he was at nightfall, in order to examine the land which ran to the east. At sunrise he saw another cape two leagues and a half to the east;...*

Columbus seems to have measured this *"two leagues and a half"* to Punta Fraile from his *"sunrise"* location, not from nearby Punta Silencio.

...having passed that, he saw that the coast trended [bolvia] to the south and inclined [tomava] to the southwest,...

Dunn/Kelley clarified this phrase to read "the coast turned south and trended southwest" east of Punta Fraile, a rendering supported by a Las Casas marginal note.

...and presently he saw a very lofty and lovely cape on the said course, and the distance between the two was seven leagues...

Las Casas neglected to transcribe the southeasterly course Columbus probably followed after rounding Punta Fraile. While *"on the said course"* Columbus could see Punta Caleta's *"very lofty and lovely cape"* marking the latitude of Cuba's south coast. Its 2010-foot peak is the highest in Oriente Province, barely edging out El Yunque, the anvil-shaped peak that had impressed Columbus at Baracoa. The *"distance between"* these two dominant heights measures a fraction more than *"seven leagues"* in a southeast direction paralleling the *"said course"* he was following.

...He would have liked to go there, but he abandoned the idea, because he wished to go to the island of Baneque, which lay to the northeast, according to what the Indians whom he had with him said. Yet he could not go to Baneque either, for the wind which he had was northeast...

Columbus must have been fuming as he imagined Martin Alonso Pinzón harvesting those imaginary gold nuggets on *"the island of Baneque."* Those contrary *"northeast"* winds were actually saving the Admiral a lot of trouble because the only "gold" his insubordinate captain would find on Great Inagua were the barren sand dunes blanketing much of that arid island.

....As he so proceeded, he looked to the southeast and saw land and it was a very large island, of which, as he says, he had already received information from the Indians, who called it Bohio, that it was populous...

Denied access to *Baneque's* "gold" by the contrary wind, Columbus continued on his *"southeast"* course to the *"very large island"* of Española instead of detouring *"south southwest"* to Jamaica. He *"saw"* Española's western peaks soon after entering the Windward Passage separating that island from Cuba.

...Of these people, he says that those of Cuba or Juana and all these other islands are much afraid, because they say that they eat men...

This *Journal* extract is the first of several revealing Columbus had originally named the island for the royal heir, an honor barely surviving the sickly prince's 1497 demise. For clarification Las Casas usually added *"Cuba"* to the island's original name of *"Juana."*

...The Indians told him by signs other very marvellous things, but the Admiral says that he did not believe them, but that the people of that island of Bohio must be more astute and have greater intelligence than they to capture them, because these men are very faint-hearted. So, as the wind was northeast northerly, he decided to leave Cuba or Juana, which up to then he had regarded as being the mainland owing to its extent,...

Columbus finally accepts the reality that Cuba is not the mainland. Next February his widely disseminated letter would confirm, "Juana...was nothing but an island" after acknowledging he had first thought it to be the mainland because "it was so extensive."

...for he had gone fully one hundred and twenty leagues along one side of it...

His February letter would reduce this claim of *"one hundred and twenty leagues"* to a somewhat more reasonable 107 leagues of coastline. It would be speculative to try matching this tempered claim to the 70 leagues of Cuba's coastline Columbus actually sailed, portions of which were variably retraced and frequently inflated by the opposing flow of the Atlantic Ocean's North Equatorial Current.

....And he departed to the southeast by east. Since the land which he had seen trended towards the southeast, this gave protection, because the wind was constantly changing from the north to the northeast and from there to the east and southeast...

Now familiar with the Caribbean's clockwise weather patterns, Columbus offset his initial course to Española by one compass point to accommodate the wind's anticipated rotation.

...The wind changed greatly, and he carried all sail, the sea being smooth and the current favoring him,...

His faulty reading of a *"current favoring him"* could have been caused by Taino maps exaggerating the width of the Windward Passage. But tomorrow's precise Taino mapping of Española makes it more likely Columbus simply made a careless calculation.

...with the result that, up to the first hour after midday, from the morning, he had made eight millas an hour, and that time was six hours, but not quite so, because he says that there the nights are about fifteen hours long...

Barely a week before the winter solstice Columbus surely realized Española's nights lasted only 13 hours. So, why did all three of his recorded measurements stretch that duration by an hour or two? Possibly his *Journal* was deliberately altered to bolster Spain's tenuous claim to continental North America.

...Afterwards he went ten millas an hour. So up to sunset he made some eighty-eight millas, which are 22 leagues, always to the southeast...

Columbus crossed the Windward Passage with favorable winds that brought him to Española's western cape shortly after the 5:20 PM *"sunset."* The Atlantic's opposing NEC inflated his estimate of today's 62-mile sail to *"22 leagues, always to the southeast."* So far, this persistent current has merely inflated some of his speed and distance estimates, but it will soon give him a major Christmas headache.

...And as night was falling, he ordered the caravel Niña, *as she was fast, to go forward in order to examine the harbor before dark. Having arrived at the mouth of the harbor, which was like the bay of Cadiz,...*

The *"bay of Cadiz"* and Española's *"harbor,"* the Baie du Môle, are comparable in size and shape; both nearly two miles wide and more than two miles in length.

...and as it was already night, she sent her boat, carrying a light, to take soundings in the harbor. Before the Admiral came to where the caravel was lying to and waiting for the boat to make signals that she should enter the harbor, the light in the boat was extinguished. The caravel, as she saw no light, ran out and showed a light to the Admiral, and when he came up with her, they told him what had occurred. Just at this point, those in the boat lit another light. The caravel went to it, and the Admiral could not and remained all that night, beating about.

THURSDAY, DECEMBER 6th — *At dawn, he found himself four leagues from the harbor; he named it* Puerto Maria **(A)**. *He saw a lovely cape to the south by west, which he named* Cape Estrella **(B)**, [Cape Foux] *and it seemed to him that this was the last land of this island towards the south, and that the Admiral was distant from it twenty-eight millas [7 leagues]. Another land appeared, like an island of small size* **(C)** [Tortuga] *towards the east, at a distance of about forty millas [10 leagues.] To the east by south, at a distance of some 54 millas [13 ½ leagues,] there lay another very beautiful and well-shaped cape, which he named* Cape Elephant **(D)** [Chaîne du Haut Piton]. *Another cape lay east southeast of him, and this he named* Cape Cinquin **(E)** [Pte Jean-Rabel]; *it was some twenty-eight millas [7 leagues] away. Southeast, easterly, at a distance of some twenty millas [5 leagues] from him, there lay a great cutting or opening or arm of the sea, which seemed to be a river* **(F)**; *it seemed that there was a wide inlet between Cape Elephant and Cape Cinquin, and some of the sailors said that it was a division of the island; that he named* Isla de la Tortuga...

These six long-range distance measurements define the *Santa Maria's "dawn"* location as *"four leagues"* north of Baie du Môle. It's impressive enough that Columbus estimated all six distances so accurately. What's especially noteworthy are errors of less than two percent for Tortuga's nearest peak, a full 30 miles to his east, and Española's Cape Elephant, to which he confidently added a fractional league in estimating its 40-mile range. To fully appreciate his stunning accuracy, consider that Cape Elephant's backlit image was equivalent to one inch and Tortuga's less than a quarter inch when viewed from a distance of 8 feet. I believe his astonishingly accurate distance estimates must have come from a map – a map of far greater accuracy than could be expected of Taino guides far from their home, especially with Columbus still halving their canoe-day estimates. One possible source for his accurate estimates is suggested in the *Journal's* October 3rd entry revealing Columbus had *"information of certain islands in that region."* Accurate mapping of the Caribbean's major islands would have been a fruitful activity for his countrymen after observing the 1477 solar eclipse at totality from the site of his 1492 landfall.

It should also be noted that these six Española coastal measurements converge for a league length of three nautical miles. This convergence rejects Morison's claim that Columbus had created a "land league" of half that length to measure the coastline of under-sized Rum Cay.

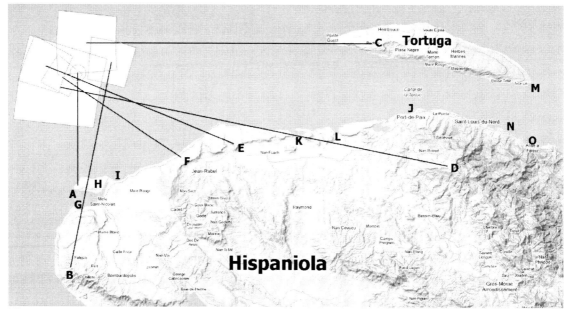

Figure 9-1. Columbus distance estimates aligned with points on northwest coast

Figure 9-2. Northwestern end of Hispaniola

...That large island seemed to be very high land, not fenced in by mountains, but level like lovely farmland, and it seemed to be entirely cultivated or a great part of it, and the crops looked like wheat does in May in the fields of Cordoba. Many fires were seen that night, and by day much smoke as if from lookouts, which seemed to be designed to guard against some people with whom they were at war...

Columbus seems to have been oblivious to how unsettling the intrusion of his majestic fleet must have been to the Caribbean's primitive population. By now, news of his Egg Island landfall had spread south to Española where Indian smoke signals tracked the fleet's movements for an apprehensive populous.

...All the coast of this land trends to the east. At the hour of vespers he entered the said harbor and named it Puerto de San Nicholas, *because it was his feast;...*

Columbus entered Baie du Môle by midafternoon, giving it a new name to replace the *"Puerto Maria"* he had recorded in his *Journal* that very morning.

...and at its entrance he wondered at its beauty and goodness, and although he had greatly praised the harbors of Cuba, yet he says that beyond doubt this is not less to be praised but rather surpasses them, and there is none like it. At the mouth and entrance it is a league and a half wide [de ancho],...

Both the Spanish and English languages can be ambiguous in defining harbor dimensions. Baie du Môle is only half a league *"wide,"* but it does measure exactly *"a league and a half"* from front to back.

...and one should steer to the south-southeast, although owing to its great breadth one can steer in whatever direction one wishes. In this way he went two leagues to the south-southeast...

Las Casas apparently failed to record the first half of Columbus's four-league tacking route to the harbor.

...At its entrance, to the southward, it forms a kind of promontory [angla] **(G)**...

A small cove just inside the harbor's southern cape became the first of five Española "anglas" identified by Columbus. It will become evident that all five of these usages describe the curving shoreline of a "cove," rather than the opposite topographical concept of "promontory" invented to accommodate conventional landfall theories.

...and from there it extends about the same distance to the end,...

It's *"a league and a half"* from this first *"angla"* to the harbor's placid north *"end"* where a narrow isthmus shields its vessels from the Atlantic's fury.

...where there is a very lovely beach and a field of trees of a thousand kinds, all laden with fruit, which the Admiral believes to be spices and nutmegs, but they were not ripe and he did not recognize them. In the center of the beach there is a river. The depth of the harbor is marvellous, since at a distance of the length of a ... from land it could not be sounded or any bottom reached at a depth of forty braças,...

Dunn/Kelley suggest *"forty braçias"* was the standard length of a sounding line, equivalent to 76 feet of depth using the generally accepted conversion factor for Columbus's 1477 tidal measurements. In Baie du Môle this depth generally carries to within a few hundred yards of shore, allowing us to speculate the unit of length lost to this ellipsis was greater than a stone's throw, but less than the range of a crossbow.

...and within that distance it has a depth of fifteen braçias [29 feet] and is very clear. And so the whole harbor within each point at a distance of five feet [una passada] from land is fifteen braçias [29 feet] deep and free from rocks. In the same way all this coast has very deep and clear water, so there does not seem to be a single shoal, and at its foot, at a distance of a boat's oar from land, there are five braçias [10 feet]...

My interpretation of this confusing passage is that Columbus took depth measurements at three distances from shore: a 10-foot depth at an oar's length, 29 feet when 76 feet from shore, and 76 feet at a few hundred yards. He may have been contrasting these ample depths with the worrisome shallows he had faced in the Bahama Islands.

...Beyond the end of the harbor, going toward the south-southeast, and within it, a thousand carracks could beat about; an arm **(H)** *of the harbor extends to the northeast, running into the land a full half-league, and everywhere of the same breadth as if it had been measured with a tape. It lay in such a manner that, being in that arm which was twenty-five paces [passos] wide, the mouth of the main entrance was invisible, as if it were an enclosed harbor. The depth of this arm from its beginning to its end is 11 braçias [21 feet],...*

While the harbor's *"northeast...arm"* is precisely *"a full half league"* in length, its width of 1800 to 2100 feet exceeds the transcribed *"25 passos"* by more than an order of magnitude. This huge discrepancy suggests transcribers misread the 76-foot nautical sounding lines recorded by Columbus as the much shorter *"passos"* familiar to landlubbers. If true, the resulting 1900 feet become a reasonable width measurement of the harbor's *"arm."*

...and it is everywhere basa *or clean sand, and at the shore and at a distance at which the gunwales could be laid against the grass, it has eight braçias [15 feet] depth...*

A century later, French cartographers would tacitly confirm the harbor arm's suitability for careening by naming it *Baie Carénage.*

...All the harbor is very breezy and unsheltered, bare of trees. All this island seems to be more rocky than any other that he had found hitherto; the trees are smaller and many of them are of the same kind as in Spain, such as oaks and strawberry trees and others, and the same is true of the plants. The land is very high and is all open country or clear; the air is very good and he had not found such cold as here; although it could hardly be described as cold, except in comparison with the other lands. Opposite the harbor there was a beautiful fertile plain and in the middle of it the river already mentioned,...

Columbus hints he will soon christen this magnificent island in honor of *"Spain."*

...and he says that in this neighborhood there must be large centers of population, judging from the appearance of the canoes in which they navigate, which are very numerous and as large as a fusta of fifteen benches. All the Indians took to flight and fled when they saw the ships. Those whom he carried with him from the smaller islands were very anxious

to go their own land, and their idea was, says the Admiral, that when he left that place, he would take them to their homes, and they already regarded it as suspicious, that he was not taking the route to their home...

His "*suspicious*" Taino guides were familiar enough with Caribbean geography to realize Columbus was not "*taking the route to their home*" in Eleuthera.

...On this account he says that he did not believe what they told him, nor did he understand them well or they him, and he says that they had the greatest fear in the world of the people of that island. To have speech with the people of that island, he would have been obliged to remain thus for some days in that harbor; but he did not do this, in order that he might discover much land, and because he was doubtful whether the fair weather would continue. He hoped in Our Lord that the Indians, whom he had with him, would learn their language and he theirs, and afterwards he would return and have speech with those people, and with Gods help, as he says, he should have some good trade in gold before his return.

FRIDAY, DECEMBER 7th — *At the passing of the quarter of dawn, he set sail and left the Harbor of St. Nicholas. He navigated with the wind southwest two leagues to the northeast, as far as a cape which the beach makes [que haze el cheranero]; a promontory [angla] lay to his southeast...*

Dunn/Kelley corrected Cecil Jane's translation of "*que haze el cheranero*" to read, "which forms the careenage," an obvious reference to the "*cape*" fronting Baie Carénage. This "*cape*" is "*two leagues*" from the "*Harbor of St. Nicholas*" and bordered "*to his southeast*" by the second "*angla*" **(I)** Columbus had found in Española. Cecil Jane had plenty of company in misreading this cove "*to his southeast*" as an imagined "*promontory.*"

...and Cape Estrella to the southwest at a distance of twenty-four millas [6 leagues] from the Admiral. Thence he navigated along the coast eastward, as far as Cape Cinquin **(E)**, *which was some forty-eight millas...*

The most prominent feature along today's route was Pte Jean-Rabel where the coast veers easterly at the foot of "*Cape Cinquin.*" From there Columbus could glance back to *Cape Estrella*, "*[6 leagues...to the southwest]*," while changing course "*eastward*" to reach an evening anchorage at Port-de-Paix **(J)**.

...In actual fact twenty were to the east by north. All that coast is very high land and there is great depth of water; close to the shore it is twenty and thirty braçias [38 to 57 feet], and it is so deep that at about a lombard's shot from land, bottom could not be reached. All this the Admiral proved that day, much to his delight, as he went along the coast with a southwest wind...

At dawn Columbus had established today's midday target as "Cape Cinquin," the 1181-foot peak now "[5 leagues]... *to the east by north.*" From there he could sail due east to Port-de-Paix, bringing the day's total sail to about 12 leagues in a following "*southwest wind.*" He had to reach Port-de-Paix by nightfall if he was going to take advantage of LPC-16, his first opportunity to measure Española's longitude. His accurate charts informed him a spit of land on the east side of Port-de-Paix would offer an unobstructed view of Jupiter as it rose at 10 PM barely one degree above the Moon.

...The promontory [angla **(I)***] mentioned above, extends, he says, within a lombard shot of the harbor of St. Nicholas, so that if that distance were pierced or cut through, an island would be formed;...*

After planning today's route to reach an LPC observation site just beyond Port-de-Paix, Columbus turned his attention to that *"angla...within a lombard shot"* of Baie du Môle. The 900-yard *"cut"* needed to form this imagined *"island"* is compatible with his *"lombard shot"* of 1000 to 1200 yards at Andros Island.

...the part cut off would have a circumference of three to four millas...

Las Casas made two errors in sizing this conceptualized *"island"* when he incorrectly recorded "the part cut off would have a circumference of 34 millas." Columbus was actually describing how a man-made isthmus would create an island having a *"circumference"* of 3 or 4 leagues. Cecil Jane, and many others, caught his numerical error, but none corrected his *"millas"* into the leagues recorded by Columbus.

....All that land is very high; it has no large trees, but only oaks and strawberry trees, like, he says, the land of Castile...

Deforestation to fuel ubiquitous charcoal cooking ovens has given airline passengers a graphic mapping of the border separating Haiti's barren slopes from the lush forests of the adjoining Dominican Republic

...Before he reached Cape Cinquin, at a distance of two leagues, he found a small opening, like a ravine in a mountain **(F)**, *through which he caught sight of a very large valley, and he saw that it was apparently sown with barley, and he thought that there must be large villages in that valley...*

This *"ravine in a mountain"* is the same *"great cutting or opening or arm of the sea"* Columbus had first seen yesterday morning *"twenty miles"* to his SSE.

....At it sides there rose great and very lofty mountains...

The highest coastal peak along his route to *"Cape Cinquin"* rises 2280 feet above sea level.

...When he reached Cape Cinquin, the head of the island of Tortuga lay to the northeast at a distance of about 32 millas [8 leagues],...

It's only 6 leagues from *"Cape Cinquin"* to Tortuga's western peak, but very nearly *"8 leagues"* when measured from that *"ravine in a mountain."*

...and near this Cape Cinquin, at a lombard shot, there is a rock in the sea which rises high and can thus be easily seen...

The *Sailing Directions for The West Indies* describe "reefs that closely fringe the western side of Pointe Jean Rabel and the shore in the vicinity of Jean Rabel Anchorage" at the foot of his *"Cape Cinquin."*

...The Admiral being off the said cape, Cape Elephant lay to the east by south, and it was some seventy millas [17½ leagues] to it...

The recorded distance is an evident transcription error. Columbus measured this *"east by south"* bearing to *"Cape Elephant"* from his position off *"Cape Cinquin,"* the peak exactly 7½ leagues west of Haut Piton.

....All the land was very high. At the end of six leagues he found a great bay [grande angla **(E-J)***]...*

Española's third *"angla"* was the *"grande"* cove stretching *"six leagues"* eastward from *"Cape Cinquin"* to Port-de-Paix.

...and saw inland large valleys and cultivated fields and very high mountains, all resembling Castile. Eight millas [2 leagues] from there he found a very deep river, but it was narrow, although it would have been possible to enter it in a carrack; the mouth was all clear, without a bar or shoals **(K)***...*

The *Sailing Directions for the West Indies* describe Baie du Port ál Ecu as "a well sheltered cove...about 7 ½ miles eastward of Pte Jean-Rabel." Columbus measured its location from his *"Cape Cinquin"* reference very nearly *"2 leagues"* to its west.

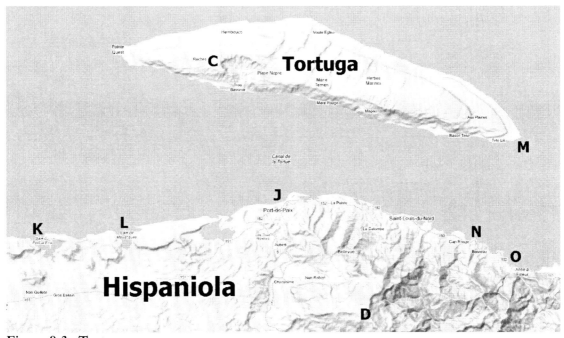

Figure 9-3. Tortuga

...Sixteen millas [4 leagues] from there he found a very wide harbor **(L)***, very deep, so that he could not find bottom at the entrance or at three passos [13½ feet] from the shore, except at fifteen braçias [29 feet], and it ran inland a quarter of a league...*

The next harbor he passed was the *"wide"* and *"deep"* Baie de Moustiques, located somewhat less than *"4 leagues"* east of *"Cape Cinquin,"* and extending *"inland a quarter of a league."* It's not surprising he found a depth of *"[13½ feet]"* within *"[29 feet]"* of shore as the *Sailing Directions* report 100 fathoms less than a quarter mile from the entrance.

...And although it was still early, about an hour after midday, and the wind was astern and fresh, since the sky showed that it was about to rain heavily, and was very overcast, which indicates danger even off a shore which is known and much more off one which is not known, he decided to enter the harbor, which he called Puerto de la Concepción **(L)**...

With a heavy overcast threatening to obscure LPC-16 at Port-de-Paix, Columbus put safety concerns ahead of measurement by terminating today's coastal route at Baie de Moustiques. This proved a correct call after it rained heavily for two days at the same time his *Ephemerides* was alerting him to LPC-17, a stronger measurement opportunity this Wednesday. Shortly after midnight Mars would rise just half a degree above the Moon, but its bearing angle of 88 degrees meant the measurements would have to be taken at mid channel.

...He made land in a river which is not very large and is at the head of the harbor; it flows through some plains and fields, the beauty of which was a wonder to see...

A small river flows through *"plains and fields"* to *"the head of the harbor."*

...He took nets to fish, and before he reached the shore a skate, like those of Spain itself, jumped into the boat. Up to that time he had seen no fish which seemed to be like those of Castile. The sailors went fishing and caught some, as well as soles and other fish like those of Castile. He went a short distance into that country, which is all cultivated, and he heard the nightingales and other birds singing, like those of Castile...

It may have been the melodious *"singing"* of mocking birds wintering in the Caribbean that reminded Columbus of *"the nightingales...of Castile."*

...They saw five men, who would not wait but took to flight. He found myrtle, and other trees and plants, which, no less than the land and mountains, recalled Castile.

SATURDAY, DECEMBER 8th — *There in that harbor they had heavy rain, with a very strong north wind. The harbor is sheltered from all winds, except the north, and that can do no damage, because the surf is heavy and prevents the ships from dragging their anchors or the water of the river from being disturbed. After midnight, the wind changed to the northeast and then to the east, from which winds that harbor is well protected by the island of Tortuga, which lies opposite to it at a distance of thirty-six millas [nine leagues].*

His *"nine leagues"* accurately give the length of yesterday's Española coasting to the *"harbor"* at Baie de Moustiques, *"which lies opposite"* Tortuga's western cape.

SUNDAY, DECEMBER 9th — *This day it rained and the weather became wintry like October in Castile. He had seen no dwelling except a very beautiful house on the harbor of St. Nicholas, which was better made than those in the other places which he had visited. The island is very large and the Admiral says that it would not be an overestimate to say that it has a circumference of two hundred leagues...*

After sailing less than one tenth of Española's perimeter, Columbus was able to estimate its *"circumference of two hundred leagues"* with an error of less than three percent! If he had read the island's dimensions from an accurate Taino chart scaled in their canoe-days, he would have halved the true conversion to leagues. For today's accurate estimate he needed a map scaled in leagues, such as one drawn by the 1477 expedition.

...He had observed that it is all well cultivated. He believed that the villages must be at a distance from the sea and that from them they saw when he arrived and so all took to flight, carrying with them all that they had and lighting warning fires, like soldiers. At its entrance this harbor is a thousand passos wide, which are a quarter of a league; there is in it no bar or shoal, but on the contrary bottom can hardly be found close to land by the seashore. Within it extends for three thousand passos; it is all clear and with a sandy bottom, so that any ship could anchor in it without fear and enter without hesitation. At its end [cabo] there are two river mouths; they bring down little water...

This *Journal* abstract doesn't record Columbus's departure from Baie de Moustiques. But the phrase *"when he arrived"* and his fresh descriptions of *"this harbor"* suggest he had now reached Port-de-Paix, the harbor that *"extends for three thousand passo"* and *"is a thousand passos wide."* On his approach Columbus could have seen *"two mouths"* of the *Les Trois Rivieres* issuing from the *"cabo"* immediately west of the harbor.

...Opposite its end there are some plains, the loveliest in the world, and as fit for sowing as the lands of Castile, and indeed they are superior. For this reason, he named the island Española.

MONDAY, DECEMBER 10th — *It blew strongly from the northeast, which caused the anchors to drag about half a cables length. At this the Admiral was surprised, and he thought that it was because the anchors were near land and the wind blew towards it...*

Columbus didn't need a copy of the *Sailing Directions for The West Indies* to confirm that Port-de-Paix's "bottom is foul in places, and the holding ground bad." He would return to the protection of Baie de Moustiques after deeming neither harbor suitable for viewing LPC-17, Wednesday morning's ascending lunar conjunction with Mars.

...And seeing that the wind was contrary for the course which he wished to follow, he sent six men, well equipped with arms, on land, to go two or three leagues inland, in order to discover if they could have speech...

Apparently Columbus wanted to avoid the multiple tacking maneuvers needed to clear Tortuga's narrow channel in headwinds *"contrary for the course,"* but rejected the simple alternative of circling the island. Schedule permitting, he would wait for a following wind rather than bypass any stretch of Española coastline where gold might be discovered.

... They went and returned, having found neither men nor houses. They found however, some huts and very wide roads, and places where many people had made fires. They saw the best lands in the world, and they found many mastic trees and brought some of it, and they said there was much, but it was not yet the time for gathering it, because it did not form gum.

TUESDAY, DECEMBER 11th — *He did not set out owing to the wind which was still east and northeast. Opposite that port, as has been said, is the isle of Tortuga, and it seems to be a large island and its coast runs almost as does that of Española, and from the one to the other it was, at the most, ten leagues, that is to say, from Cape Cinquin to the head of Tortuga* **(M)***, which is to the north of Española...*

This is yet another astonishing example of his precise cartography, because the east *"head of Tortuga"* is almost exactly *"ten leagues"* from the peak defining *"Cape Cinquin."* It was impressive enough that Columbus had accurately mapped those six distant peaks last Thursday, but today's sea level marker remained out of view more than 600 feet below his horizon! Unless transcribers later doctored this entry, Columbus may have obtained this precise measurement from an accurate map.

...Afterwards its coast runs to the south. He says that he was anxious to examine the strait between these two islands, in order to view the island of Española, which is the loveliest thing in the world and because, according to the Indians whom he had brought there, that was the direction of the island of Baneque. They told him that this island was very great and had very large mountains and rivers and valleys, and they said that the island of Bohio was larger than that of Juana, which they call Cuba, and that it is not surrounded with water. It appears that they meant that it was mainland [tierra firme] and that it is here, behind this Española, which they call Caritaba, and that it is of infinite extent,...

Columbus continues misinterpreting *"Bohio"* as a landmass instead of a native hut, now shifting its imagined location from Española to *"a mainland... of infinite extent."* He would be careful to characterize his discoveries as the "Indies" in his 1493 letter, so today's revelation of a continent *"not surrounded with water"* may have been added later to bolster Spain's New World claims.

...and it appears likely that they are harassed by an intelligent race, all these islands living in great fear of those of Caniba. "And so I repeat what I have said on other occasions," he says, "the Caniba are nothing else than the people of the Grand Khan, who must be very near here and possess ships, and they must come to take them captive, and as the prisoners do not return, they believe that they have been eaten...

Columbus had to reject these tales of cannibalism if he was going to convince his readers *"the Caniba are nothing else than the people of the Grand Khan."*

...Every day we understand these Indians better and they us, although many times there has been misunderstanding," says the Admiral. He sent men ashore; they found much mastic which was not yet gummy. He says that the rains must do this, and that in Chios they gather it in March, and that in those lands, as they are so temperate, they would gather it in January...*

Columbus was personally familiar with the harvesting of mastic trees on *"Chios."* As a young seaman in 1476 he escaped drowning when the Portuguese attacked his ship transporting the island's mastic harvest to northern Europe.

...They caught many fish, like those of Castile — dace, salmon, hake, dory, pompano, mullet, congers, shrimps; and they saw sardines. They found much aloe.

WEDNESDAY, DECEMBER 12th — *He did not set out on this day, for the reason already given of the contrary wind...*

Columbus was forced to ignore LPC-17 when the moon rose at 1:15 AM with Mars a half degree above it. Massive Haut Piton blocked the horizon at his Port-de-Paix anchorage, and the *"contrary wind"* stymied attempts to gain a clear view from Tortuga's south coast.

...He set up a great cross at the entrance of the harbor, on the western side, on a very conspicuous height, "As a sign," he says, *"that Your Highnesses hold this land as your own, and especially as an emblem of Jesus Christ, Our Lord, and to the honor of Christendom." When this had been set up, three sailors went up the mountain [por el monte] to see the trees and plants,...*

Fortress ruins west of the harbor's entrance now mark the likely location of this *"great cross."* The Dunn/Kelley translation of *"por el monte"* as "into the bush" ignores nearby Haut Piton, the highest *"monte"* within view.

... and they saw a great crowd of people, all naked like those found before. They called to them and went towards them, but the Indians took to flight. Eventually they took a woman, as they could not take any more, "For I had given orders," he says, "that they should take some, treat them well and make them lose their fear, that some gain might be made, since, considering the beauty of the land, it could not be but that there was gain to be got." So they brought the woman, a very young and lovely girl, to the ship, and she spoke to those Indians, for they all had the same language. The Admiral caused her to be clothed and gave her glass beads and hawks bells and brass rings, and sent her back to land very honorably, according to his custom. He sent some of the ships company with her and three of the Indians, whom he had with him, to talk to those people. The sailors who went in the boat told the Admiral that when they brought her to land, she did not wish to leave the ship, but to stay with the other Indian women, whom he had taken at Puerto de Mares in the island of Juana or Cuba. All the Indians who were with the Indian woman came, he says, in a canoe, which is for them a caravel, in which they navigate everywhere, and when they appeared at the entrance of the harbor and saw the ships, they turned back and left the canoe in some place there, and went towards their village. She showed them the situation of this village. This woman had a small piece of gold in her nose, which was an indication that there was gold in that island.

THURSDAY, DECEMBER 13th — *The three men, whom the Admiral had sent with the woman, returned at three o'clock at night, and they had not gone with her as far as the village, because it seemed to be far or they were afraid. They said that on the next day many people would come to the ships, since they could only be reassured by the news which the woman would give them. The Admiral longed to know whether there was anything of value in that land and to have some speech with those people, because the land was so lovely and fertile; and he also wished that they might become eager to serve the Sovereigns. For these reasons, he decided to send again to the village, trusting in the news that the Indian woman would have given that the Christians were good people, and for this purpose he selected nine men, well supplied with arms and fitted for such a business, and with them went an Indian, of those whom he carried with him. These men went to the village, which was four and a half leagues to the southeast. They found it in a very large valley, and it was abandoned, for, as soon as they perceived the Christians, all fled into the interior, leaving whatever they had. The village was of a thousand houses and of more than three thousand inhabitants. The Indian, whom the Christians took with them, ran after them, shouting, saying that they need not be afraid, for the Christians were not from Caniba, but rather came from heaven, and that they gave beautiful things to all whom they found. What he said so greatly impressed them that they were reassured, and more than two thousand of them came all together, and they all came to the Christians and placed their hands on their heads, which was a mark of great respect and friendship; yet they were all trembling until they had all been greatly reassured. The Christians said that when at last they had lost their fear, they went to their houses, one and all, and each one of them brought to them what they had to eat, which is bread of niamas, that is, of roots like large carrots which they grow, for they sow and grow and cultivate this in all these lands, and it is their mainstay of life...*

Dunn/Kelley suggest that *"niamas"* is probably a misspelling of *niames*, the Spanish word for cassava, a nutritious starchy tuber widely cultivated in the tropics.

...They make bread from these roots and boil and roast them, and they taste like chestnuts, so that no one eating them would believe that they are anything but chestnuts. They gave them bread and fish, and whatever they had. And as the Indians whom he had in the ship had understood that the Admiral wished to have a parrot, it seems that the Indian who went with the Christians told them something of this, and so they brought them parrots and gave them as many as they asked, without wishing to have anything in return. They asked them not to go back that night, and then

they would give them many other things which they had in the mountains. At the moment when all those people were with the Christians they saw a great array or crowd of people coming with the husband of the woman whom the Admiral had treated with honor and sent back, and they brought her, riding on their shoulders, and they came to give thanks to the Christians for the honor which the Admiral had shown her and the gifts given to her...

Ever a staunch Columbus booster, Las Casas may have transcribed all *Journal* excerpts demonstrating the Admiral's respectful treatment of indigenous peoples.

...The Christians told the Admiral that all these people were more handsome and of better character than any of the others whom they had found up to that time, but the Admiral says that he does not know how they could be of better character than the others, by which he means to imply that all those who had been found in the other islands were of very good character. As to their personal appearance, the Christians said that there was no comparison either for men or women and that they are fairer than the others; among them, they saw two young women as white as any that could be found in Spain. They said also, concerning the beauty of the lands which they saw, that the best lands in Castile for beauty and fertility could not be compared with these. And the Admiral saw that this was so from those lands which he had visited and from those which he had before him, and they told him that these could not be compared with those of that valley, which the plain of Cordoba did not equal, the two being as different as day and night. They said that all those lands were cultivated, and that through the middle of the valley there flowed a river, very wide and great, which could water all the lands. All the trees were green and full of fruit, and the plants all flowering and very tall, the roads very wide and good, the breezes like those in Castile in April. The nightingale and other small birds were singing as they do in that month in Spain, and he says that it was the greatest delight in the world. At night some small birds sang sweetly, and many crickets and frogs were heard. The fish were as those of Spain; they saw much mastic and aloe and cotton trees. They found no gold, nor is this surprising in the very short while that they were there...

First, the good news for his sovereigns - arguably the most lyrical description yet of his discoveries. Then the bad news - they haven't found any gold yet.

...Here the Admiral tested the length of the day and night, and from sunset to sunrise [de sol a sol] was twenty half-hour glasses, although he says that there may have been some error, either because they were not turned quickly enough or because the sand did not all pass through...

All three of his previous solar measurements defined the length of night, while this one defined the day, an important distinction lost in Cecil Jane's careless translation. The 9-day lag of his Julian calendar informs us Columbus chose today's winter solstice for his timely measurement of *"the length of the day and night."* He recorded only *"twenty half-hour glasses"* instead of the actual 22, but was aware of his undercount.

...He also says that he found by the quadrant that he was thirty-four degrees from the equinoctial line.

His final *"quadrant"* reading of Polaris repeats his October 30th mistake of interpreting its tangent scale as measuring *"degrees from the equinoctial line."* His <u>tangent</u> reading of 0.34 defines a latitude of 18.8 degrees, more than one degree too low, in contrast to an October 30th reading nearly one degree too high. Even if Columbus had understood this simple instrument, his careless reading errors were several times larger than the contemporary performance of 15-20 arcmin reported in John Gilchrist's quadrant study. Either Columbus wasn't very handy with the quadrant, or he was ignoring the daily rotation of Polaris about the North Celestial Pole.

FRIDAY, DECEMBER 14th — *He left that harbor of Concepción with a land breeze, and very soon it became calm, as had been the case every day that he had been there. Afterwards an east wind sprang up and he steered with it to the north-northeast; he reached the island of Tortuga...*

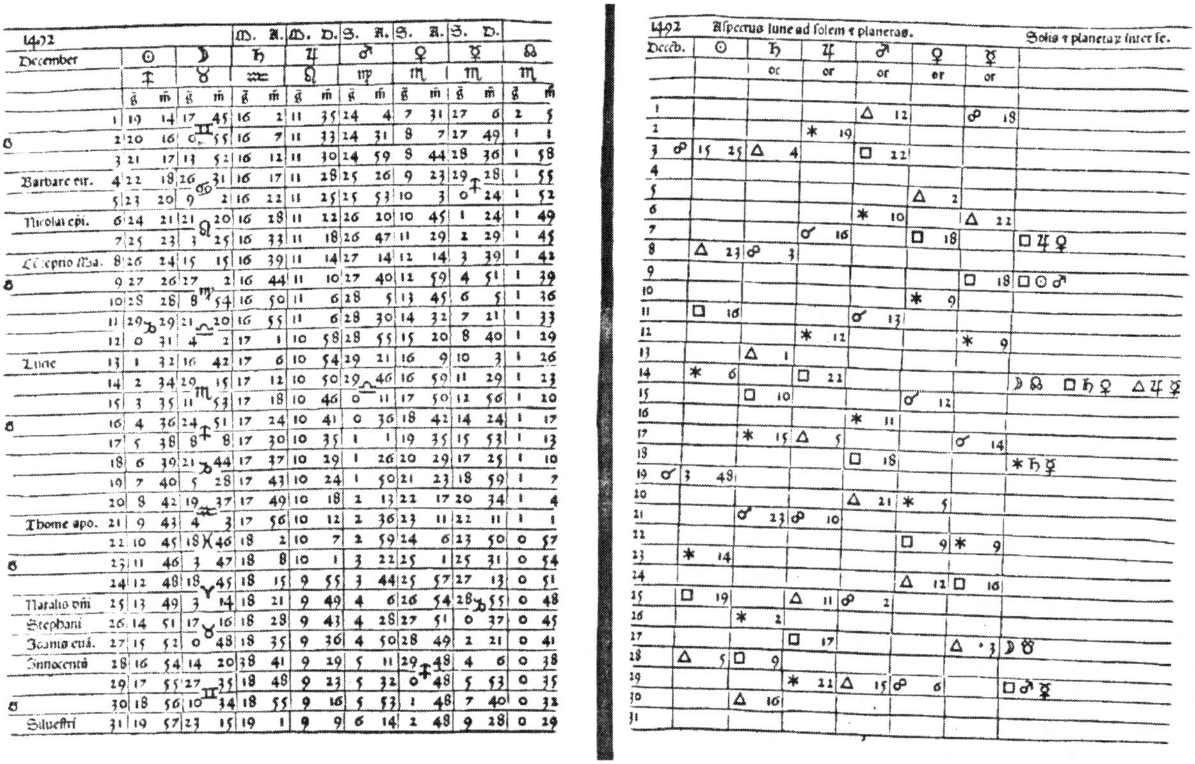

Figure 9-4. December facing pages of the *Ephemerides* created by German Astronomer Johannnes Muller (a.k.a. "Regiomontanus")

His *Ephemerides* informed Columbus that LPC-18 would occur early Sunday morning when the Moon rose 4.3 degrees below Venus. He realized this promising longitude opportunity would be wasted at Baie de Moustiques where moonrise would be blocked by massive Haut Piton. So his first measurement of Española's longitude had best be made from some anchorage on Tortuga's forbidding south coast. Accordingly, *"he steered to the north-northeast"* to reach *"the island of Tortuga,"* hoping for better luck with his third Española opportunity. But Tortuga's only secure anchorage remained out of sight near its eastern cape, leaving a disappointed Columbus unable to measure his longitude.

...and saw a point of it which he named Punta Pierna, *which was to the east-northeast of the head of the island, at a distance of twelve millas [3 leagues]. And from there he sighted another point which he called* Punta Lanzada, *in the same direction to the northeast, at a distance of some sixteen millas [4 leagues]...*

This morning's NNE course did bring Columbus to within sight of two prominent landmarks on Tortuga's south coast, both situated northeasterly of Baie de Moustiques. The modern name for Columbus's "Punta Pierna" (down stroke) is Pte de la Vallée (valley point) at the base of Tortuga's deepest valley, and *"3 leagues"* to the northeast of Baie de Moustiques. The modern

157

name for his "Punta Lanzada" (spear thrust) is Pte Grand Mahé, directly under Tortuga's sharpest peak, *"4 leagues... northeast"* of Baie de Moustiques.

....So from the head of the island of Tortuga as far as Punta Aguda it was some forty-four millas, which are eleven leagues, to the east-northeast. On that course there were some stretches of wide beach...

This first mention of *"Punta Aguda"* suggests Columbus introduced it earlier, possibly to differentiate Pte Jean-Rabel's "sharp" coastal point from Cape Cinquin's adjacent peak. *"Punta Aguda"* is barely 10.5 leagues from *"the [eastern] head of the island of Tortuga,"* but Columbus may have rounded this distance to *"eleven leagues"* to differentiate it from his *"ten leagues"* to Cape Cinquin.

...The island of Tortuga is very high land, but not mountainous,...

Tortuga's mountainous spine is indeed a *"very high land"* rising to an elevation of 2,179 feet above *"some stretches of wide beach."* Española's nearby towering Haut Piton may have influenced his misleading *"not mountainous"* description of Tortuga.

...and is very lovely and very populous, like the island of Española, and the whole island is so cultivated that it looks like the plain of Cordoba...

Whether *"cultivated"* or not, Tortuga's mountainous terrain could never pass for the *"plain of Cordoba."* This Las Casas extract obscures the likelihood Columbus intended his *"whole island is so cultivated"* to describe Española's bountiful lowlands.

...Seeing the wind was contrary and that he could not go to the island of Baneque, he decided to return to the harbor of Concepción, whence he had set out, and he was unable to make a river which is two leagues from the said harbor towards the east.

The onset of a *"contrary"* westerly wind not only prevented Columbus from reaching Great Inagua; he was even *"unable to make"* it back to Les Trois Rivieres, barely *"two leagues...east"* of Baie de Moustiques.

SATURDAY, DECEMBER 15th — *He again left the harbor of Concepción on his voyage, but on leaving the harbor, the east wind blew strongly against him and he steered toward Tortuga, which he reached. From there he went about to examine that river which he had wished to examine and reach yesterday and was unable to do so. On this occasion again he could not make it, although he anchored half a league to the leeward, off a beach, a good and clear anchorage...*

The small inlet *"half a league"* west of Les Trois Rivieres would have provided adequate day anchorage for his ships while Columbus was exploring these rivers by rowboat.

...Having secured his ships, he went with the boats to examine the river and entered an arm of the sea which is half a league short of it and was not a river mouth; he turned back and found the mouth which was not even a braçia deep and where there was a very strong current. He entered it with the boats, to reach the villages which those whom he had sent the day before yesterday had visited; he ordered the line to be thrown ashore and the sailors, pulling at it, brought the boats two lombard shots up, and it was impossible to go farther owing to the strength of the current of the river. He saw some houses and the large valley, where the villages lay, and he said that he had never seen anything more lovely,

and through the middle of that valley flowed that river. He saw people also at the entrance to the river, but they all took to flight. He says further that those people must be greatly hunted, since they live in such a state of terror, because when they arrived at any point, immediately those people made smoke signals from lookouts though out the land, and this was more the case in this island of Española and in that of Tortuga, which is also a large island [grande isla],...

Columbus probably mapped countless islands during his years as an Iberian cartographer. So his *"grande isla"* of Tortuga ought to be orders of magnitude larger than the miniature *"isleta"* describing his San Salvador landfall. Tiny Egg Island easily passes this test, but Watlings Island sprawls over an area nearly as large as Tortuga.

...than in the other islands which he had left behind. He called the valley Valle del Paraiso, *and the river* Guadalquivir, *for he says that it flows as strongly as the Guadalquivir by Cordoba, and on its edges or banks there is a beach of very lovely stones and it is all accessible.*

SUNDAY, DECEMBER 16th — *At midnight, with a light land breeze, he set sail to go out of that gulf [golpho,] and coming from the coast of the island of Española, sailing close-hauled, because presently at the hour of tierce it blew from the east,...*

Once again Columbus reveals the importance he attaches to his celestial longitude measurements. Denied a stable observation site on Tortuga, he rousts his weary crew before *"midnight"* in order to observe the Moon's 4:30 AM rising conjunction with Venus from the open *"gulf"* of the Tortuga Channel. To reach this unobstructed view of LPC-18 above the eastern horizon he had to sail *"close-hauled"* against a wind that *"blew from the east."*

...and in mid-channel [a medio golpho], he found a canoe with a solitary Indian in it...

Tonight's *"mid-channel"* encounter with *"a solitary Indian"* recalls the similar meeting of October 16th while crossing TOTO en route to Andros Island. On that occasion Cecil Jane's landfall theory compelled him to render *"golpho"* as *"channel,"* a distortion repeated here two lines after he had translated the word correctly.

...At this the Admiral was amazed, wondering how he could keep above water, the wind being high. He had him and his canoe taken on board the ship, and to please him gave him glass beads, hawks bells, and brass rings, and carried him in the ship ashore at a village which was sixteen millas [4 leagues] from there near the sea. There the Admiral anchored and found good anchorage by the beach near the village, which seemed to have been recently established as all the houses were new. The Indian at once went ashore in his canoe, and gave news of the Admiral and of the Christians as being good people, although they already held them to be so on account of the experience of the others where the six Christians had gone. Presently there came more than five hundred men, and a little afterwards there came their king. All came down to the beach near the ships, for they were anchored very close to the shore. Then one by one, and many at a time, they came to the ship, bringing nothing with them, although some wore some grains of very fine gold on their ears or noses, which they immediately gave with great readiness. The Admiral ordered honor to be done to all of them, and he says: "They are the best people in the world and beyond all the mildest, so that I have much hope in Our Lord that Your Highnesses will make them all Christians, and that they will be all yours, for I regard them as yours." He saw also that the king was on the beach and that they all showed him respect. The Admiral sent him a present, which he received with much ceremony; he was a young man of some twenty-one years, and he had an old governor and other counselors, who advised him and answered for him, and he himself said very few words. One of the Indians whom the Admiral carried with him spoke to him and told him how the Christians came from heaven and

that their journey was in search of gold and that it was their wish to go to the island of Baneque. He answered that it was well and that in the said island there was much gold, and to the alguacil of the Admiral, who carried the present to him, he showed the route which should be taken, and explained that in two days they could arrive there from this place, and if they had need of anything from his land, he would give it with very good will...

Whatever his motivation, this *"king"* wasn't about to discourage a futile quest for Great Inagua's imaginary gold. The winds must have weakened if that 60-mile detour would require *"two days...to arrive there from this place."*

...This king and all the others went naked as their mothers had borne them, and so did the women, with no trace of shame. They are the most handsome men and women whom they had found up to then, so very fair that, if they were clothed and protected themselves from the sun and air, they would be almost as white as the people of Spain, for this land is very cool and the best that tongue can describe. It is very lofty and on the highest mountain oxen could plough and all could be made like the plains and valleys. In all Castile there is no land which could be compared to this for beauty and fertility; all this island and that of Tortuga is as cultivated as the plain of Cordoba. They have sown them with ajes *[yams], which are certain slips which they plant, and at the foot of them grow some roots like carrots, which serve as bread, and they grate them, knead them, and make bread of them. Afterwards they again plant the same slip in another place and it again produces four or five of these roots, which are very savory and have the exact taste of chestnuts. Those here are the largest and best that he had seen in any land, for he also says that they are found in Guinea; these here were as thick as a leg. He says of these people that they are all stout and valiant and not feeble like the others whom he had previously found, and with very pleasant voices; they have no creed. He says that the trees there grew so luxuriantly that their leaves were no longer green but dark colored. It was a thing of wonder to behold those valleys and those rivers and fair springs of water, and the lands suited for growing bread, and raising stock of all kinds, of which they have none, for gardens, and for everything in the world that a man could desire...*

This effusive description is more suggestive of an Eden ripe for exploitation than admiration for lands supposedly under the control of a powerful Great Kahn.

...Afterwards, in the evening, the king came to the ship; the Admiral showed him due honor and caused him to be told that he came from the Sovereigns of Castile who were the greatest princes in the world. Neither the Indians whom the Admiral carried with him, and who were the interpreters, nor the king either, believed anything of this, but they were convinced that they came from heaven and that the realms of the Sovereigns of Castile were in heaven and not in this world. They placed before the king things to eat from Castile, and he ate a mouthful and afterwards gave it all to his counselors and to the governor and to the others whom he brought with him. "Your Highnesses may believe that these lands are of such extent, good and fertile, and especially those of this island of Española, that no one knows how to describe them and no one can believe it, unless he has seen it. And you may believe that this island and all the others are as much your own as Castile, so that there is lacking here nothing except a settlement and then to command them to do what you wish. For I, with these people whom I carry with me, who are not many, could go about all these islands without meeting opposition, for now I have seen three of these sailors land alone, where there was a crowd of Indians, and they have all fled, without anyone wishing to harm them. They have no arms and are all naked and without any knowledge of war, and very cowardly, so that a thousand of them would not face three. And they are also fitted to be ruled and to be set to work, to cultivate the land and to do all else that may be necessary, and you may build towns and teach them to go clothed and adopt our customs."

MONDAY, DECEMBER 17th — *That night the wind blew strongly from the north-northeast; the sea was not very rough, because the island of Tortuga, which is opposite and forms a shelter, protected and guarded it. He was there in this way for that day. He sent the sailors fishing with nets; the Indians mixed freely with the Christians and* *brought them some arrows [flechas] belonging to the Canibatos or the Cannibals, and they are made of the spikes of canes and are tipped with some small sticks, hardened in the fire and sharp, and they are very large [muy largas]. Two men showed them that some bits of flesh were missing from their bodies and gave them to understand that the Cannibals had bitten mouthfuls from them. The Admiral did not believe this...*

All eleven other *Journal* usages of *"flechas"* are paired with *"arcos"* to describe the bows *and* arrows of these more advanced cultures Columbus had found in eastern Española. This single exception may describe a spear, characterized here as *"very long"* when *"muy largas"* is precisely translated.

...He again sent some Christians to the village, and in exchange for some glass beads they secured some pieces of gold worked into a thin leaf...

Columbus seems to tolerate unfair trade whenever it brings him gold.

...They saw one man, whom the Admiral took for the governor of that province, whom they called "cacique", with a piece of gold as large as the hand, and it seemed that he wished to exchange it. He went to his house and the others remained in the square, and he caused that piece to be broken into small pieces and exchanged it, bringing one small piece at a time. When there was none left, he said by signs that he had sent for more and that the next day they would bring it. All these things, and the manner of them, and their customs and mildness and behavior showed them to be a more alert and intelligent people than the others whom he had found up to that time. The Admiral says: "In the afternoon there arrived a canoe from the island of Tortuga with quite forty men, and when it reached the beach, all the people of the village, which was near, sat down as a sign of peace, and almost all those in the canoe landed. The cacique alone rose, and with words which seemed to be threats, made them go back to the canoe, and threw them water and took stones from the beach and threw them into the water, and after that they all with great obedience settled down and embarked in the canoe. He then took a stone and place it in the hand of my alguacil, whom I had sent to land with the secretary and others to see if they could bring back anything of value, for him to throw it, and the alguacil did not wish to throw it." In this way that cacique showed clearly that he favored the Admiral. Presently the canoe went away, and after it had gone, they told the Admiral that in Tortuga there was more gold than in the island of Española, because it was nearer to Baneque. The Admiral says that he does not believe that there are mines of gold either in that island of Española or in Tortuga, but that they bring it from Baneque and they bring little, because they have nothing to give for it...

An upbeat Columbus rationalizes his disappointment in Española's limited holdings of Great Inagua's *"gold"* by blaming its deficiency on the native's unappealing trade goods.

...That land is so rich that there is no need for them to labor much to get themselves food and clothing, especially as they go naked. And the Admiral believed that he was very near the source of the gold and that Our Lord would show him where it originated. He had information that from there to Baneque it was four days journey, which would be some thirty or forty leagues, so that they could go there in one day of fair weather.

His charts informed Columbus *"he was very near...Baneque,"* the imagined *"source of the gold"* nuggets only 20 leagues from today's anchorage. His estimate of *"four days"* for the Taino to complete that round trip of *"thirty or forty leagues"* tells us he was still limiting their canoes to less than 10 leagues a day. While halving the actual speed of Taino canoes, he knew his own ships could reach Baneque *"in one day of fair weather."* A half century later Las Casas was aware of the actual speed of

Taino canoes when he added his thoughtful postil, "This does not seem to be Baneque, perhaps it was the island of Jamaica," then about 75 leagues from Columbus.

TUESDAY, DECEMBER 18th — *All this day he remained anchored by that beach, because there was no wind, and also because the cacique had said that he would bring gold — not that the Admiral set much store by the gold which he would bring, he say, because there were no mines there, but he would know better whence they brought it. Presently, when dawn came, he commanded the ship and the caravel to be decked with arms and banners for the festival which was the day of Santa Maria de la O, or commemoration of the Annunciation...*

Said to be so identified by Columbus because many of this day's hymns began with the letter "O."

...They fired many shots from the lombards, and the king of that island of Española, says the Admiral, had started early from his house, which must have been five leagues away from there, as far as he could judge, and at the hour of tierce [9 AM] came to that village, where there were already some whom the Admiral had sent from the ship to see if the gold had come. They said that the king was on his way with more than two hundred men, that four men carried him in a litter, and that he was a young man, as has been said above. Today, while the Admiral was dining below the castle, he came to the ship with all his people. And the Admiral says to the Sovereigns; "There is no doubt that your Highnesses would think well of his estate and of the respect which all have for him, although they all go naked. As soon as he came on board the ship, he found that I was eating at the table below the stern castle, and, hurrying up, he came and seated himself beside me, and he would not allow me to go to meet him or to rise from the table, but wished me to continue my meal. I thought that he would be pleased to eat of our viands; I immediately commanded things to be brought for him to eat. And when he came in below the castle, he made signs with his hand that all his men should remain outside, and they did so with the greatest readiness and respect in the world, and they all seated themselves on the deck, except two men of mature age, whom I think were his counselors and one his governor, who came and sat at his feet. And of the viands which I placed before him, he took of each kind as much as may be taken to taste it and afterwards at once sent the rest to his people, and they all ate of them. So also he did with what he was offered to drink, for he merely raised it to his lips, and then gave it to the others. All this was done with wonderful ceremony and with very few words, and such words as he did say, so far as I could understand them, were very formal and sensible, and those two men watched his face and they spoke for him and with him, and with great respect. After having eaten, a page brought a belt, which is like those of Castile in shape but of different workmanship, and this he took and gave to me, and two pieces of worked gold, which were very thin, so that I believe that here they obtain very little of it, although I hold that they are very near where it is found and where there is much. I saw that a drapery which I had above my bed pleased him; I gave it to him, and some very good amber beads which I was wearing around my neck, and some red shoes and a flask of orange flower water, at which he was so pleased that it was wonderful. And he and his governor and counselors were very grieved because they did not understand me or I them. All the same I realized that he told me that, if I required anything from there, the whole island was at my disposal. I sent for some beads of mine, among which I had as a token a gold exelente, *on which Your Highnesses are depicted, and I showed this to him, and I told him again, as I had yesterday, that Your Highnesses rule and command all the best part of the world, and that there are no princes so great, and I showed him the royal standards and the others with the cross. At this he was much impressed, and he explained to his counselors that Your Highnesses must be great sovereigns, since you had sent me from so far and from heaven without fear to this place. And many other things passed, and I did not understand anything except that I could see well that they regarded everything as wonderful." Afterwards, as it was already late, and he wished to go, the Admiral sent him in the boat very honorably, and had many lombards fired, and when he had entered his litter and went away with his men, who were more than two hundred, and his son was borne behind him on the shoulders of an Indian, a very honorable man. To all the sailors and people of the ships, wherever he found them, he commanded that they should be given to eat and that much honor should be paid to them. A sailor*

said that he had met him on the way and had seen all the things that the Admiral had given to him, and all of them carried a man, who seemed to be on of the most important personages, before the king. His son followed at a good distance behind the king, with as great an escort of people as he, and so did another, a brother of the same king, except that the brother went on foot, and two principal men held him by the arm. He came to the ship after the king, and to him the Admiral gave certain things of the articles of barter, and there the Admiral learned that in their language they called the king Cacique. *On this day they bartered little gold, but the Admiral learned from an old man that there were many islands near, at a distance of a hundred leagues or more, as far as he could understand, in which very much gold was produced,...*

This *"old man"* may have been instrumental in shifting Columbus's golden quest from Great Inagua Island to Puerto Rico, nearly 110 leagues east of today's Baie de Moustiques anchorage.

...so much that the old man told him that one island was all gold and that in the others there was so great a quantity that they gather it and sift it with sieves, and they smelt it and make bars and a thousand worked articles; he explained the making by signs. This old man indicated to the Admiral the direction and location of the gold; the Admiral resolved to go there,..

Puerto Rico appeared to be a promising source of *"very much gold,"* but it was *"a hundred leagues or more"* to the east, so an impatient Columbus *"resolved to go there...This night"* instead of waiting for dawn.

...and he says that, if it had not been that this old man was so important a subject of that king, he would have detained him and taken him with him. Or, if he had known the language, he says, he would have asked him to come, and he believes, as he was friendly with him and the Christians, that he would have gone willingly. But, as he already held those people for the Sovereigns of Castile, and as there was no wisdom in offending them, he decided to let him go. He set a very mighty cross in the center of the square of that village, in which work the Indians greatly assisted, and, as he says, they offered prayer and adored it, and from the signs which they give, the Admiral hopes in Our Lord that all those islands will become Christian.

10 - The Loss of the Santa Maria

WEDNESDAY, DECEMBER 19th *— This night he set sail, to go out of that gulf [golpho] which the island of Tortuga there makes with Española,...*

Columbus had been anchored at Baie de Moustiques nearly a fortnight waiting for a westerly wind to carry him *"out of that gulf which the island of Tortuga there makes with Española.* Cecil Jane and Dunn/Kelley both rendered *"golpho"* correctly here, freed from the constraints imposed by the lack of a *"gulf"* near Rum Cay.

...and when day came, the wind changed to east, so that all this day he could not come out from between those two islands, and at night he was not able to make a harbor which appeared there...

"When day came, wind changed to east," leaving Columbus unable *"to make"* Rade Basse Terre, *"a harbor"* five miles short of Tortuga's eastern cape. This harbor is Tortuga's "only good anchorage" according to the *Sailing Directions for the West Indies.*

...He saw near there four points of land **(N)** *and a large bay and river* **(O)***,...*

At last freed from the headwinds locking him in the Tortuga Channel, Columbus sailed past Española's *"four points of land"* bracketing Pte Vent. Directly to their east he came upon Anse a Foleur, *"a large bay,"* bisected by the *"river"* Bas de Sainte-Anne.

...and beyond he saw a very great bend [angla muy grande],...

Two months earlier Columbus had sailed past the *"grande angla"* formed by Long Island's eight miles of concave coastline. Today's *"angla muy grande"* was a concave coastline extending three times that distance to Haut du Cap-Haïtien **(P)**, seen rising above the eastern horizon.

...and there was a village and at the side a valley between many very lofty mountains: they were full of trees which he thought to be pines. Above Dos Hermanos **(Q)***, there was a very high and broad mountain, which ran from northeast to southwest;...*

Shortly after entering the *"angla muy grande,"* Columbus sailed by Fond la Grange, a deep *"valley between many very lofty mountains."* Las Casas hadn't transcribed any previous references to "Dos Hermanos," most likely the pair of small coastal heights embracing Chouchou Bay. From there Columbus had his first view of Haut du Cap-Hatien, the eastern anchor of a mountain range running *"from northeast to southwest."*

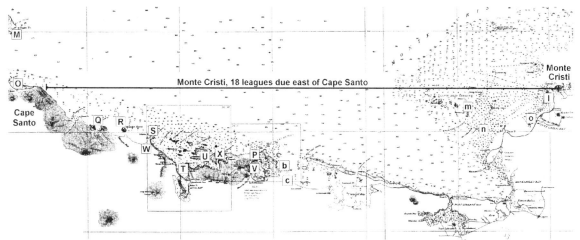

Figure 10-1. Cape Santo to Monte Cristi

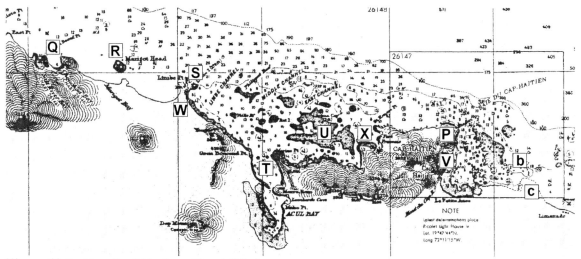

Figure 10-2. Detail of Marigot Head (R) Area

...and on the east-southeast of Cape Torres [towers] *there is a small island, which he called* Santo Tomas **(R)**, *because it is his vigil tomorrow...*

Marigot Head is the next *"small island"* to *"the east-southeast"* of "Dos Hermanos," those two pinnacles embracing Chouchou Bay. But Las Casas seems to have omitted Marigot Head from his transcript because Limbé Island has a much tighter congruence with all subsequent references to "Santo Tomas."

...The whole circuit of that island had capes and marvellous harbors, as he judged viewing it from the sea. To the westward, before the island, there is a cape which runs far out to sea, part of it being high land and part low, for which reason he named it Cape Alto y Bajo **(S)**...

Limbé Point, to *"the westward, before the island"* of Santo Tomas, is the "Cape Also y Bajo" rising 200 feet *"high"* from the *"low"* mangrove swamp connecting it with Española.

165

...To the east, east by south, from Cape Torres it is 60 millas [15 leagues] to a mountain higher than the other, which juts into the sea and from a distance seems to be an island apart, owing to a ravine which there is on the land side. He named it Monte Caribata, because that province was called Caribata...

Haut du Cap-Haïtien gives the appearance of *"an island apart"* that *"juts into the sea"* exactly five leagues *"east by south"* of those Chouchou Bay "towers." The careless recording of this distance as "15 leagues" is a reminder that no landfall theory should be rejected on the basis of a single piece of evidence transcribed from a secondhand copy of Columbus' original log.

...It is very lovely and full of trees, a vivid green, and without snow or mists round it; and it was there at that time like March in Castile so far as the breezes and temperature were concerned, and like May for the trees and plants. He says that the nights were fourteen hours.

One week after the Winter Solstice, the *"nights were fourteen hours"* in Charleston, South Carolina, one hour longer than they were in Española. This is another example of how the *Journal* may have been doctored in the early 16th Century to bolster Spain's fading claim to North America.

THURSDAY, DECEMBER 20th — *Today, at sunset, he entered a harbor* **(T)** *which was between the island of Santo Tomas and Cape Caribata, and anchored. This port is most beautiful and one in which all the ships of Christendom could lie...*

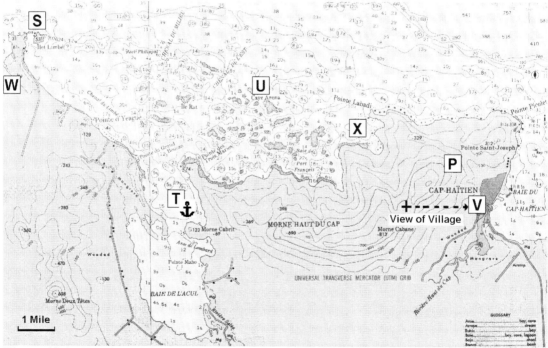

Figure 10-3. Roadstead for *"all the ships of Christendom"*, Acul Bay, and Nearby Village

Columbus had stood off Limbé Point all Wednesday night rather than risk a moonless challenge of the roadstead's forbidding reefs. Today, after surveying roughly 20 square miles of the roadstead, he judged it large enough for *"all the ships of Christendom,"* His survey completed, *"at sunset, he entered"* Acul Bay, the *"beautiful"* enclosed harbor on the roadstead's south coast where he *"anchored"* in its well-protected shallows.

...From the sea its entrance appears to be impossible to those who have not entered it, owing to some reefs of rocks which extend from the mountain almost as far as the island and which are not in a continuous line but are some here and some there, some being out to sea and others near the land. Consequently one has to be on watch to enter by some gaps which there are, very wide and good, so that it is possible to enter without fear; and all very deep, seven braças [13 feet]...

The reef's three major channels, Limbé, Middle and East, are each *"very wide and good,"* and have depths generally exceeding several fathoms. A fourth narrow channel, which Columbus would follow to his Christmas disaster, had a controlling depth of barely a dozen feet.

...and when the reefs are passed, within it is twelve braças [23 feet]...

Much of Acul Bay was too shallow for the *Santa Maria*, but it had depths up to 40 feet near its entrance. Columbus anchored in *"twelve braças,"* possibly at Anse de Lombard, a sheltered cove at Acul Bay's northeast corner.

*...The ship can be fastened with any cable against whatever wind blows. At the entrance of this harbor he says that there was a channel, which lay to the west of a sandy island [isleta]***(U)*** *and on which there are many trees, and up to the edge of it there are seven braças [13 feet]...*

Limbé Channel is the west *"entrance of this harbor...which lay to the west of a sandy [isleta]"* called Rat Island, the harbor's only islet with convenient anchorage for the *Santa Maria*. But it wouldn't be a suitable site for viewing tomorrow evening's LPC-19 when the Moon and Saturn set behind hills rising more than two degrees above the horizon.

...But there are many shoals near, and it is necessary to keep the eye open until the harbor has been entered; afterwards, there is no fear of any tempest in the world. From that harbor, a very large valley appeared, all cultivated; it ran down to the harbor from the southeast and was all fenced in by very lofty mountains, which seemed to touch the sky, and which were very beautiful, full of green trees, and without doubt there are there loftier mountains than the island of Tenerife in the Canaries, which is held to be one of the loftiest that can be found...

Columbus continues with his hyperbolic discovery claims; Española's highest elevation is actually less than a third of Tenerife's *"loftiest."*

...At a league from this part of the island [deste parte de la isla} of Santo Thomas there is another islet,...

There are numerous shoals but only two islets, Rat Island and Arena Cay, within the extensive shallows embraced by *"Santo Tomas and Cape Caribata."* Arena Cay offered a better platform than Rat Island for measurement of LPC-19 because it was twice as far from those coastal hills. But this quarter-acre sand dune was surrounded by dangerous shoals and could only be approached by rowboat. Neither viewing site was satisfactory, forcing Columbus to search for an elevated alternative.

...and within that another, and in all there are wonderful harbors, but it is essential to be on the watch for shoals. He saw also some villages [poblaçiones] and the smoke which they made.

Columbus systematically differentiated between the Indian's small "villages" (pueblos) and their "towns" (poblaçiones), a distinction frequently ignored by Cecil Jane.

FRIDAY, DECEMBER 21st — *Today he went with the ships boats to see that harbor...*

Columbus *"went in the ships boats"* to survey Arena Cay, the islet with the widest expanse of open water along LPC-19's bearing angle of 256 degrees.

...He saw it to be such that he affirms that none of those which he had ever seen equaled it. And he excuses himself, saying that he has praised those already visited so much, he does not know how to praise this, and he fears that he may be thought to extol excessively and out of proportion. He meets this charge, saying he has with him old sailors, and they say and will say the same, as will all who go to sea, that is, they will assent to all the praise which he has given to the harbors already seen, and agree that it is also quite true that this is much better than all. He goes on to the following effect; "I have spent twenty three years at sea, without coming off it for any time worth mentioning and I have seen all the east and west..."

Taken literally, to *"have seen all the east and west"* is suggestive of Columbus's claim to have sailed "100 leagues beyond the island of Thule" in 1477.

...as he says, by going on the northern voyage, which is England,...

Las Casas wasn't about to detract from his hero's 1492 accomplishment, so he may have substituted this single line of abstracted text to conceal a more detailed description of that 1477 "northern voyage."

...and I have gone to Guinea, but in all these parts I have not found the perfection of these harbors...

After possibly skirting 1477 evidence, Las Casas reverts to his verbatim transcription. But his censorship standards may have been too lax for Spanish authorities because his transcript is interrupted at this point by almost two full lines of deleted text — the *Journal's* only multi-word ellipsis. Historians might gain new insights into New World explorations by applying modern technology to the recovery of this deletion.

...having found the...better than the other, so that I considered with great care what I have written, and again I assert that I have written well,...

This *Journal* ellipsis may have lost a harbor comparison.

...and that now this harbor surpasses all, and in it all the ships of the world could lie and be secure, with the oldest cable on board a ship it would be held fast."

Today's expanded search for a satisfactory LPC-19 observation site may have revealed this *"harbor"* extended east of Cap-Haitien, moving Columbus to enlarge yesterday's capacity estimate to *"all the ships of the world."*

...From the entrance to the end of the harbor it is five leagues...

A roadstead expansion to the shallows east of Cap-Haïtien would put this "*end of the harbor...five leagues*" from its western "*entrance*" at "the island of Santo Thomas."

...He saw some very cultivated lands, although all are such, and he ordered two men to land from the boats and go to a height in order to see if there was a village [poblaçion], since from the sea none was visible,...

One more Indian "*town*" may have been of some interest, but his immediate need was an elevated viewing site with an unobstructed horizon below tonight's LPC-19. So Columbus had "*two men*" scale Haut du Cap-Haïtien to find a site better than Rat Island. Apparently he lost interest in this elevated observation site after his men saw that a 3600-foot peak would block his western horizon directly below LPC-19. From their panoramic perch these men may have observed the dominating southerly peak where three centuries later their Admiral's namesake, Henri Christophe, would erect his massive citadel. As the surviving leader of Haiti's successful slave revolt against its French overlords, Christophe would conscript 20,000 workers for its construction. These conscripts labored under the tropical sun for more than a decade before completing his formidable fortress in 1820, the year of his suicide.

...although on that night, about ten o'clock, certain Indians came to the ship in a canoe to see and marvel at the Admiral and the Christians, and he gave them of the articles of barter, at which they were much pleased...

In this delayed recording Columbus wedged a premature mention of tonight's visit into his afternoon search for an LPC-19 viewing platform. He apparently favored Arena Cay's convenience over Haut du Cap-Haitien's better western horizon, because he returned to the *Santa Maria* by "*about ten o'clock*" to greet "*certain Indians.*"

...The two Christians returned and said that from there they had seen a large village [poblaçion grande] **(V)***, at a short distance from the sea...*

This "*poblaçion grande*" at the foot of Haut du Cap-Haitien was less than two miles from the mountaintop lookout of those "*two Christians.*" The city's strategic location below those heights allowed for timely warning of Puerto Rican raiders as well as unrestricted access to fresh water. The French wouldn't establish it as the island's capital for several decades, but today's lookouts must have been impressed by its large precursor, the home of Guacanagarí, leader of Española's northern province.

...The Admiral ordered them to row towards the place where the village [poblaçion] was until they came near the land. He saw some Indians who came to the seashore, and as they appeared to do so without fear, he ordered the boats to be stopped, and the Indians, whom he carried with him in the ship, to tell them that he would do them no ill. They then came nearer the sea and the Admiral went nearer to the land, and when they had entirely lost their fear, so many came, men and women and children alike, that they covered the earth, giving great thanks. Some of them ran here and some there to bring us bread which they make of niñames, *which they call* ajes, *and which is very white and good, and they brought us water in gourds and clay pitchers, made like those of Castile, and they brought to us all that they had in the world and which they knew that the Admiral desired. They did all this with such generosity of heart and such joy that it was wonderful...*

Today's prompt offer of the drinking water *"that the Admiral desired"* contrasts with the 2-day delay at October's landfall. This delay would have been pointless at Watlings Island, but understandable at Egg Island where the Taino would need to cross Royal Island's channel carrying *"water in gourds and clay pitchers."*

...*"And it is not to be said that because what they gave was of little value, they therefore gave it liberally"*, says the Admiral, for they did the same and as freely when they gave pieces of gold as when they gave a gourd of water, and it is easy to know," says the Admiral, *"when something is given with a great readiness to give."* These are his words. *"These people have no spears or darts or any other arms, nor have the others in all this island, and I hold that this island is very large. They are as naked as when their mothers gave them birth, men and women alike; for in the other lands of Juana and of the other islands women wear some cotton articles in front with which they cover their privy parts, rather like a pair of men's drawers, especially after they pass the age of twelve years, but here neither young nor old do so. And in other places all the men endeavored to conceal their women from the Christians owing to jealousy, but here they do not. There are some very well formed women, and they were the first to come to give thanks to Heaven and to bring whatever they had, especially things to eat, bread of* ajes, chufa,...

Cecil Jane identified the *"chufa"* is a "small tubercule, produced by a reed-like plant...Apparently the Indians ate the small tubercules as we do nuts."

...*and five or six kinds of fruit,"* which the Admiral ordered to be preserved that he might bring them to the Sovereigns. He says that the women in other places did the same before they were concealed, and the Admiral everywhere ordered all his men to be careful not to offend anyone in any way, and to take nothing from them against their will, and so they paid them for everything which they received from them. Finally the Admiral says that it is impossible to believe that anyone has seen a people with such kind hearts and so ready to give and so timorous, that they deprive themselves of everything in order to give the Christians all that they possess, and when the Christians arrive, they run at once to bring them everything. Afterwards the Admiral sent six Christians to the village [poblaçion] in order to see what it was...*

Columbus wasn't about to let a visit to this newly discovered *"poblaçion grande"* disrupt plans for this evening's longitude measurement. But he wanted to establish contact with this large city, so he sent *"six Christians"* by boat to meet with Guacanagarí and map a route through the shallows for the fleet to follow a few days later.

...*To these men, they did every honor that they could and knew, and gave them whatever they had, so no doubt remained but that they believed that the Admiral and all his people had come from heaven. The same was the belief of the Indians whom the Admiral carried with him from the other islands, despite the fact that they had been already told what they ought to think. After the six Christians had gone, some canoes came bringing people to ask the Admiral, on behalf of a chief man, to go to his village when he left this place. "Canoa" is a vessel in which they navigate, and some of them are large and some small. And having found that the village of that chief was on his way, on a point of land, and that he was awaiting the Admiral with many people, he went there;...*

The *"point of land"* near this *"village"* may be the *Punta Santa* mentioned two days hence.

...*and before he set out, there came to the shore so many people that it was alarming, men, women and children shouting that he should not go away but remain with them. The messengers of the other chief, who had come to invite him, remained waiting with their canoes, so that he should not go without coming to see the chief. And he did so; and when the Admiral came to that place where that lord was awaiting him and had a great many things to eat, he commanded all his people to sit down. He ordered them to carry the food they had to the boats, where the Admiral was, close to the seashore. And as he saw that the Admiral had accepted what they had brought, all or most of the Indians started to run to the village which must have been near, to bring him more food and parrots and other things which they had, with such generosity of heart it was a wonder. The Admiral gave them glass beads and brass rings and hawks bells, not because they asked for anything, but because it seemed to him to be right, and above all, says the Admiral, because he holds them to be already Christians and to belong to the Sovereigns of Castile more than do the peoples of Castile. And he says that nothing was lacking save to know the language and to give them orders, because every order that was given to them they would obey without any opposition. The Admiral went back to the ships, and the Indians, men and women and children alike, shouted that the Christians should not go away and that they should remain with them. When they had gone, there came after them to the ship canoes full of them, to whom he caused much honor to be done and food to be given, and other things which they took with them. There had also come before another lord from the west, and many people even came swimming, and the ship was more that a full half league from land...*

This *"lord from the west"* was the second minor chieftain Columbus would entertain today.

*..."The lord, whom I mentioned, had gone back; I sent certain persons to see him and ask him of these islands." He received them very well and took them with him to his village, in order to give them some large pieces of gold; they reached a large river **(W)** which the Indians crossed by swimming; the Christians could not do so, and accordingly turned back. In all this neighborhood there are very high mountains, which seemed to reach the sky,...*

A *"large river"* flows into the roadstead 1.5 miles southwest of Limbé Island.

...so that the mountain of the island of Tenerife appears to be nothing in comparison with them, in height and in beauty,...

Columbus continues to have trouble containing his enthusiasm: Haut Piton, the highest Española peak he had seen yet, rises less than one third the height of Tenerife's volcanic cone.

...and all are green, full of woods, so that it is a thing of wonder. Between them there are very fair plains, and at the end of this harbor, to the south there is a plain, so extensive that eyes cannot see its end; there is no mountain to interrupt it and it seems that it must be fifteen or twenty leagues. Through it runs a river and it is all populated and cultivated, and is as green now as if it were in Castile in May or June, although the nights are fourteen hours long and the land is so far north...

This measurement of *"fourteen hours"* repeats the one-hour exaggeration recorded two days earlier. Spanish authorities, apprehensive of English encroachment on their New World discoveries, may have again deliberately altered Columbus's measurement; this time embellishing their deception with the misleading observation *"the land is so far north."*

...This harbor is good whatever winds may blow, protected and deep, and all inhabited by a people very good and gentle, and without arms, good or ill. In it any ship may lie without fear that other ships might come by night to attack her, because, although the mouth may be more than two leagues wide, it is to a great extent closed by two reefs of rock [restringas de piedras], which scarcely appear above water...

The implication here may be that *"restringas de piedras"* usually rose well *"above water."* If true, this identical phrase during the inspection of San Salvador's harbor fits Royal Island's exposed limestone ridge, but not the submerged reefs fronting Watlings Island.

...In this reef, however, there is a very narrow passage, which looks as if made by hand, leaving an opening wide enough for ships to enter. At the mouth, there is a depth of seven braçèas, [13 feet] so far as the foot of a flat islet, which has a beach and trees at its foot...

The roadstead's *"very narrow"* East Channel is only 200 yards wide, but its lined edge provided a useful guide from Rat Island to the harbor's mouth. Columbus demonstrated some consistency here by repeating yesterday's description of *"seven braçias"* and *"trees"* for this islet. When Columbus returns to this solitary islet tomorrow he will christen it *"La Amiga,"* perhaps because it was also the roadstead's best anchorage for awaiting a westerly wind.

...On the west side, there is an entrance; a ship can without fear come near enough to touch the shore near the rock. On the northwestern side, there are three islands,...

Limbé Channel, the roadstead's western passageway, has adequate depth near the shore's *"rock"* ledge. Several closely spaced *"islands"* on the *"northwestern side"* of this roadstead confirm its identity.

...and there is a great river a league from the end of this harbor...

The *"great"* Rivière Salée meanders into Acul Bay's headwaters almost *"a league"* south of the inner harbor's entrance.

...It is the best in the world; he named it Puerto de la Mar de Santo Tomas, *because today is his day; he called it "mar" because of its great extent.*

SATURDAY, DECEMBER 22nd — *At daybreak, he set sail to proceed on his way, in search of the islands which the Indians told him had much gold, and some of which they declared to have more gold than earth. The weather was not favorable, and he was obliged to anchor again,...*

"At daybreak," Columbus sailed from Acul Bay, but he would have to wait until the wind shifted westerly before threading his way eastward through the roadstead's narrow channel. So he dropped *"anchor"* at Rat Island, well positioned for an easterly track through the shallows when the wind turned favorable. The island's name suggests it may share a dubious distinction with the Rat Island Columbus explored at his October landfall — the New World's first breeding grounds for Old World rats escaping their shipboard confinement.

...and he sent the launch to fish with the net. The lord of that land, who had his village [lugar] near there, sent him a large canoe, full of people, and in it one of his principal servants, to ask the Admiral to go with the ships to his land, telling him that he would give him all that he possessed...

Las Casas appended a helpful postil here identifying this *"lugar"* (place) as Guacanagarí's town "where the Admiral made the fortress and left the 39 Spaniards."

...He sent with that servant a girdle which had hanging from it, in place of a purse, a mask of which the two ears, which were large, the tongue and the nose were of beaten gold. And as these people are of a very generous disposition, so that they give whatever is asked of them with the greatest goodwill in the world, and so it appears that anyone who asks something from them does them a great favor, as the Admiral puts it, they came up to the launch and gave the girdle to

a ships boy, and then came in their canoe alongside the ship to perform their embassy. Some part of the day passed before he understood them, nor did the Indians, whom he carried with him, understand them well, since they had somewhat different words for the names of things. Finally, by means of signs, he succeeded in understanding their invitation...

The *"Indians, whom he carried with him"* were now a greater distance from their Eleuthera homeland than Barcelona is from Genoa, so Columbus shouldn't have been surprised that Española's *"people"* had *"somewhat different words for the names of things."*

...He resolved to leave that place on Sunday, although he was not accustomed to set out on a Sunday, solely as a result of his piety and not on account of any superstition. But, he says, in the hope that those people will turn Christian, on account of the goodwill which they show, and become subject to the Sovereigns of Castile, as he holds them already to be, and that they may serve him with zeal, he wishes and endeavors to do everything to please them. Before he departed today he had sent six men to a very large village [poblaçion muy grande], three leagues from there, towards the west, because on the previous day the lord of that place came to the Admiral and told him that he had some pieces of gold...

Columbus reminds us that last night *"he had sent six men to a very large village, three leagues from there, towards the west."* The transcribed direction is in error; those six men had been sent to Guacanagarí's town, *"three leagues"* to the <u>east</u> of Rat Island.

...When the Christians arrived there, the lord of the place took the hand of the Admirals secretary, who was with them. The Admiral had sent him in order that he might prevent the others from doing anything unjust to the Indians. For as the Indians were so liberal and the Spaniards so greedy and unrestrained, it was not enough for them that for a lace tip and even a bit of glass and of earthenware and other things of no value, the Indians would give them whatever they desired, but without giving anything to them, they wished to have and to take everything...

Their unbridled greed would spell disaster for the 39 eager volunteers soon to establish the settlement of La Navidad, Spain's first colony in the New World.

...This the Admiral always forbade, although the things they gave to the Christians, except the gold, were also many things of small value. But the Admiral, considering the generous hearts of the Indians, who for six glass beads would give and gave a piece of gold, on this account ordered that nothing should be accepted from them without something being given in exchange. So the lord of the place took the hand of the secretary and brought him to his house with all the people, who were very numerous and who accompanied him, and caused them to be given to eat, and all the Indians brought to them many things of cotton, worked and wound into small balls. Later in the afternoon, the lord of the place gave them three very fat geese and some small pieces of gold. A great number of people came with them and carried all the things which they had exchanged there, and contended among themselves for the honor of carrying them on their backs, and in fact they did so carry the Christians across some rivers and through some marshy places. The Admiral ordered some things to be given to the lord of the place, and he and all his people were very content, firmly believing that they had come form heaven, and they regarded themselves as fortunate in having seen the Christians...

At this point Columbus turned his attention from his six emissaries to trading activity at his Rat Island anchorage.

...On this day more than one hundred and twenty canoes came to the ships, all being full of people, and they all brought something, especially their bread and fish, and water in small earthenware jars, and seeds of many kinds, which are

good spices. They threw a grain into a mug of water and drank it, and the Indians whom the Admiral carried with him, said that it was a most healthy thing.

SUNDAY, DECEMBER 23rd — *For lack of wind the Admiral could not leave with the ships for the land of that lord who had sent to ask him to come, but with the three messengers who waited there, he sent the launches with people and the secretary...*

      While becalmed at Rat Island, Columbus *"sent the launches with people and the secretary"* ahead to Guacanagarí's large town at Cap-Haitien.

...While these were on their way, he sent two of the Indians, whom he had with him, to the villages [poblaçions] which were near there close to the station of the ships, and they returned with a lord to the ship with news that in the island of Española there was a great quantity of gold, and that they came from other places to buy it, and they told him that there he might have as much as he wished. Others came who confirmed the statement that in it there was much gold, and they showed him the method which they used to collect it. All this the Admiral understood with difficulty, but yet he regarded it as clear that in those parts there was a very great quantity of gold and that, if the place where it was procured were found, he would get it very cheaply and, as he imagined, for nothing. And he repeats that he believes there must be much, because during the three days he was in that harbor he had secured good pieces of gold, and it could not be believed that they brought it here from another land...

      These reports of *"a great quantity of gold... in the island of Española"* were all it took for Columbus to shift his single-minded quest from Puerto Rico.

..."Our Lord, Who holds all things in His hand, be pleased to aid me and to give whatever may be for His service." These are the words of the Admiral. He says that at that hour he believes that more than a thousand persons had come to the ship, and that all brought some of the things they possess, and that, before they have come within a half a crossbow shot of the ship, they stand up in their canoes, and take what they bring in their hands, crying Take! Take! He also believes that more than five hundred came to the ship swimming, because they had no canoes; and the ship was anchored about a league from shore...

      These *"five hundred"* Indians swam *"a league"* from their village to his Rat Island anchorage.

...He estimated that five lords and sons of lords with their whole household, women and children, had come there to see the Christians. The Admiral ordered something to be given to all, for he says that this was all well spent, and he says: "Our Lord in His Goodness guide me that I may find this gold, I mean their mine, for I have many here who say that they know it." These are his words. In the night the boats arrived, and they said that their journey had been a long one, and that at the mountain of Caribata they found many canoes with many people, who came to see the Admiral and the Christians from the place to which the latter were going,...

      Their "long" trip to Guacangarí's town would have required about six hours each way, assuming a rowing speed of 1½ knots. The crowd at *"Caribata"* may have delayed their arrival at the Guacanagarí's town until late Saturday morning. If these men explored the town until midafternoon Sunday, they could have arrived back at Rat Island that *"night."*

...and he was sure that if he could be in that harbor on the feast of the Nativity, all the people of that island, which he now estimated as being larger than England, would come to see them...

Española is only 60 percent the area of England.

...All these returned with the Christians to the village [poblaçion], which, he says, they declared to be larger and better laid out in streets than any of those previously found up to then. He says that this village **(V)** *lies about three leagues to the southeast of Punta Santa [es de parte de la punta Sancta al sueste quasi tres leguas],...*

Dunn/Kelley corrected Cecil Jane's mistranslation to read, *"...in the direction of the Punta Santa almost three leagues southeast."* This change made it clear Guacanagarí's town was *"almost three leagues to the southeast"* of the Rat Island anchorage, and could be reached only by following an indirect route *"in the direction of Punta Santa."* There's no habitable site in the mangrove swamps *"three leagues to the southeast of Punta Santa,"* so Jane's careless translation may have helped mire the perceived location of Guacanagarí's town in soggy Caracol Bay, more than four league beyond Punta Santa.

...and as the canoes can be rowed fast, they went ahead to give the news to the "cacique", as they call him there. Up to that time the Admiral had not been able to understand whether by this they meant king or governor. They use also another name for a grandee, whom they call nitayno; *he did not know if by this they mean king or governor or judge. The cacique finally came to them, and they gathered in the square, which was very clean; the whole village, which contained more than two thousand men, was there. The king did much honor to the people from the ships, and the common people, each one of them, gave them something to eat and drink. Afterwards, the king gave to each one some cotton cloths, which the women wear, and parrots for the Admiral, and some pieces of gold. The common people also presented some of the same cloths and other things from their houses to the sailors, in return for a trifle which they gave them and which, judging from the way they received it, they seemed to regard as relics. When it was evening and they wished to depart, the king asked them to wait until the next day, as did all the people. When it was clear that they were resolved to go, the Indians went a long distance with them, carrying the things which the cacique and the others had given them on their backs to the boats, which remained at the mouth of the river.*

MONDAY, DECEMBER 24th — *Before sunrise, he weighted anchor with a land breeze. Among the many Indians who had come yesterday to the ship and who had indicated to them that there was gold in that island and had named the places where it was collected, he saw one who seemed to be better disposed and more attached to him, or who spoke to him with more pleasure. He flattered this man and asked him to go with him to show him the mines of gold. This Indian brought another, a friend or relation, with him, and among the other places which they named where gold was found, they spoke of Cipangu, which they called "Cibao", and they declared that there was a great quantity of gold there, and that the cacique carries banners of beaten gold, but that it is very far to the east. The Admiral here says these words to the Sovereigns: "Your Highnesses may believe that in all the world there cannot be a people better or more gentle. Your Highnesses should feel great joy, because they will presently become Christians and will be educated in the good customs of your realms, for there cannot be a better people or country, and the number of the people and the extent of the country are so great that I no longer know how to describe them. For I have spoken in the superlative of the people and land of Juana, which they call Cuba, but there is as great a difference between that and this as there is between night and day. Nor do I believe that any one who had seen this would have done or said less than I have said and say. For it is true that the things here are a wonder, and the great peoples of this island of Española, for so I call it, and they call it "Bohio", all display the most extraordinarily gentle behavior and have soft voices, unlike the others, who seem to threaten when they talk; and they are, men and women, of good height and not black. It is true that they all paint themselves, some black, and others with some other color, and the majority red. (I have learned that they do this on account of the sun, so that it may not harm them so much.) The houses and villages are so lovely, and in all there is government, with a judge or lord of them, and all obey him so that it is a wonder. And all these lords are men of few words and excellent manners, and their method of giving orders is generally to make signs with the hand, and it is understood, so that it is a marvel." All these are the words of the Admiral. Anyone who has to enter the sea of*

Santo Tomas must steer a full league over the mouth of the entrance, by a small flat island which lies in the middle of it, which he called La Amiga, keeping the bow towards it. After coming within a stones throw of it, he must pass to the west of it and leave it to the east, and must keep near it and not go in the other direction, as a very large reef [restringa muy grande] stretches from the west and even out to sea;...

This "*restringa*" is similar to the underwater reef Columbus would have found at Watlings Island. Both differ from the "*restinga de piedra*" describing the exposed rock shelf lining the south coast of Royal Island.

...beyond it, there are three shoals, and the reef comes to within a Lombard shot of La Amiga. He must pass between the reef and the island, and he will find at the shallowest point seven braçias, and gravel beneath, and within he will find a harbor for all the ships in the world, where they may lie without cables. Another reef and shoals extend from the east of the island of La Amiga, and are very large and stretch far out to sea and come within two leagues of the cape, but between them it appeared that there was a passage, at two lombard shots from La Amiga;...

Those six sailors who had rowed to Guacanagarí's town may have mapped this "*passage*" through the navigable shallows girding Punta Santa.

*...and at the foot of Mount Caribata, towards the west, there is a very good harbor **(X)** and very large.*

Port Francais is the well-protected "*harbor...at the foot of*" Haut du Cap-Haitien "*towards the west.*"

TUESDAY, DECEMBER 25th — *He navigated with little wind yesterday from the sea of Santo Tamas towards Punta Santa, from which he was distant one league when the first quarter had passed, that is, eleven o'clock at night, and he decided to lie down to sleep, because for two days and a night he had not slept...*

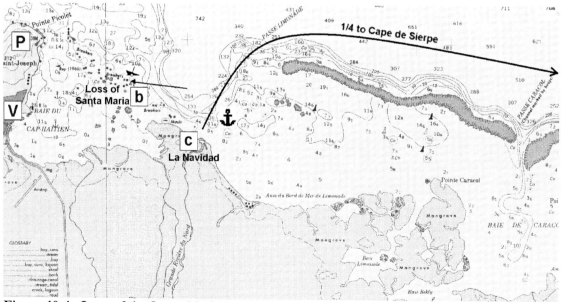

Figure 10-4. Loss of the Santa Maria

Fernando Columbus resolved this directional ambiguity by specifying the *Santa Maria's* *"eleven o'clock"* position as *"a league beyond Punta Santa."* This informs us the Admiral had *"navigated with little wind"* to enter a circular two-mile basin. Soundings quickly warned Columbus the basin was too deep for anchoring, and he surely realized the coast's pervasive westerly current would quickly carry the unanchored *Santa Maria* back onto those dangerous shoals. Despite this obvious threat, the weary Admiral took to his bed as the moon slipped below the horizon, leaving the *Santa Maria* adrift in unfamiliar waters illuminated only by starlight.

...As it was calm, the sailor who was steering the ship, decided to go to sleep, and he left the steering to a young ships boy, a thing which the Admiral had always strictly forbidden during the whole voyage, whether there was a wind or whether it was calm, that is to say, they were not to leave the steering to ships boys...

As Columbus recorded the night's disastrous events, his evident priority was to deflect future criticism of his questionable command decisions. He made his first target *"the sailor who ...left the steering to a young ships boy."* But Columbus should have come to anchor because he surely realized the danger of drifting in the Atlantic's relentless NEC.

...The Admiral felt secure from banks and rocks, because on Sunday, when he sent the boats to that king, they had passed a full three leagues and a half to the east of Punta Santa, and the sailors had seen all the coast and shoals from Punta Santa to the east-southeast for a full three leagues, and they had found where it was possible to pass, which he had not done during the whole voyage...

His next targets for blame were the half dozen *"sailors"* responsible for charting his course *"where it was possible to pass."*

...Our Lord willed that at midnight, as they had seen the Admiral lie down and rest, and as they saw that it was a dead calm and the sea was as in a bowl, all should lie down to sleep, and the rudder was left in the hands of that boy, and the currents carried the ship upon one of those banks **(b)**;...

In this *"dead calm"* his sense *"the sea was as in a bowl"* reminds us of his *"water in a well"* describing Royal Island's placid harbor. He applied tonight's metaphor to that deep two-mile-wide *"bowl"* of sheltered water, likely blasted out of the shallows eons ago by a large meteorite. Columbus had felt secure when he retired *"at eleven o'clock"* with the *Santa Maria* in a *"dead calm"* near the center of that *"bowl."* But he wouldn't have been so confident had he recalled the westerly current constantly sweeping Española's northern coast. Shortly after he retired for the night the unrelenting NEC silently carried his flagship a mile westward through the darkness, before noisily depositing it on the barrier reef fronting Cap-Haïtien. Centuries later Morison would also ignore this westerly current by misdirecting the attention of marine archeologists to the improbable <u>eastern</u> edge of that *"bowl"*.

...the sea breaking on them made so much noise that it could be heard and seen, although it was night, at a full leagues distance...

In his third effort to shift blame for this morning's disaster, Columbus exaggerated the utility of the reef's audible and visual warnings. In a *"dead calm"* a current of less than one knot couldn't produce breakers loud enough to be *"heard...at a full league's distance,"* nor could they have been *"seen"* with the moon now below the horizon. Morison correctly mapped most of the harbor's breakers to the west side of the *"bowl,"* but ignored their role in the *Santa Maria's* disaster.

...The ship went upon it so gently that it was hardly noticed. The boy, who felt the rudder ground, and heard the sound of the sea, shouted, and at his cries, the Admiral came out and was so quick that no one had yet realized that they were aground. Immediately the master of the ship,...

This *"master of the ship"* was the same Juan de la Cosa who had stayed awake the entire night of October 12th to give us the landfall's only surviving cartography. This night he demonstrated much less interest in the survival of his ship.

...whose watch it was, came out, and the Admiral told him and the others to launch the boat which they carried at the stern, to take an anchor and throw it out astern, and he with many others jumped into the boat, and the Admiral thought that they were doing what he had ordered them to do. They only thought of escaping to the caravel, which was lying half a league to windward...

If these men *"only thought of escaping to the caravel,"* Columbus's fourth attempt to shift blame for the disaster has merit. Juan de la Cosa's apparent lack of interest in his Admiral's desperate efforts to save the *Santa Maria* suggests he was well insured against the loss of his vessel.

...The caravel would not take them aboard, therein acting rightly, and so on this account they returned to the ship, but the boat of the caravel reached her first. When the Admiral saw that they were running away and that it was his crew, and that the water was growing shallower and the ship was now lying broadside on to the sea, as he saw no other remedy, he ordered the mast to be cut and the ship to be lightened as far as possible to see whether they could draw her off. And as the water became shallower still, he was unable to save her,...

Prospects for saving the *Santa Maria* couldn't have been bleaker after it grounded at high tide. Within two hours the sea level had fallen by 2 inches – producing a buoyancy loss of 6 tons — a staggering weight that would double within the hour. By now it had become impossible to lighten the ship quickly enough to refloat its groaning timbers in the ebbing tide.

...and she lay on her side, broadside to the sea, although there was little or no sea running, and the seams opened, but the ship remained whole. The Admiral went to the caravel, in order to place the crew of the ship in safety on the caravel, and as a light breeze was no blowing from land, and there also still remained much of the night and they did not know how far the banks extended, he hung off until it was day and then went to the ship from within the line of the bank. He had first sent the boat ashore with Diego de Arana of Cordoba, alguacil of the fleet,...

"Diego de Arana" was cousin to Beatriz de Arana, the mistress who gave Christopher his bastard son Fernando, the author of his biography. Diego became a Columbus favorite after introducing him to Beatriz in 1487.

...and Pero Gutierrez, butler of the royal household, to inform the king who on Saturday night had sent him an invitation and asked him to come to his harbor with the ships, and who had his own town a league and a half away from the bank **(c)**...

The *"bank"* where the *Santa Maria* had foundered lay only *"a league and a half"* from Guacanagarí's *"población grande,"* site of the modern city of Cap-Haitien. This is the same *"large town"*

178

those *"two Christians"* had seen from their mountaintop lookout last Friday. The Taino had several reasons for making this their capital city; most notably its ample fresh water, a sheltered harbor for their canoes, and elevated lookouts to warn of hostile raiding parties. The fortuitous transcription of this *Journal* segment by Las Casas pinpoints the *Santa Maria's* final resting place as a small cluster of rocks almost *"a league and a half"* directly east of Cap-Haitien.

Samuel Eliot Morison, and most other historians, have overlooked this *Journal* evidence, claiming that distant Caracol, rather than nearby Cap-Haitien, was Guacanagarí's *"poblaçion grande."* Their choice implies those *"two Christians"* were able to make that assessment from wisps of smoke and the glimpse of a few tall structures penetrating the dense jungle canopy from a distance of 14 nautical miles. Even if such a sighting were possible, Caracol was an unlikely site for a *"large town"* because it had little fresh water and tillable land, and lacked the elevated lookouts for maintaining a durable settlement in a hostile environment. Morison himself exposed some of its deficiencies by citing Columbus's 1493 rejection of "all the low, damp shores of Caracol Bay" for the rebuilding of La Navidad. Morison's choice of Caracol made Limonade Bord-de-Mer the only feasible site for the original La Navidad. But this site fails the *"league and a half"* test because it's two leagues as the crow flies from Limonade to Caracol, and more than three by the shortest route.

Finding any remains of La Navidad is strongly dependent on identifying the reef where the *Santa Maria* foundered. This identification depends largely on two factors: the flow of the Atlantic's NEC and the *Santa Maria's* location when *"the young ships boy"* took the helm. Assuming Columbus and the sailor were ignorant of the NEC, the "safest" place to transfer control would have been near the center of the harbor's *"bowl,"* a mile from its ominous encircling reefs. From there it would take the Atlantic's NEC less than two hours to silently carry the *Santa Maria* to its destruction on the reefs fronting Cap-Hatiien. Fruitless searches for the ship's remains along the <u>eastern</u> rim of this *"bowl"* have demonstrated a total disregard for the direction of the NEC's flow. If the *Santa Maria* foundered near the bowl's western rim, a logical site for La Navidad becomes the mouth of the *Grande Riviére du Nord* **(c)**, exactly *"a league and a half"* from Guacanagarí's *"own town."*

...When he heard the news, they say he wept and sent all his people from the town, with many large canoes to unload the ship. This was done and everything was taken from the decks in a very short space of time. So great was the haste and diligence which that king showed! And he in person, with his brothers and relatives, was active both on the ship and in guarding what was brought to land, so that everything might be very safely kept. From time to time, he sent one of his relatives in tears to the Admiral, to console him, telling him that he must not be troubled or annoyed, that he would give him whatever he possessed. The Admiral assures the Sovereigns that nowhere in Castile could he have been able to place everything in greater security, without the loss of a shoestring. He commanded everything to be placed near the houses, while some houses which he wished to give were emptied, that there everything might be placed and guarded. He ordered armed men to be set round everything to keep watch all night. "He and all the people with him wept. They are," says the Admiral, "a people so full of love and without greed, and suitable for every purpose, that I assure Your Highnesses that I believe that there is no better race of better land in the world. They love their neighbors as themselves, and they have the softest and gentlest voices in the world, and they are always smiling. They go naked, men and women, as their mothers bore them. But Your Highnesses may believe that in their intercourse with one another they have very good customs, and the king maintains a very marvelous state, of a style so orderly that it is a pleasure to see it, and they have good memories any they wish to see everything and ask what it is and for what it is used." All this says the Admiral.

WEDNESDAY, DECEMBER 26th — *Today at sunrise the king of that land, who was in that village, came to the caravel* Niña, *where the Admiral was, and, almost in tears, told him that he must not be grieved, for he would give him whatever he had, and that he had given to the Christians who were on shore two very large houses, and that he would give them more if it were necessary, and as many canoes as they needed to load and unload the ship and bring to land as many men as he might wish, as had been done yesterday without a crumb of bread being taken or anything else at all. "They are so loyal," says the Admiral, "and without greed for what is not theirs, and so above all the others was that virtuous king." While the Admiral was talking with him, another canoe came from another direction [de otro lugar,]...*

Cecil Jane had translated *"de otro cabo"* as *"from another [direction]"* in his attempt to force fit Rum Cay into congruency with the *Journal's* precise *"from another cape."* Today, for no obvious reason, he gave the same misreading to *"de otro lugar [place]."*

...which brought certain pieces of gold, which they wanted to give for a hawk's bell, because they wish for nothing so much as for hawk's bells. So while the canoe had not yet reached the ships side, they called out and showed the pieces of gold, crying "chuque, chuque," meaning hawk's bells, for they almost go crazy for them...

These same coveted *"hawk's bells"* were soon to measure the Indian's mandatory daily quota of gold dust panned for their Spanish overlords.

...After they saw this and the canoes which came from other places were about to leave, they called the Admiral and asked him to have a hawk's bell kept until next day, since they would bring him four pieces of gold as large as the hand. The Admiral rejoiced to hear this, and afterwards a sailor, who came from ashore, told the Admiral that it was wonderful to see the pieces of gold which the Christians who were on land were getting in exchange for nothing; for a leather thong they gave pieces of gold worth more than two castellanos,...

These Indians eagerly traded a third of an ounce of gold for *"a leather thong,"* a clearly unfair exchange at which Columbus *"rejoiced."*

...and this was nothing to what it would be at the end of a month. The king was greatly delighted to see the Admiral joyful and understood that he desired much gold, and he told him by signs that he knew where there was very much in great abundance near there, and that he should be of good cheer, for he would give him as much gold as he might desire. He says that he explained this to him, and more particularly that in Cipangu, which they called Cibao, it was in such quantity that they regard it as of no account, and that he would bring it from there, although in that island of Española, which they call "Bohio", and in that province of Caribata, there is also very much. The king ate in the caravel with the Admiral, and afterwards landed with him, and on land did the Admiral much honor, and gave him a repast of two or three kinds of ajes and with them shrimps and game, and other foods which they had, and some of their bread which they call "cacabi"...

This was the cassava, a tuberous New World root, eventually to become one of Africa's major sources of carbohydrates.

...Thence he took him to see some groves of trees near the houses, and about a thousand people, all naked, went there with him. The king now wore a shirt and gloves, which the Admiral had given him, and he rejoiced more over the gloves than over anything which had been given to him. In his eating, by his decent behavior and exquisite cleanliness, he showed clearly that he was of good birth. After having eaten, as he remained at the table for some while, they brought him some herbs with which he rubbed his hands a great deal. The Admiral believed that he did so in order to

make them soft, and they gave him water for his hands. After they had finished eating, he brought the Admiral to the beach, and the Admiral sent for a Turkish bow and a handful of arrows, and caused a man of his company to shoot them; he was skillful, and the chief very much impressed, as he did not know what weapons are, since they neither have nor use them. The Admiral says, however, that the beginning of it all was talk about the people of Caniba, whom they call "Caribs", who come to capture them and carry bows and arrows, without iron; for in all these lands there is no knowledge of it or of steel, or of any other metal, except gold and copper, although the Admiral had only seen a little copper...

This *"Turkish bow"* with a reported effective range of 500 yards immediately *"impressed"* Guacanagarí as a potent weapon to unleash against marauding Caribs.

...The Admiral told him by signs that the Sovereigns of Castile would order destruction of the Caribs and would have them all brought with their hands bound. The Admiral ordered a lombard and a musket to be fired, and seeing the effect which their force had and what they pierced, the chief was left wondering; and when his people heard the firing, they all fell on the ground. They brought to the Admiral a large mask, which had great pieces of gold in the ears and eyes and other places, and this was given to him with other gold ornaments, which the king himself had placed on the Admirals head and round his neck; and to the other Christians who were with him he also gave many things. The Admiral was greatly pleased and consoled with these things which he saw, and the grief and pain which he had suffered and continued to suffer for the loss of the ship was assuaged, and he recognized that Our Lord had caused the ship to run aground there in order that a settlement might there be formed. "And," he says, "in addition to this, so many things came to hand, that in truth it was no disaster, but rather great good fortune; for it is certain," he says, "that had I not run aground there, I should have kept out to sea without anchoring at this place, because it is situated within a large bay and in that bay are two or more sandbanks; and on this voyage I should not have left people here, and, had I desired to leave them, I could not have given them so many supplies, stores and provisions, nor the material needed for making a fort...

By now a chagrined Columbus must have realized the NEC's western current was responsible for the *Santa Maria's* loss. To assuage his guilt he managed to convince himself this wreck was a *"great good fortune"* essential to the establishment of Spain's first New World settlement.

....And it is very true that many of the people who are with me have asked and petitioned that I give them permission to remain...

Ready access to Taino maidens and golden nuggets swelled the ranks of volunteers hoping to man this idyllic outpost. Within a year all of these eager volunteers would be dead, many surely suffering from Syphilis, then endemic throughout the Caribbean.

...Now I have ordered a tower and fortress **(c)** *to be built, all very well done, and a large moat,...*

The Grande Riviere near the *Santa Maria's* wreck offered several projecting peninsulas as promising *"fortress"* locations. But its *"large moat"* couldn't protect the men from the internal bickering that quickly led to the colony's collapse, apparently at the hands of Guacanagarí's Indian foes. When Columbus returned a year later he would find all of the colonists dead and their settlement in ruins. Guacanagarí felt so guilty about his failure to protect the colony that he lavished several expensive gifts on Columbus, including a golden crown and several pounds of panned gold.

...not that I believe it to be necessary for these people, for I take it for granted that with these men whom I have with me I could subdue all this island, which I believe to be larger than Portugal and with more than twice the population...

Columbus boldly overstates all three of his claims for Española. First, by his assertion a small force *"could subdue all this island."* Second, in claiming Española was at least *"larger than Portugal,"* if not *"England."* And third, by asserting Española had *"twice the population"* of Portugal, when the opposite was true according to *The Christopher Columbus Encyclopedia.*

...But they are all naked and without arms and very cowardly beyond hope of change. It is right, however, that this tower should be built, and it must be as it must be, being so distant from Your Highnesses and what they can do, so that they may serve them with love and fear. So they have boards with which to construct the whole fortress, and provisions of bread and wine for more than a year, and seeds to sow, and the ships boat and a caulker and a carpenter and a gunner and a cooper, and many men among them who are very zealous in the service of Your Highnesses, and who will give me the pleasure of finding the mine where the gold is collected. Thus, then, all has happened greatly to the purpose that a beginning may be made, and above all, when the ship ran aground, it was gently that the shock was hardly felt, and there was no sea or wind." All this the Admiral says...

Because *"there was no... wind,"* the *Santa Maria's* wreck was due entirely to the Atlantic Ocean's NEC, the relentless half knot current supposedly ignored by Columbus.

...and he adds more, in order to show that it was great good fortune and the predestined will of God that the ship should run aground there, so that he would leave people there; and if it had not been for the disloyalty of the master, and of the crew, who were all, or most of them from his district, in being unwilling to throw out the anchor from the stern in order to drag off the ship, as the Admiral had commanded them, the ship would have been saved, and so he would not have been able to learn about the land, he says, as he learned in those days that he was there, and as he will learn later, through those that he resolved to leave there. For it was always with the intention of discovering that he voyaged and not delaying more than a day in any place, save for lack of wind, but he says that the ship was very slow and not suited for the work of discovery. He says that it was the men of Palos who caused such a ship to be taken, for they did not fulfill what they had promised to the King and Queen in supplying ships suitable for that voyage...

Columbus wanted to have it both ways: the wreck was a *"great good fortune"* he could blame on *"the men of Palos."*

...The Admiral ends by saying that of all that was in the ship not a leather thong nor a plank nor a nail was lost, because she remained as sound as when she set out, except that she was cut and split to some extent in order to get out the water butts and all the cargo, and they brought everything to land and had it well guarded, as has been said...

Many of the *Santa Maria's* surviving artifacts may await recovery at the site of La Navidad. The site's only significant find was made in 1493 when Columbus and Dr. Chanca recovered one of the *Santa Maria's* anchors at the mouth of Grande Rivière du Nord. This ignored candidate for La Navidad's location would have been a logical choice because of its proximity to the wreck, copious fresh water, and a solid footing lacking in the mangrove swamps lining most of that coast.

...And he says that he trusts in God that on his return, which he intended to make from Castile, he would find a barrel of gold, which those whom he had left there should have obtained by barter,...

Fernando Columbus provided additional detail in his *Biography* for this passage, explaining how his father had left orders "to clean out the well of the fort during his absence; for at the time of his departure for Castile, fearing some untoward event, he had directed all the gold that was found to be thrown into the well." When Columbus returned in 1493 he found the well empty without a glimmer from his eagerly anticipated *"barrel of gold."*

...and they would have found the gold mine and the spices, and in such quantity, that the Sovereigns, within three years, would undertake and prepare to go to the conquest of the Holy Places, "For so," he says, "I protested to Your Highnesses that all the gains of this my enterprise should be expended on the conquest of Jerusalem, and Your Highnesses smiled and said that it pleased them, and that without this they had that inclination." These are the words of the Admiral.

THURSDAY, DECEMBER 27th — *At sunrise, the king of that land came to the caravel and told the Admiral that he had sent for gold and that he desired to clothe him in gold before he departed; but rather, he begged him not to depart. And with the Admiral there were the king and his brother and another relative, very high in favor, and these two men told him that they wished to go to Castile with him. At this juncture, certain Indians came with the news that the caravel* Pinta *was in a river at the end of that island. The cacique at once dispatched a canoe there, and in it the Admiral sent a sailor;...*

Five weeks earlier, Martin Alonso Pinzón had deserted Columbus for the delightful prospect of harvesting "all those golden nuggets" blanketing Great Inagua Island. We don't know how quickly Pinzón realized his disappointment, but he left enough time to redirect his golden quest to the reported riches of Española, and possibly Puerto Rico. When Columbus learned Pinzón was closer than him to Spain, he may have feared his insubordinate lieutenant would hurry home to steal credit for his discoveries. But Pinzón showed no stomach for a risky solo crossing of the Atlantic and had already begun coasting Española westward to rejoin his Admiral.

A 146-league roundtrip to "*the end of that island*" in what proved to be slightly more than five days was beyond the capabilities of Indian canoes, even if rowed around the clock. This "sailor" may have truncated his search after sensing Pinzón was either slowly working his way westward to rejoin Columbus, or already racing home to claim credit for the discoveries. One likely limit to his five-day search is the prominent headland at Cabo Francis Viejo. Pinzón's link-up with Columbus wouldn't occur until January 6th, indicating he found the first crack at Española's gold more inviting than facing his Admiral's wrath. In route to their link-up this brash captain christened the Río Bajabonico as "*Río de Martín Alonso*," a place name ignored by Columbus though somehow surviving forty years later in the Chaves Rutter.

...for he so greatly loved the Admiral that it was a marvel. The Admiral already intended to prepare for his return to Castile with as much speed as he could.

FRIDAY, DECEMBER 28th — *In order to direct and hasten the completion of the building of the fortress and to give directions to the people who were to remain in it, the Admiral landed, and it appeared to him that the king had seen him while he was still in the boat, for he at once went into his house, dissembling, and sent his brother to greet the Admiral and bring him to one of the houses which he had given to the Admiral's people, the largest and best in that town. In it they had prepared a dais of the inner bark of palm trees, where they caused him to seat himself. Afterwards, the brother sent one of his pages to tell the king that the Admiral was there, as if the king was unaware that he had come, although the Admiral believed that he had made pretense to do him much great honor. When the* *page delivered his message, as he says, the cacique hurried to come to the Admiral, and placed round his neck a great plate of gold which he carried in his hand. He remained there with him until evening, considering what was to be done.*

SATURDAY, DECEMBER 29th — *At sunrise, there came to the caravel a nephew of the king, very young and of good understanding and courage, as the Admiral says, and as he always endeavored to learn where they gathered the gold, he asked every one, for by means of signs he now understood something. And so this youth told him that four days journey to the east there was an island which was called "Guarioné,"...*

A *"four days journey"* for the remaining 92 leagues to Puerto Rico suggests *"this youth"* had given Columbus a realistic distance estimate.

...and others which were called "Maricorix" and "Mayonic" and "Fuma" and "Cibao" and "Coroay" in which there was infinite gold...

These five *"others"* appear to have been regions of eastern Española, a relationship supported in a Las Casas postil asserting, "These were not islands, but provinces of Española." Today's only surviving place name is *"Cibao"* on the north coast of the Dominican Republic.

...The Admiral wrote these names down, and when the brother of the king heard what the youth had said, he rebuked him, as the Admiral gathered. On other occasions also the Admiral had understood that the king endeavored to prevent him from learning where the gold originated and was collected, in order that he might not go elsewhere to barter for it or buy it. "But there is so much and in so many places, and in this island of Española itself," says the Admiral, "that it is a wonder." When it was already night, the king sent him a great mask of gold, and sent to him also to ask for a hand basin and a jar. The Admiral believed that he asked this so as to have others made, and so he sent him what he asked for.

SUNDAY, DECEMBER 30th — *The Admiral went ashore to eat, and he arrived just as there had come five kings, subject to him who was called Guacanagarí, all with their crowns, an indication of very high estate, so that the Admiral tells the Sovereigns that their Highnesses would have been pleased to see their bearing. As he reached land, the king came to receive the Admiral and led him by the arm to the same house as yesterday, where there was a dais and chairs, on which he placed the Admiral, and immediately took the crown from his own head, and placed it on that of the Admiral. And the Admiral took from his neck a collar of good bloodstones and very beautiful beads, of very fine color, which appeared very good in every way, and placed it round his neck, and he took off a cloak of rich scarlet cloth which he was wearing that day, and dressed him in it. And he sent for some colored buskins...*

Buskins were thick-soled laced foot coverings with leggings reaching at least halfway to the knee.

...which he made him put on, and placed on his finger a large silver ring, because they had told him that he had seen a sailor with a silver ring and he had tried to obtain it. He was very pleased and very content, and two of those kings, who were with him, came to where the Admiral was beside him, and brought to the Admiral two large plates of gold, each bringing one. And just then, there came an Indian, saying that two days before he had left the caravel Pinta *to the east in a harbor...*

If this *"Indian"* traveled alone, a likely candidate for the *Pinta's* *"harbor"* would be the Rio Bajabonico **(f)**, 20 leagues east of La Navidad. With companions it could have been 10 leagues further east at Puerto Plata **(g)**. In either case Pinzón had made barely a day's progress from Point

Engamo in nearly a week. Perhaps he intended to assuage his Admiral's wrath by presenting him with samples of Española's gold deposits.

...The Admiral went back to the caravel, and Vincent Yañez, her captain, declared that he had seen rhubarb and that it was in the island Amiga, which is at the entrance of the sea of Santo Tomas, six leagues from there,...

Columbus was in no hurry to gather *"rhubarb;"* he would wait until midnight tomorrow before sending harvesters on a day-trip back to *"the island Amiga... at the entrance of the sea of Santo Tomas."* His estimate of *"six leagues"* must have been for a round trip to *"Amiga"* because a dozen leagues within 18 hours was beyond the capability of his men. The roundtrip from Limonade Bord-de-Mer measures 8.8 leagues, almost half again longer than estimated by Columbus, while the roundtrip from Grand Riviere is a closer fit at 7.6 leagues.

...and that he had recognized the branches and root. They say that rhubarb throws out small branches from the ground, and that it has some fruit which looks like green mulberries, almost dry, and that the stalk in the part near the root is as yellow and as fine as the best color there can be to paint; and underground it has a root like a large pear.

MONDAY, DECEMBER 31st — *On this day, he concerned himself with ordering water and wood to be taken in his departure for Spain, in order to give speedy news to the Sovereigns, that they might send ships to discover what remained to be discovered, since already the matter appeared, says the Admiral, to be so great and of such moment as to be a marvel. And he says that he did not wish [quisiera] to depart until he had seen all that land which there was towards the east and gone along all the coast, in order to learn also the length of the journey from Castile there, he says, for the purpose of bringing stock and other things...*

His *Ephemeredes* revealed LPC-22 would offer an outstanding opportunity to measure *"the length of the journey from Castile"* when the Moon *eclipsed* Venus on the morning of January 14th. Columbus had not wished *"to depart until he had seen all that land which there was towards the east,"* but *"as he was left with only one ship, it did not seem reasonable to expose himself to the dangers."* He didn't need to sail *"along all the coast"* of Española to find a suitable viewing site; his accurate charts informed him Samaná Bay **(h)** was ideally configured for observing LPC-22. After completing this important longitude measurement he could begin his return voyage to Spain.

...But, as he was left with only one ship, it did not seem to him reasonable to expose himself to the dangers which he might encounter in the course of discovery; and he complained that all this evil and inconvenience was the result of the caravel Pinta *having parted from him.*

Columbus had two full weeks to find a suitable LPC-22 viewing site in Samaná Bay, an objective within a few days reach. His relaxed schedule might allow him to reestablish contact with the *Pinta*, rather than *"expose himself to the dangers...with only one ship"* for his return voyage. At the least it gave him time to prepare his tongue-lashing of Pinzón free of nautical distractions.

TUESDAY, JANUARY 1st — *At midnight he dispatched the boat to the islet of Amiga to fetch the rhubarb. It returned at vespers with a basket of it. They did not bring more, because they had no spade to dig; he brought this as a specimen to the Sovereigns...*

Allowing two hours for lunch, rest and "rhubarb" harvesting, "the boat" completed its 23-mile circuit at an average rowing speed of 1.5 knots.

...The king of the land said that he had sent many canoes for gold. There returned the canoe, which went to get news of the Pinta, *and the sailor, and they had not found her...*

There are no concealed harbors between El Morro and Samaná Bay, so the sailor's 5-day search for the *Pinta* apparently was aborted short of the Indian's Puerto Plata sighting.

...The sailor said that twenty leagues from there **(i)** *they had seen a king who wore two large plates of gold on his head, and immediately the Indians in the canoe had spoken to him, he took them off. He also saw much gold on other persons...*

At Rio Bajabonico, *"twenty leagues"* east of La Navidad, *"the sailor... had seen a king who wore two large plates of gold on his head."* This must have been an especially impressive display of gold because 40 years later the Chaves Rutter still referred to this river as the *Rio de Martin Alonso* (Pinzón).

...The Admiral believed that King *Guacanagarí must have forbidden all to sell gold to the Christians, in order that all might pass through his hands. But he had learned the places, as he said the day before yesterday, where it was in such quantity that they held it to be of no account. Moreover the spice, which they eat, says the Admiral, is in large amount and more valuable than pepper or allspice. He left orders to those whom he wished to leave there that they should procure as much as they could.*

WEDNESDAY, JANUARY 2nd — *He landed in the morning in order to take leave of king Guacanagarí and to set out in the name of the Lord, and he gave him one of his shirts. And he showed him the power which the lombards had and the effect which they produced, and for this purpose he ordered one to be loaded and fired at the side of the ship which was aground. This was as a result of a conversation concerning the Caribs, with whom they were at war; and he saw how far the lombard carried, and how it pierced the side of the ship, and how the charge went far out to sea...*

This display of *"the power which the lombards had"* may have impressed Guacanagarí, but it wasn't effective enough to protect La Navidad.

...He also had the people of the ship arm themselves and engage in a sham fight, telling the cacique that he was not to fear the Caribs even if they should come. All this the Admiral says that he did, that the king might regard the Christians whom he left as friends and might be frightened and have fear of them. The Admiral took him with him to eat at the house where he was lodged, and the others who went with him. The Admiral greatly recommended to him Diego de Arana and Pero Gutierrez and Rodrigo Escovedo, whom he was leaving as his joint lieutenants over the people who remained there, in order that all might be well regulated and organized for the service of God and of their Highnesses...

This awkward tripartite division of leadership may have contributed to the settlement's rapid demise.

...The cacique showed great affection for the Admiral and great grief at his departure, especially when he saw him go to embark. A favorite of that king told the Admiral that he had commanded a statue of pure gold, as large as the Admiral himself, to be made, and that in ten days they would bring it. The Admiral embarked with the intention of setting out at once, but the wind would not permit him to do so...

Columbus would have left this well-protected harbor today on an ebbing tide, but the trade winds *"would not permit him to do so."*

...He left in that island of Española, which the Indians call "Bohio", thirty-nine men in the fortress, and he says that they were very friendly with that king Guacanagarí. Over them, as his lieutenants, he left Diego de Arana, a native of Cordoba, and Pero Gutierrez, butler of the king's dais, a subordinate of the despensaro mayor, and Rodrigo de Escovedo, a native of Segovia, nephew of Fray Rodrigo Perez, with all his powers which he held from the Sovereigns. He left with them all the merchandise which the Sovereigns had commanded to be brought for purposes of barter, and this was much, in order that they might deal and exchange it for gold, with all that had been brought from the ship. He left them also bread, biscuit for a year, and wine, and much artillery, and the ships boat, in order that they, being sailors as most of them were, might go, when they saw a suitable time, to discover the mine of gold, so that, when the Admiral returned, much gold might be collected by his coming, and a place found where a town might be established, because this was not a harbor after his heart, especially because the gold which they brought there came, as he says, from the east, and the more they were to the east, the nearer they were to Spain...

Columbus already had misgivings about La Navidad's location. When he *"returned"* to *Española* on his second voyage, he planned to order a new *"town...established"* near the Rio Bajabonico discovered by Martin Alonso Pinzón. This eastward move made sense partly because La Navidad lacked a *"harbor after his heart,"* but *"especially because the gold which they brought there came...from the east."*

...He left them also some seeds to sow, and his officials, the secretary and the alguacil, and with them a ships carpenter and a caulker and a good gunner, who well understood machines, and a cooper, and a doctor, and a tailor, and all, as he says, seamen.

11 - The Venusian Gift of Longitude

THURSDAY, JANUARY 3rd — *He did not set out today, because at night, he says, three of the Indians whom he brought from the islands, and who had remained, came and said that the others and their women would come at sunrise...*

The real reason Columbus *"did not set out today"* was *"because at night"* this anchorage was well situated for observing LPC-20. At 7:45 PM the Moon stood 15 degrees above his unobstructed ENE horizon and less than two degrees below Jupiter.

...The sea also was rather rough and the boat could not go to land. He resolved to depart on the next day, the grace of God allowing. He said that if he had had with him the caravel Pinta, *he would certainly have been able to bring back a barrel of gold,...*

Columbus must have anticipated a bitter confrontation when he and Pinzón presented the Crown with conflicting reports of their voyage. Here he strengthens his hand by claiming the *Pinta's* unauthorized excursion had cost Spain *"a barrel of gold."*

...for he would have dared to go along the coasts of these islands, a thing which he did not dare to do being alone, lest some accident should occur to him and prevent him from returning to Castile and from informing the Sovereigns of all the things which he had found...

Next month, during a terrible storm in the Azores, Columbus would float a wax-sealed record confirming his discoveries in case he should perish at sea. The record was never recovered, but the *Journal's* 19th century publication stimulated a booming market for a number of obvious fakes.

...And if it were certain that the caravel Pinta, *with that Martin Alonso Pinzón, would reach Spain safely, he said that he would not abandon doing what he desired; but, since he heard nothing from him, and because, when he went, he might tell lies to the Sovereigns in order to avoid the punishment which he deserved, as he had done and was doing so much harm in going away without permission and in preventing the good which might have been achieved and learned at that time, says the Admiral, he trusted that Our Lord would give him fair weather and that all would be remedied.*

FRIDAY, JANUARY 4th — *At sunrise, he weighed anchor with a light wind, and the boat led the way...*

"At sunrise, he raised anchor with a light wind" so a *"boat"* might help ease the *Niña* through the reef opening at Limonade Pass.

...towards the northwest, in order to get outside the reef by another channel, wider than that by which he entered...

The exit *"channel"* between Cap-Haitien and Limonade Pass was indeed *"wider than that by which he entered"* the harbor from the west on Christmas Eve.

...This channel and others are very good for going beyond the town of La Navidad, and everywhere there the least depth which he found was from three to nine bracias [6 to 17 feet]. These two extend from the northwest to the southeast, for those shoals were great and stretch from Cape Santo to Cape de Sierpe, which is more than six leagues,...

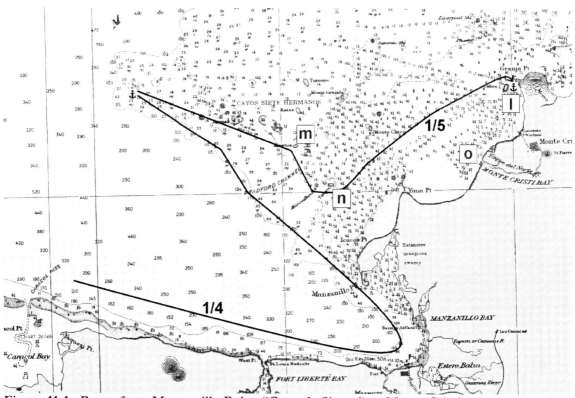

Figure 11-1. Route from Manzanillo Point ('Cape de Sierpe') to Monte Cristi

His *"Cape de Sierpe"* aptly describes the coiling peninsula terminating at Manzanillo Point. Columbus measured *"more than six leagues"* for his 6.3 leagues of coasting from Limonade Point to this serpentine cape, but his *Journal* incorrectly ties this measurement to Cap-Haitien, 8 leagues to the west.

...and outside to sea is a good three bracias [6 feet], and by Cape Santo, at a league distance, there is not more than eight bracias [15 feet] depth,...

From its La Navidad anchorage, the *Niña* had sailed first *"towards the northwest,"* passing along the shoals that extend *"a leagues distance"* east of Cap-Haitien.

...and within the said cape, to the east, there are many shallows and channels by which to pass through them...

And, in fact, Columbus had successfully passed *"through them"* a few hours before he lost the *Santa Maria*.

...All that coast trends to the northwest and southeast, and is all sandy [toda playa]...

Cecil Jane had mistranslated *"todas playas"* as *"all the coasts"* when he needed to accommodate Long Island's limestone cliffs. In today's entry he was free to accurately describe this coast's *"sandy"* beach.

...and the land very flat, as far as a full four leagues inland. Afterwards, there are very high mountains,...

Once again Columbus demonstrates his uncanny ability to estimate distances. Those *"high mountains"* paralleling this coast created a dramatic backdrop behind a *"full four leagues"* of intervening coastal flats.

...and all is thickly populated with large villages [poblaçiones grandes], and they are good people, as they proved themselves to be towards the Christians. So he navigated to the east, in the direction of a very high mountain, which appears to be an island, but is not, for it has a very low-lying isthmus uniting it with the shore. It is shaped like a very lovely pavilion, and he called it Monte Cristi; it lies exactly to the east of Cape Santo, and at a distance of eighteen leagues...

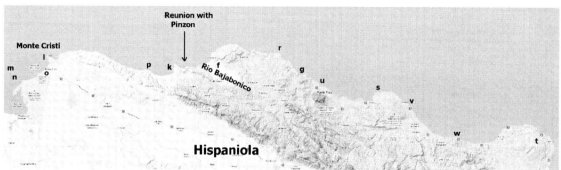

Figure 11-2. Columbus coasts central Hispaniola to the east, January 5th through January 11th

"Cape Santo" has two problems with this identification; *"Monte Cristi"* is only *"at a distance of"* 11 leagues, and clearly not *"exactly to the east"* of that cape. A stronger candidate for this benchmark *"Cape"* is the western terminus of the *"angla muy grande"* Columbus had entered in his *Journal* on December 19th. Although unlabeled in that day's extract, this coastal feature matches today's positioning of *"Monte Cristi...exactly to the east...at a distance of eighteen leagues."* This congruence in both distance and direction makes it likely Las Casas substituted today's *"Cape Santo"* for whatever untranscribed place name Columbus had given to the western end of this *"angla muy grande."*

...On that day, since the wind was very light, he could not come within six leagues of Monte Cristi. He found four very low sandy islets,...

As *"the wind was very light,"* Columbus *"could not come within six leagues of Monte Cristi."* But this was close enough to discover *"four"* of the *Siete Hermanos*; a cluster of seven *"low sandy islets"* extending several leagues west of that *"very high mountain."*

...with a reef which stretched far to the northwest and went far to the southeast. Within it, there is a very large gulf, which extends from the said mountain to the southeast a full twenty leagues,...

This *"very large gulf"* was Samaná Bay, an anchorage oriented for convenient measurement of LPC-22 when the moon rose to the ESE on January 14th. Its distance of 42 leagues was probably mapped accurately by the Taino, but reduced by Columbus to *"a full twenty leagues"* as he continued his halving of their canoe-day.

...and this must be all very shallow and have many banks. Within it on all the coast there are many rivers, not navigable, although that sailor whom the Admiral sent with the canoe to learn news of the caravel Pinta, said that he saw a river into which ships might enter...

If this *"sailor"* had cut his search short of Puerto Plata, the best anchorage along his route would have been Bahia Isabela **(k),** two leagues west of Rio Bajabonico. It has "good holding ground in 4 ½ fathoms" according to the Sailing Directions for the West Indies.

...The Admiral anchored there six leagues from Monte Cristi, in nineteen braças [8.6 fathoms], having put out to sea in order to keep away from the many shoals that were there, and he remained there that night...

Almost *"six leagues"* due west of *"Monte Cristi"* the *"many shoals"* are too deep for safe anchorage except near their southwest corner where one small sea mount rises to within 20 feet of the surface. Columbus did well to find this tiny anchorage in the late afternoon daylight.

...The Admiral warns that he who has to go to the town of La Navidad when sighting Monte Cristi, should keep two leagues out to sea, etc....

Columbus had foreseen the need to instruct future pilots seeking the shortest route to *"La Navidad."* So he alerted them to Monte Cristi Shoals, a shipping hazard still mapped exactly *"two leagues"* north of *"Monte Cristi."*

...But, because that land is already known, and more in that direction, it is not set down here. He concludes that Cipangu is on that island, and that there is much gold and spice and mastic and rhubarb.

SATURDAY, JANUARY 5th — *When the sun was about to rise, he set sail with a land breeze; afterwards the wind changed to the east, and he saw that south-southeast of Monte Cristi, between it and a small island* **(l)***, there seemed to be a good harbor in which to anchor for the night....*

A *Journal* copyist misread "oeste" as "este," because there's no *"small island"* to the *"south-southeast"* of Monte Cristi. Columbus was describing Isla Cabra, a 40 acre islet 600 yards south-south<u>west</u> of that prominent landmark. He would have needed a detailed chart to characterize this narrow opening as *"a good harbor"* while he was still several leagues to its west. Today's Sailing Directions for the West Indies reinforce that need with the observation that "vessels approaching from westward will find it difficult to distinguish the islet from the land until close to."

...He steered to the east-southeast, and afterwards to the south-southeast, a good six leagues towards the mountain, and he found, when the six leagues had been accomplished, seventeen braças [7.7 fathoms] depth and soft bottom **(m)***, and so he went three leagues with the same depth...*

Superimposing Columbus' route to Isla Cabra on a depth chart of the intervening shoals reinforces our appreciation of his keen nautical judgment. At daybreak he followed the shoal's edge nearly 2½ leagues *"east-southeast"* to a point **(m)** just south of *Muertos*, one of *The Seven Brothers*. His path blocked there by shallows, he changed course to *"south-southeast"* for nearly a league until he found a depth of six fathoms beyond *Tororu* **(n)**, the southernmost islet of that archipelago. There he turned northeasterly for *"three leagues"* to reach Isla Cabra through depths uniformly charted as six fathoms by an unknown vessel retracing his route four centuries later. A southwesterly breeze must have favored Columbus today because he executed all three legs in a caravel incapable of sailing within five points of the wind.

...Afterwards, the depth lessened to twelve braçias [23 feet] in the direction of the head of the mountain,...

The ocean bottom gradually reduces to a depth of *"twelve braçias"* a half league beyond the mouth of the *Yaque del Norte River* **(o)**.

...and off the head of the mountain, at a leagues distance, he found nine braçias [4.1 fathoms], and all clear, with fine sand...

This combination of distance and depth identify his location as *"a league"* southwest of Monte Cristi and 1,000 yards from shore.

...So he followed his course, until he entered between the mountain and the islet, where he found three and a half braçias [1.6 fathoms] depth, at low tide, and a very remarkable harbor, where he anchored...

Columbus noted that the shallows directly south of Isla Cabra provided added protection for the *"very remarkable harbor"* between it and Monte Cristi.

...He went with the boat to the islet, where he found a fire and evidence that fishermen had been there. He saw there many colored stones of various shades, or a quarry of such stones, naturally shaped, very lovely, he says, for church buildings or other royal works, like those he found in the islet [isleta] of San Salvador...

It might be instructive to compare this *"quarry of such stones"* with those found at the several candidates for *"the islet of San Salvador,"* especially the water-worn boulders anchoring Egg Island's sandy southern beach. It's worth noting that Cecil Jane felt free to correctly translate *"isleta"* in this excerpt.

...He also found in this islet many roots of Mastic. He says that this Monte Cristi is very beautiful and lofty and accessible, of a very attractive form, and all the land near it is very low, very fair cultivable land, and it alone is so high that, being seen from a distance, it looks like an island without connection with any land. Beyond the mountain, to the east, he saw a cape at a distance of twenty-four millas [six leagues], which he called Cape Becerro **(p)**,...

Columbus could see a 1350-foot pinnacle at *"six leagues"* rising slightly higher above the eastern horizon than its 1500-foot partner two leagues beyond. He dubbed this matched pair *"Becerro,"* likening them to the immature horns of a yearling calf.

...and from it as far as the mountain some reefs with shallows stretch out to sea a good two leagues [passa en el mar bien dos leguas unas restringas de baxos]...

Dunn/Kelley clarified Cecil Jane's murky translation to read "he passed in the sea a good two leagues of reefs and shoals." Punta Buen Hombre, at the foot of Becerro's nearest "horn," marks the end of a coastal reef extending eastward from Monte Cristi.

...It seems, however, that there were between them channels by which an entry might be made, but it is well that it should be by day and that the attempt should be made with the boat going ahead to take soundings. From this mountain, to the east, towards Cape Bezerro, for four leagues, it is all beach, and the land is very low and beautiful, and for the rest the whole country is very high, and there are great mountains, cultivated and lovely, and inland a chain runs from the northeast to the southeast, the most lovely that he had seen, so that it seemed like the sierra of Cordoba. Very far away there appeared also other mountains, very lofty, towards the south and the southeast, and very large valleys, very green and very beautiful, and many streams; all this is in such delightful quantity, that he did not believe that he had exaggerated a thousandth part. Afterwards, he saw to the east of the said mountain a land, which seemed to be another mountain, like Monte Cristi in greatness and beauty, and from there, to the northeast by east, the land is not so high and it must be a full hundred millas [25 leagues], or about that.

SUNDAY, JANUARY 6th — *The harbor is sheltered from all winds, except the north and northwest, and he says that they prevail little in that land, and that even from these winds they can be protected behind the islet; there is from three to four braças [1.4 to 1.8 fathoms] depth. At sunrise, he set sail to go farther along the coast, which trended continually eastward, only it is necessary to give wide berth to the many reefs of rock [restringas de piedra] and sand which are on this coast...*

Columbus implies the elevated rock shelves lining Española's coast near Rio Bajabonico are similar to the *"restringas de piedra"* encountered during his exploration of Royal Island. But he differentiates their character by reporting how today's rock shelf was resting on *"sand"* whereas Royal Island's rose directly from the water.

...It is true that within them there are good harbors and good entrances through their channels. After midday, the east wind blew freshly; and he ordered a sailor to go up the mast to watch for shallows. He saw the caravel Pinta *coming towards him from the east, and she reached the Admiral, and since there was nowhere to anchor, as it was shallow water, the Admiral returned to Monte Cristi, going back the ten leagues which he had made, and the* Pinta *with him...*

Their afternoon reunion *"ten leagues"* east of Cabras Island was only a league from Pinzón's overnight anchorage at Rio Bajabonico. His scant headway in a favorable *"east wind"* suggests he was anchored when his lookouts spotted the *Niña's* sails on the western horizon. He knew Columbus would be seething over his unauthorized excursion to Great Inagua Island, and may have thought it prudent to reunite while actively seeking contact instead of gathering Rio Bajabonico's gold..

...Martin Alonso Pinzón came to the caravel Niña, *in which the Admiral was, to excuse himself, saying that he had parted from him against his will and giving reasons for this. But the Admiral says that they were all false, and that he had gone away that night when he had left him with much haughtiness and greed; and the Admiral says that he did not know the cause of the arrogance and disloyalty with which he had used him during that voyage. This the Admiral wished to pass over in order not to give room for the evil works of Satan, who greatly desired to hinder the voyage, as he had done up to that time. But an Indian, one of those whom the Admiral had entrusted to him, with others whom he carried in his caravel, had told Martin Alonso that in an island which was called "Baneque" there was much gold, and as he had a handy and light vessel, he wished to part company and to go by himself, leaving the Admiral, but the*

Admiral was anxious to wait and to coast along the islands of Juana and Española, since all that voyage would be to the east...

Columbus has forgotten how he had contended with unfavorable winds for more than a week in his own fruitless attempts to join in the harvesting of Great Inagua's *"much gold."*

...After Martin Alonso had gone to the island of Baneque, he says, and found no gold, he came to the coast of Española, as a result of information received from other Indians, who told him that in that island of Española, which the Indians called Bohio, there was a great quantity of gold and many mines, and on this account he arrived near the town of La Navidad, some fifteen leagues from it,...

It wouldn't have taken long for Pinzón to discover that Great Inagua's only *"gold"* was its mantel of arid sand dunes. He then should have rejoined his Admiral on Cuba's northeast coast, but *"information received from other Indians"* redirected his fixated quest to Española's *"great quantity of gold."* To reach that island's *"mines"* ahead of Columbus he had sailed eastward in search of Monte Cristi, the beacon marking the route to Española's gold deposits. After spotting that marker he took the safe route circumventing its shallows instead of risking the direct crossing Columbus would later follow. His southeasterly course along the edge of those shallows brought Pinzón to Española's north coast at Loma Rucia, a point *"fifteen leagues"* east of La Navidad.

...and that was more than twenty days ago...

Given that Pinzón was AWOL for 46 days, it seems likely he had been busily harvesting Española's golden nuggets for almost twice the "twenty days" he confessed to Columbus.

...From this it seems that the news, which the Indians gave, was true, on account of which king Guacanagarí sent the canoe and the Admiral the sailor, and that he must have gone away when the canoe arrived...

The lack of concealment along that stretch of coastline suggests *"the sailor"* had failed to carry out orders to explore the island's entire length.

...And the Admiral says here that the caravel bartered for much gold, so that for a lace tip they gave good pieces of gold, the size of two fingers, and sometimes the size of a hand, and Martin Alonso took half and divided the other half among his men...

Although Columbus must have resented Pinzón's golden harvest, he apparently made no attempt to expropriate this unauthorized booty, neither for himself nor his Sovereigns.

...The Admiral goes on telling the Sovereigns: "Thus, Sovereign Princes, I realize that Our Lord miraculously ordained that the ship should remain there, because it is the best place in all the islands for forming a settlement and nearest to the mines of gold"...

By several measures Monte Cristi was hardly Española's *"best place in all the islands for forming a settlement."* Columbus's reason for favoring this tiny exposed harbor may have been its proximity *"to the mines of gold"* discovered by Pinzón. In a few months Pinzón would be dead, freeing Columbus to move *La Navidad's* replacement even further east to Rio Bajabonico. Within a few years this replacement site was also abandoned after a permanent settlement was established at Santo Domingo on the island's south coast.

...He says also that he learned that he learned that behind the island of Juana, towards the south, there is another great island, in which there is a greater quantity of gold than in this, to such an extent that they collected nuggets larger than beans, and in the island of Española they gathered pieces of gold from the mines as large as grains of wheat. That island, he says, was called "Yamaye"...

Although Jamaica never produced much *"gold,"* the discovery of its bauxite ore in 1942 soon made it the world's leading source of aluminum. Today, this island's most noteworthy *"beans"* are the Blue Mountain variety favored worldwide by coffee connoisseurs.

...The Admiral also says that he learned that towards the east, there was an island where there were none save women only, and he says that he learned this from many persons, and that the island of Española or the other island of Yamaye was distant from the mainland ten days journey in a canoe, which must be sixty or seventy leagues, and that there the people were clothed.

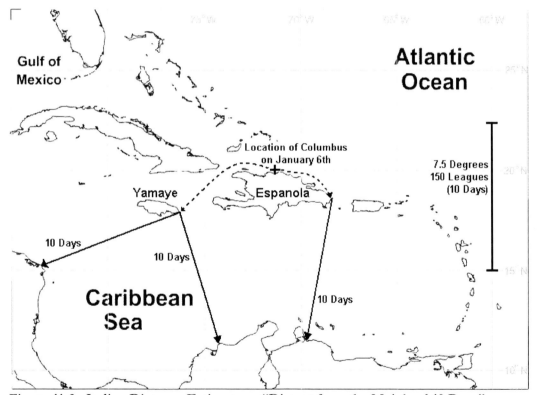

Figure 11-3. Indian Distance Estimates – "Distant from the Mainland 10 Days"

Whatever this measurement's source, *"ten days journey in a canoe"* was impressively accurate given that *"Española"* and Jamaica ("*Yamaye*") are both about 145 leagues from the nearest *"mainland."* This casual mention of a *"mainland"* 200 leagues from his route contrasts with his apparent failure to mention Florida when he was within a quarter of that distance. This dichotomy suggests his original *Journal* was more thoroughly scrubbed by Spanish authorities than indicated by the apparent excisions in his 21 December entry. In any event, Columbus was continuing to halve the length of the Taino's canoe-day, so he misinterpreted those *"ten days"* as only *"sixty or seventy leagues."* His 1493 letter would conceal this important discovery, but three months later the Royal Capitulations were updated to add the *"mainland"* to the list of *"what he hath discovered"*. Columbus wouldn't actually set foot on South America until 1498, but even this delayed arrival preceded Cabral's "discovery" by two years.

MONDAY, JANUARY 7th — *This day he had the caravel, which was leaking, pumped and caulked, and the sailors went ashore to collect wood, and he says that they found much mastic and lignaloe.*

Teredos had been burrowing into the *Niña's* hull since its early November careening, leading Columbus to have it *"caulked"* again in anticipation of an arduous Atlantic crossing.

TUESDAY, JANUARY 8th — *As there was a strong east and southeasterly wind blowing, he did not set out on this day. Accordingly, he ordered that the caravel should take in supplies of water and wood and all that was necessary for the whole voyage, because, although he was anxious to coast along the whole shore of Española, which, keeping to his course, he could have done, yet those whom he had placed in the caravels as captains, who were brothers, that is to say, Martin Alonso Pinzón and Vincente Yañez, and others who followed them, considering with haughtiness and greed that all was now their own, disregarding the honor which the Admiral had done and given to them, had not obeyed and did not obey his commands, but on the contrary did and said many unjust things against him, and Martin Alonso had left him from the twenty-first of November until the sixth of January without cause or reason, but only out of disobedience. All this the Admiral had suffered and overlooked in order to bring his voyage to a good conclusion; therefore, in order to free himself from such evil company, in which, he says, he was compelled to dissemble, although they were a disobedient people and although he had with him many men of goodwill, but it was not the time to consider punishment, he resolved to return with the greatest haste possible, and not to delay any further...*

Columbus ignored today's *"strong east and southeasterly wind,"* so favorable for a return to Spain *"with the greatest haste possible."* Instead, he chose to remain in Española another week to measure its longitude accurately using the Moon's rare occultation of Venus.

...He entered the boat and went to the river, which is near there, a full league towards the south-southeast of Monte Cristi, where the sailors had gone to take water for the ship,...

There's no river to the *"south-southeast"* of Monte Cristi: Columbus must have been referring to the Yaque del Norte River that empties into Monte Cristi Bay *"a full league"* south-south<u>west</u> of his anchorage. A Las Casas postil incorporating "yaqui" in his description of this "gold-bearing" stream supports this assumption.

...and he found that the sand at the mouth of the river, which, he says, is very large and deep, was all full of gold and of such quality that it was a wonder, although it was very small. The Admiral believed that in coming down that river it crumbled on the way, although he says that in a little space he found many grains as large as lentils, but the smaller size, he says, was in great abundance. And, as the sea was at high tide...

With the moon a week past full, Columbus would have observed *"high tide"* near midday.

...and the salt water mingled with the fresh, he ordered the boat to go up the river a stones throw. They filled the water butts from the boat, and returned to the caravel, they found caught in the hoops of the barrels small pieces of gold, and

the same thing in the hoops of the cask. The Admiral called the river Rio del Oro, and within, when the entrance has been passed, it is very deep, although the entrance is shallow, and the mouth is very wide, and it is seventeen leagues from the town of La Navidad...

This excerpt suggests Las Casas had more difficulty transcribing the *Journal's* place names than its sailing distances. Four days earlier he had recorded how *"Monte Cristi...lies exactly to the east of Cape Santo...at a distance of eighteen leagues."* Today, after sailing one league west of Monte Cristi to the *"Rio del Oro"* (Yaque del Norte), he wrote that this river is *"seventeen leagues from the town of La Navidad."* These mutually consistent distances to two different place names suggest Las Casas was still groping for the one Columbus apparently had assigned to the far west end of that *"angla muy grande."* Four days ago he had substituted *"Cape Santo"* for that missing place name, but today he mislabeled it as *"La Navidad."*

...In the interval there are other large rivers, and especially three, which he believed must have much more gold than that, because they are larger,...

There are only two *"large rivers"* between the Yaque del Norte River and *"La Navidad."* The Admiral's use of *"especially three"* confirms those *"seventeen leagues"* extended well beyond both *"Cape Santo"* and *"La Navidad"* to encompass the Riviére Salée flowing into Acul Bay.

...although this is as large as the Guadalquivir at Cordoba,...

To establish a meaningful comparison, Columbus chose a location midway between the Guadalquivir's headwaters and its mouth, a scene familiar to many of his countrymen.

...and from them to the mines of gold it is not twenty leagues...

These Indian *"mines of gold"* were apparently near the headwaters of the Bajabonico River, *"twenty leagues"* from the mouth of the Yaque del Norte River.

...The Admiral says further that he did not wish to take any of that sand which contained so much gold, because their Highnesses had it all under their absolute control and at the gate of their own town of La Navidad, but first to come at full speed to bring them the news and to escape from the evil company which he had, and he had always said that they were a disobedient people.

WEDNESDAY, JANUARY 9th — *At midnight he set sail...*

"At midnight he set sail" while Mars was rising two degrees behind the Moon. Columbus may have delayed his departure until convinced cloud cover wouldn't clear in time to allow measurement of LPC-21, potentially one of the better opportunities of his voyage.

*...with the wind southeast and steered to the east-northeast. He reached a headland, which he called Punta Roja **(r)**, which is exactly to the east of Monte Cristi, sixty millas [15 leagues] away...*

The *"southeast"* wind was well-suited for a return to Spain, but the opportunity to measure next Monday's LPC-22 from Samaná Bay trumped yesterday's wish to return home *"with the greatest haste possible."* Instead, Columbus coasted eastward to Punta Patilla, the *"headland...exactly to the east of*

Monte Cristi" at a distance of *"15 leagues."* Morison resurrected his short "land league" to suggest Columbus's *"Punta Roja"* was Punta Rucia, a "gray point" only 8 ½ leagues from Monte Cristi. Not only does Punta Rucia fail the distance test, its name doesn't match the ruddy hue implied by *"Roja."*

...and in the shelter of it he anchored in the afternoon at approximately three hours before nightfall. He did not dare to leave there by night, because there were many reefs, until they were known, for afterwards they would be an advantage, if they had channels, as they must have, and would have great depth of water and good anchorage, secure from all winds...

Samaná Bay, where he planned to observe LPC-22 next Monday morning, was less than a day's sail from Punta Patilla. His leisurely schedule allowed Columbus to anchor behind Punta Patilla *"three hours before nightfall"* rather than needlessly expose his ships to its *"many reefs"* at night.

...These lands from, Monte Cristi, to the point where he anchored, are high and smooth and very fair champaign, and at the sides there are very lovely mountains, which run from east to west, and are all tilled and green, so that it is a wonder to see their beauty, and there are many streams. In all this land there are many tortoises, some of which, as they come ashore to lay their eggs, the sailors took at Monte Cristi, and they were as large as a wooden shield. The day before, when the Admiral went to the Rio del Oro, he said that he saw three sirens, who rose very high from the sea, but they were not as beautiful as they are depicted, for somehow their faces had the appearance of a man...

It's generally agreed that these *"three sirens...not as beautiful as depicted"* were actually Manatee.

...He says that on other occasions he saw some in Guinea on the coast of Manegueta...

A Cecil Jane footnote reads, "The Malagueta Coast (Liberia, Sierra Leone) was named after a variety of pepper, the *malagueta*, which grows there." Columbus had sailed that coast a decade earlier under a Portuguese flag.

...He says that this night, in the name of Our Lord, he will set out on his voyage, without delaying longer for anything, since he had found what he had been seeking,...

This excerpt may have been intentionally distorted by one of the copyists. In fact, Columbus will be *"delaying"* his return voyage until after the longitude measurement *"he had been seeking"* through observation of LPC-22.

...because he did not wish to have further controversy with that Martin Alonso, until their Highnesses learned the news of his voyage and what he had accomplished: "And afterwards," he says, "I will not endure the acts of evil persons and men of little virtue, who with small consideration presume to do what they will in opposition to him who did them honor."

THURSDAY, JANUARY 10th — *He set out from that place where he had anchored and at sunset arrived at a river to which he gave the name Rio de Gracia* **(g)**, *three leagues to the southeast...*

The winds must have been unfavorable if Columbus could only make it as far as Puerto Plata, the harbor he identified as "Rio de Gracia" and accurately mapped *"three leagues to the southeast"* of Punta Patilla. Morison missed the impossibility of sailing any distance "southeast" from Punta Rucia, his flawed choice for the "Punta Roja" of Columbus.

...He anchored at its mouth, where there is a good anchorage, on the east side. Going inside, there is a bank which has no more than two braçias [0.9 fathoms] of water and is very narrow. Within, there is a good closed harbor, except that there are many shipworms...

Teredos were becoming an increasing concern for Columbus as he visualized the pounding his ships might endure on their return voyage to Spain.

...From them the caravel Pinta, *in which was Martin Alonso, suffered great damage, for he says he remained there trading for sixteen days, and there they bartered much gold, which was what Martin Alonso desired...*

Martin Alonzo Pinzón's report of *"trading for sixteen days"* at Puerto Plata is consistent with his January 6th claim that he arrived at Española *"more than twenty days ago."* But his partial accounting must have left Columbus ruminating about his other activities during his unauthorized absence.

...When he had learned from the Indians that the Admiral was on the coast of the same island of Española, and that he could not avoid him, he came to him, and it is said that he wished all of his men in the ship to swear that he had only been there six days. But he said that his wickedness was a thing so notorious that it could not be concealed, and, says the Admiral, he had made rules by which half the gold which was bartered or procured was for him, and when he came to leave that place, he took four Indian men and two girls by force, and the Admiral ordered clothing to be given to them and had them returned to land that they might go to their homes: "This," he says, "is for the service of your Highnesses, for these men and women are all your Highnesses' and it is so especially in this island, as in the others. But here, where your Highnesses already have a settlement, more honor and favor ought to be done to the people, since in this island there is so much gold and good lands and spices."

FRIDAY, JANUARY 11th — *At midnight he set out from Rio de Gracia with the land breeze: he steered as far as a cape which he called Bel Prado* **(s)**, *a distance of four leagues,...*

Cabo Macorís is the modern name for the *"cape which he called Bel Prado, a distance of four leagues"* east of Puerto Plata.

...and from there to the southeast is the mountain which he named Monte de Plata, and he says that it is eight leagues from there...

"Monte de Plata," a solitary 2700-ft peak centered on Española's silver-bearing region, is *"eight leagues"* southeast of Cabo Macorís. In his postil, Las Casas mistook it for Pico Duarte, the Caribbean's highest mountain, concealed from Columbus behind the Cordillera Septentrional paralleling Española's north coast. Las Casas paved the way for modern tourist brochures showing Pico Duarte's 10,500-foot peak shrouded by clouds when he incorrectly speculated it was "...called de Plata because it is very high and there is always a mist above its peak which makes it white or silvery."

...From Cape del Prado, to the east by south, is the cape which he called del Angel **(t)**, *distant eighteen leagues,...*

There's no cape *"eighteen leagues"* from Cabo Macorís, and neither is there any height visible *"to the east by south"*. But this combination of distance and direction do define the relationship between two important coastal features – the Punta Patilla Columbus had departed yesterday morning and Cabo Francés Viejo, the 1500-foot peak emerging into view as he rounded Cabo

Macorís. In his *Journal* abstract Las Casas may have overlooked the way Columbus sometimes aggregated measurements linking prominent coastal features, such as his January 4th entry referencing Monte Cristi's location to the east end of that "*angla muy grande.*"

...and from this cape to Monte de Plata there is a gulf and the best and most lovely lands in the world, all fit for cultivation, high and beautiful, and they run far inland, and afterwards there is a range of mountains which stretches from east to west, very large and very lovely, and at the foot of the mountain there is a very good harbor **(u)**, *and at the entrance there are 14 braçias [6.3 fathoms]...*

Rio Muñoz at the west end of Punta Bergantin is the only "*very good harbor*" between Puerto Plata and Cabo Francés Viejo. It has a depth of 30 feet "*at the entrance.*"

...This mountain is very high and lovely, and all is very populous, and the Admiral believed that there must be good rivers and much gold. From Cape del Angel to the east by south it is four leagues to a headland which he called del Hierro **(v)**, *and four leagues in the same direction there is a headland which he called Punta Seca,***(w)**...

Having defined the distance to his Cape del Angel objective, Columbus identifies two points along the route. His "*del Hierro*" is the modern Punta Cabarete, located slightly more than "*four leagues...east by south*" from Rio Muñoz, not the "*Cape del Angel*" misread by Las Casas. His "*Punta Seca*" is today's Playa Gen, another "*four leagues in the same direction.*"

...and six leagues from there in the same direction is the cape which he called Redondo,...

It's "*six leagues... in the same direction from*" Punta Cabarete to the 1500-foot peak capping "rounded" Cabo Francis Viejo, the dominant feature of today's coasting.

...and from there to the east is Cape Francés, and at this cape, on the east side, there is a large bay [angla grande] **(x)**, *but it did not seem to have an anchorage...*

Española's fifth "*angla*" was an exposed bight more than two leagues wide to the southeast of Cabo Francis Viejo. Because "*it did not seem to have an anchorage,*" Columbus turned northeasterly from this threatening coastline before nightfall.

...A league from there is Cape del Bueno Tiempo **(y)**: *from this to the south by east, there is a cape which he called Trajado* **(z)**, *at a full leagues distance...*

Columbus measured the bight's embracing capes from the southern limit of his coasting: one "league" north to Punta La Estella, and "south by east... a full leagues distance" to Punta Laguna Grande.

...From this towards the south he saw another cape **(aa)**, *and it seemed to be fifteen leagues away...*

Columbus had first detected 1990-foot Cabo Cabrón "*towards the south*" earlier today as he was rounding Cape Francés Viejo. At a distance of "*fifteen leagues*" it rose only a tenth of a degree above his horizon, leading him to needlessly soft-pedal what proved to be his accurate distance estimate. Other nearby peaks rose higher to view, but his charts may have identified Cabo Cabrón as a guide to Samaná Bay, the harbor where he hoped to measure longitude three days hence.

...Today he went a great distance, as the winds and currents were with him...

Today's westerly *"winds"* had driven Columbus 20 leagues eastward from Puerto Plata to Cabo Francés Viejo. Despite his loss of the *Santa Maria* to the Atlantic Gyre, he continued to believe this opposing *"current"* was flowing *"with him."*

...He did not dare to anchor for fear of the shallows; and so he jogged off and on all night.

SATURDAY, JANUARY 12th — *At the quarter of dawn he steered to the east with a fresh wind, and so went until day, and in this time he made twenty millas [5 leagues], and in the following two hours twenty-four millas [6 leagues]. From there he saw land to the south, and went towards it; it was forty-eight millas [12 leagues] away and he says that, keeping out to sea, he went this night twenty-eight millas [7 leagues] to the north-northeast...*

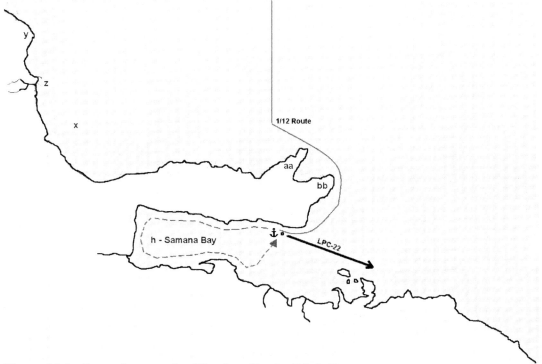

Figure 11-4. Cayos Levantados Viewing Site for LPC-22

From 3 A.M. until dawn Columbus *"steered to the east"* 11 leagues at hull speed under *"a fresh wind."* At daybreak *"he saw"* Cabo Cabrón *"to the south"* at nearly 13 leagues, a distance he mapped as *"twelve leagues"* by ignoring the push of the Atlantic Gyre. Columbus then remembered to record those earlier *"seven leagues to the north-northeast"* he had made *"this night"* before 3 A.M. The consistency of these distances suggests yesterday's final recording, that *"he jogged off and on all night,"* was a mistake.

...When he saw the land, he named a cape, which he sighted, Cabo de Padre y Hijo, because at its point, on the east side, there were two projections, one being greater than the other...

After sailing south almost halfway to Cabo Cabrón **(aa)**, Columbus could see its smaller neighbor, Cabo Samaná **(bb),** rising to its east. His choice of name for this mismatched pair, "*Cabo* *de Padre y Hijo (Father and Son),"* was apt, but apparently forgotten well before Las Casas began transcribing the *Journal.*

....Afterwards to the east, at two leagues, he saw a great and very lovely opening between two large mountains, and he saw that it was a very large harbor, good and with a very good entrance,...

Sailing *"two leagues"* southeast brought Columbus to the harbor with the *"very good entrance"* bracketed by "Padre y Hijo."

...but because it was very early in the morning [por ser muy de maña]...

After his dawn sighting of Cabo Cabrón, it took Columbus at least 5 hours to sail the 14 leagues to Padre y Hijo. So it must have been nearly noon, not *"very early in the morning,"* when he finally reached this *"very large harbor."*

...and in order not to delay his journey, for during most of the time it blows there from the east and so carries a ship north-northwest [entonces le lleva nornorueste],...

Dunn/Kelley corrected Cecil Jane's misleading translation to read, "most of the time in that region, east winds blow, and at that time he had a north-northwesterly."

...he would not wait longer. He followed his course to the east as far as a very high and very beautiful cape, all of jagged rock, to which he gave the name Cape del Enamorado, it was to the east of that harbor, which he called Puerto Sacro, thirty-two millas [8 leagues] distant. When he reached it, he discovered another cape, much more lovely and much higher and rounded, all of rock like Cape St. Vincent in Portugal; it was twelve millas [3 leagues] east of Cape del Enamorado...

His afternoon search for a backup site isn't fully documented in the Las Casas extract of the *Journal.* It seems likely Columbus conserved his remaining daylight hours by following the 111-degree bearing line from Cayos Levantados. After almost *"8 leagues"* his angled crossing of Samaná Bay's wide opening would have brought him to the foot of *"Cape del Enamorado,"* a *"beautiful"* 1092-foot coastal peak, *"to the east of that harbor."* *"When he reached it, he discovered another"* (2080-foot peak) emerging from behind it *"much higher and rounded...[3 leagues] east of Cape del Enamorado."*

...After he had come abreast of Cape del Enamorado, he saw between it and the other [otro] cape a very large bay, which had a breadth of three leagues, and in the middle [en medio] of it a tiny islet [isleta pequeñuela]...

Samaná Bay's wide mouth extends *"three leagues"* south from Punta Balandra to Punta Maguá. Columbus used *"en medio"* to position the *"tiny islet"* of Cayo Levantado which offered the bay's best-protected anchorage having a clear view of LPC-22. "Cayo Levantado" (Lifted or Raised) may derive its name as the observation site when the Moon and Venus "rose" together on a bearing angle of 111 degrees.

...The depth is great at the entrance near the land; he anchored there in twelve braças [23 feet]...

Morison thought Columbus chose a 12-fathom anchorage fully exposed to hostile Caribs and the eastern trade winds battering Samaná Bay. However, Columbus avoided both of these threats when "*he anchored...in twelve bracias*" between Cayo Levantado and Cayo Pascual.

...He sent the boat to land for water and to see if they could have speech, but the people all fled. He also anchored in order to see if all that land was one with Española and if what he called a gulf did not form a separate island. He was amazed that the island of Española was so large.

SUNDAY, JANUARY 13th — *He did not go out of this harbor because there was no land breeze with which to do so. He was anxious to leave in order to go to a better harbor, since that was somewhat exposed...*

His Cayo Levantado anchorage was indeed *"somewhat exposed"* to the trade winds, but Columbus would lose his unobstructed view of tomorrow morning's LPC-22 if he anchored any deeper within Samaná Bay.

...and because he wished to observe the conjunction of the moon with the sun, which he expected on the seventeenth,...

Columbus would have risked permanent retinal damage by recklessly trying *"to observe the conjunction of the moon with the sun."* The transcriber responsible for concocting this gibberish apparently forgot that the *Niña* would be at sea *"on the seventeenth."*

...and the moon in opposition with Jupiter, and in conjunction with Mercury, and the sun in opposition to Jupiter, which is the cause of great winds...

The only *"conjunction"* of interest to Columbus wasn't *"the cause of great winds;"* it was tomorrow morning's LPC-22 allowing measurement of his longitude. Las Casas took this silly *Journal* distortion seriously when he noted "...by this it seems that the Admiral knew something of astronomy even though not well expressed because of the transcriber's bad handwriting."

...He sent the boat to land at a beautiful beach,...

This *"beautiful beach"* immediately east of Puntas de las Flechas was less than a mile from his Cayo Levantado anchorage.

...in order that they might take ajes to eat, and they found some men with bows and arrows, with whom they paused to talk, and they bought two bows and many arrows, and asked one of them to go to speak with the Admiral in the caravel, and he came. The Admiral says that he was more ugly in appearance than any whom he had seen. He had his face all stained with charcoal, although in all other parts they are accustomed to paint themselves with various colors; he wore all his hair very long and drawn back and tied behind, and then gathered in meshes of parrots feathers, and he was as naked as the others. The Admiral judged that he must be one of the Caribs who eat men and that the gulf, which he had seen yesterday, divided the land and that it must be an island by itself. He questioned him concerning the Caribs, and the Indian indicated to him that they were near there to the east, and the Admiral says that he sighted this land yesterday before he entered the bay. The Indian told him that in that land there was much gold, and pointing to the poop of the caravel, which was very large, said that there were pieces of that size. He called gold "tuob," and did not understand it by "caona," as they call it in the first part of the island, or by "nozay," as they name it in San Salvador and in the other islands...

The only *"gulf"* within view was Samaná Bay, which Columbus had *"sighted...yesterday before he entered the bay."* Lacking adequate time for exploration he assumed its huge embracing peninsula was *"an island by itself,"* separate from *"the first part of the island"* of Española.

...In Española they call gold or copper of poor quality "tuob." Of the island of Matinino, the Indian said that it was entirely peopled by women without men, and that in it there is very much tuob, *which is copper or gold, and that it is further to the east of Carib...*

The *Journal* mentions these islands of *"Matinino"* and *"Carib"* half a dozen times over the course of the following week. Most historians have correctly identified *"Carib"* as Puerto Rico, while ignoring how this island would soon warp Columbus's homeward route. But almost all have skirted identification of the second island, described by Columbus as *"Matinino...the island east of Carib."* One bold exception was Cecil Jane, who incorrectly guessed it was Martinique. In fact, *"Matinino"* was the Indian's name for St. Croix, the largest of the Virgin Islands, not discovered by Columbus until his second voyage to the New World. Las Casas recorded how Columbus gave this numberless archipelago the glorious name, "Santa Ursula y las Once Mil Virgines (Saint Ursula and the Eleven Thousand Virgins)." Many historians have romanticized his choice of name, but Columbus was simply recalling how this island supposedly *"was entirely peopled by women without men."*

...He spoke also of the island of "Goanín," where there is much tuob. *Of these islands, the Admiral says that he had been told some days before by many persons. The Admiral says further that in the islands which he had passed they were in great terror of "Carib;" in some islands they call it "Caniba," but in Española, "Carib;" and they must be a daring people, since they go through all the islands and eat the people they can take. He says that he understood some words, and from them he says that he gathered other things, and the Indians whom he carried with him understood more, although they found a difference of languages, owing to the great distances between the lands. He ordered food to be given to the Indian, and gave him pieces of green and red cloth and glass beads, to which they are very much attached, and sent him back to shore. And he told him to bring him gold, if there was any, which he believed to be the case from certain small ornaments which he was wearing. When the boat reached the shore, there were behind the trees quite fifty-five men, naked, with very long hair, as women wear their hair in Castile. At the back of the head, they wore tufts of parrot feathers and feathers of other birds, and each one carried his bow. The Indian landed and caused the others to lay aside their bows and arrows and a short stick, which is like a very heavy [...] and which they carry in place of a sword...*

A Las Casas postil clarifies the *Journal's* final lacuna as a *bludgeon* fashioned in the form of an iron shovel carved from a palm's trunk

...Afterwards they came to the boat and the people from the boat landed, and they began to buy from them their bows and arrows and other weapons, because the Admiral had ordered this to be done. When two bows had been sold, they would not give more, but prepared rather to assault the Christians and capture them. They went running to collect their bows and arrows, where they had laid them aside, and came back with ropes in their hands, in order, as he says, to bind the Christians. Seeing them come running towards them, the Christians, being on guard, as the Admiral always advised them to be, fell upon them, and they gave an Indian a great slash on the buttocks and they wounded another in the breast with an arrow. When they saw that they could gain little, although the Christians were not more than seven and they were fifty and more, they turned in flight, so that not one remained, one leaving his arrows here and another his bow there. The Christians, as he says, would have killed many of them, if the pilot who went with them as their captain had not prevented it. Afterwards the Christians returned to the caravel with their boat, and when the Admiral learned of it, he said that on the one hand he was sorry, and on the other hand not, since they would be afraid

of the Christians, for without doubt, he says, the people there are, as he says, evil doers, and he believed that they were those from Carib and that they eat men; accordingly, if the boat which he had left with the thirty-nine men in the fortress and town of La Navidad should come there, these would be afraid to do any ill to them. And he says that if they were not Caribs, at least they might be neighbors of them and have the same customs, and they are a fearless people, not like the others of the other islands, who are cowardly beyond reason and without weapons. All this the Admiral says, and that he wished to take some of them. He says that they made many smoke signals, as they were accustomed to do in that island of Española.

MONDAY, JANUARY 14th — *He wished to send this night to look for the houses of the Indians, in order to take some of them, believing that they were Caribs, and owing to the strong east and northeast wind and to the high sea running, he did not do so...*

Columbus was anticipating a more productive use of the darkness than the capture of a few *"Caribs."* For his *Ephemerides* predicted LPC-22 would offer an exceptional opportunity to measure longitude when Venus rose at 3:21 AM Monday morning only 1½ degrees below its impending lunar occultation. Yesterday's moonrise had confirmed Cayo Levantado as his best location for viewing LPC-22 over an unobstructed ocean horizon: if he had anchored even a few miles further within Samaná Bay, Española's eastern peaks would have obstructed his 111-degree bearing line to LPC-22. So he waited patiently this morning at Cayo Levantado for Venus to follow the Moon, already rising from the ocean's ESE horizon. As the Moon climbed alone in the eastern sky, each arc minute of agonizing delay in the arrival of Venus pushed his celestially computed longitude 27 miles closer to Africa. Columbus must have been stunned when Venus finally rose almost three full degrees below the Moon, an angular separation he would have expected 800 leagues (40 full degrees!) east of Samaná Bay. Simultaneous occultation measurements in Seville would later resolve tonight's huge discrepancy, but we shall soon see how this morning's incredibly misleading longitude measurement would alter his homeward course.

...But as soon as it was day, they saw many Indians on land, and the Admiral therefore ordered the boat to go there with people well equipped. And immediately they saw them, they all came to the stern of the boat and especially the Indian who had come to the caravel the day before and to whom the Admiral had given some articles of barter. He says that with him there came a king, who had given some beads to the said Indian to present to those in the boat, as a sign of security and peace. This king, with three of his people, entered the boat and came to the caravel, and the Admiral ordered that they should be given biscuit and honey to eat, and he gave him a red cap and beads and a piece of red cloth, and to the others he also gave pieces of cloth. The king said that next day he would bring a gold mask, declaring that there was much there and in Carib and Matinino. Afterwards, he sent them to land well pleased. The Admiral says further that the caravels were leaking much at the keel, and he complains greatly of the caulkers who at Palos caulked them very badly, and when they saw that the Admiral had noticed the poorness of their work and that he wished to make them put it right, they fled. But, despite the fact that the caravels were taking much water, he trusted that our Lord, who brought him there, in His pity and mercy would lead him back, for His High Majesty well knew how much controversy he had experienced before he was able to set out from Castile, and that no other had been in his favor save Him alone because He knew his heart, and after God, their Highnesses; and all the others had been contrary to him without any reason. And he says further as follows: "And they have been the cause that the royal crown of Your Highnesses has not a hundred millions more revenue than it has, since the time that I came to serve you, which is now seven years ago the twentieth day of January, this present month,...

This accurate dating was challenged in a Las Casas postil asserting the Enterprise of the Indies wasn't proposed until 1489. But Columbus always dated his service to the Crown from his

1486 arrival at the royal city of Cordova *"seven years ago the twentieth day of January."* He knew this date well because a few months later Fray Hernando Talavera, Isabela's confessor, would organize a committee to consider the merits of his *Enterprise*.

...plus the accumulation which would result from now on; but the mighty God will make all well." These are his words.

TUESDAY, JANUARY 15th — *He says that he wished to depart because now there was no profit in remaining, owing to those disagreements which had occurred; he must mean the dispute with the Indians...*

At 4 AM Venus stood seven degrees above the rising Moon, still close enough for Columbus to confirm yesterday's stunning longitude measurement. Today's *Ephemerides* entry would have shrunk yesterday's huge longitude error, but only to the still considerable distance separating Los Angeles from Savannah, Georgia. After completing this morning's measurement *"there was no profit in remaining"* in Española, which was more to do with the fading utility of LPC-22 than with Sunday's "dispute with the Indians."

...He says also that today he has learned that all the abundance of gold was in the district of the town [villa] of La Navidad of their Highnesses, and that in the island of Carib and in Matinino there is much copper,...

An abundance of *"copper...in the island of Carib and in Matinino"* implies extensive trading activity with mainland communities separated by several hundred miles.

...although there would be difficulties in Carib, because that people is said to eat human flesh. Their island was in sight from there, and he resolved to go to it, as it was on his course, and to the island of Matinino, which is said to be entirely peopled by women without men, and to see both and to take some of them, as he says...

The *"Carib... island"* of Puerto Rico wasn't *"in sight from there;"* its tallest peak, Cerro de Punta, was well below Samaná Bay's horizon. But the claim of discovery was important to Columbus, so he *"resolved to go to it"* even though it was hardly *"on his course"* for Spain.

...The Admiral sent the boat ashore and the king of that land had not come, because, he says, the village [poblaçion] was distant, but he sent his gold crown, as he had promised. And there came many other men with cotton and bread and ajes, all with their bows and arrows. After all had been bartered, there came, as he says, four young men to the caravel, and they seemed to the Admiral to give so good a description of all those islands which were towards the east on the same course, which the Admiral had to take, that he decided to carry them to Castile with him...

These *"four young men"* gave Columbus *"a good description of all those islands which were towards the east."* With their guidance he would covertly bend his return route just enough to discover Puerto Rico without alarming his homesick crew.

...There he says that they have no iron bar nor has he seen any other metal, although in a few days it is impossible to learn much concerning a country, owing to the difficulty of the language, which the Admiral only understood by guesswork, and because they did not understand what he asked of them in a few days. The bows of that people, as he says, were as large as those of France and England; the arrows are like the spears of the other peoples which he had visited previously, for they are of the stalks of canes, when they are seeding, which are very straight and a vara and a half and two varas in length,...

These shafts ranging from 4 to 5 ½ feet were as long as the *"spears"* they had acquired at Egg Island.

...and afterwards they fix at the end a piece of sharp wood, a palm and a half long, and into this piece of wood some insert a fish tooth and some, the majority, put poison there. They do not shoot them as in other parts, but in a peculiar manner so that they cannot do much harm. There was there much cotton, very fine and long, and there is much mastic, and it seemed to him that their bows were of yew, and that there was gold and copper. There is also much axi, which is their pepper, which is worth more than pepper, and all those people eat nothing without it, for they find it very healthy. Fifty caravels could be loaded with it every year in Española. He says that he found much seaweed in that bay, of the kind which they found in the gulf when he came to the discovery [en el golpho quando venia al descubrimiento], on which account he believed there were islands lying directly to the east, from the point where he began to find them, since he regards it as certain that this weed grows in shallow water near the land,...

Cecil Jane was free to render *"golpho"* correctly in 1930 because no one had yet proposed a landfall candidate actually fronting a *"gulf when he came to the discovery."* This situation changed in 1980 after I identified Egg Island's Northeast Providence Channel as the only *"golpho"* shown on a 16th century Spanish mapping of the Bahama Islands. In 1989 Dunn/Kelley neutralized this important finding by warping their translation to accommodate *every* landfall candidate with *"in mid-sea when he came [on his voyage of discovery]."* Not only did their strained translation reduce the Atlantic Ocean to a *"gulf,"* it also assumed Columbus somehow confused the Sargasso Sea's rootless seaweed with Egg Island's uprooted Benthic weed which *"grows in shallow water near the land."*

...and he says that, if this be so, these Indies were very near the Canary Islands, and for this reason he believed that they were less than four hundred leagues distant...

Today's second measurement of LPC-22 was a slight improvement over yesterday's, but still 600 leagues short of true! A half century later Las Casas probably knew these huge longitude errors were a result of faulty *Ephemerides* data, so he defended Columbus with a postil praising the Admiral for his *"bien juzgava."* That *"good judgment"* honored the impressive accuracy of his celestial measurements after their adjustment by Spanish astronomers also observing LPC-22. His measurement accuracy would be validated when his second voyage found landfall near the eastern rim of the Greater Antilles, establishing a preferred route to the New World that would endure for centuries to come. The precision of his second landfall would be a tribute to his careful LPC-22 observations, the corrections applied by Seville's astronomers, the accuracy of Indian maps, and his skillful navigation.

Part V – Homeward Bound

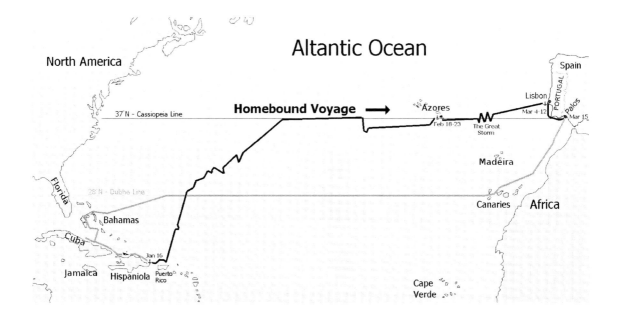

12 - On to the Azores

WEDNESDAY, JANUARY 16th — *He set out from that gulf, which he called Golfo de las Flechas, three hours before day with a land breeze, and afterwards with a west wind, steering to the east by north, in order to go, as he says, to the island of Carib,...*

Columbus was confronted with a troubling dilemma as he set out upon his return voyage. He knew his men were anxious to return home before losing their battle with the ship worms feasting on their vulnerable fleet. While he shared their survival concerns, he was anxious to sight *"the island of Carib,"* both to broaden his claim for what he *"discovered and gained in the Ocean Sea,"* and to identify the best route for future voyages to the New World. Today's initial *"east by north"* course is an evident recording error, because in *"a west wind"* Columbus was free to sail *"east by <u>south</u>"* towards Puerto Rico on a direct route barely skirting Española's coastal bulge. Normally it would have been risky to sail that darkened coast by compass. But when he *"set out from (the) Golfo de las Flechas, three hours before day"* the third-magnitude star Sabik was well positioned to guide him *"east by <u>south</u>"* from its perch 10 degrees above the pitch-black horizon. Within the hour a slender crescent moon rose directly below Sabik, taking over its guidance role until the dawn's first light illuminated Española's rugged silhouette paralleling his route to Puerto Rico.

...where lived the people of whom all those islands and lands were in so great fear, because it is said that with their innumerable canoes they go about all those seas and it is said that they eat the men whom they can take. He says that some Indians, of the four whom he had taken yesterday in the harbor of las Flechas, had shown him the course. After having gone, in his opinion 64 millas [16 leagues], the Indians indicated to him that the island lay to the southeast...

After sailing *"[16 leagues]"* to the *"east by <u>south</u>,"* the fleet cleared Española's coastal bulge, ominously identified on modern maps as *Playa del Muerto*, perhaps for the many ships grounded there by an unrelenting Atlantic Gyre. Now, with open water to the *"southeast,"* Columbus could head directly for the Carib's island of Puerto Rico.

...He wished to take that route, and ordered the sails trimmed, and after having gone two leagues, the wind became stronger, very good for going to Spain. He observed among the people that they began to grow sad because they were turning aside from the direct course, owing to the fact that both caravels were taking much water, and that they had no remedy save in God...

Columbus was faced with a delicate balancing act. His men, fearing a watery grave in their leaking caravels, were anxious for an expeditious ocean crossing, while he needed a sighting of Puerto Rico to validate his 10 percent claim to its riches under the Articles of Capitulation. He would resolve this dilemma through the deception of appearing to maintain a homeward course during the day while covertly edging his fleet within viewing distance of Puerto Rico at night.

...He was forced to abandon the course which he believed led to the island, and he went about to the direct course for Spain, northeast by east,...

Prior to LPC-22 Columbus had been confident an E by N course would carry him back to the Canary Islands. But that conjunction's huge longitude error predicted such a course would intercept the African coastline far to the south of the Canary Islands, not only intruding on Portuguese territory, but also adding a hundred leagues to his already precarious return voyage. He surely doubted this unexpected *Ephemerides* finding, but realized its surprising *"northeast by east"* course wouldn't impose a significant distance penalty. In the likelihood subsequent LPCs proved it false, the constellation Cassiopeia would simply guide him home along the 37th parallel with an eastward boost from the Atlantic's clockwise winds and current.

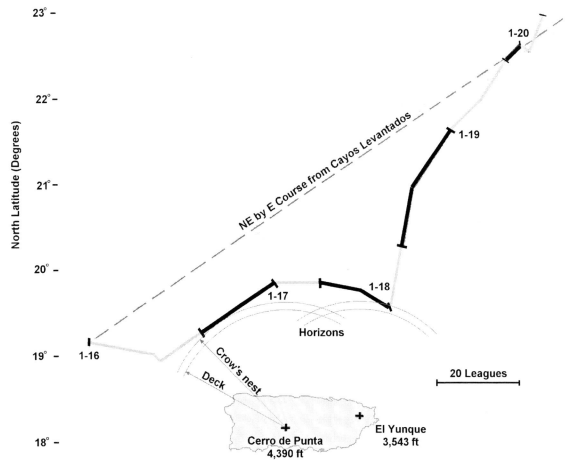

Figure 12-1. Sighting of Puerto Rico's "El Yunque" at 18 January Sunrise before regaining NE by E course "home"

...and so he went 48 millas, which are twelve leagues, until sunset...

His early afternoon order to turn homeward as *"the wind became stronger"* must have bolstered his men's sagging spirits. But Columbus still needed to verify the Taino's mapping of Puerto Rico's easternmost mountains, both to validate his claim of discovery and to establish a landmark for follow-up voyages. If his Taino maps proved accurate, he saw he could avoid alarming his crew by skirting the island beyond detection range on a course keeping its easternmost peaks out of view until Friday's sunrise.

...The Indians told him that by that route he would find the island of Matinino, which is said to be peopled by women without men, and which the Admiral greatly desired to visit, in order, as he says, to take to the Sovereigns five or six of them. But he doubted whether the Indians knew the course well, and he could not delay on account of the danger from the water which the caravels were shipping. But he says that it was certain that there were these women, and that at a certain time of the year men came to them from the island of Carib, which he says was ten or twelve leagues from them. And if they gave birth to a boy, they sent him to the island of the men, and if to a girl, they kept her with them...

The "*island of Matinino*" was probably St. Thomas, the largest of the Virgin Islands, situated 11 leagues east of Puerto Rico, a distance the Taino approximated as "*ten or twelve leagues.*" Although Columbus "*greatly desired to visit*" this island "*peopled by women without men,*" he wouldn't reach this archipelago of the fanciful (yet durable) name until his second voyage.

...The Admiral says that both islands cannot be over xv or xx leagues from where he had set out, and he believed that they were to the southeast and that the Indians did not know how to indicate the direction to him...

Columbus was still cutting the actual length of the Taino's canoe-day in half — Puerto Rico was almost 40 leagues "*from where he had set out*" this morning, not the "*xv or xx*" he recorded. This stubborn misconception contrasts with his several impressively accurate "guesses" about some of the region's major cartographic features. These include Española's circumference, his landfall's distance to that island's western peaks, and today's distance from Puerto Rico to St. Thomas. One possible explanation for this striking cartographic dichotomy is that Columbus possessed accurate individual maps of "*certain islands in that region,*" but had to depend on the Taino for the unmapped distances between them. His comment "*that the Indians did not know how to indicate the direction to him*" suggests increasing self doubt he was correctly interpreting those unmapped distances.

...After having lost sight of the cape on the island of Española which he called Cape de Sant Teramo, *which lay sixteen leagues to his west, he went twelve leagues to the east by north. He had very good weather...*

This 1980-foot peak on the north "*cape*" abutting his Samaná·anchorage slipped below his western horizon near the end of this morning's "*sixteen leagues.*" Today's *Journal* excerpt reinforces his prior claim he made "*twelve leagues, until sunset,*" but introduces directional uncertainty by rotating this course segment two compass points clockwise from "*northeast by east*" to "*east by north.*" Either course makes sense; the former accommodating his 600-league longitude error, and the latter defining the true direction to the Canary Islands. I'm inclined to the latter interpretation because it allows for an otherwise impossible sighting of eastern Puerto Rico on Friday morning.

THURSDAY, JANUARY 17th — *Yesterday at sunset...*

On his outbound journey Columbus began his daily *Journal* recordings at sunrise. But on his return voyage most will open with "*this night,*" and only occasionally "*yesterday, after sunset*" those few times he apparently delayed recording until the following morning.

...the wind fell somewhat. He went for 14 sand glasses, each of which marks one half hour, or a little less,...

This revelation of *"little"* timing uncertainties suggests why Columbus (in 1477) and Magellan (in 1520) both made use of solar eclipses occurring within one half hour of the local horizon. Not only were large elevation angles difficult to measure accurately with 15th century instruments, but interval timing errors as small as one percent could distort an otherwise perfect zenith measurement by nearly 50 miles of longitude.

...until the passing of the first quarter, and he made four millas an hour [3 knots], that is, 28 millas [7 leagues]...

Shortly after midnight the fleet passed within 20 miles of Cerro de Punta, Puerto Rico's highest mountain. If their passage had occurred during daylight hours this peak would have alerted the wary crew to their Admiral's subterfuge.

...Afterwards the wind became fresher, and so he went all that quarter, which makes ten half hour glasses, and afterwards for another six, until sunset [salido el sol] at eight millas an hour [6 knots],...

This is the first of several instances where Cecil Jane mistranslated *"salido el sol"* as *"sunset"* rather than *"sunrise."*

...and so he made in all eightyfour millas, which are 21 leagues,...

There are some troubling inconsistencies between tonight's recorded distances, speeds and times. Robert Fuson pointed out that *"ten half hour glasses"* must be read as *"eight"* to arrive at tonight's correct total of *"21 leagues."* This correction still leaves a worrisome over count of tonight's sand glasses, which Columbus may have tried to explain by lamely asserting that each glass marked *"one half hour, or a little less."*

...to the northeast by east,...

This night Columbus averaged almost five knots on a *"northeast by east"* heading, his *"direct course"* to the Straits of Gibralter according to his suspect LPC-22 findings.

...and up to sunset, he made a further forty-four millas, which are eleven leagues, to the east...

January winds in this region of the Atlantic Ocean are predominantly northeasterly. A NE by E wind at daybreak would have given Columbus the excuse he needed to change his heading to due *"east."* He continued on this course until sunset, far enough from Puerto Rico's coast to conceal his intentions from his apprehensive crew.

...A booby came to the caravel, and afterwards another, and he saw much weed of the kind that is in the sea.

This is the *Journal's* second demonstration that Columbus knew the difference between naturally floating Sargassum weed "of the kind that is in the sea," and the uprooted benthic weed "they had found in the gulf [Northeast Providence Channel] when he came to the discovery [of Eleuthera]."

FRIDAY, JANUARY 18th — *This night he navigated with little wind to the east by south, forty millas, which are 10 leagues, and afterwards 30 millas, which are 7 and a half leagues, to the southeast by east, until* sunrise *[salido el sol]...*

At sunset Columbus took advantage of a moonless night to covertly turn the Niña's heading another point clockwise to the *"east by south"* for a distance of *"10 leagues."* After midnight, with most of the crew presumably asleep, he boldly turned the Niña three more points to the "southeast by east," holding this course for *"seven and a half leagues"* until *"sunrise."* If this unexplained course change had been dictated by the wind, Columbus could have nearly doubled his homeward progress by instead sailing a close-hauled tack to the N by E. The likely objective of this surprising course was confirmation of the mapped location for El Yunque, the eastern terminus of Puerto Rico's mountainous Cordillera Central. At *"sunrise"* his lookouts must have been startled to find themselves within sight of this solitary 3500-foot peak just piercing their southern horizon. Its sighting legitimized the Admiral's claim to his share of Puerto Rico's riches, and would give him the confidence to launch his second New World voyage in the direction of the Leeward Islands, whose existence, until then, had been suggested only by Indian maps and uprooted seaweed.

...After sunrise *[salido el sol] he navigated all day with little wind east-northeast and northeast, and to the east, more or less, turning her prow sometimes to the north and sometimes to the north by east and north-northeast, and so, taking it all in all, he believed that he may have made sixty millas, which are 15 leagues...*

Having surreptitiously validated his claim to Puerto Rico's riches, Columbus could now reassure his apprehensive crew by ordering an abrupt counter clockwise of 10 full compass points, intending to regain his *"direct route for Spain,"* now 40 leagues to his north. The Dunn/Kelley translation clarifies Cecil Jane's ambiguous reading by identifying *"east-northeast... northeast...east"* as wind directions rather than headings sailed by Columbus. Absent an aggregated direction for today's *"15 leagues,"* his headings of *"north and sometimes to the north by east and north-northeast"* can be averaged as N by E without introducing significant latitude error.

...Little vegetation appeared in the sea, but he says that yesterday and today the sea seemed to be choked with tunny-fish, and the Admiral believed that from there they must go to the duke's fisheries at Conil and to the Cadiz fisheries. On account of a fish called rabiforcado [frigate-bird], which followed in the wake of the caravel, and afterwards went in the direction of the south-southeast, the Admiral believed that there must be some islands there,...

Cecil Jane's careless translation is incorrect. This *"fish"* was actually a frigate-bird that *"followed in the wake of the caravel"* before winging *"south-southeast"* in the late afternoon to its nest somewhere in the nearby Virgin Islands.

...and he said that to the east-southeast of the island of Española lay the island of Carib and that of Matinino and many others.

This morning's sighting of Puerto Rico must have given Columbus increased confidence in the Taino mapping of St. Thomas, the island of *"Matinino...to the east-southeast of Española."* Those *"many"* other islands mapped by the Taino probably included Deseada, the "desired" future landfall as the Caribbean island closest to Spain. Next December Columbus would make landfall at Dominica, less than 30 miles south of Deseada.

SATURDAY, JANUARY 19th — *This night...*

"This night" Saturn was only one degree above the Moon's slender crescent when both slipped below the horizon at 6:40 PM. Columbus may have book marked this marginal LPC in planning his voyage, while realizing it might be difficult to detect Saturn within a dozen degrees of the setting Sun.

...he went fifty-six millas [14 leagues] to the north by east, and 64 [16 leagues] to the northeast by north. After sunrise [de sol salido] he navigated to the northeast with the wind east-southeast, with a fresh wind, and afterwards to the northeast by north and he went 84 millas, which are twenty-one leagues. He saw the sea thick with small tunny-fish; there were boobies, tropicbirds and frigate birds.

SUNDAY, JANUARY 20th — *This night the wind dropped and at intervals there were some gusts of wind, and he went in all twenty millas [5 leagues] to the northeast. After sunrise he went eleven millas [2¾ leagues] to the southeast; afterwards to the north-northeast 36 millas, which are nine leagues...*

"This night the wind dropped," leaving Columbus to contend with the slowest progress of his return voyage. *"After sunrise"* he struggled to accommodate the Atlantic's unfavorable northeasterly winds by tacking 2 ¾ leagues *"to the southeast."* But those persistent head winds soon convinced Columbus he would have difficulty maintaining his imagined *"direct course for Spain, northeast by east."* So he finished the day by sailing *"nine leagues...to the north-northeast"* on his way to establishing a NE course more compatible with the opposing winds. To facilitate future mapping of his discoveries this new course would also be tied to Hispaniola's Golfo de las Flechas.

...He saw innumerable small tunny-fish; he says that the breezes were very soft and sweet, as in Seville in April or May; and "The sea," he says, "was always very smooth, many thanks be given to God." Frigate birds and petrels and many other birds were seen.

MONDAY, JANUARY 21st — *Yesterday, after sunset, he navigated to the north by east, with an east and northeast wind. He went 8 millas an hour [6 knots] until midnight, which will be fifty-six millas [14 leagues.] Afterwards he went to the north-northeast at 8 millas an hour, and so in the whole night it came to a hundred and four millas, which are 26 leagues, towards the northeast by north...*

January 30th would have been this entry's date in the modern Gregorian calendar. The Nautical Almanac reveals the "whole night" of January 30th lasts almost exactly 13 hours at the fleet's latitude of 24 degrees. Over the next five weeks their northward progress would lengthen the nights at roughly the same rate as the calendar shrunk them, leading Columbus to continue recording 11 hours of daylight and 13 hours of night for the remainder of his voyage. Tonight's 13 hours at a steady 6 knots gave him exactly "xxvi leagues, towards the northeast by north."

...After sunrise, he steered to the north-northeast with the same east wind, and at times to the north by east, and he went 88 millas in the eleven hours of daylight, that is 21 leagues, deducting one which he lost, because he fell off towards the caravel Pinta *in order to speak with her...*

"After sunrise" Columbus maintained an average speed of 6 knots for the *"eleven hours of daylight,"* but lost one of those potential 22 leagues to a half hour rendezvous with Pinzón's *Pinta*. This loss recalls his reluctance to sacrifice progress to a prompt collection of longitude

measurements in September, so today's meeting with the *Pinta* must have been important. Perhaps he felt it necessary *'to speak with her"* about how their rotation to a NE base course dictated an easterly search for the Canary Islands once they reached the 28th parallel.

...He found the breezes very cold, and he thought, as he says, that he would find them more so every day, as he arrived farther to the north, and also on account of the nights being longer owing to the narrowness of the sphere. Many tropicbirds and petrels and other birds were seen, but not so many fish, owing, as he says, to the water being colder. He saw much weed.

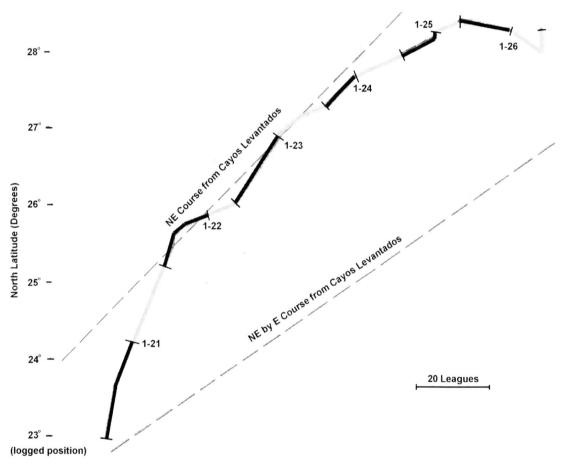

Figure 12-2. Easterly headwinds induce a northerly course rotation, interrupted on January 26th by a premature search for the Canary Islands

TUESDAY, JANUARY 22nd — *Yesterday, after sunset, he navigated to the north-northeast with an east wind which veered to the southeast; he made 8 millas an hour [6 knots], until five half-hour glasses had passed and three before watch was begun...*

Their progress during the *"three* [glasses] *before* [tonight's] *watch was begun"* was already included in yesterday's *"eleven hours of daylight."* Those redundant 1½ hours suggest his brief rendezvous with the *"Pinta"* ended around 4:00 PM. After deducting this double count of *"three"* glasses from tonight's total, the *Journal* records the appropriate total of 26 *"half-hour glasses"* for the 13 hours between 5:30 PM and 6:30 AM.

...which comes to eight half-hour glasses, and so he may have gone seventy two millas, which makes eighteen leagues...

The fleet's maximum speed of 3 leagues an hour exposes *"eighteen leagues"* between 4:00 and 8:00 PM as an incorrect transcription. If Columbus had simply continued those four hours at his last recorded speed of 6 knots he would have covered 8 leagues, only 5 of which represented progress after 5:30 PM. It's not clear from this entry whether Columbus or a copyist added those extra 10 leagues.

...Afterwards he went to the north by east for six half-hour glasses, which will be another 18 millas [4½ leagues]...

During the *"six half-hour glasses"* between 8 and 11 PM they covered only *"4½ leagues"* when their average speed dropped to 4½ knots in tonight's dying winds.

...after that, for the four half-hour glasses of the second watch to the northeast, at six millas an hour, which comes to three leagues to the northeast;...

Between 11 PM and 1 AM they continued at 4 ½ knots in adding *"three leagues"* to tonight's headway on their new base course *"to the northeast."*

...afterwards, until sunrise, he went to the east-northeast for eleven half-hour glasses, six league an hour, which makes seven leagues;...

During those remaining *"eleven half-hour glasses"* of the night they made *"seven leagues"* at an average speed of about 4 knots, rather than the impossible *"six leagues an hour"* transcribed by Las Casas. He apparently converted a recorded speed of 1½ leagues per hour into 6 millas per hour while forgetting to record his change of units.

...after that, to the east-northeast, until eleven o'clock, 32 millas [8 leagues]; and so the wind fell, and he went no farther that day...

After 6:30 AM they made better than 5 knots for 4½ hours until they could go *"no further"* when the *"wind fell"* at 11:00 AM.

...The Indians went swimming; they saw tropicbirds and much weed.

WEDNESDAY, JANUARY 23rd — *This night he found many variations in the winds. Being on the watch for everything and giving the attention which good seamen are accustomed and ought to give, he says that he went that night to the northeast by north 84 millas, which are 21 leagues. He waited many times for the caravel Pinta, because she went badly close-hauled, since she found little help from the mizzen, owing to the mast not being good; and he says that if her captain, who is Martín Alonso Pinzón, had taken as much care in the Indies to provide himself with a good mast, where there are so many and of such a kind, as he had been zealous to part company with him, thinking to stuff the ship full of gold, he would have done well...*

Tonight a strengthening wind allowed the fleet to average almost 5 knots despite waiting *"many times for the caravel Pinta."* Columbus groused that they could have done better if Pinzón had provided *"himself with a good mast"* instead of *"thinking to stuff the ship full of gold."*

...Many tern were seen and much weed;...

Three straight days of *"much weed"* indicate the fleet was now well within the Sargasso Sea's carpet of seaweed.

...the sky was all overcast during these days, but it has not rained, and the sea has always been as smooth as a river, "Many thanks be given to God." After sunrise [del sol salido] he went due northeast for thirty millas, which are seven leagues and a half, for some part of the day, and afterwards for the rest he went to the east-northeast a further 30 millas, which are seven leagues and a half...

"After sunrise" they averaged better than 4 knots on a composite course totaling 14.7 leagues to the northeast by east. The slight clockwise rotation of today's course from NE suggests Columbus was sailing a great circle route instead of a rhumb line.

THURSDAY, JANUARY 24th — *He went all this night, taking into account the many variations which there were in the wind, to the northeast 44 millas, that is, eleven leagues. After sunrise until sunset, he went to the east-northeast fourteen leagues.*

Tonight *"the many variations...in the wind"* reduced the fleet's average speed to 2½ knots. *"After sunrise"* they managed nearly 4 knots on an *"east-northeast"* course, enough (Columbus mistakenly believed) to regain the Canary Islands' latitude of 28 degrees at *"sunset."* In September, Ursa Major had guided him westward along this same latitude line. But with the change of seasons this constellation's lower culmination was invisible in the bright light of day, so his latitude estimates now depended on accurate records of hull speed <u>and</u> the risky assumption of negligible ocean currents. While Columbus could estimate his water speed accurately, he had no way of knowing the unrelenting Atlantic Gyre had been driving him northwesterly 10 to 15 miles each day. Unaware the fleet was already a hundred miles north of Tenerife; his uneasy crew kept scanning the pitch-black eastern horizon for signs of its 12,180-foot fiery cone. They would have been devastated to learn it was still more than 2,000 miles beyond their increasingly desperate grasp.

FRIDAY, JANUARY 25th — *He steered this night to the east-northeast for a part of the night, which was thirteen half-hour glasses, for nine leagues and a half; afterwards, he went to the north-northeast another six millas [1½ leagues]. From sunrise, during the whole day, because the wind fell, he went to the east-northeast 28 millas, which are 7 leagues...*

Columbus wasn't ready to give up his search for Tenerife. To improve his chances of detection he turned his heading *"to the east-northeast...for nine leagues and a half"* until headwinds forced an unproductive *"1½ leagues"* to the *"north-northeast."* After sunrise he made an additional *"7 leagues...to the east-northeast"* before *"the wind fell."*

...The sailors killed a dolphin and a very large shark, and he says that they had much need of them, because they had now nothing to eat except bread and wine and ajes from the Indies.

SATURDAY, JANUARY 26th — *This night he went to the east by south, for 56 millas, that is, fourteen leagues. After sunrise, he steered sometime to the east-southeast and sometimes to the southeast. Up to eleven o'clock he went forty millas [10 leagues];...*

Tonight Columbus anxiously ordered an abrupt course change *"to the east by south,"* waiting for that fiery Tenerife peak to pierce the eastern horizon. By now he may have suspected this volcanic beacon was 2,000 miles out of range, but he doggedly continued scanning the horizon for its glow. After sunrise he turned even more southerly *"to the east-southeast and sometimes to the southeast"* until his Tenerife detour had squandered a full 10 leagues of potential homeward progress.

...after that, he made another tack and then went close to the wind, and by night he went towards the north 24 millas, which are six leagues.

It was late morning before Columbus reluctantly gave up his quest for Tenerife and turned *"towards the north"* to resume his homeward course. After wasting the morning's strong winds on his fruitless search for Tenerife, he managed less than three knots for the remainder of the day.

SUNDAY, JANUARY 27th — *Yesterday, after sunset, he went to the northeast and north by east, and made five millas an hour, and in thirteen hours 65 millas, which are 16 leagues and a half;...*

"Yesterday, after sunset" is an unusual recording delay suggesting Columbus retired early yesterday evening to recover from the ordeal of his 36-hour search for Tenerife.

...after sunset [sol <u>salido</u>], he went towards the northeast 24 millas, which are six leagues, up to midday, and from that time, until sunset, he went three leagues to the east-northeast.

After "<u>sunrise</u>" a refreshed Columbus resumed command and promptly ordered a return to their NE base course. But by *"midday"* he had made a crucial decision. Yesterday's failure to detect Tenerife must have convinced him his LPC-22 longitude measurement grossly underestimated the length of their tenuous return voyage. This left him two options. Either he could continue due east possibly 2000 miles to Tenerife, or he could angle northward that same distance to Porto Santo, at a latitude of 33 degrees in the Madeira Islands. Columbus had at least three reasons for favoring the Porto Santo route: the island was 150 miles closer to Spain, he knew it well from several years there with his late wife Dona Felipe Perestrello e Moniz, and it was still his father-in-law's fiefdom. That afternoon the fleet edged slowly towards Porto Santo on a revised base course to *"the east-northeast."*

MONDAY, JANUARY 28th — *All this night he steered east-northeast; he made 36 millas, which are 9 leagues. After sunrise, he went until sunset, to the east-northeast, 20 millas, which are five leagues. The breezes he found to be temperate and sweet; he saw tropicbirds, and petrels and much weed.*

TUESDAY, JANUARY 29th — *He steered to the east-northeast, and went in the night, with a south and southwest wind, 39 millas, which are 9 leagues and a half; in the whole day, he made 8 leagues. The breezes were very temperate as in April in Castile; the sea very smooth. Fish, which they call dorados, came to the side.*

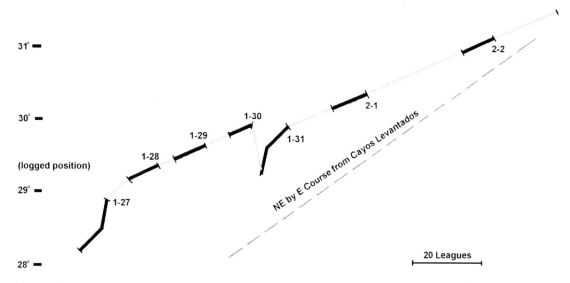

Figure 12-3. Regaining of baseline NE by E Course, interrupted January 30th by possible search for the Canary Island of Lanzarote

WEDNESDAY, JANUARY 30th — All this night he made 7 leagues to the east-northeast. During the day, he ran to the south by east, for thirteen leagues and a half...

       At dawn Columbus ordered a drastic course change *"to the south by east for thirteen leagues and a half."* By sundown this course had brought him about 20 leagues north and 75 east from the start of Saturday's search for Tenerife. These distances approximate that island's location relative to Lanzarote, suggesting Columbus was still groping for the peak that had guided him to the Canary Islands in August.

...He saw tropicbirds and much week and many dolphins.

THURSDAY, JANUARY 31st — He steered this night to the north by east, for thirty millas [7 ½ leagues], and afterwards to the northeast for 35 miles [8 ¾ leagues] which are sixteen leagues...

       Columbus realized a nighttime search for Lanzarote's dormant peak would be problematic, lacking the guidance of an active volcano. So he abandoned his futile quest at sunset and turned *"to the north by east"* to regain his course for Porto Santo. An hour before sunrise LPC-23 rewarded him with the most accurate longitude measurement of his return voyage when Jupiter set 3.8 degrees behind the nearly full moon. He must have had mixed feelings when his *Ephemerides* reduced his huge longitude error by a factor of six, not an entirely satisfactory result, but enough to free him from the gross distortions of LPC-22.

...After sunrise, until night, he went for 13 leagues and a half to the east-northeast. They saw tropicbirds and petrels.

Now confident of the distance to Porto Santo, Columbus resumed "the east-northeast" course he believed would carry him to his search latitude of 33 degrees. He had yet to realize the Atlantic Gyre had already carried him well north of that latitude.

FRIDAY, FEBRUARY 1st — *He went this night to the east-northeast, for sixteen leagues and a half...*

The Dunn/Kelley transcript interprets this distance as "10 leguas y media," more likely the actual value.

...During the day he ran on the same course for 29 leagues and a quarter. The sea was very smooth, thanks be to God.

SATURDAY, FEBRUARY 2nd — *This night he went to east-northeast forty millas, which are 10 leagues. In the day, with the same wind astern, he ran 7 millas an hour [5 ¼ knots]; so that in eleven hours he made 77 millas, which are 19 leagues and a quarter. The sea was very smooth, thanks to God, and the breezes very soft. They saw the sea so choked with weed that, if they had not seen it, they would have feared shoals. They saw petrels.*

SUNDAY, FEBRUARY 3rd — *This night, the wind being astern with the sea very smooth, thanks to God, they went 29 leagues. The north star appeared very high, as at Cape Vincent; he could not take its altitude with the astrolabe or quadrant, as the roll did not permit it...*

From his log and his compass readings, Columbus had reckoned his latitude as slightly more than 31 degrees, almost 2 degrees short of his planned LS route to Porto Santo. He didn't want to overshoot this route, so he turned to the heavens tonight for confirmation of his latitude. He must have been stunned when the *"north star appeared very high, as at Cape Vincent,"* fully six degrees higher than he had expected. But he refused to accept a measurement ballooning his carefully estimated latitude progress by nearly 50 percent, so he ignored its unsettling finding by claiming, *"the roll did not permit"* a reliable measurement. But the ship's *"roll"* wasn't responsible for this unsettling latitude discrepancy; it was actually caused by the unrelenting Atlantic Gyre. This powerful circular current had silently carried his fleet 200 miles northwesterly during the past fortnight! The huge latitude error caused by this undetectable current demonstrates why Columbus had relied on LS instead of DR to follow the 28th parallel on his outbound voyage.

...In the day he steered on his course to the east-northeast, and he made ten millas an hour [7 ½ knots], and so in eleven hours 27 leagues...

Columbus was too proud a navigator to respond to a single anomalous latitude warning: instead he would continue his *"course to the east-northeast"* until his recorded track indicated he had reached Porto Santo's latitude of 33 degrees. Once there he would sail east to monitor Cassiopeia's elevation angle from a constant-latitude course. If the constellation confirmed he was already far north of Porto Santo he could shift his target to the Azores island of Santa Maria without incurring much of a distance penalty.

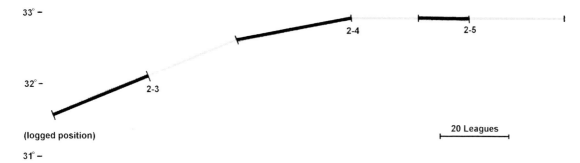

33° –

2-4

2-5

32° –

2-3

(logged position)

31° –

20 Leagues

Figure 12-4. Due east course change suggests Columbus now aware an ocean current may have carried him northward

MONDAY, FEBRUARY 4th — *This night he steered east by north; for some part of it, he made 12 millas an hour [9 knots], and for some part, ten [7 ½ knots]. So he made 130 millas, which are 32 leagues and a half...*

Columbus would have made those *"32 leagues and a half"* in exactly 13 hours at 7 ½ knots. This suggests the *"some part of...This night"* at 9 knots lasted barely long enough to confirm the wisdom of his *"east by north"* route selection.

...The sky was very overcast and rainy, and it was somewhat cold, on which account he says that he knew that he had not arrived at the islands of the Azores...

The *"overcast and rainy"* night prevented the measurement of latitude from the height of Cassiopeia's lower culmination. This left Columbus free to deny yesterday's *"north star"* latitude warning. So he boldly asserted, *"he knew he had not arrived at the islands of the Azores."*

....After the sun had risen, he changed his course, and went to the east; he went in the whole day 77 millas, which are 19 leagues and a quarter.

The morning after his Polaris warning, Columbus's faulty plotted track finally indicated he had reached Porto Santo's latitude. So he boldly *"changed his course, and went to the east."* But if future readings of Cassiopeia should confirm he was already several degrees north of that haven, the worrisome condition of his ships demanded he forgo Porto Santo and sail for home on a higher latitude course within reach of the Azores.

TUESDAY, FEBRUARY 5th — *This night he steered east; in the whole of it, he went 54 millas, which are fourteen leagues less a half...*

The lack of any reference to *"overcast"* suggests Columbus had his first opportunity to confirm Sunday's unsettling view of the "north star" when he measured the lower culmination of Cassiopeia.

...During the day he ran 10 millas an hour, and so in eleven hours they went 110 millas, which are 27 leagues and a half. They saw petrels and some small sticks, which was a sign that they were near land.

These *"petrels and some small sticks"* may have bolstered the fleet's hopes, but Flores, the nearest island, was still 700 miles to their east.

Figure 12-5. The fleet continues eastward as evidence of latitude error mounts

WEDNESDAY, FEBRUARY 6th — *This night he navigated to the east;...*

This evening's LPC-24 gave Columbus another opportunity to measure longitude when the Moon rose less than two degrees under Mars. If he did observe this conjunction he may have withheld its disappointing 10-degree *westerly* bias from his uneasy crew. More likely his celestial focus was on confirmation of last night's measurement of Cassiopeia's lower culmination. If that reading proved a fluke he would continue on to Porto Santo; but if confirmed he might sail directly for Palos de la Frontera, the port where he had launched his momentous voyage six months earlier.

...he made eleven millas an hour [8 ¼ knots] in thirteen hours of the night; he went 143 millas, which are 35 leagues and a quarter...

Columbus recorded a constant speed of 2.75 leagues per hour to make 35.75 leagues in 13 hours. Las Casas converted both speed and distance to millas correctly, but seems to have misread that distance as 35.25 leagues.

...They saw many birds and petrels. During the day he ran 14 millas an hour, and so on that day he went 154 millas, which are 38 leagues and a half, so that, day and night together, they went 74 leagues, a little more or less. Vincent Yañez found that today in the morning the island of Flores lay to his north and the island of Madeira to the east...

This evening the clearing skies allowed Columbus to confirm yesterday's finding that his fleet was more than 250 miles northwest of his plotted track, which was mostly based on DR. He was now confident enough of his surprising latitude readings to criticize his pilots' faulty readings. His first victim was *"Yañez Pinzón,"* whose careless DR and ignorance of the Atlantic Gyre continued to incorrectly map *"the island of Madeira to the east."*

...Roldán said that the island of Fayal or that of San Gregorio lay to the north-northeast, and Porto Santo to the east. Much weed was seen.

Tonight's second victim was Bartolomé Roldán, an assistant pilot from Palos. His longitude estimate supported Vincente Yañez, but Roldán's latitude estimate agreed with the one Columbus had recorded prior to his accounting for the Atlantic Gyre.

THURSDAY, FEBRUARY 7th — *He navigated this night to the east; he made 10 millas an hour, and so in thirteen hours 130 millas, which are 32 leagues and a half; during the day, he made eight millas an hour [6 knots]; in eleven hours he made 88 millas, which are 22 leagues. On this morning the Admiral was 75 leagues south of the island of Flores,...*

It's clear that none of his pilots were measuring Cassiopeia's lower culmination because they still believed they were sailing the 33rd latitude, 160 leagues *"south of the island of Flores."* If sailing directions for the following week were correctly recorded, the Admiral's estimate of only *"75 leagues"* proved to be impressively accurate. But Flores wasn't accurately charted in 1492; raising the possibility Columbus adjusted this estimate after reaching the Azores.

...and the pilot Pero Alonso, steering north, passed between Tercera and the island of Santa Maria, and steering east, passed to the windward of the island of Madeira, twelve leagues to the northward...

Tonight Columbus singled out his third patsy, Pero Alonso Niño of Andalucia, whose brother Juan was owner of the Niña. Pero had also neglected to correct his latitude using Cassiopeia, so it's not surprising that his faulty longitude estimate supported the other pilots.

...The sailors saw weed of a different kind from that previously seen, and of which there is much in the islands of the Azores; afterwards, they saw the same kind as before.

Yet another demonstration of seaweed's importance to 15th century pilots.

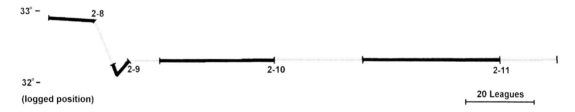

Figure 12-6. Fleet continues eastward with a slight southerly adjustment

FRIDAY, FEBRUARY 8th — *He went this night three millas an hour [2 ¼ knots] to the east for a while, and afterwards east by south. In the whole night he made 12 leagues...*

Twelve leagues in 13 hours suggest they picked up a little wind after adjusting their course to the *"east by south."*

...From sunrise to midday he ran 27 millas [6 ¾ leagues,] afterwards, until sunset, he ran as many more, that is thirteen leagues to the south-southeast.

This *Journal* excerpt doesn't give any reasons for tonight's abrupt course change *"to the south-southeast."* If its purpose had been to reach the Azores' westerly winds, Columbus would have taken a *northerly* tack according to his logged position. Perhaps he now knew his actual latitude and was adjusting his route to reach the Azores. If not, his target may have been Madiera.

SATURDAY, FEBRUARY 9th — *During part of the night he went three leagues to the south-southeast, and afterwards to the south by east. Afterwards, he went to the northeast, until ten o'clock, for a further five leagues, and then, until night, he went nine leagues to the east.*

From sunset until the following morning they made less than half a league an hour, partly because Columbus was attempting to establish the latitude he had specified for his return course. Careful measurement of Cassiopeia's culmination that night would have revealed they had slightly overshot their new course 90 leagues south of Flores. By *"ten o'clock"* next morning they regained that latitude and ended the day by sailing *"nine leagues to the east"* at better than 3½ knots.

SUNDAY, FEBRUARY 10th — *After sunset, he steered all night for 130 millas, which are 32 leagues and a half; the sun having risen, he went 9 millas an hour [6 ¾ knots] until night, and so in eleven hours he made 99 millas more, which are 24 leagues and three quarters. In the caravel of the Admiral, Vincent Yañez and the two pilots, Sancho Ruiz and Pero Alonso Niño and Roldán, charted their course or fixed their position. They all made it much beyond the islands of the Azores to the east according to their charts, and navigating to the north, no one touched the island of Santa Maria, which is the last of all the islands of the Azores, but rather they would be five leagues beyond it and in the neighborhood of the island of Madeira or in that of Porto Santo. But the Admiral found himself much out of his course, making his position very far behind theirs. This night the island of Flores lay to his north,...*

Only the entry's first sentence covers today's 24 hours of sail; the remainder describes an extraordinary night meeting Columbus called for *"Vincent Yañez and the two pilots, Sancho Ruiz and Pero Alonso Niño and Roldán."* While tonight's lower culmination of Cassiopeia apparently convinced the pilots their latitude records had been distorted by the Atlantic Gyre, they forgot it had also reduced their longitude progress by 70 leagues. So they optimistically claimed they had sailed *"five leagues beyond...the island of Santa Maria."* Columbus understood the opposing effect of the Gyre when he correctly made their position *"very far behind theirs"* so that by midnight *"the island of Flores lay to his north."*

...and to the east he was going in the direction of Nafe in Africa, and passed to the windward of the island of Madeira,...leagues to the north...

Recovery of the *Journal's* eighth and final missing textual gap might confirm Columbus was sailing *"to the east"* on a course *"[60] leagues to the north"* of Madeira. *"Nafe"* (Casablanca) then lay within half a compass point of that course.

...They thus made themselves 150 leagues nearer Castile than he did. He says that, by the grace of God, when they see land, it will be known who took their position the more accurately...

The pilots' spurious finding of a position *"five leagues beyond... the island of Santa Maria"* informs us Columbus had accurately measured it as 145 leagues short of *"the island."* He alone realized they were still SSW of Flores, allowing him to smugly anticipate a demonstration of *"who took their position the more accurately."*

...He says here that he went 263 leagues beyond the island of Hierro, on the outward voyage, before he saw the first weed, etc.

Las Casas had recorded the outbound fleet's first reported sighting of *"weed"* on September 16th. By that morning they were 247 leagues *"beyond the island of Hierro"* according to the daily progress transcribed by Las Casas. Over the next 24 hours they added 39 leagues, so it's likely the fleet had gone *"263 leagues beyond...Hierro"* by late that afternoon. The consistency of these data should increase our confidence in the accuracy of the Las Casas transcription.

MONDAY, FEBRUARY 11th — *He went this night twelve millas an hour [9 knots] on his course, and so in the whole night he reckoned 39 leagues,...*

These *"39 leagues"* in 13 hours tell us the fleet had raced eastward all night at its hull speed of 9 knots. His *Journal* had recorded this rate for a full day's sail only on September 16th and October 2nd.

...and in the whole day he ran 16 leagues and a half. He saw many birds, on account of which he believed that he was near land.

TUESDAY, FEBRUARY 12th — *He navigated to the east at six millas an hour this night, and by daybreak he went 73 millas which are eighteen leagues and a quarter. Here he began to experience heavy seas and stormy weather, and he says if the caravel had not been very good and well equipped, he would have feared to be lost...*

Las Casas lined out his original transcription of *"63 millas, which are 15 leagues and three quarters,"* apparently after finding another 2½ leagues in the *Journal.* At *"six millas an hour"* Columbus would have made those *"eighteen leagues and a quarter"* in 12 hours and 10 minutes, suggesting *"stormy weather"* terminated tonight's measurements *"by daybreak."*

...During the day he ran eleven or twelve leagues with great toil and danger.

For the next three days the fleet would be battered by a fierce storm threatening the very survival of Columbus and his "Enterprise of the Indies." Under these terrible conditions he could only estimate his progress as one league per hour for the *"eleven or twelve"* hours of daylight.

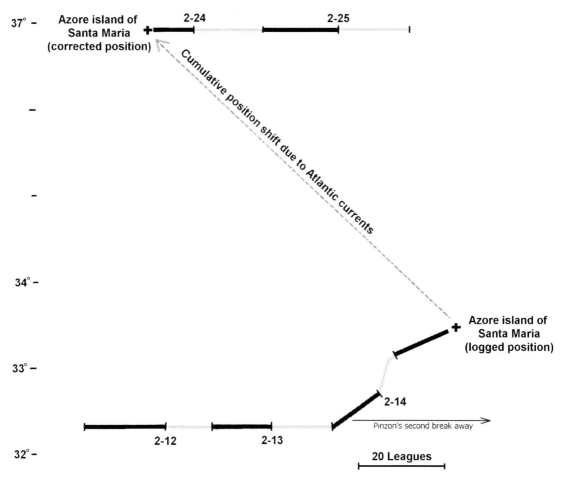

Figure 12-7. Columbus follows sea birds to Azores Island of Santa Maria

WEDNESDAY, FEBRUARY 13th — *After sunset, until day, he experienced great difficulty from the wind and from the very high sea, and the stormy weather. It flashed with lightning three times to the north-northeast; he said that this was an indication of a great storm which would come from that direction or against him. For most of the night, he went with bare poles;...*

LPC-25 occurred at 4:15 this morning when Venus rose only a few degrees ahead of the Moon. But Columbus needed to focus his attention on survival even if this conjunction had been visible during this "*great storm.*"

... afterwards, he hoisted a little sail and went 52 millas, which are thirteen leagues...

Once again, Columbus could only estimate his speed at one league per hour over the "*thirteen*" hours from sunset to sunrise.

...This day the wind moderated a little, but presently it increased, and the sea became terrible, and the waves met each other, so that they strained the ships. He made 55 millas, which are thirteen leagues and a half.

Las Casas should have converted those recorded *"thirteen leagues and a half"* into 54 millas.

THURSDAY, FEBRUARY 14th — *This night the wind increased and the waves were terrible, one meeting another, so that they crossed and held back the ship, which could not go forward or come out from the midst of them, and they broke over her. He carried the mainsail very low, merely in order to escape to some extent from the waves; so he went for three hours and ran 20 millas [5 leagues]...*

The ferocity of *"the wind"* can be judged from the *Niña's* 5-knot run with *"the mainsail very low."*

...The sea and the wind increased much, and, seeing that the danger was great, he began to run before the wind where it bore him, as there was no other recourse. Then the carvel Pinta, *in which was Martin Alonso, also began to run before the wind and disappeared, although all night the Admiral made flares and the other vessel answered, until, as it seems, she could do no more owing to the violence of the storm and because she was very far out of the course of the Admiral...*

Columbus never saw Martín Alonso Pinzón again. Early this stormy night his insubordinate lieutenant took advantage of the *Pinta's* speed to race homeward well ahead of the Admiral. Pinzón probably reached the Iberian Peninsula north of Lisbon, skirting that busy Portuguese port by sailing north to the closest Spanish harbor at Bayona. He wasted little time requesting a royal audience to proclaim "his" discoveries, but Isabela politely informed him she would wait to hear directly from Columbus himself. On March 15th Martín Alonso would slink into Palos harbor a few hours behind a triumphant Columbus. Ignored by the town's overjoyed celebrants, a heart-broken Martín Alonso returned home to a lonely death three weeks later.

...This night the Admiral went to the northeast by east...

It wasn't a coincidence that the nearby island of Santa Maria lay directly to *"the northeast by east."* The *"many birds"* that had signaled they were *"near land"* on Monday were now guiding the battered Niña to this solitary haven. With his survival at stake, Columbus realized he would have to risk the hostility of its Portuguese inhabitants.

...54 millas, which are 13 leagues...

Exactly *"13 leagues"* in 13 hours suggests Columbus was still approximating his progress in today's tempest; incorrectly converted into *"54 millas"* by Las Casas.

...The sun having risen, the wind and sea were greater, the cross waves more terrible. He set only the mainsail and carried it low, in order that the ship might get out from among the waves which crossed, and threatened to sink her. He followed the course to the east-northeast, and afterwards, to the east by north. He so went for six hours, and in them made 7 leagues and a half...

This morning Columbus estimated his speed had slightly increased to almost four knots.

...He ordered a pilgrimage to be vowed, that some one should go to Santa Maria de Guadalupe and carry a wax candle of five pounds, and all should vow that he, upon whom the lot should fall, should perform the pilgrimage. For

this purpose, he commanded as many chickpeas to be taken as there were persons in the ship, and that one should be marked with a knife, making a cross, and that they should be placed in a cap and well shaken. The first to put in his hand was the Admiral, and he drew out the pea marked with the cross, and so the lot fell upon him, and from that moment he regarded himself as a pilgrim and as bound to go to fulfill the vow...

If they survived today's tempest Columbus would covet the honor of a pilgrimage to Extramadura's shrine of *"Santa Maria de Guadalupe."* It would have been easy to notch that chickpea deep enough for him to detect it as the *"first to put in his hand."*

...Lots were cast again to send a pilgrim to Santa Maria de Loreto, which is in the March of Ancona, the land of the pope, and which is the house where Our Lady has done and does many and great miracles, and the lot fell upon a sailor from Puerto de Santa Maria, who was called Pedro de Villa, and the Admiral promised to give him money for his expenses...

Columbus was probably relieved to hire Pedro for an arduous pilgrimage to Ancona, an Adriatic seaport northwest of Rome.

...He decided that another pilgrim should be sent to watch for one night at Santa Clara de Moguer and cause a mass to be said, and for this purpose they once more used the chick peas, and that marked with the cross, and the lot fell on the Admiral himself...

Columbus clearly deserved the honor of leading a pilgrimage to the church in Palos de la Frontera if they returned safely to that harbor. But it should be noted that his chances of winning both the coveted pilgrimages in a fair drawing were less than one in 500.

....After this, the Admiral and all the people made a vow that, on reaching the first land, they would all go in their shirts in procession to pray in a church dedicated to Our Lady. Besides the general vows or those made in common, each one made his own individual vow, because no one expected to escape, all regarding themselves as lost, owing to the terrible storm which they were experiencing. It contributed to increase the danger that the ship was short of ballast, as the cargo had been lightened, the stores of food having been already eaten and the water and wine drunk; owing to his eager desire to avail himself of the fine weather which they experienced among the islands, the Admiral did not provide ballast, intending to have it taken in at the island of the women, where he proposed to go...

Ever adept at shifting blame, Columbus now claims he had planned to take on the needed *"ballast"* at *"the island of women, where he proposed to go."* If he had really anticipated this need he should have ballasted while still anchored for LPC-22.

....The remedy which he found for this need was, when they were able to do so, to fill the casks full with sea water, they being empty of water and wine, and in this way they supplied that need...

It must have been common practice to maintain ballast by simply refilling empty water barrels *"with sea water."*

...Here the Admiral writes of the reasons which caused him to fear that Our Lord willed that he should perish there, and of other reasons which gave him hope that God would bring him in safety, so that such news, as he was bearing to the Sovereigns, should not be lost. It seemed to him that the great desire which he had to bring this momentous news and to show that he had been proved a truth teller in what he had said and had offered to discover,...

His 1477 voyage to the Bay of Fundy had shown Columbus that a New World awaited discovery less than a 1000 leagues west of the Canary Islands. He had argued his case against Court astronomers, apparently ignorant of 1477 findings, who realized a westerly route to the Orient was beyond reach at more than 3000 leagues. Columbus was understandably eager to have *"been proved a truth teller in what he had said and had offered to discover."*

...inspired him with the greatest fear that he would not achieve this, and he says that he feared that the most trifling annoyance might interrupt and prevent it. He assigns this to his little faith and to his lack of confidence in the divine providence; on the other hand, he drew comfort from the blessings which God had shown to him in giving him so great a victory, in the discovery of what he had discovered, and God had fulfilled all his desires, after he had experienced many adversities and much opposition in Castile at his setting out; and as in the past he committed his fate and entrusted all his undertaking to God, and He had heard him and had given him all that he sought, so he must believe that He would finish what had begun and bring him to safety, more especially because on his outward journey, when he had greater reason to fear, God had delivered him from the difficulties which he had with the sailors and with the people whom he had with him, all of whom with one voice were resolved to rise against him and return, making protests; and the everlasting God had given him strength and courage against them all,...

The Las Casas transcript of the outbound journey contains no hint of impending mutiny, but Fernando's *Biography* describes how the crew's growing fears had led to "grumbling, lamenting and plotting." He records how some plotters had even agreed by late September "if the Admiral would not turn back, they should heave him overboard and report in Spain that he had fallen in accidentally while observing the stars." When Columbus got word of this mutinous planning he "threatened punishment to any who hindered his voyage" and managed "to calm their fears and check their machinations" by diverting their attention to the search for signs of land.

...and there were other things of great wonder which God had shown forth in him and for him on that voyage, beyond those things which their Highnesses knew about from the members of their household. So that he says that he should not have feared the said storm;...

This mysterious reference to his Sovereigns' knowledge from *"members of their household"* doesn't appear in Fernando's apparently verbatim quote from this section of the *Journal*.

..."But his weakness and anxiety," he says, "did not permit his mind to be soothed." He says that he felt also great anxiety for two sons whom he had in Cordoba at school, for he would leave them orphaned of father and mother in a strange land,...

Columbus's only legitimate offspring, Diego Colón, was now nearly a teenager while his bastard son, Fernando, wouldn't reach his 5th birthday until September. Diego's birth mother, Dona Felipe Perestrello, was from a royal family that had immigrated to Lisbon from Italy in the 14th century. She died shortly after Diego's birth on the island of Porto Santo. Columbus never remarried, but took Beatriz Enríquez de Harana as his mistress and mother of Fernando. In a 1506 codicil to his will Columbus requested Diego "to see that Beatriz Enríquez, mother of Don Fernando my son, is put in a way to live honorably, as a person to whom I am in so great debt, and thus for discharge of my conscience, because it weigheth much on my mind." This concern for Beatriz may have given Fernando added incentive to write his father's biography.

...and that the Sovereigns would not know the services which he had rendered to them on that voyage and the most favorable news which he was bearing to them, so that they might be moved to succor his sons. For this reason, and that their Highnesses might know how Our Lord had given him the victory in all that he desired in the matter of the Indies, and that it might be known that in those parts there is no storm, which, he says, may be gathered from the grass and trees which take root and grow almost into the sea,...

Columbus hadn't reached Cuba until after the hurricane season, but he would experience a severe one on his second voyage when he lost three ships to a storm that broke their anchoring cables. His unrealistic claim of *"no storm"* in the Indies may have been inspired by the region's extensive mangrove forests *"which take root and grow almost into the sea."*

...and that, if he were lost in that tempest, the sovereigns might have news of his voyage, he took a parchment and wrote on it all that he could about all the things he had found, earnestly begging whomsoever might find it to carry it to the Sovereigns...

According to a verbatim transcript in Fernando's *Biography*, this *"begging"* was augmented by "a written promise of 1,000 ducats to whoever should deliver it sealed... to your Highnesses."

...This parchment he enclosed in a waxed cloth, very carefully fastened, and he commanded a large wooden barrel to be brought, and placed it in it, without any one knowing what it was, for they thought that it was some act of devotion, and he ordered it thrown into the sea...

This sealed *"parchment"* was never recovered, opening the door to the many obvious forgeries that have surfaced during the past century. Morison wrote of one fly-by-night London publisher who had "the impudence to claim that he had secured it, as recently picked up by a fisherman off the coast of Wales! It was written in English, he explained lamely, because the Admiral thought that the manuscript would stand a better chance of being understood if couched in the universal maritime language."

...Afterwards with showers and storms, the wind changed to the west, and he went before it with only the foresail set for five hours, the sea being very rough, and he made two leagues and a half to the northeast...

The foresail had only 20 percent the mainsail's area, so its function was similar to that of a modern storm jib — provide enough speed (1.5 knots in this instance) to maintain a safe heading in the storm.

...He had taken down the square sail from the mainmast, fearing that some wave from the sea might carry it away.

13 - Home by Way of Portugal

FRIDAY, FEBRUARY 15th — *Yesterday, after sunset, the sky began to clear towards the west, and showed that it was about to blow from that quarter. He added the bonnet to the mainsail. The sea was still very high, although it was lessening a little. He went to the east-northeast at four millas an hour [3 knots], and in thirteen hours of the night they went thirteen leagues. After sunrise, they sighted land, which showed itself ahead of them to the east-northeast; some said that it was the island of Madeira, others that it was the rock of Cintra, in Portugal, near Lisbon. Presently the wind changed to a head wind from the east-northeast, and the sea to the west became very high; the caravel was about 5 leagues from land. The Admiral, according to his navigation, found that he was off the islands of the Azores, and he believed that land to be one of them; the pilots and sailors found themselves already off the coast of Castile.*

After two full days of frightful battering the *Niña's* crew awoke to a double blessing; abatement of the fierce storm and their first glimpse of land in nearly a month. Seabirds returning to their nightly roosts on the Azores' island of Santa Maria had guided Columbus to within *"5 leagues"* of its 1870-foot peak. This thrilling sight encouraged the more hopeful *"pilots and sailors"* to believe they were *"already off the coast of Castile."* While today's *"head wind"* would slow progress to this remote haven, it gave Columbus time to compose a detailed letter describing his discoveries. Unlike yesterday's desperate floated message, this letter would be carried home to ignite the passions of discovery throughout Europe. Its upbeat message makes no mention of the terrifying storm that had threatened their survival. But it does confirm his *Eleuthera* landfall as "distant from the equinoctial line twenty-six degrees," not the 24 degrees he would have measured at Watlings Island.

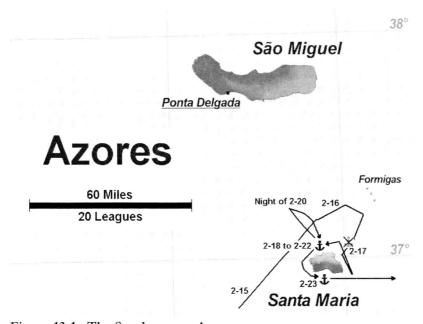

Figure 13-1. The Southeastern Azores

SATURDAY, FEBRUARY 16th — *He beat against the wind all this night in order to reach land, which he already realized was an island. At times he went to the northeast, at others to the north-northeast, until sunrise, when he steered southward in order to arrive at the island, which they could no longer see owing to the very cloudy weather. He saw astern another island at a distance of eight leagues...*

Morison speculated Columbus could somehow see the 15 leagues to São Miguel in this *"very cloudy weather."* A more likely alternative, Ilhéus Formigas, was much smaller, but *"astern"* of the Niña, and exactly *"eight leagues"* northeast of the island of Santa Maria.

...After sunrise until night, he continued making attempts to reach land, there being a high wind and a heavy sea. At the saying of Salve, which is the beginning of night, some saw a light to the leeward, and it seemed that it must be the island which they saw first yesterday,...

Columbus's omission of a **"SUNDAY"** heading in his *Journal* may be due to exhaustion following the lengthy storm vigil and today's intensive search for an anchorage.

...and all night he was beating about and drawing as near to it as he could, to find whether at sunrise he would sight some of the islands...

Morison asserted Columbus anchored this night at the exposed NE corner of the island, but he actually spent *"all night...beating about,"* hoping to *"sight some of the islands... at sunrise."*

...This night the Admiral took some rest, for since Wednesday he had not slept nor been able to sleep, and he was very crippled in his legs, owing to having been constantly exposed to the cold and water, and owing to the small amount that he had eaten...

His first *"rest"* in several days may account for this two-day *Journal* entry.

...At sunrise, he steered to the south-southwest, and at night he reached the island, and owing to the heavy clouds he could not recognize what island it was.

"At sunrise he steered to the south-southwest," a course reversal leading Columbus back to the island of Santa Maria, now obscured by *"heavy clouds."*

MONDAY, FEBRUARY 18th — *Yesterday, after sunset, he went on, rounding the island, in order to find where he might anchor and have speech; he cast anchor with an anchor which he lost at once; he sailed on once more and beat about all night. After sunrise, he again reached the northern side of the island, anchored where it looked best,...*

Morison correctly identified Punta Matos, *"on the northern side of the island,"* as the first Columbus anchorage on Santa Maria. It may have *"looked best,"* but it was exposed to the prevailing westerlies and located four arduous overland miles from the island's nearest settlement.

...and sent the boat ashore, and had speech with the people of the island, and learned that it was the island of Santa Maria, one of those of the Azores,...

Las Casas reinforced his admiration for Columbus in noting "He thought the island to be Santa Maria and thus succeeded in his navigation while all the others were in error."

...and the inhabitants indicated to them a harbor where they should bring the caravel...

This alternative *"harbor"* was shielded from the Atlantic Gyre by Punta Frades, and was only a mile from the nearest settlement.

...The people of the island said that they had never seen such a storm as that which there had been for the last fifteen days, and they marveled how they had escaped. He says that they gave many thanks to God and rejoiced greatly upon learning that the Admiral has discovered the Indies...

This was a much friendlier greeting than Columbus had expected from the Portuguese, but we shall soon see he wisely remained skeptical of their intentions.

...The Admiral says that this navigation of his had been very sure and that he had charted his course well, for which many thanks should be given to Our Lord, although he had made it a little farther on; but he had been certain that he was in the neighborhood of the Azores, and that this island was one of them. And he says that he pretended to have gone a greater distance in order to confound the pilots and sailors who did the charts, that he might remain master of that route to the Indies, as in fact he did remain, for no one of all those was certain of his course, with the result that no one could be sure of the route to the Indies.

Columbus never *"pretended to have gone a greater distance."* He actually began under-reporting his daily progress on September 10th *"in order that the crew might not be dismayed if the voyage were long."* Las Casas may have garbled this *Journal* entry while adding his own observation that *"in fact he did remain... (master of that route to the Indies.)"*

TUESDAY, FEBRUARY 19th — *After sunset, there came to the shore three men of the island and called. He sent the boat to them and they came in it, and brought fowls and fresh bread, and it was Carnival day, and they brought other things sent by the captain of the island, who was called Juan de Castañeda who sent word that he knew him very well, and that, as it was night, he did not come to see him, but would come at daybreak and bring more refreshment, and he would bring with him three men from the caravel who remained there, whom he had not sent on account of the great pleasure which he had with them, in hearing the details of the voyage. The Admiral ordered great honor to be done to the messengers, commanding beds to be given to them, in which they might sleep that night, because it was late and the settlement was at a distance...*

The only settlement then on the island's north coast was *Nossa Senhora dos Anjos*, a village established by the island's first colonists a half century earlier. Two of the coast's three anchorages lay within a mile of this *"settlement,"* but Columbus was already anchored *"at a distance"* behind the third at Punta Matos.

...And because on the previous Thursday, when he found himself in the anguish of the storm, they had made a vow and the vows mentioned above, and the vow that in the first land where there was a house of Our Lady, they would go in their shirts, etc., he decided that one half of the people should go in fulfillment to a small house, which was near the sea and like a hermitage, and he would go afterwards with the other half...

Columbus was uncertain about his hosts' intentions, so he shrewdly kept *"the other half"* of his crew ready for a possible emergency exit.

...Seeing that the land was safe and trusting in the offers of the captain and in the peace which there was between Portugal and Castile, he asked the three men to go to the village, and have a priest come to say mass for them. They went in their shirts, in fulfillment of their pilgrimage, and as they were at prayer, there fell upon them the whole village on horse and on foot, with the captain, and made them all prisoners...

Dunn/Kelley clarified the ambiguous identity of those who *"went in their shirts."* Columbus was referring to his *"one half of the people,"* not just the *"three men of the island."*

...Afterwards, the Admiral, being without suspicion, awaited the boat in order to fulfill his pilgrimage with the remaining people. At eleven o'clock, when he saw that they did not come, he suspected that they had been kept or that the boat had been wrecked, because all the island is surrounded by very high cliffs. The Admiral could not see the affair, because the hermitage was behind a point. He weighed anchor and sailed directly towards the hermitage, and saw many men on horseback, who dismounted and entered the boat in arms and came to the caravel to arrest the Admiral. The captain stood up in the boat and asked a safe conduct from the Admiral. He replied that he granted it to him, but what change was this that none of his people were in the boat? And the Admiral added that if he would come and enter the caravel, all would be done as he desired. The Admiral was trying to draw him on board with smooth words, that he might take him and recover his men. He did not believe that he was breaking faith by giving him a safe conduct, since the captain had offered peace and security and had not kept his word. The captain would not trust himself on board because, as he says, he had evil intentions. Having seen that he would not come to the caravel, the Admiral asked him to explain why he detained his men, adding that this would offend the King of Portugal, and that in the territory of the Sovereigns of Castile the Portuguese received much honor, and entered it and were as safe as in Lisbon; and since the Sovereigns had given him letters of credence for all the princes and lords and men in the world, he would exhibit them to him, if he would come on board, and as he was their Admiral of the Ocean Sea and viceroy of the Indies which now belonged to their Highnesses...

Ferdinand and Isabela probably wouldn't have supported this voyage unless they were confident the Pope would modify the Treaty of Alcáçovas to allow Spain dominion over all its discoveries.

...he would show their provisions, signed with their signatures, and sealed with their seals, and he showed them to him at a distance. And he said that the Sovereigns were in great love and friendship with the King of Portugal, and they had commanded him to show all the honor he could to the ships of Portugal which he might encounter,...

Columbus hadn't forgotten the September 6th warning that *"three caravels of Portugal"* were trying to intercept him.

...and supposing the captain would not give up his men to him, he would not on that account refrain from going to Castile, since he had sufficient men to navigate to Seville, and the captain and his men would be well punished for having committed this offense. Then the captain replied that he and the others did not recognize the King and Queen of Castile, or their letters, nor did they fear them; on the contrary, they would have him understand that this was Portugal, saying this in a rather threatening manner. When the Admiral heard this, he was greatly concerned, and he says that he thought that some dispute must have occurred between the one kingdom and the other after his departure, and he could not refrain from making that reply to them which was proper. Afterwards, as he says, the captain again stood up at a distance and told the Admiral that he should go with the caravel to the harbor and that all he was doing

and had done, the King his master had sent him orders to do. The Admiral called those who were in the caravel to witness this, and the Admiral again called to the captain and to them all, and gave them his faith and swore that he, such as he was, would not land or leave the caravel until he had carried a hundred Portuguese to Castile and depopulated all that island. And so he returned to anchor in the harbor where he had first been, as the weather and wind were very unsuitable for him to do anything else.

After his bold threat to carry *"a hundred Portuguese to Castile,"* Columbus returned to his anchorage at Punta Matos with half of his crew still in custody.

WEDNESDAY, FEBRUARY 20th — *He commanded the ship to be refitted and the casks to be filled with seawater as ballast, because he was in a very poor harbor, and he was afraid that his cables might be cut, and so it happened. On this account, he sailed towards the island of San Miguel, although in no one of the islands of the Azores is there a good harbor for such weather as there then was, and he had no recourse but to escape out to sea.*

THURSDAY, FEBRUARY 21st — *Yesterday he set out from that island of Santa Maria for the island of San Miguel to see if he could find a harbor in which to endure such bad weather as he was experiencing, with high wind and a heavy sea. He went on until night without being able to see land in one direction or the other, on account of the thick clouds and darkness caused by the wind and sea. The Admiral says that he was not contented, because he had only three sailors who knew the sea, since most of those who were with him knew nothing of the sea...*

Columbus sailed from his anchorage with a short-handed crew while the other half of his men remained in custody.

...He beat about all night in a very severe storm and in great danger and toil, and in this Our Lord showed mercy to him in that the sea or its waves came from one direction only, because, if they had crossed one another as had been the case before, he would have suffered much greater distress. After sunrise, having found that he could not see the island of San Miguel, he resolved to return to Santa Maria, to see if he could recover his people and the boat and the cables and anchors which he had left there. He says that he was amazed at the very bad weather which he experienced in those islands and in that neighborhood, because in the Indies he navigated all that winter without dropping anchor, and had always good weather, and for not a single hour did he find the sea such as he would have been unable to navigate, and in these islands he had endured so great a tempest, and the same had befallen him on his outward voyage to the islands of the Canaries, but when he had passed them, he had found the breezes and the sea always temperate...

Las Casas hadn't considered that *"tempest"* worthy of mentioning in his abstract of the outbound route to the Canary Islands. But Fernando's *Biography* confirms this storm by describing a "heavy" sea on August 4th and "the wind blew so hard" on August 7th.

...In conclusion, the Admiral says that the sacred theologians and learned philosophers were right in saying that the earthly paradise is at the end of the east, because it is a very temperate place, so those lands which he had now discovered are, he says, "the end of the east."

FRIDAY, FEBRUARY 22nd — *Yesterday he anchored at the island of Santa Maria in the place or harbor where he had first anchored,...*

Columbus again returned to his Punta Matos anchorage.

...and immediately there came a man who called from some rocks which were opposite that place, saying that they should not go away from there. Afterwards came the boat with five sailors and two priests and a notary; they asked for safe conduct, and when it had been given by the Admiral, they came on board the caravel and as it was night they slept there, and the Admiral showed them such honor as he could. In the morning they required him to show them his commission from the Sovereigns of Castile, in order to prove to them that it was by their authority that he had made that voyage. The Admiral felt that they did this in order to make some show of not having done wrong, but of being right, because they had not been able to take the person of the Admiral, whom they obviously meant to get into their hands since they came armed in the boat; but they found that the game was not turning out well for them and they feared what the Admiral had said and threatened, which he intended to do and believed that he could succeed in doing. Finally, in order to recover the people whom they held, he had to show to them the circular letter of credence from the Sovereigns for all princes and lords, and other provisions, and he gave them of that which he had, and they went ashore satisfied, and afterwards released all the people with the boat, from whom he learned that if they had taken the Admiral, they would never have let him go free, for the captain said that the King, his master, had so commanded him.

Columbus played his weak hand well during today's delicate negotiations. After showing the islanders his "letter of credence from the Sovereigns" they reluctantly released all his "people with the boat."

SATURDAY, FEBRUARY 23rd — *Yesterday the weather began to improve: he weighed anchor and rounded the island to seek some good anchorage, in order to take in wood and stone for ballast, and he could not find anchorage until the hour of complines.*

Friday evening Columbus found his fourth and final Santa Maria anchorage by the light of a gibbous moon *"after he rounded the island"* to reach its south coast.

SUNDAY, FEBRUARY 24th — *Yesterday he anchored in the afternoon to take in wood and stone,...*

Morison identified a pair of possible anchorages on the island's south coast.

...and as the sea was very high, the boat could not reach the shore, and at the passing of the first watch of the night, it began to blow west and southwest. He ordered the sails to be hoisted, on account of the great danger that is in those islands to lie at anchor with a south wind, and because when it blows from the southwest, it afterwards blows from the south. And having found that the weather was good for going to Castile, he abandoned the taking in of wood and stone, and had them steer to the east,...

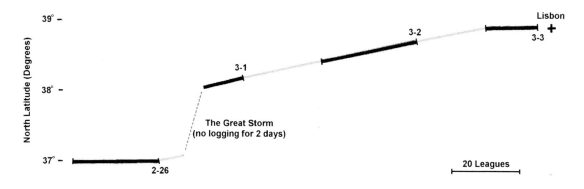

Figure 13-2. The Route from the Azores to Lisbon

From his charts Columbus knew the island of Santa Maria straddled the 37th parallel of Cape Vincent, his guidepost to Palos de la Frontera, the home port where he would proudly proclaim his discoveries to its thrilled citizens.

...and by sunrise, which was six hours and a half, he went 7 millas an hour [5 ¼ knots], which comes to 45 millas and a half [11 3/8 leagues]. After sunrise until sunset, he made 6 millas an hour [4 ½ knots], so that in eleven hours they went 66 millas [16 ½ leagues], and with forty-five and a half in the night, they went 111 and a half, and thus 28 leagues.

MONDAY, FEBRUARY 25th — *Yesterday, after sunset, he steered to the east on his course at five millas an hour [3 ¾ knots]; in thirteen hours of this night, he made 65 millas, which are 16 leagues and a quarter...*

This is the *Journal's* final reference to *"thirteen hours of...night."* In little more than two weeks the Vernal Equinox would universally shorten its duration to 12 hours.

...After sunrise until sunset, he went a further sixteen leagues and a half, with a smooth sea, thanks to God. There came to the caravel a very large bird, which appeared to be an eagle.

This *"very large bird"* was probably a European Osprey (aguila pescadora) on its northerly migration from a winter home in Africa. This bird is slightly smaller than the *"eagle" [aguila].*

TUESDAY, FEBRUARY 26th — *Yesterday, after sunset, he navigated on his course to the east, the sea being smooth, thanks to God. During most of the night he went 8 millas an hour [6 knots]; he made 100 millas, which are 25 leagues. After sunrise, with a light wind, he met with rain showers; he went a matter of eight leagues to the east-northeast.*

"After sunrise" Columbus ordered a surprising course change. Instead of continuing due *"east"* towards Spain, he inexplicably turned two compass points to the *"east-northeast,"* a route that would deliver his ship to Portuguese authorities in Lisbon. Morison dismissed "the ungenerous and preposterous charge" of many modern writers that Columbus headed for Lisbon "with the express purpose of selling out his discovery to the king of Portugal." But with the "W and NW" wind assumed by Morison, Cape Vincent would have been as easy a target as Lisbon and within a day's coasting to Columbus's home port of Palos. What makes this course change especially intriguing is that Columbus and Pinzón (adjusting for his large latitude bias) both may have made Lisbon their objective.

WEDNESDAY, FEBRUARY 27th — *This night and day he went out of his course, owing to contrary winds and heavy waves and sea, and he found himself one hundred and twenty five leagues from Cape St. Vincent, and eighty from the island of Madeira, and a hundred and six from that of Santa Maria...*

This morning Columbus apparently used LPC-26 to take the final longitude measurement of his voyage when Jupiter rose six degrees above the Moon at 2:30 AM. By now he realized large errors in his *Ephemerides* would likely dwarf the *"hundred and six"* leagues he had sailed from Santa Maria. But measurement of LPC-26 could still have served a useful purpose as a longitude training exercise to be monitored by Spain's astronomers observing the same event. While Las Casas neglected to transcribe the distance made good this night, a reasonable 13 leagues would have brought Columbus' total mileage since Santa Maria to his recorded *"a hundred and six leagues"* by sunrise.

Today's three distance estimates also help us assess the accuracy of the charts provided for his journey. That assumed 13 leagues to the ENE would have brought Columbus about eight leagues north of the Santa Maria/Cape Vincent parallel, or 11 leagues further north of Madeira than the 80 he estimated from his charts. These same charts put Santa Maria 231 leagues west of Cape Vincent, or 26 leagues less than their actual separation. A longitude mapping error 2½ times as large as its latitude error seems consistent with 15th century measurement capabilities.

...He was very grieved at so great a storm when he was on the threshold of home.

THURSDAY, FEBRUARY 28th — *He went in the same way for this night. With shifting winds, he went to the south, to the southeast, and to one side and the other, and then to the northeast and east-northeast, and all in the same way this day.*

Uncertainties in Columbus' heading and distance over the past 48 hours limit our ability to reconstruct his route from Santa Maria to Lisbon. A reasonable speculation for his progress over these two days is 12 leagues to the north and 40 leagues east.

FRIDAY, MARCH 1st — *This night he went to the east by north, for twelve leagues; during the day he ran to the east by north, for 23 leagues and a half.*

SATURDAY, MARCH 2nd — *He went on this course to the east by north, this night for 28 leagues, and in the day he ran 20 leagues...*

The storm now past, Columbus could have sailed directly east for Spain by way of Cape Vincent. But for some unexplained reason he rejected this obvious option and continued on his route to Portugal's capital, equidistant to the *"east by north."*

SUNDAY, MARCH 3rd — *After sunset, he navigated on his course to the east...*

Upon reaching Lisbon's latitude Columbus changed *"his course to the east"* in search of its harbor entrance.

...There came a squall which tore all the sails, and he saw himself in great peril; but God willed to deliver them. He cast lots to send a pilgrim, as he says, who should go in his shirt to Santa María de la Cinta in Huelva, and the lot fell on the Admiral...

Something other than luck probably chose Columbus for all three Iberian pilgrimages; the odds against this result if only by chance were greater than 15,000 to one!

...They all also made a vow to fast on bread and water on the first Saturday after they reached land...

It would prove impossible for Columbus to fulfill this vow on March 9th. That day Portugal's King João would be receiving him with "great honor".

...He made sixty millas [15 leagues] before the sails were torn; afterwards they went with bare poles, owing to the great storm of wind and sea which from two sides broke over them. They saw indications that they were near land; they found themselves to be very near Lisbon.

These *"indications that they were...very near Lisbon"* could have included benthic seaweed, driftwood and the flotsam of heavy coastal traffic.

MONDAY, MARCH 4th — *Last night they experienced a terrible storm, so that they thought that they were lost owing to the seas which came upon them from two sides, and the winds, which seemed to lift the caravel in the air, and the water from the sky and lightning from many sides. It pleased Our Lord to sustain them, and so he went until the first watch, when Our Lord showed him land, the sailors seeing it....*

At 7 PM a rising full moon back lit the dramatic 1700-foot peaks at Sintra marking the entrance to Lisbon's harbor. Three centuries later Lord Byron would celebrate these verdant heights as his "glorious Eden," and tonight those dark silhouettes on the eastern horizon must have looked especially glorious to the *Niña's* desperate crew.

...And then, in order not to come to it until he might know it and see if he could find some harbor or place where they might be safe, he hoisted the mainsail, having no other resource, and went some way, although with great danger, keeping out to sea, and so God preserved them until day, as he says, with infinite labor and terror...

The *Niña* must have been dangerously close to Portugal's rockbound coast when the rising moon finally plucked Sintra's silhouette from the storm's darkness. The threatening lee shore severely limited Columbus' options in his deadly struggle with this *"terrible storm,"* apparently the fiercest of his entire voyage.

...When day came, he recognized the land as being the rock of Cintra, which is close to the river of Lisbon,...

Sintra lies two leagues north of the Tagus River's narrow opening to Lisbon's beautiful harbor, arguably the finest in all of Europe.

...where he resolved to enter, because he could do nothing else, so terrible was the storm which prevailed...

Columbus was already sailing Lisbon's latitude when beset by this *"terrible"* storm conveniently concealing his true motives for not returning directly home to Palos de la Frontera.

...at the town of Cascaes which is at the entrance of the river. He says that the people of the place were all that morning offering up prayers for them, and after he was within, the people came to see them in wonder that they had in any way escaped...

The residents of Cascaes, a fishing village just two leagues outside the harbor's mouth, had ringside seats for this morning's epic struggle with the raging storm.

...And so at the hour of terce, he came to rest at Rastelo within the river of Lisbon,...

By mid-morning the *Niña* was safely anchored *"at Rastelo,"* two leagues inside the harbor's mouth. Columbus could now revel in his safe return to the Europe he had left 213 days earlier to lead the most important voyage in the history of mankind.

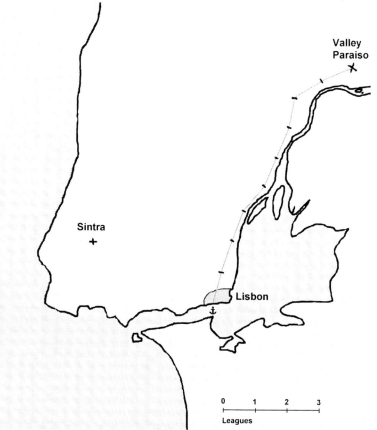

Figure 13-3. Lisbon and 9 League Route to Valley Paraiso to Visit the King

...where he learned from the mariners that never had there been a winter with so many storms, and that 25 ships had been wrecked on the coast of Flanders, and that other vessels were lying there which for four months had not been able to put out to sea. The Admiral wrote at once to the King of Portugal, who was nine leagues from there,...

The winter residence of Portugal's King D. João II at Vale do Paraiso was almost 27 nautical miles NNE of Lisbon by way of the shortest carriage route. This distance confirms the *"leagues"* of Columbus were three nautical miles in length, both at sea *and* on land, despite the contrary claims of Morison.

...that the Sovereigns of Castile had commanded him not to fail to enter the harbors of His Highness to ask for what he might need in return for payment, and he begged the King to give him permission to proceed with the caravel to the city of Lisbon, because some rogues, thinking that he was carrying much gold,...

In the *Journal's* preamble Columbus ignored the quest for *"gold"* as a possible motivation for his voyage. Instead he proclaimed his objective was *"to see those princes and peoples and lands...of India... and bring about their conversion to our holy faith."* While his *Journal* reasserted this missionary focus in only two subsequent entries, the primary mission of his voyage is suggested by its 153 references to *"gold."* The first of these occurred during the October 13th meeting with the Indians as Columbus *"labored to know if they had gold."* These Indians had only a few trinkets, but these were enough to set his future course to the *"south-west"* in search of a king who supposedly *"had large vessels of it."*

...might set themselves to commit some villainy against him, being in a deserted harbor, and also that the King might know that he did not come from Guinea but from the Indies.

Columbus needed to reassure the Portuguese he had not intruded upon their African territories. Secretly he must have relished this opportunity to remind them of their failure to support his Enterprise of the Indies.

TUESDAY, MARCH 5th — *The great ship of the King of Portugal was also anchored at Rastelo; she was the best equipped with cannon and arms of any ship that had ever been seen, and her master was called Bartolomé Díaz of Lisbon. This master came in the armed boat [batel armada]...*

Today's ambiguous usage of *"batel armada"* might be better translated as a less-threatening "fleet's launch." Pinzón had already informed Ferdinand and Isabela of the discoveries, so any hostile action against Columbus surely would have provoked their powerful neighbor.

...to the caravel and told the Admiral that he should enter the boat to go to give account to the factors of the King and to the captain of the said ship. The Admiral replied that he was Admiral of the Sovereigns of Castile and that he did not render accounts of such a kind to such persons, and that he would not leave the ships or vessels where he was, unless it was under compulsion of force which he could not resist. The master answered that he should send the master of the caravel. The Admiral said that neither the master nor any other persons should go save by force, since he regarded it as the same thing to permit anyone to go as to go himself, and that it was the custom of the Admirals of the Sovereigns of Castile to die before they would yield or allow their people to yield. The master moderated his tone, and said that, since he was so determined, it should be as he wished, but he asked him to have the letters of the Sovereigns of Castile, if he had them, shown to him. The Admiral was pleased to exhibit them, and the master at once returned to his ship and gave an account to her captain, who was called Alvaro Damán. He came to the caravel in great state with drums and trumpets and pipes, making a great display, and talked with the Admiral and offered to do all that he might command him.

WEDNESDAY, MARCH 6th — *When it was known today that the Admiral came from the Indies, so many people came from the city of Lisbon to see him and to see the Indians, that it was a thing of wonder. They all marveled, giving thanks to Our Lord, and saying that it was owing to the great faith of the Sovereigns of Castile, and their desire to serve God, that the Divine majesty had given them all this.*

THURSDAY, MARCH 7th — *Today there came an infinite number of people to the caravel and many gentlemen, and among them the factors of the King, and they all gave infinite thanks to Our Lord for the great good and increase of Christendom...*

The *"factors of the King"* must have been gratified Columbus had demolished the single-ocean paradigm by discovering an entire continent *"for the great good and increase of Christendom."* Their *"infinite thanks"* may have been stimulated by its location within the region that had been ceded to Portugal by the Treaty of Alcáçovas.

...which Our Lord had given to the Sovereigns of Castile, and he says that they attributed this to the fact that their Highnesses labored and exercised themselves for the furtherance of the religion of Christ.

FRIDAY, MARCH 8th — *Today the Admiral received a letter from the King of Portugal by Don Martín de Noroña...*

Cecil Jane noted that "This distinguished family descended from a bastard son of King Henry II of Castile, who had married the daughter of King Ferdinand I of Portugal."

...in which he asked him to come to the place where he was, since the weather was not suitable for the departure of the caravel. And so he did, in order to disarm suspicion, although he did not wish to go, and he went to sleep at Sacabén...

By now Columbus must have heard that Pinzón had anchored several weeks earlier at the Galician port of Bayona, and was now boldly claiming credit for the voyage discoveries. But he must have been confident Isabela would deny his disloyal captain a hearing when he delayed his return home in order to meet with Portugal's King João. Columbus left for Paraiso that afternoon, stopping for the night at Sacabén, a small town almost two leagues north of Lisbon on the west bank of the Tagus.

...The King commanded his factors that they should give without payment everything the Admiral and his people and the caravel might need, and that all should be done as the Admiral desired.

SATURDAY, MARCH 9th — *Today he left Sacabén to go where the King was, which was in the valley of Paraiso, nine leagues from Lisbon...*

If Columbus had used Morison's manufactured "land league" to inflate Rum Cay's tiny dimensions, he surely would have doubled today's distance to Paraiso as 18 "land leagues" instead of confirming his March 4th estimate of *"nine leagues from Lisbon."*

...As it was raining, he could not reach there until night...

A dozen soggy hours on muleback to make today's seven remaining leagues may have led Columbus to reflect on the relative speed and comfort of his nautical ventures.

...The King commanded the chief persons of his household to receive him very honorably, and the King also received him with great honor, and showed him much favor and commanded him to be seated. He spoke very amiably, offering to command all to be done which might be of use to the Sovereigns of Castile and for their service, completely and more so than if it were for himself, and he showed that he was very pleased that there had been a successful conclusion to that voyage and that it had been accomplished,...

The wily king tested Columbus' claim of discovery by calling one of the Indians aside to construct a table top map of the Caribbean with a handful of dried beans. When completed, the king swept the beans away and ordered a second Indian to duplicate the map. The similarities of their maps convinced the unhappy king of his error in rejecting the Columbus' proposal for his Enterprise of the Indies.

242

...but he understood that according to the capitulation which had been made between the Sovereigns and himself, that conquest belonged to him. To this the Admiral replied that he had not seen the capitulation...

Columbus may not have actually *"seen the capitulation,"* but he surely knew the Treaty of Alcáçovas, as written, would give Portugal dominion over all of his discoveries. However, King João must have sensed this treaty would be impossible to enforce against the will of a powerful neighbor supported by a Spanish Pope in the Vatican.

...nor did he know anything save that the Sovereigns had commanded that he not go to La Mina or any part of Guinea, and so it had been proclaimed in all the ports of Andalusia before he set out on his voyage. The King graciously answered that he was sure that in this matter there would be no need for arbitrators; he handed him over as a guest to the Prior of Crato, he being the most important personage who was there, and from him the Admiral received much honor and favor.

A Cecil Jane footnote defines *"Crato"* as "A priory belonging to the order of St. John of Jerusalem (Knights of the Hospital). It was very wealthy and included in its territory twelve towns and twenty-nine parishes. Its prior was usually a prince of royal blood or a member of the aristocracy."

SUNDAY, MARCH 10th — *Today, after mass, the King repeated to him that if he had need of anything, it should be immediately given to him, and he had a long conversation with the Admiral concerning his voyage, and always ordered him to be seated and did him much honor.*

MONDAY, MARCH 11th — *Today he bid farewell to the King who told him certain things which he was to say to the Sovereigns on his behalf, showing him always great affection. He departed after eating, and His Highness sent with him Don Martín de Noroña, and all those cavaliers came to accompany him and to do him honor for a considerable distance. Afterwards he came to a monastery of San Antonio, which is near a place called Villafranca, where the Queen was,...*

The monastery of San Antonio de Castanheira lay five leagues to his SSW on the return route to Lisbon.

...and he went to do her reverence and to kiss her hands, because she had sent to him to say that he was not to go away until he had seen her. With her were the duke and the marquis,...

A Cecil Jane footnote explains "The duke was evidently the Queen's brother, Dom Manuel, Duke of Beja, and heir to the throne. He succeeded John II in 1495. As for the marquis, Morison thinks he might have been Martín de Noroña's father."

...the there the Admiral received much honor. The Admiral left her at night and went to sleep at Alhandra.

Alhandra is a small town less than a league beyond Vila Franca de Xira.

TUESDAY, MARCH 12th — *Today, being ready to leave Alhandra for the caravel, there came a squire of the King who offered him on his behalf that, if he wished to go to Castile by land, he would go with him to arrange for lodging and to order that beasts should be supplied and all that might be needed. When the Admiral parted from him, he commanded a mule to be given to him and another to his pilot whom he had with him,...*

The offer of two mules came a day late, apparently leaving the ocean-weary Indians to trudge back to Lisbon on foot.

...and he says that the squire ordered a present of twenty espadims to be made to the pilot, as the Admiral learned. He says that all was reported to have been done so that the Sovereigns might know of it. He reached the caravel at night.

These *"twenty"* gold coins were a substantial reward duly reported to Ferdinand and Isabela.

Figure 13-4 – From Lisbon to Saltes (Palos)

WEDNESDAY, MARCH 13th — *Today, at eight o'clock, at ebb tide and with a north-northwest wind, he weighed anchor and set sail to go to Seville.*

Twenty-four hours after returning to his caravel Columbus *"weighted anchor"* with an *"ebb tide and with a north-northwest wind"* well suited for his return to Palos.

THURSDAY, MARCH 14th — *Yesterday, after sunset, he followed his course to the south, and before sunrise he found himself off Cape St. Vincent, which is in Portugal...*

Columbus and his crew must have been exulting in their good fortune as the Atlantic Gyre's clockwise current helped a brisk NNW wind drive them down Portugal's east coast at the fastest clip of their entire voyage – nearly 35 leagues in less than eleven hours.

...Afterwards he sailed to the east, to go to Saltés, and he went all day with a light wind, until now when he is off Faro.

After rounding Cape Vincent the winds had abated, so by sunset they made less than 20 leagues to reach Faro, a Portuguese seaport midway between the Cape and Palos.

FRIDAY, MARCH 15th — *Yesterday, after sunset, he went on his course until day with little wind, and at sunrise, he found himself off Saltés, and at midday, with a rising tide,...*

With the winds still weak, they needed 18 hours to make those last18 leagues to Palos de la Frontera. The slow pace that must have frustrated the ship's entire complement, so eager to replace the sounds of flapping sails with a welcoming roar from the multitude gathered at dockside.

...he entered by the bar of Saltés into the port from which he had departed on the third day of August in the previous year...

Coincidentally the *Pinta* arrived a few hours later on the same tide. Still commanded by Martín Alonso Pinzón, she had escaped the storm off the Azores and had made port at Bayona (Galicia) toward the end of February. Martín Alonso survived the storm, but was dead within a month, and without the glory he sought.

...And so he says that here ends this writing, save that he intended to go to Barcelona by sea, having had news that their Highnesses were in that city, and this in order to give them an account of all his voyage which Our Lord had permitted him to perform, and to which He had inspired him. For certainly, besides the fact that he knew and held firmly and securely without a trace of doubt that the Divine Majesty brings all good things to pass, and that all is good, save sin, and that nothing can be imagined or thought save with His consent, "Of this voyage", says the Admiral, "I know that this has been miraculously shown to be so, as can be understood from this writing, by the many notable miracles which He has shown forth on the voyage and for me, who for so long a time was in the court of Your Highnesses with the opposition of so many chief persons of your household and against their opinion, for they were all against me, regarding this undertaking as a jest, and I hope in Our Lord that it will be the greatest honor for Christendom to have been brought forth so easily."...

This final entry transcribed from the *Journal* reveals the bitterness Columbus still held against those in court who *"were all against"* his Enterprise of the Indies.

...These are the last words of the Admiral Don Christopher Columbus concerning his first voyage to the Indies and their discovery, and he had assuredly much reason and spoke as a very prudent man and almost as a prophet, although carnal men have not appreciated the goods which God offered to Spain, both spiritual and temporal; but for her ambition and greed Spain was not worthy to enjoy the spiritual good, save for some servants of God.

Thanks be to God

Bartolomé de Las Casas and his fellow Dominicans had struggled for half a century to curtail the greed and cruelty of those Spanish settlers and conquistadors who followed Columbus to the New World. Even if these *"servants of God"* had been successful in their humanitarian efforts, its indigenous population was doomed to near extinction by European diseases, including smallpox, having a far deadlier effect than Syphilis, the New World's exchange "gift" to Europeans.

Appendix – The Celestial Measurement of Longitude

During his 1492-93 expedition Columbus had access to three different celestial methods for measuring longitude, all of them capable of better accuracy than available terrestrial methods. To obtain useful celestial measurements Columbus needed both an ephemeris compiling the predicted daily longitudes of the moon and planets and also an instrument for measuring their actual longitudes. We know he satisfied the first requirement with his copy of Johannes Mueller's 750-page *Ephemerides* tabulating daily celestial predictions to the closest arc minute over a 30-year interval extending through 1506. But the only angle measuring instruments we're certain he carried were the quadrant and astrolabe designed for latitude measurements for which their accuracy of about 15 arc minutes was normally adequate.

A total of 26 lunar-planetary conjunctions (LPCs) occurred near the horizon during the 1492-3 voyage from which Columbus could measure longitude, and for which he frequently measured. He likely measured longitude using a cross-staff, but had to accommodate these factors:

- Horizon is an accurate longitude reference but has large obvious distortions (detectable and measured by observations at Sagras).
- Raising measurements 5 degrees from the horizon reduces differential refraction errors by a factor of 7. Another 2 degrees would increase that factor to 10, but would also increase the non-linearities that make overhead measurements so difficult.
- Differential refraction errors disappear when measuring longitude from solar or lunar eclipses. 1477 and 1520 eclipse measurements were both made at roughly a 5 degree elevation angle, so this seems a reasonable assumption for measurement of lunar-planetary conjunctions.

1492 Outbound Longitude Estimates

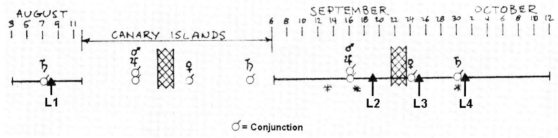

Figure A-1. Outbound Correlations of Longitude Entries and Conjunctions

In Figure A-1 above, the four longitude-related log entries (L1-L4) are indicated by the solid triangles. Note that 3 of the 4 are directly preceded by lunar-planetary conjunctions. The cross hatches indicate insufficient lunar crescents for lunar distance measurements, and the asterisks mark Polaris sights. All four outbound log entries relating to longitude are shown below.

Longitude Log Entry 1 – *"Among the pilots of the three caravels there were different opinions concerning their position, and the admiral proved to be nearest to the truth."*

Longitude Log Entry 2 – *"Here the pilots gave their position. The pilot of the Nina made it 440 leagues from the Canaries; the pilot of the Pinta, 420; and the pilot of the vessel in which the admiral was, 400 exactly."*

Longitude Log Entry 3 – *"The admiral asked him to send the chart to him, and, when it had been sent on a line, the admiral began with his pilot and sailors to fix his position on it."*

Longitude Log Entry 4 – *"The admiral's pilot on this day at dawn calculated that they had gone from the island Hierro up to then 578 leagues westward."*

1493 Homebound Longitude Estimates

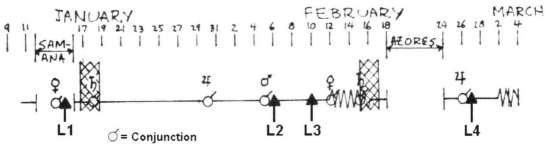

Figure A-2. Homebound Correlations of Longitude Entries and Conjunctions

In Figure A-2 above, the four longitude-related log entries (L1-L4) are indicated by the solid triangles. Note that 3 of the 4 are also (6 of 8 also counting Westbound entries) directly preceded by lunar-planetary conjunctions, strongly indicating that the coupling was more than coincidental. The cross hatches indicate insufficient lunar crescents for lunar distance measurements, and the saw teeth indicate severe late-winter storms that probably obscured conjunctions. All four log entries relating to longitude are shown below for his homeward part of the voyage.

Longitude Log Entry 1 – *"These Indies are very near the Canary Islands, and for this reason he believed that they were less than 400 leagues distant."*

Longitude Log Entry 2 – *"Vincente Yanez found that today in the morning the island of Flores lay to his north and the island of Madeira to the east. Roldan said that Fayal or San Gregorio lay to the NNE, and Porto Santo to the east."*

Longitude Log Entry 3 – *"In the caravel of the admiral, Vincente Yanez and the two pilots, Sancho Ruiz and Pero Alonso Nino, and Roldan, charted their course or fixed their position...But the admiral found himself much out of his course."* (150 leagues further away)

Longitude Log Entry 4 – *"He found himself 125 leagues from Cape St. Vincent, 80 from the island of Madiera, and 106 from that of Santa Maria."*

Bibliography

Author's Papers and Presentations

Columbus Landed Here – Or Did he? Americas, October 1981

Columbus's First Landfall: A New Theory. The Bahamas Historical Society meeting in Nassau, October 1981

Interviewed by Susan Stamberg, All Things Considered, On National Public Radio, Columbus Day 1985

The Columbus Landfall Question – A Northern Viewpoint. Encuentro, A Columbian Quincentenary Newsletter, Latin American Institute, The University of New Mexico, Fall 1986

Egg Island is the Landfall of Columbus – A Literal Interpretation of His Journal. Proceedings of the First San Salvador Conference, Watlings Island, November 1986

The Rediscovery of San Salvador. National Aeronautics and Space Administration Engineering Symposium at the Goddard Space Flight Center, October 1987

The Signature of Christopher Columbus. Encuentro, A Columbian Quincentenary Newsletter, Latin American Institute, The University of New Mexico, Fall 1988

Una Nuova Interpretazione della Firma di Colombo. Columbus 92, Genoa Italy, September-October 1989

The Case for a Northern Landfall. The Columbus Landfall Workshop at The Johns Hopkins University, October 1989

Columbus was a Latitude Sailor. Encounters, Spain '92, Foundation and the Latin American Institute of the University of New Mexico, Summer 1990

Did Seaweed Lead Columbus Back to the Antilles? (with Dr. James Norris of the Smithsonian Institution) Encounters, Summer 1991

The Journal of the Bahamas Historical Society
- Volume 4 – October 1982. *The Search for San Salvador.*
- Volume 6 – October 1984. *Ponce de Leon Belongs to the Bahamas.*
- Volume 8 – October 1986. *The Martyrs of Ponce de Leon.*
- Volume 11 – October 1989. *Did Columbus Forever Memorialize the Bahamas?*
- Volume 14 – October 1992. *No More Disturbed than Water in a Well.*

The Society for the History of Discoveries
- *A New Approach to the Columbus Landfall.* pp. 113-149 of "In the Wake of Columbus, Islands and Controversy" Wayne State University Press, 1985.
- *Columbus and the Method of Lunar Distance.* pp. 65-78 Terrae Incognitae, Volume XXIV, 1992.
- Presentations at Annual Meetings of The Society for the History of Discoveries.
  - *Exploring the Bahamas with Ponce de Leon.* November 1982
  - *Latitude Sailing: The Arabs, Vikings and 16th Century Explorers.* 11/2/84.
  - *The Mystery of the Cantino Map.* 10/18/86
  - *Espejo Navagantes of Alonso de Chave,* 9/3/87
  - *The Northern Route – Fernandina to Isabela.* 10/14/88
  - *The Columbus Journal Translations – A Northern Perspective.* 6/9/89
    - *Christopher Columbus – Navigator and Mapmaker.* 10/11/90

o *Cartographic Evidence of the Columbus Landfall.* 11/23/91
o *Did Columbus Utilize Lucayan Maps?* 10/2/92
o *Christopher Columbus: The Long Voyage Home.* 9/23/94
o *North America on Amerigo Vespucci's Cantino Map.* 11/4/95
o *Juan de la Cosa's Landfall Map.* 11/1/96
o *How William C. Coker can solve the Columbus Landfall Question.* 10/13/09

The Journal of the Institute of Navigation
- Volume 44, No. 4, winter 1997-98, *The Celestial Navigation of Christopher Columbus.* pp. 401-410
- Volume 46, *Columbus's Method of Determining Longitude: An Analytic View.*

The Washington Map Society
- *The Rediscovery of San Salvador.* Presentation at Society Meeting at Folger Library, October 1983
- *The Mystery of the Cantino Map.* The Portolan, Number 5, May 1989, pp. 15-26.
- *Cartographic Interpretation of the Columbus Signature.* The Portolan, Number 22, Fall 1991, pp 15-17.
- *Juan de la Cosa's Mapping of the Columbus Landfall.* The Portolan, Number 42, Fall 1998, pp 12-20.
- *The 1477 Columbus Voyage to North America.* The Portolan, Number 48, Fall 2000, pp.31-41.

Other Authors

Agassiz, Alexander, *A Reconnaissance of the Bahamas and of the Elevated Reefs of Cuba in the Steam Yacht Wild Duck, January to April, 1893.* Bulletin of the Museum of Comparative Zoology at Harvard College. Vol. XXVI. No. 1. December 1894

Almgren, Bertil, et al. *The Vikings.* Cagner & Co., Gothenburg, Sweden, 1966

Boland, Charles M. *They All Discovered America.* Doubleday, Garden City, 1961

Bourne, William. *A Regiment for the Sea.* The Hakluyt Society. Ed. E.G.R. Taylor 1990

Casteeda, P., M. Cuesta y P. Herndez. *Alonso de Chaves y el Libro IV de su Espejo de Navigantes.* Madrid, 1977

Columbus, Christopher et al. *The Four Voyages of Columbus.* Trans. Cecil Jane. Dover, New York, 1988

Columbus, Ferdinand. *The Life of the Admiral Christopher Columbus.* Trans. Benjamin Keen. Rutgers University Press, New Brunswick, 1992

De Alcedo, Don Antonio. *The Geographical and Historical Dictionary of America and the West Indies.* Trans. G. A. Thompson, Esq. London, 1812

Fields, Meredith Helleberg, ed. *The Yachtsmans Guide to the Bahamas.* Tropic Isle Publishers, North Miami, Fla., 1988

Fernadez-Armesto, Felipe. *Ferdinand & Isabela.* Dorset Press, New York, 1975

Formisano, Luciano. *Letters from a New World, Amerigo Vespuccis Discovery of America.* Trans. David Jacobson. Marsilio, New York 1992

Gilchrist, John H. *Latitude Errors and the New England Voyages of Pring and Waymouth*. The American Neptune, Vol. L, 1990. pps. 5-17

Hansen, Jens Peder Hart, Jorgen Meldgaard and Jorgen Nordqvist. *The Greenland Mummies*. Smithsonian Institution Press, Washington, D.C., 1991

Harrisse, Henry. *The Discovery of North America*. 1892; rpt. Amsterdam: N. Israel, 1969

Las Casas, Fray Bartolom de. *The Diario of Christopher Columbus First Voyage to America*. Trans. Oliver Dunn and James E. Kelley, Jr. University of Oklahoma Press, Norman and London, 1989

Las Casas, Bartolom de. *The Journal of Christopher Columbus*. Trans. Cecil Jane. Bramhall House, New York, 1960

Majid al-Najdi, Ahmad. *Arab Navigation in the Indian Ocean before the Coming of the Portuguese,* Trans. G. R. Tibbetts. The Royal Asiatic Society of Great Britain and Ireland. London, 1971

Marcus, G. J. *The Conquest of the North Atlantic*. Oxford University Press, New York, 1981

Morison, Samuel E.
- *Admiral of the Ocean Sea.* Little, Brown and Co., Boston. 1942
- *The European Discovery of America, The Northern Voyages, A.D. 500-1600.* Oxford University Press, New York, 1971
- *The European Discovery of America, The Southern voyages, A.D.1492-1616.* Oxford University Press, New York, 1974

Mueller, Johann (Johannes Regiomontanus), *"Ephemerides"* (for 1475 to 1505), Nuremberg, c1474

North, J. D. *The Astrolabe*. Scientific American, January 1974, pps. 96-106

Ptolemy, Claudius. *The Geography*. Trans. Edward Luther Stevenson. Dover, New York, 1991

Randles, W. G. L. *Portuguese and Spanish Attempts to Measure Longitude in the 16th Century*. Instituto de Investigao Cientifica Tropical, Coimbra 1985

Seaver, Kirsten A. *The Frozen Echo: Greenland and the Exploration of North America ca A.D 1000-1500*. Stanford University Press, Stanford, CA, 1996

U. S. Naval Oceanographic Office. *Sailing Directions for The West Indies. Vol 1: Bermuda, Bahamas and Greater Antilles.* Third edition, 1958

Villiers, Alan. *Men, Ships and the Sea.* The National Geographic Society, Washington, D.C., 1973

Wiesenthal, Simon. *Sails of Hope.* Macmillan, New York, 1973

Wilford, John Noble:
- *The Mapmakers.* Vintage Books, New York, 1982
- *The Mysterious History of Columbus.* Vintage Books, New York,1992